MEN
OF WATERLOO

MEN

OF WATERLOO

by

John Sutherland

Prentice-Hall, Inc., Englewood Cliffs, N.J.

Library of Congress Catalog Card Number: 66-19886

Printed in the United States of America

T 57574

Prentice-Hall International, Inc., London
Prentice-Hall of Australia, Pty. Ltd., Sydney
Prentice-Hall of Canada, Ltd., Toronto
Prentice-Hall of India (Private) Ltd., New Delhi
Prentice-Hall of Japan, Inc., Tokyo

For my wife, Virginia

Acknowledgments

A book is the effort of hundreds, and without the kind assistance I received from so many persons, *Men of Waterloo* would still be just an idea. In particular, I wish to thank the following:

Yann LeRoux and his two friends, Stephan Buffington and Maria Brun, who supplied hard-to-find material from Paris and Brussels; Mrs. E. W. Mulligan, who typed the manuscript and supervised the proofing; Lt. Col. John R. Boatwright, Jr., A.U.S., Ret., who read the manuscript and offered many valuable suggestions; Pienette Spiegler who translated books and documents; Saville Allnutt, Esther Bass, Jean Cruise, Thomas Hussey, Douglas Lawson, Mrs. George C. Scott, Betty Wanamaker and Mrs. William Wood, who helped with research, wrote letters and performed other necessary tasks.

In addition, there was the valuable help I received from historians, libraries, regiments and Waterloo enthusiasts. My gratitude is extended to those who were of critical importance in the development of this book:

Numerous employees of the Alexandria Public Library; Maj. A. S. C. Blackshaw, M.B.E., British Forces; Peter A. Brannon, director, State of Alabama Department of Archives and History; Brown University Library, Providence, R.I.

L. C. Cameron, Brigadier, Ret., British Forces; W. M. Cashman, M.D., Warren, Pa.; John Chase, New Orleans *States-Item;* Brigadier P. F. Claxton, O.B.E., British Forces; Colonel H. J. Darlington, O.B.E., regimental secretary, The King's Own Royal Border Regiment; James M. Day, director of State Archives, Texas State Library; Eva Denby,

Waterloo, Ala.; Leon de Valinger, Jr., state archivist, Delaware Public Archives Commission.

Barbara Elkins, Oregon Historical Society; Colonel D. A. D. Eykyn, D.S.O., the Royal Scots; the late Margaret Findlay of Scotland and the United States; Lt. Col. Patrick Forbes, O.B.E., D.L., the Gordon Highlanders; various officials in the French government; Lida L. Greene, Iowa State Department of History and Archives.

Mary Kay Hannaman, Louisiana Department, New Orleans Public Library; the late William F. Howell, former director of administration, International Bank for Reconstruction and Development; Donald Kent, director of research, Publications and Records, Pennsylvania Historical and Museum Commission; Charles E. Lee, director of South Carolina Archives Department; the Library of Congress; William R. Mitchell, Jr., historian, Georgia Historical Commission; the National Archives of the United States; Lt. Col. J. R. Palmer, M.C., Ret., the Royal Hussars.

H. Paterson and family, Dyce, Aberdeen, Scotland; William S. Powell, librarian, University of North Carolina Library, North Carolina Collection; Lt. Col. E. A. Priestley, the Welsh Regiment; Mildred Seydell of Belgium and the United States.

Colonel T. E. Stoneham, M.B.E., British Forces; Brigadier D. A. Turner, Royal Army Service Corps; Lt. Col. J. G. Vyvyan, The Royal Welsh Fusiliers; Clyde C. Walton, state historian, Illinois State Library; parish priests and city officials in and around Waterloo, and especially those who permitted the church registers of Braine L'Alleud, Charleroi, Genappe, Gosselies and Quatre Bras to be studied.

Lt. Col. H. S. R. Watson, 13th/18th Royal Hussars (Q.M.D.) British Forces; officials of the West German Government.

Finally, I must thank all those in Building 918, Parkfairfax, and many of my other friends who were so helpful: the Boatwrights, Butchers, Duffs, Duncans, Fishers, Foisies, Hogans, Howells, Knights, Lawsons, Laytons, Lenoxes, Malones, Mannings, Shockleys, and especially the Basses, who were beneath the whole plot. Then, of course, there were Cleo and Greta.

Preface

Perhaps in Valhalla the Iron Duke still may be muttering about the efforts of writers to produce satisfactory books on the battle of Waterloo. The Duke of Wellington opposed the whole idea of writing about the battle from the very start, and since his opposition to a great number of things was said to be eternal, we can assume that his opposition to books about the battle still holds.

On August 2, 1815, barely six weeks after the struggle, Sir Walter Scott wrote the Duke to say that he planned a history of the battle. Although the Duke agreed to help him, he tried to discourage Sir Walter from writing a book.

The Duke wrote: "The object which you propose to yourself is very difficult of attainment, and, if really attained, is not a little invidious. The history of a battle is not unlike the history of a ball. Some individuals may recollect all the little events, of which the great result is the battle won or lost; but no individual can recollect the order in which, or the exact moment at which, they occurred, which makes all the difference as to their value or importance."

But Sir Walter persisted. On August 17, 1815, the Duke sent him some material on the battle, but enclosed this warning: "You may depend upon it, you will never make it a satisfactory work."

Few writers took the Duke's warnings seriously. But the Duke was mostly right. Authors have found the going exceedingly rough.

Students of the battle never find all the answers they are looking for in any one book. Practically every work on the battle creates a storm of dissent. And errors abound in many books.

Men of Waterloo is certainly no effort to correct any of these deficiencies, and I hope that the book has no more than the usual errors which I have found in most books about the battle. Judgments have to be made, and in many cases the judgments turn out to be incorrect when new evidence turns up.

In *Men of Waterloo* I attempt to handle the story differently from the way it is generally done. I am concerned more with the men who fought the battle than with the mistakes in timing, tactics and strategy, although these things, too, are there. Yet I do not dwell upon them extensively, or lecture upon them at all since I feel that the book, which is mostly a narrative, would lose something in the telling. My main concern is to develop the drama of the 100 days and the battle as effectively as I can.

Deficiencies will be found here, too. For one thing it has been necessary on occasion to accept at face value some of the stories related by the men and their regiments. It was natural for them to inflate their deeds in the struggle. Nevertheless, almost any act of heroism was possible in this amazing battle, and if the roles of some men and some regiments seem overplayed, then let my descriptions of them serve as tributes to the unknown heroes of the action. At Waterloo, as in every other battle, there were hundreds of them.

Some readers may feel that British and French soldiers, especially the British, receive more attention than troops of other nationalities. Part of this is intentional. First, no perfect balance seemed possible to me. Second, the battle of Waterloo itself was a long duel between an army under British command (Wellington) and forces under Napoleon. The Prussians, led by Marshal Blücher, did not come up in force until late in the day.

Although Wellington's army was a mixture of nationalities, it seems hardly likely that the army could have lasted through the long hours if other troops had been substituted for the tough, unyielding British regiments.

Finally, I must admit that my reading on Waterloo through the years has been heavily concentrated on British books. However, I make a determined effort to give Napoleon, his troops, old

Blücher, his Prussians, and soldiers of other nationalities full credit for what they did.

Men of Waterloo is also an effort to convince readers that they should examine the Waterloo period for themselves. It is a source of endless pleasure for those of us who do.

Alexandria, Virginia
August 10, 1965

Contents

List of Maps

MEN
OF WATERLOO

Chapter One

The Stage Is Set

THE day was hot for June, but in the late afternoon a breeze had begun to stir. On a small knoll a horseman dismounted with the sun catching the splendor of his uniform as he moved out of the shade of a tall oak. Behind him more horsemen appeared. Some dismounted. Others remained in the saddle. All of them carefully scanned the countryside, some with telescopes.

Spring had been good to the land around them. Bountiful crops of rye, wheat, oats and barley shimmered in the sun. An occasional cottage was an island in the fields. To the west was a forest where a lark took flight. Winging southwest he flew low, but if his course were followed, huge restful clouds could be seen in a soft blue sky. To the north was a crossroads.

There had been some fighting in the south and southeast. But certainly there was no enemy here, thought the commander. The horsemen relaxed as if reading their captain's mind, and a flask of cognac was passed around. Some of the men lit pipes. Finally, the commander ordered one last reconnaissance of the area, but they found nothing to alarm them. Another short rest and they all remounted to ride south to rejoin their army.

The horsemen were members of an advance guard of Polish lancers attached to Napoleon's army, which was invading Belgium.* The date was June 15, 1815. The forest was Bois de Bossu.

---

* Napoleon's Polish lancers were an elite corps which had been formed by the Emperor in Poland.

1

The crossroads was Quatre Bras, twenty miles south of Brussels.

In the next three days three battles would be fought, but the men who were there would recall it as one struggle. History would choose one name for everything that happened.

Waterloo! The battle of Waterloo! It was undoubtedly the single most dramatic event of the nineteenth century. The date of the battle, June 18, 1815, became the benchmark of the century, with people of all walks of life using it to calculate the yesterdays of their triumphs and tragedies. In sumptuous London townhouses or in humble Scottish cottages, mothers would mention that their daughters had married, not in 1825, but "ten years after Waterloo." Or sons would recall that their fathers had died "five years before Waterloo."

The curious rushed to the scene the day after the battle. The cavalcade has continued throughout the decades, and each year more people visit its site than many of Europe's World War I and World War II battlegrounds.

To examine Waterloo is to gaze through a kaleidoscope. The struggle of Napoleon's forces against the allied armies, commanded by the Duke of Wellington and Marshal Blücher, presents an endless variety of pictures for anyone who cares to look. Through the years historians have disagreed on practically everything that happened there, except on the final outcome.

Waterloo has become a hallmark for the romanticist. Perhaps it is still the essence of war for him—a single battle coming closest to his most imaginative idea of what a battle should be like. Surely it had all the ingredients associated with the romance of war, which has fascinated men throughout history.

There were courageous men in colorful uniforms, magnificent chargers dashing everywhere, flags and pennants, trumpets and drums. A terrible clash of musketry and cannon, bayonet and sabre smashed regiments and destroyed whole cavalry squadrons.

There have been few battles where men from both sides died so obligingly or so heroically. Gallantry was as common as bullets. The suspense was overwhelming. The outcome of the battle was in doubt until almost the final shot. As the drama unfolded there were French and British cavalry actions that eclipsed the charge of the Light Brigade for sheer madness. There was brilliance and there was stupidity. There were lost messages and lost chances.

The stakes waged in a single battle on a single field could hardly have been higher—the destiny of Europe, an Empire, the power of a leader who had terrorized the Continent for almost twenty years.

Many of Napoleon's admirers insist that much more was at stake. They argue that, if left to carry out his destiny, Napoleon would have eventually produced an enlightened Europe where men could have pursued culture and commerce without national interference or royal regulation. They saw Napoleon in imperial robes, walking hand in hand with the common man over the smashed thrones of kings and princes to genuine liberalism. To many, the principles of the French Revolution became Napoleon's legacy only to go up in smoke at Waterloo when the Emperor was vanquished. Indeed, some modern admirers of Napoleon argue that Waterloo was, in effect, the first battle of World War I. They maintain that Napoleon's defeat opened a Pandora's box of nationalism which finally whipped Europe into the frenzy of total war.

It is not necessary to examine the validity of these arguments to realize that they have added to the lure of Waterloo. The very fact that so many men in so many places have argued so stoutly for their idol and what his loss meant to the world has always intensified interest in the battle.

The battle itself turned men into adventurers. Soldiers who were not there sought the romance of war where and when they could, on every continent, in scores of forgotten skirmishes around the globe. Many Waterloo veterans savored their moments of honor and wondered when the next big test would come. It came, of course, for the United States in 1861. The stirring events of the Civil War created a traffic jam on the glory road, with a handful of old Waterloo veterans making their final marches for both the Blue and the Grey. Europe's turn came again in 1914. But for many, glory began to die after Waterloo. For many the ultimate battle had been fought.

Napoleon's last gamble was his first battle against Wellington, although the Duke had systematically beaten the Emperor's armies in Spain. The clash between them was a duel of contrasts. Both were incurable egotists; both admired lovely women and beautiful horses. Except for the additional fact that they were superb soldiers, it is difficult to find another quality or fault they shared.

Napoleon was a rebel against any established system that was not his own. He had been for most of his life. Wellington was nursed by the Establishment from childhood, and he defended it to the grave. He was stunned by the French Revolution, not because of its terror, but because he was confounded by its resounding challenge to authority. He feared change and worshipped tradition, but like all great commanders, he challenged orders if he thought they were wrong. He managed to be atrocious to kings, princes and his superior officers even before his exploits in war made his position impregnable.

Writers of the period vainly attempted to picture Wellington as the kind of hero the people could love, as they did indeed love Lord Nelson. But this was impossible. "By God, sir," he would say to almost any admirer who approached him without a formal introduction, and with an icy, penetrating stare (the kind that broke brave subordinates and occasionally made them weep) he would back off as though a plague were in the air.

The Duke took life as he found it in the eighteenth and nineteenth centuries. He made the most of it, and never thought of questioning any part of it. The cruelties he saw in the British Army he accepted as a matter of course. If a chap deserved a flogging, "By God, sir," he got it, and if the crime called for a hundred lashes or more, well and good.

Although Wellington had great respect for the fighting qualities of the British soldier, he considered the rank and file "sots" and "ne'er-do-wells." He spoke haughtily of the "rabble" that he had to contend with in and out of the army. He often described his soldiers as "the scum of the earth," and maintained that most of them had "enlisted for drink." He despised men who betrayed their emotions. He was formal, stiff, stern, cool, calm and husbanded any emotions he had for the scorching rebukes he gave officers and men.

Bravery was an ordinary merit in a soldier, the Duke felt, and to exert it was only doing one's duty. To abandon it was to fail in one's duty. Consequently, a brave soldier could expect no special homage from him. But he did not let this stand in the way when honors for his exploits were heaped at his own feet. He himself accepted every award and purse a grateful nation could bestow upon him for his successful soldiering.

Infantry, often called the "Queen of Battles," was indeed his queen on the battlefield. He respected it above all other arms. Unlike many other officers of the era, he guarded it with careful commands, high ground, trees, bushes, rocks, buildings and sunken roads. He gave it every advantage he could. Artillery was good to have, but not nearly as dependable as tough infantry, deployed on a reverse slope, the Duke found. For some reason, he treated artillery officers with a special curtness. Cavalry was a luxury and he never had enough of it. But often his opinion of the dashing young gentlemen of his horse regiments couldn't have been much lower. Once in Spain after sharply rebuking cavalrymen for a rash charge, he said, "The only thing that they can be relied on to do is to gallop too far and too fast." [1] These words were prophetic for Waterloo.

Burdened on many a field with unreliable allies, Wellington took to using some of their troops on occasion as an umbrella to shield his dependable British infantry. Since many of the forces he had to work with had very little *esprit de corps* even under ordinary circumstances, their terror was magnified many times when they were used as a buffer. In Spain he found that the Spanish soldier, although exceptional in guerilla warfare, was not the kind of fighter who could stand still while the enemy moved relentlessly upon him. He blamed this mostly on their officers. Once speaking of the Spanish army, he said: "Their army amounts at most to thirty or forty thousand men, and they have not an officer amongst them—not one—not one, I believe, who is fit to command even a regiment!" [2] Wellington also said, "They are really children in the art of war, and I cannot say they do anything as it ought to be done, with the exception of running away, and assembling again in a state of nature." [3] He later added that he didn't know what effect they had on the enemy "... but, by God, they frighten me!" [4]

The Duke would most assuredly have lost his earlier battles and would never have had the command at Waterloo if he hadn't fought as he did. Like many British commanders throughout history, Wellington not only had to fight the enemy, he had to fight Parliament. He never had enough of anything, and throughout most of his career, he was always in danger of losing his command. Consequently, he had to fight with great skill and great economy. Risks had to be taken, of course, but rashness could never be afforded, since he never had enough men, guns or supplies to gamble recklessly. A disastrous drain on his manpower would not do, for Parliament would recall him.

His armies were always smaller than those that Napoleon commanded. Because of this he could keep a tight rein on his troops in the field. He roamed the positions and even on occasion posted companies. He had no chief of staff, was jealous of his power and delegated it only infrequently. He wrote his own general orders and, in a battle, would issue scores of verbal commands and rest serenely in the saddle, watching their execution. The Duke maintained that his personal supervision was the secret of his victories. "The real reason why I succeeded in my own campaigns is because I was always on the spot—I saw everything and did everything myself." [5] As flexible in a clash as he was inflexible in his beliefs, the Duke would not hesitate to tear up plans, improvise, retreat or attack. A countercommand rested on his own quick survey of the field and spur-of-the-moment judgment, always his own judgment, since he became a tiger if a subordinate sought to influence either a strategic or tactical situation which was before him. The Duke insisted that Napoleon's marshals planned their campaigns "like a new set of harness." But he said his plans were made of "ropes." "If anything went wrong I tied a knot and went on," he said.[6]

Wellington's troops were quick to obey him. The harsh discipline of the day was only part of the reason. The Duke looked after his troops constantly. He went to extreme efforts to see that they were paid on time and as well-fed and housed as conditions would permit. The men knew that their commander was as fair as he was tough. He punished them by adhering strictly to the military code, but if he felt a soldier was being unduly persecuted he would stand up for him in a court martial. Most of all, his men knew that the Duke kept an anxious eye on the casualty list. They also knew that they could count on their leader to be with them no matter how hot the battle. They respected him and would die for him, but they could not love him. No one, it seems, could ever love the Duke.

Even his mother saw him as "food for powder." [7] His wife, Dollie, lived in awe of him. He learned to despise her, and committed the grave marital sin of criticizing her in the company of more intelligent and exciting women. His tastes in women shocked some of the young ladies from London who were vacationing in Brussels before the battle, and they wrote their mothers and aunts about women of loose character who attended his parties. At social events the Duke could be charming or a great bore, depending on his moods and the company. He could hold a small group spellbound with his observations on events of the day, but he was an uninspired speaker if he faced large audiences. His repartee was mostly limited to the hammer. Should a conversation start to move beyond his scope, he would quash the fellow leading the mental ambuscade with a "By God, sir," and that would be that.

No, he was not loved for his wit, or for any other reason. After the battle of Waterloo even his horse, Copenhagen, kicked him.

Napoleon had a magic about him which made his soldiers love him even though he often treated them poorly and deserted them in Egypt and Russia. They forgave him everything. Even after Waterloo they would have fought for him again. There were mutinies in some regiments when the soldiers heard that he could no longer lead them, and that they were now to serve France. Many could die for Napoleon, but would not wear a uniform in the service of their country. In the beginning, he had been careful with them. His victories came from skill and daring, but later when he had a whole world to watch, he turned his armies over to others. He asked for victory. The blood it cost did not seem to matter. The swift maneuver which had won for him the admiration of military men in every respectable army was forgotten. With a seemingly inexhaustible supply of manpower, he became a squanderer on the battlefield. When he was in action, if a costly frontal assault was the easiest thing to do, he did it, and as the drums rolled for the charge, his mind often turned elsewhere—to politics, to Paris, to a hundred other things. By the time of Waterloo, he found it hard to fight economically, as Wellington did, and as he once did himself. As Emperor, of course, he could not always remain a professional soldier with the relatively limited responsibility of supervising an army.

Much has been written about the magic that made men worship him. It was said by Stendhal that "Napoleon was our only religion"; perhaps he put it best of all since no one has really been able to analyze properly the personal magnetism of Napoleon. Generals would risk their armies and their careers to gain a simple compliment from him. When he said, "Vous n'avez pas mal fait," * many preferred this indirect tribute to a castle in Spain or a flattering title. Horribly mangled soldiers would, in one last torturous effort, scream, *"Vive l'Empereur!"* just before they died. Napoleon used the love of his soldiers to excess—for without it he could never have traveled from Elba to Paris and thence to Waterloo. His return from banishment was incredible, and the love he had from his troops was the most important factor of all.

There were many women in Napoleon's life. His affairs, it is said, began with a streetwalker, who lured him to her flat when he was a junior officer. They ended with those who comforted him in the final years of his life at St. Helena. In all, there could have been as many as fifty women in his life. Many loved him, many did not. The one woman he is said to have sincerely loved, Josephine, was an incorrigible demirep, who could not give him an heir.

He heard of the death of his divorced wife at Elba. No one knows what really went through his mind when he did, but the news could have been one of those incalculable things that helped him to decide to take his last gamble. His life, of course, was a steady procession of great risks. He met them dramatically and often rashly. A phrase from Machiavelli was his compass: "It is better to be brutal with Fortune than to approach her with respect; for Fortune is a woman, and he that seeks to win her must use violence rather than diplomacy." [8]

Unlike Wellington, Napoleon was a man who eagerly read historians and philosophers, poets and playwrights. He was a complex, sophisticated man who could and did converse with all the intellectuals of his time. Although his critics charge that these interests were a dictator's way to self-glorification, there are many counterarguments. It is known that he had been interested in the classics since his school days and that he enjoyed acting out tragedies with his brothers and sisters behind closed doors. He was a devoted playgoer, a severe critic of the theater. He was a serious student of dramatics, secretly taking elocution lessons

---

* You have not done badly.

from the great tragedian of the period, Talma. A talented speaker, Napoleon, in contrast to Wellington, displayed emotions unashamedly. He would pout, storm, and even show remorse. He was jealous of all great men and demonstrated it openly by brutal, unjust criticism. Napoleon criticized the campaigns of Alexander, Hannibal, Caesar; the plays of Shakespeare; the histories of Tacitus; the poetry of Virgil. He had an opinion on practically every human endeavor, and found time to rant about it or to praise it. Probably no world leader rewarded bravery and talent so lavishly as he did. As Emperor, he was a man who would even try to influence the destiny of a departed soul by rewarding one of his favorite dancing girls with a Christian burial. His friends never tired of telling the story of Mademoiselle Chameroi. When this notorious beauty from the Opera died suddenly, the Vicar of Saint-Roch refused to conduct services for her because of her sin-filled life. Napoleon ordered the Archbishop of Paris to suspend the Vicar for three months. His reason, he said, was "to give him time to meditate on the fact that Jesus Christ had taught men to pray for poor sinners, and to cultivate the divine attribute of charity to all." [9] Before his fortunes waned, Napoleon, fond of plays with a tragic theme, had hoped to award a grand prize to the composer of the greatest tragedy of the age. Wellington, it seems, should have been in the running.

The Duke, of course, had formidable help at Waterloo. There was the army of Marshal Blücher, the angry, old Prussian who had battled Napoleon before. He passionately hated Napoleon and hoped to preside over a grand execution of the Emperor. The seventy-three-year-old soldier was always dreaming of Napoleon dangling from the gallows in front of the entire Prussian army. He fought viciously to accomplish this objective, charging boldly, brawling like a sergeant, riding with his dragoons like a corporal. If it had not been for the resolute marshal whose army arrived to support the Duke in the final hours of the battle, the outcome could have been reversed.

Napoleon's lieutenants did not show the same drive as old Blücher until it was too late. Many historians believe that if they had, the Emperor would probably have won—perhaps to be engulfed later by vastly superior numbers, but carrying the day at Waterloo, nevertheless. Marshal Ney, who commanded the left flank of the Emperor's forces in the campaign, was forty-six, the same age as Napoleon and Wellington. Nicknamed "old Red Peter" by his troops because of his bright red hair, the marshal, "the bravest of the brave," was one of the most daring officers to wield a sword for Napoleon. But something happened to him in the campaign. At times he became overly cautious, a dreaded military disease from which he had always seemed safe. Marshal Grouchy, forty-nine, was on the right flank. He finally was given a special force under his personal control with the task of making sure the Prussians did not join their English allies. Grouchy was miscast as an independent commander. Prior to Waterloo he had never held such a command. Forty-six-year-old Marshal Soult was a crack field commander who also seemed out of his element at Waterloo. He served Napoleon as chief of staff during the battle, and managed to complicate or confuse the orders to Ney and Grouchy which were given to him by the Emperor.

The fact that in any account of Waterloo it is necessary to spend more time discussing Napoleon's subordinates than Wellington's emphasizes the difference in battle techniques between the two men. Wellington's lieutenants could not lose the battle for him because they were under such tight control by their commander that Sunday. Consequently, they were of less importance. Napoleon's subordinates, with much more freedom of choice, could lose for him. But just how much Napoleon contributed to his own disaster is one of those perpetual riddles that hundreds of writers have tried to answer. The real beginning of the end for Napoleon had begun many months earlier with the first snowflakes of the terrifying Russian winter of 1812. The Emperor lost over 400,000 men to the winter and the Cossacks. It was a blow from which he never recovered. In the following months, until his first abdication in April 1814, the remainder of his troops were in and out of numerous desperate engagements with English, Prussian, Austrian and Spanish armies. The allies were all exuding confidence because of his disaster in the North. Pressed on all sides by generals quite willing to fight a war of attrition, since he was outnumbered everywhere, the Emperor was forced slowly back to Paris. There his political power was dissolving due to his military reverses. His control finally melted entirely away and his huge empire shrank to a 20,000-acre island. The allies allowed

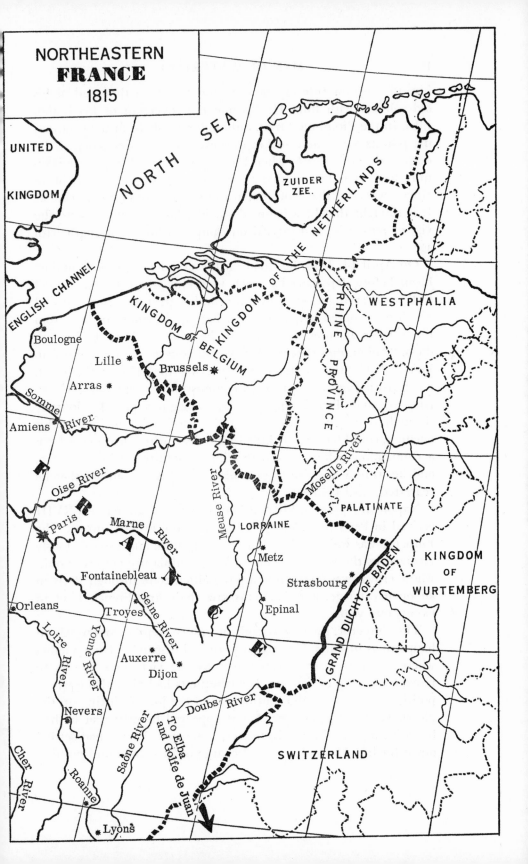

NORTHEASTERN
FRANCE
1815

UNITED
KINGDOM

NORTH SEA

ZUIDER
ZEE.

KINGDOM OF THE NETHERLANDS

ENGLISH CHANNEL

KINGDOM OF BELGIUM

RHINE PROVINCE

WESTPHALIA

Boulogne

Lille

Brussels

Arras

Somme

Amiens River

Oise River

Meuse River

Moselle River

PALATINATE

Paris

Marne River

LORRAINE

Metz

KINGDOM

OF

WURTEMBERG

Fontainebleau

Strasbourg

Orleans

Troyes

Seine River

Epinal

GRAND DUCHY OF BADEN

Auxerre

Dijon

Yonne River

Loire River

Doubs River

Nevers

Saône River

To Elba and Golfe de Juan

SWITZERLAND

Cher River

Roanne

Lyons

him to keep his title as Emperor and to take a thousand of his old soldiers with him. He became the sovereign of his island, Elba, in the Piombino Strait, although officials from the conquering powers were there to keep an eye on him. The story of the despair that seized him when his world exploded has never been fully told. It is known that he was gravely ill at Fontainebleau after it was clear that banishment from France was his only course. It is thought that he attempted suicide, failing only because the vial of poison he had carried on campaign lost its strength with age.

On April 14, 1814, he stood on the grand terrace of Fontainebleau before departing by coach to Fréjus where he was to sail to Elba. Wearing a general's uniform, his great grey overcoat and his three-cornered hat, which had become a symbol of fear from the English channel to the Don, he said good-bye to his soldiers. "Adieu, mes enfants! Mes voeux vous accompagneront toujours!" [10] He then entered a coach for the trip to the coast, accompanied by the four allied commissioners, representing Austria, England, Prussia and Russia, to begin a perilous journey through southern France. Along the way mobs, incited by his enemies, could have easily killed him. Fear, which had never been a companion before, was with him constantly during the trip, and he wore a disguise to save his life. This was an act that he regretted until his death.

Napoleon landed in Elba on May 4, two days after Louis XVIII arrived in Paris preparatory to assuming the French throne. The Emperor was welcomed with a 101-gun salute and was graciously received by the whole population of his miniature empire. Louis, whose crown was guaranteed by the allies, rode through Paris in an open carriage, and Parisians saw their first French king in twenty-one years.

The Emperor, through friends in France, kept a close watch on happenings in Paris. He carefully studied dispatches from Vienna where a Congress had been called by the victorious powers to remake the map of Europe. His conquests had altered the whole political structure of the continent, and the job of picking up the pieces was not an easy one. Yet it appeared in Elba that he had had his fill of political adventures. It seemed that he had settled down for life. He took personal charge of the island and nothing seemed too trivial to escape his attention. He set about to improve the place's agriculture, its laws, administration, trade and environment. He urged his soldiers to marry the attractive dark-haired girls, who seemed more than willing to take up with them. He presided at colorful, if somewhat heavily regulated social functions which he himself organized. It seemed that he had found the last dregs of his cup the most flavorful of all.

Napoleon's enemies sometimes wondered if they had done enough to guarantee his exile. Some would have sent him to a more distant island. Others wanted to kill him. The Emperor's special couriers kept him informed of all the intrigue against him. Meanwhile, he was angered by broken promises. The French government had promised him an annual income of two million francs, but it was not forthcoming. Since it had cost billions in gold and an estimated two million lives to banish the Emperor, it seems strange that his promised income should have been denied him, especially if there was any thought at all that it might curb his restlessness.

The Austrians refused to permit his wife, Marie-Louise, and his son, the King of Rome, to join Napoleon, or even to visit him. Even if they had given her permission to go, she would have refused. The Austrian-born princess he had married to provide him with an heir had cooled toward him. Aside from a mild concern for his safety, she preferred to forget the past.

But the news that reached Napoleon was not all bad. In the early weeks of his exile some of it even amused him. Problems for his enemies who had gathered around the conference table in Vienna seemed insurmountable. Disputes among the allied representatives over what nations considered just compensation for their long wars with France raged constantly. The negotiations seemed endless.

Word traveled swiftly from Paris that Louis was a laughingstock. Napoleon heard that the situation in the capital was ridiculous, with word circulating everywhere that the Bourbon king, very fat and very unpopular, might have to make another hasty exit to Belgium or England. But Louis seemed oblivious to the whisperings, the gossip and the tittering which went on behind his back. Many Parisians, their nerves already exposed and quivering, because the city vibrated with the boots, hooves and wheels of foreign armies, grimaced anew every time they saw their king don *petit chapeau à la Wellington*. They felt this was an unwarranted tribute to their British enemy.

On occasion, Louis decreed, as his ancestors had done, that the people should have the privilege of watching him eat. Curious peasants thronged Paris to view the spectacle of their king at table. The show seemed better than any at the comic opera. Farmers, tanned and lean from heavy work in the fields, gawked at their corpulent majesty as they trudged past slowly, hats in hand. The king sometimes acknowledged their presence with a benign smile, but mainly concentrated on the business at hand, devouring gargantuan amounts of food from the golden imperial plate, one of his legacies from Napoleon, and drinking huge splashes of champagne from the imperial goblets. Sometimes wheeled or carried to dinner when his gout was raging, he was an immense picture in his light blue coat with epaulets and gilt buttons, red velvet gaiters, velvet boots and powdered wig. "The king's favourite dish of fifteen mutton cutlets—all of which, *sautées au jus,* he daily despatches at breakfast, and again at dinner, varied by a *sauce à la champagne*—appears as usual, and as usual, soon disappears," wrote one observer of the royal appetite in action.[11]

His majesty seemed ignorant of the temper of the people and continued to remind them of the Revolution at a time when it would have seemed wiser to shroud its apparent failure with less antagonizing royal behavior. Millions of Frenchmen were galled every time they remembered that the bloody efforts of '89 had apparently come to nothing. Louis constantly harped about the divine right of kings, and insisted that his first year's reign should be recorded as his nineteenth year in power, although he had emigrated since the French Revolution. He ordered a search for the heads and bodies of Louis XVI and Marie Antoinette, the Revolution's favorite victims. When some skulls and bones were found in a corner of the old cemetery of the Madeleine, they were given a solemn and splendid royal funeral. Frenchmen groaned.

The king's unpopularity was not lost on Napoleon. As the *gros goutteux,* which the French nicknamed Louis, continued his reign, signs of unrest in France reached the Emperor's ears. Many of his old soldiers who had been made to serve under the white cockade of the Bourbons were deserting. Some of those who remained in the army at half-pay grumbled and organized secret Napoleonic societies. Crude imperial eagles, hastily scrawled *Ns,* and occasionally a red, white and blue cockade, the emblem of the French Revolution, appeared on walls and on the sides of churches and other buildings. Prints and small busts of Napoleon were bootlegged at fairs and by street peddlers. Some buyers were daring enough to place them conspicuously in their workshops. The violet was adopted as a Napoleonic emblem. Young women wore violets in their hair. Men wore them in their lapels. Actors and actresses took seemingly innocent lines in their plays and with an inflection here or there or a slight mispronunciation, turned them into tributes to the Emperor. In the audiences there would be a mixture of applause and hisses. Mademoiselle Mars, one of the most popular actresses in Paris, often delivered a line or two in tribute to the Emperor during her performances. She would often wear a violet in her dress as well.

Although there was unemployment in Paris and other large cities in France, Napoleon's partisans made the problem appear much worse than it was, since travelers were pouring into the country, especially from Britain. At least the cafés and inns were doing a booming business. In fact, French restaurateurs hadn't enjoyed such a turnover in years, and they sincerely hoped that they had heard the last of the Emperor. French shopkeepers were getting their revenge against the English in the market place, often charging ridiculous prices for the bric-a-brac they were seeking.

Nevertheless, a peace-time economy lag had set in and many workers who had been employed in war production were looking for jobs. Even if the allies had permitted it, Louis had no burning interest in building up France's military preparedness, since it was France's enemies who guaranteed him his place in the sun. The allies, in fact, carted out millions of dollars worth of military supplies which had been stored by Napoleon in dozens of fortresses and arsenals. The unemployed who watched the dismantling of France's might gossiped about it in their cafés.

Meanwhile, Louis was lavishly spending Napoleon's treasure, which was given to him by the allies who had captured it. Amounting to over 60 million francs, the legacy was shrinking fast.

If the report on the squandering of his fortune didn't jar the Emperor, other messages reaching Elba did. Many of his marshals had been feting his enemies since his downfall. They were using the treasures which he had heaped upon them during the Empire to give balls and banquets in their palatial estates. Marshal Ney, bearing the title Prince de Moskowa, which had been created for him by Napoleon because of his valor, was among the more entertaining hosts. He was a social lion during the brief festive period in Paris when many crowned heads of Europe and their armies made the city occupation headquarters. The rulers of Austria, Russia, Prussia and many minor kings and princes, all with splendid corps of servants and retainers, paraded through the city. Their arrivals and departures were marked by massive displays of military pomp and ceremony with troops of the victorious nations lining the streets and boulevards.

Josephine, too, was swept up in the glitter. Before her death, early during Napoleon's exile in Elba, she entertained the Czar Alexander enthusiastically. She did so, although her former husband's enemies had claimed much of her imperial inheritance as well as his. The Duchess d'Angoulême promenaded grandly in all the famous salons, wearing earrings which had decorated Josephine at her coronation as Empress. Great pear-shaped brilliants within a circle of the finest diamonds, they had cost Napoleon 250,000 francs.

On Elba, often windy, rainy and cloudy, there were few portents that the Emperor would ever attempt a coup. He played cards with Madame Mere, who had joined him. He took brisk horseback rides around the countryside, enjoyed scalding baths, and continued an active interest in the affairs of his little nation. Those who knew the Emperor well might have read something in the fact that he chose a number of residences on the island before settling down. This would seem to indicate a certain restlessness. At night he retired to a bedroom which was decorated to resemble a tent. Occasionally he would hint to his soldiers that there were better times ahead.

No one in authority possessed the imagination to envision Napoleon back on the throne of France. Although many people still feared him, and there was still talk that he might make an attempt to regain his old power, the whole idea seemed too preposterous as the months passed. Even if he did attempt to return to France, was not the King's army ready to arrest him? What of the British fleet that patrolled the Mediterranean?

But in Paris, Madame de Krüdener, a prophetess in vogue in many high places, began forecasting dire events. Finally, in January 1815, she mysteriously announced that Napoleon would return. He would escape "for the chastisement of the allies and the punishment of guilty France, as decreed by the Eternal," she said.[12]

Her prophecy was not long in coming true. No one really knows when Napoleon made up his mind to march on Paris. The idea could have been with him from the very moment he was forced from the throne of France. It could have come when his coach was jostled by the mobs as he traveled to the Southern Coast, to what his enemies hoped was oblivion. Or he could have thought of it during one of his lonely rides around the island. It is believed, however, that no preparations were made to return to France until nearly February of 1815.

On February 10, Sir Neil Campbell, the British commissioner, left for a twelve-day holiday on the mainland. French writers insist that Sir Neil, a handsome, towering Scot, went there and on to Florence to keep a rendezvous with a lovely woman. Her name and nationality remain mysteries, although a dozen charming courtesans have been gossiped about as the temptress who enticed Sir Neil to her side. It is said that such a woman might well have been in the service of the Emperor.

Napoleon brilliantly used the time of Sir Neil's absence to prepare for the dash to France. Stores of flour, potatoes and salt-beef were hoarded. Provisions were made for the secret removal of what was left of the Emperor's treasure. Minute plans for organizing a flotilla were carried out by Napoleon's lieutenants. Stores of extra clothing and gunpowder were put aside. Horses were reshod. Even Napoleon's two Berlin carriages were disassembled and packed.

The tiny Elba fleet, assigned to the Emperor by the treaty of Fontainebleau, was made ready. There were the *Inconstant,* Napoleon's sixteen-gun flagship; the *Caroline,* a one-gun sloop; one large open boat; and two oar-and-sail-propelled feculias, the *Mouche* and the *Etoile.* But the "armada" was not enough to carry the Emperor's 1,250 soldiers and sailors, the horses and the provisions. Shortly before departure his men seized a 196-ton commercial vessel, the *Saint-Esprit*.

Napoleon stood on the deck of the *Inconstant* during embarkation, which was just after midnight on February 26. His flag, the banner of Elba with its orange diagonal band decorated with three bees, barely stirred on the mast above him. The winds would not be with him for hours, and his fleet hugged the shores for what must have seemed like an eternity. Finally, the winds came and the Emperor was on his way to what must be considered the greatest comeback in history. Perhaps this in itself is the main reason why the battle of Waterloo was such a glorious adventure. No one in history had fallen so far to rise again so magnificently.

On Tuesday, February 28, Sir Neil Campbell, the British commissioner, had definitely established that Napoleon had escaped from Elba. Warned by a British sea captain that something sinister was afoot, he hastened back to Elba from Italy. So fraught with concern was Sir Neil that when the sails slackened a few miles from the island, he ordered a small boat lowered and was rowed in. He was too late. Although he sounded the alarm and sent warnings to every British post he could think of in Europe, he could not guess where the Emperor had headed.

Chapter Two

The News Breaks

SEEN anywhere from a distance that day, the Golfe-Juan was a hazy blue. But toward the shore the sea was a lively green as it washed smooth white pebbles in the sand and made whirlpools in scars on the beaches. It was cold and blustery. The mistral, which comes down from the Maritime Alps, had whipped over fresh snow on its way to the sea. It dropped the temperature and spun the waves with white froth. The sky was grey. Clouds moved rapidly to the north where the Vallauris mountains and the Vallée d'Or lay, with the Maritime Alps rising in the distance.

Small cottages of fishermen, potters and peasants could be seen inland. White, blue and brown boats, pulled up on the beaches, pointed their prows everywhere. Here and there were black kettles used for boiling fishing nets clean. Away from the beaches were olive groves and orange trees.

Nearing this lovely stretch of coastline as dawn broke on March 1, 1815, was Napoleon's fleet. It had come from Elba almost without incident. Once, when a French man-of-war had approached, the soldiers had stretched out on the decks to avoid being seen. But now, with the sun rising, France was in sight. The adventure was about to begin.

The Emperor emerged from below deck. The soldiers and sailors watched him closely. It seemed that they could not take their eyes off him. He had grown somewhat heavier in exile, but his great grey coat and the three-cornered hat flattered his figure. He seemed almost slender. The Emperor looked toward France. He talked to no one. It was noticed that he was wearing a tricolor cockade.

The men followed his example. There was laughter and cheering. Some of the younger men grappled with one another in exhilaration. They pulled out cockades from knapsacks, hats, pockets. The Elba pennant, familiar in all nearby waters, was rapidly lowered. Skimming up the mast went the blue, white and red flag of the French Republic and the Empire.

Later, many would say that his return to France was his greatest campaign. They would say, too, that if he had acted with the same dispatch at Waterloo, he would have won a stunning victory.

His return to France was the most delicate campaign in his career. Force was completely out of the question. A careless shot, a hasty blow could throw France into revolution. Any bloodshed and the adventure might end before it had begun. Napoleon warned his men time and time again to forget their muskets and pistols.

France must be won with words! Proclamations were ground out in Elba and aboard the *Inconstant*. They were filled with fire that molds men's emotions. There were all kinds. Some appealed to the civilian population, others to officials. But Napoleon's main target was the king's soldiers. The impact of the message had to be tremendous if he were to succeed: "Soldiers, rally round the standard of your chief. He lives but for you, his rights are but those of the people and your own. Victory, swift, triumphant, lies before us. From village spire to village spire the eagle shall bear the nation's colors, even to the towers of Notre Dame."

Proclamations had to be posted as soon as the landing was secure. Although there were supplies aboard, more were needed. Horses and donkeys would have to be bought. Passports would be necessary for agents who would head for scores of cities and towns to rally support for the Emperor.

It was still many hours to a landing. Ashore there was no sign that a cloudburst of excitement was about to break. The noises of the dawn were the usual ones—a baby crying, a donkey braying, a cock crowing. Near the Gabelle Tower, where Napoleon was to make his landing, were the quarters of the customs official. He could not know how futile his day would be.

In many nearby villages and towns, old soldiers, retired or on half-pay, dreamed their adventures. They soon would be swept up in the greatest one of all.

In Cannes, seven miles to the northeast, the mayor slept fitfully. It was his custom. Here and there, people began to stir for breakfasts of milk or wine, soup and bread. A weary sentry may have imagined a routine day ahead. He was stationed just a short distance away at the fortress of Antibes.

Napoleon had his plans ready. Not a minute could be wasted. Not a thing could be left undone, if he were to succeed. Most of the details of the landing and the rush to Paris were firmly fixed in his mind. Communications to Paris would have to be disrupted as long as possible. Blockades had to be erected, post-offices seized, coaches impounded. All these things had to be done, and not a shot could be fired.

To win France, it would be better to take a route to Paris through the lower Alps. It was a section where Napoleon was popular. Another way, although shorter and less difficult, would lessen his chances, and the risks against a successful return were great as it was.

The hours passed. The end of the voyage seemed the longest part of the journey. To the men in the cramped boats, so loaded that the sea nearly lapped at the gunwales, the distance to the shoreline seemed endless. Anxiety mounted. Had the king's troops been warned? Would there be fighting on the beaches? It seemed impossible that nothing could have gone wrong.

The noon hour had passed. Fishermen and cottagers had taken their second meal of the day. Some had eaten sardines and bread along the quay areas, and wondered about the strange fleet. No one had any idea that Napoleon was about to make his appearance. But a rumor spread that the ships carried Algerian pirates who sometimes raided along the coast. Men, women, children disappeared from the beaches. Doors were locked. Shops were barricaded. A British tourist is said to have braved the weather with his family to picnic in the area. The tricolor on the *Inconstant* is said to have made him curious since he knew that the flag had been outlawed by the Bourbons and their allies. He is reported to have finally guessed that the fleet was Napoleon's and was one of the first to reach London with the news.

It was 1:00 P.M. when the first small boat was lowered to carry ashore an advance party. Shortly before, Napoleon grouped his officers around him and gave them their final orders. He was coatless now, and as he spoke he pointed out the landmarks and punctuated his commands with a flurry of gestures.

As the first small boat approached shore and then another, and another, some of the men, gleeful to be back in France once more, plunged into shallow water and raced to land. They said the fragrance of France was overpowering and that it was impossible to stay in the boats any longer. The fragrance of France was delightful. The strong smell of the sea was softened by the wind crossing through the orange trees, eucalyptus, rose laurel and bougainvillea, cactus and agave.

The only opposition to the landing came from the customs official who had slept so soundly in the dawn. He stood on the beach shouting that no one could land until his health regulations were satisfied. In his semi-military uniform of dark green—frock coat, white cross belt, huge hat and short boots—he was a dot of sobriety in a melee of mirth. *"C'est Napoléon, c'est Napoléon,"* grinning troops shouted. The customs official's authority was demolished by laughter.

All the planning, which had been so carefully detailed by Napoleon, went into effect. All the military precautions of a beachhead on alien soil were in force. The unloading began, and the beach started to pile up swiftly with packages, barrels, boxes, cases and chests. Some of the troops, delirious with the fact that they were back on French soil, broke out bottles of wine to celebrate. Their officers, after a few minutes of attending to superfluous matters so the men could have *joie de vivre,* got them back on the job again.

Napoleon remained aboard until after 5:00 P.M. It was after the horses and cannon and most of the supplies were ashore that the Emperor decided to disembark. A thunderous cheer went up from his men when he arrived in a barge. Curious peasants had gathered now that their fear of pirates had disappeared. They were held back by squads of soldiers, but the Emperor met with a group of children before he took a nap on his camp bed, which had been set up in the open. A cottage had been cleared for him, but he preferred to take his place near an olive grove, a sign of good luck to the Old Guardsmen.

But there was one bad omen, or so it seemed to many. One of the Emperor's officers, Captain Lamouret, with a dozen grenadiers, had been captured by the 87th Regiment at Antibes. This was the garrison that Napoleon felt should be neutralized. Lamouret and his men were allowed into the fortress and then surrounded and disarmed. They fought as best they could with words and threats, but remembering Napoleon's orders that no shots could be fired, they finally surrendered.

The news of the landing began to sweep through France. A mixture of rumors and half-truths preceded the fact that Napoleon himself had arrived. Some of Napoleon's troops had landed, but the Emperor remained in Elba! Napoleon's Imperial Guard had deserted him! The Emperor was dead and his men were returning to France! The rumors flew along every road leading out of Cannes. In headlong flight rode the constable from Cannes. He flew to Fréjus in the west to warn the gendarmerie. He reported that some of Napoleon's troops had arrived without the Emperor. This news was started up the chain of communications and command to Paris.

A coach carrying the duc de Valentinois to his principality of Monaco was halted by Napoleon's troops and the duc was detained. But one of Valentinois' servants managed to flee eastward. He reached Monaco some hours later, and from there the news sped to Italy.

The truth that Napoleon himself was among the landing party followed closely behind the first warnings. Napoleon's agents, headed for all sections of France where there were signs of resistance to the king, were supposed to keep the landing secret from the public. But often the news spilled out in conversations at taverns and inns. Official messages of the Emperor's landing, sent by mayors and other officials loyal to the king, moved by courier in all directions. In a matter of hours after Napoleon's landing was confirmed, the word was flowing slowly (but swiftly for the times) to Italy, Spain, England, Prussia, Austria, Russia and the United States.

Napoleon's troops had eaten on the run, but toward evening

they had a decent meal—thick soup—the Old Guard's staple made from whatever ingredients happened to be on hand. It was supplemented by fresh supplies purchased from the surrounding neighborhood: fruit, bread, olives and fish.

Napoleon held another meeting with his staff. His officers reported one by one that his orders had been carried out. Some suggested that soldiers should be sent to rescue Captain Lamouret and his men, but the Emperor wouldn't hear of it. He explained that he and his small force had spent enough time in the area, and that to delay longer would be disastrous. Napoleon's last order before marching was to give Captain Cambronne, one of his crack officers, command of an advance guard.

The drums began to beat. Cambronne and his grenadiers started the long march to Paris. Napoleon followed shortly with his troops. There were additions to his force: some half-pay officers living in semi-retirement in the area, a few officers and men from the 87th regiment, the unit which had captured some of his own men earlier. This was the first of the defections from the Loyalists to the Emperor. Napoleon had greeted each "recruit" personally. He was to greet many more.

The route Napoleon chose was a surprise for his enemies. A simpler way, which they fully expected him to take, would have played into their hands. With Cambronne's vanguard flying before him, demanding excessive rations to exaggerate the strength of the Emperor's force, Napoleon marched for Grasse. By dawn of March 2, he was there. Just a few hours later, he struck out on a rugged path for Castellane, arriving in the early morning of March 3.

The march was difficult. Napoleon and his troops slipped in the mud, fell in the snow. A mule carrying cases of gold coins crashed over a ravine. Some supplies were abandoned. The artillery and carriages had been left behind.

On the night of March 3, Napoleon was in Barrème. That same night the news of his arrival in France was buzzing through Marseilles. It had arrived earlier in the day. An official message addressed to the king was hurried north to Lyons by relays of couriers on horseback. There, the message would be put on the aerial telegraph for Paris.

The aerial telegraph was a remarkable system of communica-

tions, and had been adopted by the French government for sending messages between distant points twenty-three years before.*
By 1815 the system had been improved and it was possible if conditions were right, for news to travel nearly 500 miles an hour.
The system consisted of chains of relay towers on high ground.
Each relay tower was manned by signalers. Their tower was a tall post with a crossbar at the top. On each end of the crossbar were small semaphore arms moving on pivots. The positions of these arms represented letters or complete words, and could be hurriedly manipulated from the ground. Observers manning the next tower three to four miles away would read messages with their telescopes and then repeat the whole process for the benefit of another signaler down the line. There was a connecting line from Paris to Lyons, one of the terminal points.

By Saturday, March 4, Napoleon was in Digne. Arriving at noon, he spent over eight hours there to give his troops a rest.
He continued his march in the evening. As he lunched at the Hôtel du Petit-Paris,[1] some of his grenadiers managed to slip away to the basilica of Notre-Dame-du-Bourg, the beautiful and ancient Romanesque church. They lit candles to the Virgin for the Emperor's success, but they didn't want him to know about it, because they felt he would think them superstitious.

On Sunday, an exhausted courier arrived at the aerial-telegraph tower in Lyons with the message from Marseilles. Minutes later, it was being flashed through the heart of France northwest to Paris. In the early morning Cambronne reached Sisteron, with the Emperor not far behind. The cicadas were chirping shrilly as the battalions slogged along. This seemed another good omen to the soldiers as they talked with their new companions who had joined the Banner of the Eagle. The ranks had not yet been swelled with new recruits. But more and more half-pay and retired officers were falling in and gaspingly trying to maintain the pace of the long-legged Guardsmen.

In the rear of the columns, mothers found time to stem their tears, to curse Napoleon for attracting their sons to his colors.
For here and there, young men wrapped lunches in their shirts and scurried away to join up.

* The device was invented by two brothers, Claude and Ignace Chappe, and remained in use in France until replaced by the electric telegraph system.

The Emperor and his troops marched over the red soil, past sil-very trees bearing grey-green olives, past the hillsides of carefully-tended terraces into Sisteron. The little army moved through the fascinating narrow streets of the city, past the Cathedral of Notre-Dame, with its priceless gilt wood. Napoleon's soldiers would have liked to pause, but they did not. The march continued to Upaix.

There, enthusiasm for the Emperor exploded. Until that point, his receptions were generally lukewarm. But at Upaix, on the road to Gap, it was a carnival. A delegation of mayors from nearby villages, old soldiers who had taken the trouble to put on the remnants of their uniforms, women with bouquets of flowers, laughing children swarmed around him. *"Vive l'Empereur!, Vive l'Empereur!"* was heard everywhere.

A short pause and the march was resumed. Children skipped along to the beat of the drum. Young girls jumped up and down to get a better look at their Emperor. Women scuffled and el-bowed to get closer to him. Bottles and pitchers of wine were passed to the soldiers, some of it hand over hand from windows to the crowds, to the marching columns. Nervous donkeys brayed in protest. Some of the horses shied and pranced. The soldiers were ecstatic. They pounded each other on the back, winked at the girls and shouted *"Vive Napoléon!"*

In Paris, the message from Marseilles had arrived at the city's telegraph receiving point in Montmartre at noon on Sunday. It had been hastily transcribed by surprised codemen and rushed to Ignace-Urbain-Jean Chappe, the director of telegraphs. The news shattered Chappe, but he managed to follow the proper pro-tocol. The message was carefully written for the king's eyes and officially sealed. Then Chappe headed for the Tuileries Palace as fast as he could. Sweating and puffing, his bulging stomach seem-ingly about to burst, he managed to present himself at the office of Baron de Vitrolles, the king's secretary.

At first, Chappe could say nothing, but in a moment or two he sputtered that there was an emergency. He begged de Vitrolles to act, although he said he knew the king was ill. Louis was again having a serious attack of the gout, but the message was taken to him. With difficulty, his puffed fingers tore open the envelope, and he began to read to himself slowly. Finally, he announced the news to de Vitrolles and ordered the telegram taken to the Minister of War.[2] The king did not delude himself. He knew at once that Napoleon's escape meant war or exile for him, or probably both.

Napoleon had left the Durance River, which sparkles its way through the Alps. The cool water filled his soldiers' canteens and bathed their feet. The battalions were on the last miles to Gap. The day was ending. The Olan and Sirac peaks and the ridges south of the Massif des Ecrims were beautiful in the twilight.

The Emperor arrived in Gap at 11:00 P.M. Another carnival awaited him. This time an illuminated one. Lights were lit in every home. There were bonfires in the streets and in the squares. Napoleon felt that the shouts of *"Vive l'Empereur!"* had turned to thunder. He predicted he would be in Paris on March 20.

The government tried to suppress the news, but it began to be known in Paris the night of the 5th. Officials and officers whispered the word confidentially to their friends. At glittering parties in fashionable residences along Rue Vivienne, Saint Denis and Rue de la Paix, the matter was discussed. For the most part Parisian society took the news lightly. "The man will surely be killed," lovely women in pink and ivory-white gowns said to their escorts. Some of the men made mental notes to visit the stock market. Perhaps it would be just as well to sell, although there was no question that Napoleon would be quickly dealt with by Louis' troops, they noted. Saturday's transactions on the Bourse saw shares of the Bank of France selling at 1,200 francs. Five percent bonds were moving at 78.75 francs.

On Monday, March 6, Napoleon sped on, hoping to arrive in Grenoble as soon as possible. Camps were broken up quickly, but there was still time for the soldiers to grill trout and the lake fish which mountaineers gave them: lavarets, ombles and feras. Meanwhile, in Paris, important ambassadors and ministers had received the news of Napoleon's landing from the king's couriers. They sent off messages to their home governments. William H. Crawford, the United States minister in Paris, was informed, but decided to wait until the news was printed in the newspapers so he could include them with his dispatch. It was on March 7 when the story broke in *Le Moniteur Universel.** On that date the news also reached Vienna. It had come up by way of Italy and was

* This newspaper was the official government publication.

based on the first warnings of Sir Neil. There was no word there
yet that Napoleon had landed in Provence and was on his way to
Paris. The Duke of Wellington, England's representative at the
Congress of Vienna, heard of the escape in a letter from a British
official in Florence. Austrian Minister Metternich on hearing the
news predicted that Napoleon would march straight for Paris.

It was reveille in Paris. Dispatches moved back and forth between Chief of Staff Marshal Soult, quartered in the capital, and
far-flung battalions, squadrons and batteries. Marshal Ney hurried
from Besançon to confer with Soult, arriving on the 7th. A proclamation was rushed all over France calling for Napoleon to be
captured "dead or alive." Warnings were posted which stated that
any Frenchman who aided Napoleon in any way would suffer stiff
penalties. The news struck Parisians like a thunderclap. The stock
market began to fall, but there was enough buying by those who
expected a quick end to the Emperor to keep it from nosediving.
Shares of the Bank of France were selling at 1,100 francs. Five
percent bonds dipped to 75.50 francs. To the poor this didn't
matter, but they did wonder if the government would make good
their lottery tickets. But good news was being whispered through
the back streets of Paris. On March 1, the day Napoleon landed
in France, the winning numbers were drawn, as usual, on Neuve
des Petits Champs. The five winning tickets were numbers 59,
61, 71, 67 and 20. Word spread that winners would continue to
be paid.

The views of the man in the street differed widely, as they always do. Some at first thought the news was false, many welcomed
it, and others started planning on a quick exit from the capital.
Many, however, fully expected the king's troops to stop Napoleon
before he got much further. Thousands of British tourists were
in Paris. Some of them decided to get back to England as fast as
possible. The passport office, which had become a babble with
the influx of tourists since Napoleon's abdication, now became
completely impossible.

With the first news a great exodus got underway. Exasperated
pages struggled with mounds of luggage. Many families had spent
months exploring French shops, a treat the British hadn't had in
years. Many were determined to take all their purchases with
them: old cabinet work, escritoires, gueridons, old lace, ivories,

china, pictures, statuary, old books. Coachways took on the appearance of auction houses. There was a run on Mademoiselle Chaumeton's salon at 8, Rue Cerutti as ladies stocked up on her famous face cream, *L'Eau de Minon,* and rouge, *Le Serkis.* Fashionable British women crowded the famous goldsmith stores of Auguste, Simon and Pito for jewelry. They snatched up Van Dyke hats, lemon-colored capotes, velvet coats, cashmere wraps and pink gossamer gowns at all the smart shops.

Napoleon was running into his first real difficulty. Near Laffrey, a Loyalist battalion assembled to arrest him. Tension mounted as the Emperor approached. A young Loyalist officer grew nervous as Napoleon and his small legions continued their march. He fingered his pistol and pulled at his collar.

Finally, Napoleon was within range. The marching stopped. There was a pause, and then the proclamation was read. The final sentence ended, "From village spire to village spire the eagle shall bear the nation's colors, even to the towers of Notre Dame." There was another pause and Napoleon, standing very still and very straight, said: "If there is any man among you who wants to kill his Emperor, here I am." For a second there was nothing —no sound that anyone could ever remember.

Then a Loyalist captain ordered his troops to fire. The command was lost in a volley of cheers. The men were joining the Emperor. Loyalist officers were running away. The battalion tore off white cockades and threw them on the ground. Old Guardsmen and Polish lancers passed the soldiers bottles of wine. Men who a moment before had been ordered to fire on Napoleon were at his side pledging themselves to his cause. The march continued.

On the evening of the 7th, Napoleon was in Grenoble. He was to remain there until the afternoon of the 9th. The resolution of all Loyalist officers melted away before him when they found that their troops would never fire on the Emperor. In Grenoble, the people themselves forced the gates for him.

The city went on holiday. The reception, complete with bands and singers, was his best so far. Hundreds of troops pinned on the tricolor cockade. Among them was the 4th artillery, his regiment of twenty-five years before. Later, speaking of Grenoble, Napoleon was to say that until then he had been an adventurer, but from then on he was a prince.

Now Napoleon had an unorganized mass of soldiers. His strength had multiplied seven times in seven days. At Grenoble, he took time to organize them properly. He also wrote Marie Louise on March 8, noting that he soon would be in Paris, and that she and their son could join him. She had already heard that he had escaped and trembled at the thought.

Meanwhile, Paris still shook with the news. Mr. Crawford in the Hôtel d'America wrote Secretary of State James Monroe in Washington that Napoleon had landed and that it appeared he was directing his march through Digne, Gap and Grenoble:

"It is impossible to foresee the result of their movement. Everything depends upon the fidelity of the troops, who are marching to oppose him. It is said that MacDonald * and Ney are to command them.

"We know nothing of the immediate exciting course of their desperate effort. It may be the result of the measures in retaliation to him about to be adopted by the Congress of Vienna. A short time will dissipate the storm, or give it a terrific force which will overturn the throne of the Bourbons. I will not indulge in conjectures. My next letter will give the result." [3] The letter was labeled dispatch No. 38. After copies were laboriously made with pen and ink by a clerk, the dispatch was sealed and placed in the hands of an American friend who was returning to Washington.

A few streets away from the American Ministry, Louis was receiving reports in the Tuileries that some Loyalist troops had defected to the Emperor. Assistants assured him that such desertions were only isolated cases, and that Napoleon would soon be in chains. The king didn't believe them for a moment and told them so. In the poorer sections of Paris the people were gathering around friends who could read and listening to accounts of the march. Many were intoxicated with the Emperor's success. They began to harass officers and soldiers, shouting *"Vive l'Empereur!"* and tugging at their white cockades. Posters calling for volunteers to serve in the king's army were torn from the walls. Workmen were sometimes seen gathering along the docks of the Seine to shout their defiance to the king's soldiers.

The days seemed to telescope. Rumors flew everywhere. Napo-

* Despite his name he was French. He remained loyal to the king.

leon was dead! The king had abdicated! Paris would become a battleground! Napoleon left Grenoble on the afternoon of the 9th. Twenty-four hours later he was approaching Lyons.

On the morning of March 10 MacDonald, who had arrived in Lyons, tried to appeal to his troops to stop Napoleon. It was useless. The marshal headed back to Paris. The crowds went wild. They ripped down Bourbon flags, smashed windows, threatened the lives of nobles and attacked their homes. Roads leading into the city were choked with people from scores of nearby villages who came to cheer the Emperor. Meanwhile, Napoleon's old officers were leading troops from numerous garrisons to join him.

Soldiers in or near Paris were showing signs of going over to Napoleon. Non-commissioned officers met in secret to drink to his success while Loyalist commanders assured themselves that the troops would fight for the king.

In numerous other regiments, the men were secretly making tricolor flags when they were off duty. At Lyons, the whole garrison went over to Napoleon. There, he issued a stream of orders. He took the title of Emperor and abolished on paper practically every vestige of royalty, including its flags, decorations, titles, its holdings and troops. For the men, the old city gave them a respite. They walked on the quays of the Rhône and Saône or in the park of the Tête-d'Or with the girls they had met. They enjoyed gourmet dinners, whether in camp or in the excellent cafés. They ate sausage prepared with truffles, finely minced pike served with a sauce of crawfish, boiled chicken and various cheese dishes, sauces and pastries, They drank Beaujolais, which had been given them on the march. They downed gallons of the red wines of the Côtes-Rôties, and the white wines of Château-Grillet and Condrieu, which had been carted into the city.

In Paris the stock market was erratic. But shares in the Bank of France had rallied by 60 points, and on March 10 were selling at 1,160. Five percent bonds, however, were still sinking. They had now hit 68, a loss of nearly 14 points in a week.

It was on Saturday, March 11, that the news of Napoleon's landing appeared in the London *Times*. Officially and unofficially the news had arrived a bit sooner, but London had heard mostly rumors. Some time before, on the 6th, Nathan Rothschild, of the banking family, had received the news from France. It enabled him to make hundreds of thousands of pounds on the stock market.

That week one of the biggest signs of activity was in Change Alley near the stock exchange. Traders and jobbers gathered in Garraway's coffeehouse and dozens of others to discuss the news and what its impact would mean. In the heart of the city, at the Exchange itself, at Mansion House, near the Bank of England and other large banks, up Broad and Threadneedle Streets, and in Throckmorton Street, stockholders rushed by carriage to place orders with their brokers, some to buy and others to sell.

Congestion was intolerable. Donkey carts loaded with bread and beer, omnibuses crowded with passengers, and cabs and carriages filled with London's elite were in one great mash. Taverns did a landoffice business—the Ship and Turtle on Leadenhall Street, the Spread Eagle Inn near Gracechurch Street, the Queen's Head on the west corner of Mark Lane, the Saracen's Head Inn on Friday Street, and dozens of others in the area. On Fleet Street, always a meeting place for Londoners, the pubs were full—the Grecian, the Rainbow, the King and Keys, the Cheshire Cheese, the Sergeants Inn and Peele's at the corner of Fetter Lane.

Mail piled up at the general post-office on Lombard Street, with many customers missing the deadline in the evening and paying extra fees of sixpence so their letters could get out by coach as soon as possible. From London, the news sped quickly all through England. At the Bull and Mouth, a coaching inn near the post-office, travelers changed plans, and then changed them again.

The same thing was happening at the White Horse Cellar near Piccadilly, where coaches set out to the west of England. On Brook Street, at Mivart's, London's favorite luxury hotel, later to become the famous Claridge's, reservations had started to come in slowly. The high and the mighty were converging on London.

The news affected the whole city. Every citizen, whether poor or rich, had something at stake. London received an economic impetus from the Napoleonic wars. Now it would get an extra push, and some of the money would even dribble down to such sections as Field Lane, one of the notorious neighborhoods crammed with thieves and prostitutes. More cattle would run through Smithfield market opposite Old Bailey. Whitbread's brewery would produce more beer. In the prisons, at old Millbank, at Tothill Fields, at Marshalsea, a few inmates would have a chance to see daylight if they would be willing to march off to war.

There would be more money for the theaters, for Drury Lane and its gin houses, and the Olympic, the Adelphi, the Lyceum.

Many young officers would draw heavily on their accounts at Gosling's Bank for new uniforms, additional horses, and all the personal, expensive impedimenta of war.

In the fashionable sections, young officers home on leave or living in plush bachelor quarters were delirious with expectation. They felt that war had passed them by, and now they had their chance. The news was discussed everywhere. Toasts were drunk to the Crown in all the posh clubs: in White's Club on the east side between Piccadilly and Jermyn Streets, in Boodle's below Jermyn Street, in Brook's between Bennet Street and Park Place, at Almack's on King Street, and in dozens of other establishments for gentlemen.

On secluded Stratton Street and in the smart residential sections of Berkeley, Bryanston, Grosvenor and St. James Squares, the news of "Boney's escape" dominated parties, teas and dinners. London's entire population of over a million, crowded in an area from Hyde Park in the west to Mile End and Limehouse in the east, must have heard the news within hours of the announcement by the *Times*. It was relayed by the towncriers, at the toll gates, and in the taverns.

In Parliament, the news exploded while many members, irritated by the failure of British arms at New Orleans in January, were investigating the reason why the Duke of Wellington's peninsular veterans could be turned back by the American general, Andrew Jackson.

As the lamplighters made their rounds through the streets that night to turn on London's new gaslights, the city fathers wondered what the approaching war would do to construction in London. Construction of Regent Street would be delayed, but construction on the Mint would continue. Work on the new bridge being built across the Thames wouldn't suffer. No one had a name for it yet. It would be dedicated Waterloo Bridge on June 18, 1817.[4]

On March 12, news of the fall of Lyons reached Paris. On the

same day the Duke of Wellington received word from his government that he could remain in Vienna as Britain's representative
at the Congress, or take command of the army. The Duke and all
of Vienna also received word that Grenoble had fallen. By this
time, the news had traveled to every capital in Europe: Berlin,
Moscow and all the rest. The whole civilized world was shocked.

On March 13, the Emperor left Lyons, and his string of successes continued. On the same day, he was branded an outlaw by
the allies. Napoleon's representatives had contacted Marshal Ney
at Lons-le-Saulnier. Ney, marching with his army to stop Napoleon, was the King's last hope. For Napoleon, a clash with his old
comrade-in-arms would end the campaign. All would be lost if
blood were spilled.

The Emperor had to stop him. He sent Old Guardsmen to
present his case and to exaggerate his successes. Besides, he had
written a flattering letter to Ney. "I shall receive you as after the
battle of the Moskowa," the letter exclaimed. The marshal's opposition wilted. Yes, he, too, would join the Emperor.

Napoleon continued his dash to Paris. The 15th and 16th
passed in a clamor of trumphs in every village and town along
the route.

In the capital on the night of the 15th, Mr. Crawford, the
American minister, closeted himself with a dependable diplomatic
source. The American hoped to get some accurate information on
the state of the army since the Paris newspapers were boasting of
its "zeal and devotion," and he didn't trust them. He got it, and
included the information in dispatch No. 39, which was written
on the 16th: "I was informed ... that no reliance was placed in
the garrison of Paris. That when the barracks were visited by the
Princes, they would say to each other, let us cry 'vive le Roi,' and
that their demonstrations were immediately given, and as soon as
the Princes had left them, they would look at each other and
laugh." [5]

Mr. Crawford made a number of other points. He said that
Le Moniteur had admitted that the people were in Napoleon's
favor in a number of cities, but he added, "It is stated, however,
that none but the dregs of the people have participated in the in-
surrection." [6] But, he said that one couldn't put much assurance
in the newspapers.

The National Guard in Paris was dispersing "all collections or groups of people, whether ambulating or standing in the streets of public places," he said. He added that the king, on the 16th, was appearing before the Chamber of Deputies to make an appeal, but explained, "The sovereign who presumes in the 19th century to reign by divine right must not expect any enthusiasm in the support of his pretensions." [7]

Louis, who felt all along that the Emperor would succeed, was completely convinced the game was up when he received the news on the 17th that Ney had gone over to Napoleon.

Dispatches, one after another, told of the Emperor's success. High officers who had served the king were, at this very moment, approaching the Emperor and swearing their lives to him. The Emperor would assign them commands and say, "Follow me, follow me!" By now, the Emperor was in Auxerre, only ninety-eight miles from Paris. The next day, the 18th, he was still there, but time was short for anyone who wanted to flee the capital.

The retreat of British tourists, which had begun several days before, was in full swing now. Small fortunes were paid to rent coaches and horses. Roads leading to the Channel, Belgium and Holland also carried numerous officials whose loyalty to the king seemed less important than escape.

On Sunday, March 19, Napoleon had left Auxerre and was marching for Fontainebleau. It was only a matter of hours until he would arrive in Paris. The city seemed to hold its breath. The church bells rang. The morning hours seemed never to pass.

After Mass, many of the people returned to their homes to stay indoors. The cool, sunny day dragged on, and finally, it was nearing 5:00 P.M. Those near the Place du Carrousel, between the Tuileries Palace and the Louvre, heard a clatter. The king in his coach, escorted by aides and cavalry, was returning from a drive. The rumors that the king had left Paris were not true, people murmured. Later, there were official denials that the king planned on leaving Paris at all. But in the middle of the night, Louis, gout-ridden and miserable in his coach, was fleeing the city. At that same time, Mr. Crawford's dispatch No. 40 was making its way slowly to Washington. He said it looked like Napoleon would reach Paris on March 20.

The white flag of the Bourbons drooped in the icy Monday

rain. It was still atop the Tuileries. Early that morning, some public official, who had stuck at his post, ordered all obscene references to Napoleon cleaned from the walls and urinals of Paris. A brigade of workmen with pails, brushes, soap and water took over the city, which seemed deserted for the moment.

Later, country people started coming into the capital. They brought their own wine and lunches. Some had bouquets of violets, the symbol of the Emperor. On side streets, in little crowded rooms, men and women rushed to complete their stocks of tricolor cockades, which they would sell for two sous apiece. In other rooms, young women, at the behest of cranky madams, plucked away all signs of the Bourbon dynasty, ripping white cockades from rugs, removing pictures and mementoes of royalty. Years later, old hags, burdened by the ravages of time and disease, would chuckle over their wine when they remembered how they drove their "darlings," so Napoleon's soldiers could be received properly.

By noon, the white flag had been torn down and the tricolor was up. Hundreds of retired and half-pay soldiers had started to assemble in the Tuileries to welcome the Emperor. The roads leading to Paris from every direction were filled with troops, country people and workmen on their way to welcome him. Some had spent the night in the open.

Schoolmasters gave up trying to get their pupils' attention and emptied their classrooms. In hundreds of shops, *souvenirs de Napoléon* miraculously began to appear. At one o'clock, flying down the Place Vendôme, came part of Napoleon's vanguard. The party was small: some cavalry, some artillery. But it was a coach filled with the Emperor's cooks that thrilled the old soldiers who were gathering. Who could defeat *le petit corporal* when he can take the greatest capital in the world with a company of cooks? [8]

The hours passed slowly, and finally it was night. But the people waited. The crowds were so tremendous that the Emperor's carriage was delayed for hours. At 9:00 P.M. the Emperor, wearing his grey coat, stepped out of a carriage near the Quai du Louvre. He was smiling. Soldiers and officials broke into tears at the sight of him. The cheers shook Paris. No one could recall such a reception.

Chapter Three

An "Uncircumcised Triumph"

IN the United States on April 26, 1815, it rained in Vermont, Massachusetts and New Hampshire; great patches of the western wilderness had unusually dry weather. Docking at New York harbor in the afternoon was the *Sine-Qua-Non*, mastered by Captain Pond. The ship was twenty-four days out of La Rochelle, France. Besides her usual cargo of exotic French goods, wine, furniture, lace, glassware, clothing and a general list, she bore the news of Napoleon's landing and his triumphant march to Paris.

No one knows when the news first reached American soil. Days earlier a ship's complement could have rowed ashore to some desolate coastline for fresh supplies. The news could have been told to a disinterested tavern keeper who buried it with some trapper headed for the interior. Or it could have come from the lips of a drunken sailor in one of a score of ports along the Eastern Seaboard, and his listeners could have missed the point. But it was the *Sine-Qua-Non* that carried heavy mail from Americans abroad who reported on the happenings in France. And Captain Pond had taken the trouble to stock up on French newspapers before casting off. From the *Sine-Qua-Non* the news was rushed to newspapers in New York.

Editors tore greedily at the dispatches. The news was bulletin matter. The fact that Napoleon was back in France would be of major interest, not only to merchants who kept fleets of American ships plying the oceans but to the average citizen along the eastern coast who depended on imports of all kinds of things, from Holland gin to Paris percales. What would happen now? Was there danger of another war with Great Britain? Would the flow of goods to France again be curtailed by British ships? What would the French do? What supplies would they need? What would Napoleon's policy be toward the United States?

The United States had just weathered its second war with Great Britain. Although the White House had been burnt to the ground by the English, and U.S. troops hadn't fared too well except at the battle of New Orleans, the United States, officially just thirty-four years old, was like most new countries. She carried a chip on her shoulder. She was proud, quick to be insulted, seemed willing to take on anybody and anything—British soldiers and British ships, French men-of-war, Barbary pirates or Indians. This hard-nosed attitude added to the desire for news from abroad. Besides, although few Americans would admit it, the fifteen-state nation was a backwater in the civilized world. News from Europe was fascinating, and heated discussion about events there was endless. The story of Napoleon's escape would be sure to start a lively moral debate among readers, editors felt. There would be those who would welcome the news because of the recent clash with the English. But there would be others who would denounce Napoleon as a tyrant and a dictator.

The New York *Evening Post* hit the streets with the news on the same day the *Sine-Qua-Non* arrived in port. Reporting on "the astonishing fact," the *Post* covered the Emperor's landing, the Bourbon family's escape to Belgium, and charged Marshal Soult with engineering the coup.[1] All the cities along the Eastern Seaboard carried the story as soon as they could. Among the first newspapers to have the story was the Philadelphia *Gazette*. "The stupendous event," it shouted in heavy black type, "is of a nature to divest the mind of all reflection, leaving it for a while completely wrapt in astonishment." [2] Entranced, the *Gazette* went on: "It may be truly said that we live in an age of revolutions. Centuries have rolled away without witnessing such wonderful events as have occurred during the last few years: and we know not what still mightier and more astonishing revolutions are teeming in the womb of time." [3]

The Baltimore *Telegraph* "roasted" the fair weather friends of

King Louis and turned its ire on Paris' *le Moniteur*.[4] It castigated the paper for changing sides: "The *Moniteur* for instance, the very paper, and the very editor, who formerly denounced the Emperor as an insufferable tyrant, is now equally loud and clamourous against the tyranny of Louis." [5] The *Telegraph* rejected the idea that Napoleon alone was responsible for his triumph: "Some are disposed to consider the return of Napoleon as a measure dictated by his own genius alone, without any preconcerted design. We are inclined strongly to suspect the reverse. It might have been a plan concerted even before the Emperor's banishment to Elba." [6]

Up and down the coast the news broke—in Boston where sixty-year-old Gilbert Stuart was being deluged with commissions while neighbors gossiped about him because of his poor business judgment. They said he never really knew, or seldom cared, whether a painting had been paid for or not. The news broke in New Orleans where Andrew Jackson, a major general in the United States army, had taken his first big step toward the White House by beating "them English." His mind was already on Washington, although he had no intention of competing for the Presidency against his friend, Secretary of State Monroe.

At the moment the Secretary of State had a perfect right to wonder why official dispatches always seemed to come in a poor second when there was a race with the news. For Secretary Monroe had to depend on the newspapers for his initial information on Napoleon's triumph. One of the first newspapers circulating in Washington with complete coverage of the event was the Alexandria *Gazette*.

The little city where the paper was printed was part of the Federal District in 1815, but in its own right it was a thriving port on the Potomac, the main one for the area, and was a crossroads for the young nation. Diplomats on their way to the Federal City of Washington, a mudflat in 1815, docked at Alexandria, which was just six miles south of the gutted White House. Many congressmen traveling to Washington arrived in Alexandria first. Although considered a Southern community, citizens from across the Union had taken up residence there because of commercial ties. A picture of the city in 1815 was a reflection in miniature of the bustling nation. It was here, too, where the news of Napoleon's escape arrived by ship on April 30. The crossroads city became a message center and the news was relayed into the interior by horseback, to coastal points by ship.

Samuel Snowden, publisher of the Alexandria *Gazette,* heard of the events in France the evening of April 30. It was too late to do anything about it then, but he planned to announce it the next day, although there was such a demand for advertising, space would be limited.

Anyone walking along the docks near the newspaper office that morning of May 1 would have found it difficult not to notice how swiftly the Potomac seems to flow to the sea. Before 5:00 A.M. the river is not in competition with any other real movement. The ships are moored securely, and they bob gently. There is no traffic to detract from the rush of the river. Near the docks that dawn were scores of silent ships, ready in a few hours to discharge cargo or to load. Captain Moran's *Fair American* was waiting to take passengers to England. The *Union* had advertised for passengers to New York. The *American Hero* had just been brought in from New Bedford by Captain Clark. She had a load of Swedish iron and domestic shirting and ginghams. Captain Delano was about ready to sail the *Pallas* to Cork. The schooner *Kremlin* was ready to go anywhere in the seven seas as soon as she received a cargo. Other ships from many foreign ports waited to unload cargoes of Irish whiskey, molasses, sugar, tin and tar, silk and satins.

Along the docks there was the aroma of coffee and baking bread. Westward from the docks were cobblestone streets, a contribution of Hessian soldiers during the Revolutionary War. About the only thing stirring on them was an occasional cat and dog returning home from a night of prowling.

In Alexandria, the sun rises from the Maryland shore. In spring the sun seems to burn with the intensity of noon shortly after dawn. Its light had crossed the river and was touching the church spires and the slate roofs, and was shining through a thousand windows. The city began to come alive. John A. Stewart, merchant, had just received a large shipment of playing cards from England. He also had a new supply of Holland gin, West India rum, sugars, butter, beef and pork in barrels. He was to advertise in the *Gazette* that day. So was P. G. Marsteller, the proprietor of the Vendue Store and the biggest merchant in town. He sold everything from hats to slaves. Joseph Spear, coffin maker, was to advertise that he made his product "as called for." [7]

On Queen Street eight-year-old Robert E. Lee was still in bed. He didn't need to get to school until 8:00 A.M. William H. Fitzhugh, owner of Ravenworth estate near the city, was in ill sorts that morning. Beck Parker, his "bright mulatto" of "about 20 years of age," had been gone for several days now.[8] Fitzhugh had his manager advertise for information concerning Beck who was believed to have disappeared with "a white waggoner from the other side of the ridge." [9] Fitzhugh offered $25 for the return of his slave and $50 for the conviction of the waggoner whose name was thought to be Newby.

That morning James Patton, Acting Vice Consul of His Britannic Majesty for Alexandria, was at work on Prince Street. The war with Britain was over, and Mr. Patton wanted to inform American merchants as often as possible that he had the authority to grant consular certificates for trade with Britain and her colonies. He had written an ad stating that merchants need only apply to him.

The war between England and the United States had officially ended on December 24, 1814, when a treaty was signed at Ghent. But there had been many clashes at sea since then, and the battle of New Orleans had been fought in January. Numerous stories of American victories at sea were in most American newspapers.

It wasn't until Mr. Snowden got to his office that morning that he was informed that the final treaty, which had been ratified by President Madison and the U. S. Senate had arrived in London. The publisher read a short story from the London *Gazette,* dated the Foreign Office, March 14, 1815: "The honorable Capt. Maude, of his Majesty's ship *Favorite,* arrived at this office at half past nine last night, being the bearer of the Ratification by the President and the Senate of the U. S. of America, of the Treaty of Peace, concluded at Ghent, between his Majesty and the said U. S. on the 24th of December last." [10] The publisher marked it for use in the paper that day.

In the afternoon, the first copies of the newspaper appeared on the street. The story about Napoleon was on page three, headlined "Bonaparte's Restoration!" [11]

One of the stories noted that Captain Pond had left France

earlier than expected because "an embargo was expected immediately." [12] Another story was a direct translation of Paris' *le Moniteur* of March 20. It told of the king's departure from Paris and
Napoleon's arrival. The Alexandria *Gazette* also carried Napoleon's proclamation of March 18 in Lyons which abolished the
white cockade and various royal decorations. In later editions it
took an editorial position on Napoleon's return, calling his ascen-
sion as Emperor an "uncircumcised triumph indeed," and went
on to say:

> Well, rejoice on. We have no disposition to damp your generous,
> honest feelings. That Providence by whom Napoleon is brought
> forward again for its inscrutable purposes, has in its infinite mercy
> given US a peace.
>
> Here is the true subject for thanksgiving, and although the dread-
> ful tragedy may be acted over again, and Europe deluged in blood;
> yet if our dear bought experience be properly husbanded, and we do
> not once more sell our birthright, our situation, in a local and com-
> mercial point of view will be enviable indeed—we shall only have
> to "look on and see the salvation of the Lord."
>
> We did suppose that at Elba this scourge of God might die a
> natural death—his doom will now probably be accelerated in the
> great end for which he is again taken in hand.[13]

President Madison scheduled an early meeting with Secretary
Monroe as soon as he heard the news. Despite Madison's enemies
who claimed he would support France against England, it seemed
that a policy of strict United States neutrality would be maintained. And, of course, it was. Luckily for Mr. Madison, Congress
had adjourned several weeks before, on March 3, and his enemies
in the House and Senate did not have a sounding board. Congress
didn't convene again until December 4, and by that time Europe
was at peace once again.

Some of the jabs at Mr. Madison in Congress and the newspapers had been provoked by those who considered the War of
1812 a major mistake. Much trade had been lost, and the President was often under severe criticism. A little poem called *Im-
promptu* circulated in the newspapers:

> Says Jemmy Madison to James Monroe,
> I've flogg'd the British rascals Jim, by Jo,
> Have you so? says Monroe: And after all what's gaine'd?

What by your war, good sir, have you obtain'd?
Gain'd says Jim; why, since for this you call,
I'll tell you—Gain'd? why, nothing—that's just all.[14]

Meanwhile what of the dispatches from Paris to the Secretary of State? Mr. Crawford's latest reports, written on March 19 and 20, along with all of his earlier ones on the crisis, didn't arrive in Washington until May 3. The March 19th dispatch, No. 40, said the Emperor would be in Paris the following day. No. 41 had been written while the cannons were booming the Emperor's arrival. In it Mr. Crawford predicted war, saying that "the seizure of Belgium (by France) will produce a war with England, who will not fail to make every exertion to form new coalitions against France." [15] He reported that the diplomatic corps had received an invitation to join the king's government in exile, but that he would remain in Paris to learn what the Emperor's views were toward the United States. He ruled out a revolution in France. He stated that the Emperor was welcomed to Paris with cries of *"A bas le pristes,"* along with *"Vive l'empereur!"* [16] Recounting Napoleon's "miraculous" triumph and detailing the blunders of the king, Mr. Crawford expressed amazement at the abilities of the Emperor. "Almost every circumstance attending this extraordinary man baffles the boldest efforts of human reason." [17]

The news, which eventually was to reach every settlement and village in the United States even if it took all year, was moving across the land. The impact lost its sting in direct proportion to miles traveled into the interior of the country. It seemed to be of only passing interest in Cooperstown, New York, where twenty-six-year-old James Fenimore Cooper was contemplating the life of a country gentleman instead of a writing career.

In the wilderness the news was a postscript to more important matters, such as how much the latest shipment of store-bought goods would cost. This was certainly so in the vast reaches of Tennessee where twenty-nine-year-old David Crockett was boasting that it was better to rely on his "natural born sense instead of law learning." Or in Hardin County, Kentucky, around Knob Creek, where six-year-old Abraham Lincoln was in a backwoods school. Or in any community within miles of the mouth of Osage Creek in Missouri Territory, where eighty-one-year-old Daniel Boone had settled with his son, Nathan.

Chapter Four

War or Peace?

ONE spring evening in Paris a young officer and his fiancée knocked at the door of Miss Lenormand on the Rue de Tournon. Could she see them? She could, but they would have to wait. In a few minutes another couple, just as gay and as handsome as the one that was waiting emerged from an inner room. Miss Lenormand was now ready for the second couple. Yes, she would read their fortunes. A pertinent question: would the young officer live or die in the war that he felt was about to begin? He would live, Miss Lenormand said, after some minutes of occult consideration. Francs were pressed into her hands, and the young couple almost danced through the door and onto the street. Miss Lenormand was a famous witch. Her prophecies were guaranteed, or at least so thought the young couples who rushed to her door that spring of 1815. Her reputation would soon suffer serious damage.

The king was gone. Napoleon had returned. But life for Paris went on in its beautifully enchanting fashion. Couples strolled past the unfinished Arc de Triomphe and along the Seine. They drank chocolate and coffee in the Café des Arts on the Rue du Coq, and sipped wine at the Café Zoppi at 13, Rue des Fosses Saint Germain, a favorite with them. They saw Molière comedies at the Gaiety, the Odéon, and the French Theatre. They heard *Armide* at the Opéra. They dined at the Billiotte at 612, Rue du Bac, and the Café d'Apollon on the Boulevard du Temple. Soldiers walking in favorite public gardens caught admiring glances from young ladies who seemed a little ashamed of their civilian escorts. Young civilians sometimes taking the hint traded their long black jackets and blue trousers for uniforms.

In the public halls, and in the mansions which had not been emptied by those who fled Paris, couples danced *la gavotte, le boléro* and *la valse. La mazurka, la contredanse* and *le quadrille* were stylish, too, but often it was better to watch the fine dancers in the theaters execute these routines than to try them. Mademoiselles Gosselin, Legros and Taglioni were superb on the stage. To copy their style the young ladies of Paris took instruction from Tremis, Gardel, Saint Amant or Abraham. After a dance it was delightful to go to a favorite café to watch a group of singers and song writers at work. They met in all the famous restaurants, and every young person in Paris had his preference. There were so many of them it was hard to choose, but the Lazy Group, the Lyric Group, and the Apollon's Friends Group had large followings. The tinkling pianos invited everyone inside.

Officers and soldiers who were not acquainted in Paris could quickly find companionship by strolling through the Palais Royale, along the Rue de Richelieu, the Rue des Petits Champs, or by heading for the Jardins des Tuileries. Some of the girls (*chattes en poche* *) were very attractive and very expensive. They were available for an hour, or a night, or, in some cases, wealthy officers could purchase their services for a complete military campaign. It required an exorbitant sum for the pretty ones, and this was only the beginning. To hide the girl from a superior officer or Napoleon himself it often would be necessary to dress her in regimentals and buy her a horse. Only a very wealthy young fool would consider taking his own *chatte* on campaign, but it was often done for one's sweetheart or mistress. A tempting young female could be quite attractive in the tight uniform of a hussar. If one didn't have enough money, and the prospect was appealing enough, there was always the roulette table. A string of gaming houses operated in the Palais Royale, and they were all over Paris, on Rue Saint Honoré, Boulevards Saint-Martin and Montparnasse or the Avenue des Champ-Elysées.

During the day little street organs played while old men sunned

* *Chattes en poche:* literally "cats in the pocket."

themselves in the parks or played chess in the cafés. Their wives haggled in the markets: Les Halles, Saint Germain, Saint Martin and Saint Honoré. The beef looked good, but it seemed over-priced at 70 centimes a kilogramme, although it was less expen-sive than the mutton chops which sold for 10 centimes more. Butter was 15 centimes per kilogramme. Charcoal was costly, but it was necessary shrugged the housewife as she deposited seven francs for a five-kilogramme bag. Children sent for bread tightly clutched their seven sous. Coaches clattered through the streets and boulevards carrying young matrons to the couturiers—to Le-roy's at 12, Rue Maudar for dresses and lingerie, or Despeaux's at 11, Rue Graumont, to Sandoz's on the Boulevard des Italiens for hats. And perhaps later they would go to the hairdressers: Joly's, Plaisir's or Majesté's. They would return home with the fragrance of vanilla about them, for that was the favorite scent the perfumers were selling that spring.

There were American tourists in Paris. One of them was forty-eight-year-old John Quincy Adams. Destined to become the sixth President of the United States, Mr. Adams was making the rounds of the city like most Americans. Meanwhile Minister Crawford was preparing to return to Washington because of illness. He would appoint Henry Jackson to serve as *chargé d'affaires* in his absence. Messages between Washington and the American Minis-try dribbled to almost nothing. Events were moving too fast for communications to keep up. The best informed man in the United States on what was happening in Paris was not Mr. Madison, but former president Thomas Jefferson. Living in retirement at Mon-ticello in Virginia, Mr. Jefferson kept up an elaborate correspond-ence with his friends in France. They informed him of everything, including the stock market.

The Bourse was shaky. Shares in the Bank of France plunged to 900 francs on March 13 when it looked like a revolution was inevitable. Then the stock made a comeback, and after Napoleon's arrival in Paris it had almost hit 1,100, but there were major fluctuations. Five percent bonds hovered in the sixties. The stock market wondered, Paris wondered—what would it be, war or peace?

Napoleon wanted peace at least until he could consolidate his position, yet he started preparing for war within hours after ar-

riving in the capital. The Emperor knew that an early clash with
the allies was almost certain. But there was always the chance that
there would be a slip at the conference table, and he would be
given a long enough respite to consolidate his power at home
and mold an invincible army.

Paris seemed like a stranger to him. In the eleven months he
had been away many things had changed. Although he was back
in the Tuileries and was once more the ruler of France, he found
that he was not her master. It would take time to gather power
in his hands. At Lyons, in order to win support from the people,
he had promised a more liberal government, including a new constitution. He had to present a new image to the masses, at least
for a while. He abolished the slave trade, censorship of the press,
and invited his political enemies to work with him for the good
of France. Some liberals who would not have been tolerated in
his court before his abdication were now cloistered with him
daily. Emissaries, including Marshal Ney, were sent throughout
France to spread word that all the Emperor wanted for the nation was freedom and peace. To win support, Napoleon was lavish
with decorations and pensions. He visited colleges, workrooms,
public establishments to show himself. He moved through Paris
in an open carriage, and sometimes on horseback. He appeared on
the balcony at the behest of crowds, and for once in his life he
went to Mass regularly.

The Emperor tried hard to convince all of Europe that peace
was uppermost in his mind. He wrote personally to heads of state,
stating emphatically that France had no ambitions beyond solving
her domestic problems. Secret messages were sent to his wife,
Marie Louise, in Vienna. If she would but join him, Austria
would be neutralized. Perhaps the rest of Europe would hesitate
to strike France while the daughter of the Austrian Emperor,
Francis I, was at his side. But no one would listen, least of all
Marie Louise, who had become the mistress of Count von Neip-
perg, a member of the Austrian court. He had been assigned to
her as an escort and traveling companion. The Prince Regent of
England * left unopened Napoleon's messages calling for peace.

---

* The Prince Regent was the English ruler because his father, George III,
was considered mad. After his father's death the Prince Regent became
George IV.

The Emperor's communications to the sovereigns of Prussia and Russia fell on deaf ears. Europe, it seemed, had had its fill of Napoleon. Representatives of the four great powers who had beaten Napoleon's armies the previous year—Austria, Britain, Prussia and Russia—plus numerous representatives of small powers had started assembling in Vienna as early as September 1814, to work on a massive treaty for all of Europe. Napoleon's adventures had cut up the map of the Continent like a newly-plowed field. The task seemed endless, especially when nationalistic tempers were fanned again and again by claims and counterclaims. But with the Emperor loose again the four major powers set aside any disputes arising at the conference table to deal with him once and for all. They had declared him an outlaw on March 13 at Vienna. Later, the four nations put teeth into their declaration by pledging 600,000 men and the necessary treasure to banish him forever from Europe. Napoleon was to admit that his flight from Elba was ill-timed. It came while all the great powers were meeting in Vienna, and this permitted them to act with dispatch. At another period he might well have succeeded in stretching the peace for six months or more. By then he would have been ready for anything, he felt. But now after his amazing success in reaching Paris everything seemed to be going wrong. The only ally he had, King Joachim of Naples, provoked Austria into a premature war and was badly beaten at Tolentino on May 2-3. The King, married to Napoleon's sister Carolina, was Marshal Joachim Murat, who had served the Emperor in a score of battles. His movement against Austria at a time when Napoleon was doing his utmost to convince the world that he wanted peace was an act the Emperor couldn't forgive. When a defeated Murat came to Paris to seek a command in the Grand Armée, Napoleon wouldn't see him.

Then there was the nagging worry about conscription. Louis had done only one thing that was popular in France. He had stopped drafting civilians into the army. At a time like this, with Europe arming for war, it was madness not to demand conscription so a proper army could be mobilized. But it was also madness to try it until the Emperor was sure he could convince the public that it was needed, or until he had enough power to do it safely even if he had to move against the will of the people. Conscription finally came in June, but by that time it was too late to help the Emperor at Waterloo.

Around him were traitors, sycophants, mountebanks, turncoats, fence sitters and jealous partisans who fought one another for his favor. To form his government he had to take what was quickly available. His worst inheritance was Joseph Fouché, who became his Minister of Police. It would have been better if Napoleon had chosen a soldier from the ranks. The lean fifty-two-year-old Fouché smelled of intrigue. He had helped fan revolutionary anger which resulted in the guillotining of King Louis XVI. There were those who credited him with the head of Robespierre. Minister of Police twice before for Napoleon, he had been dismissed in 1810 for conducting secret negotiations with the British. Landing on his feet when Louis returned to Paris, he went to work for the gout-ridden king who seemed ignorant of his venom. Now with the Emperor again, he would be discovered plotting with Metternich to overthrow Napoleon. The Emperor would have liked to have him executed. But then Napoleon's troubles would be evident to all of France. Napoleon was to die regretting the decision to spare Fouché's life.

There were other crises. Some Loyalists still remained in France urging an uprising for Louis. Troops had to be dispatched to Lyons, to La Vendée. In Marseilles and Bordeaux it was dangerous to show a tri-color cockade. And what of the army itself? Louis had let it go to ruin. The allies had carted out munitions and weapons. Everything from shakos to boots seemed shoddy. Spare parts for artillery trains didn't exist. The horses were all on the farms, or so it appeared.

The Emperor, of course, hadn't let his appeal for peace stand in the way of preparation for battle. The day after he arrived in Paris, he met with the man he chose to be his Minister of War, Marshal Louis Nicolas Davout. One of the few men he could trust, Davout had distinguished himself in numerous battles, including Austerlitz and Wagram. He knew that conscription was impossible because he was familiar with the mood of France. The war machine would have to be built with regulars, volunteers, and the nucleus of the Imperial Guard. Finally even sailors were trained as infantrymen. The hard core of Napoleon's army, as always, would be the Guard and he took steps swiftly to restore its prestige and privileges. This enticed a flood of veterans to the colors. They detested civilian life anyway and had found it hard to make ends meet after years of carrying muskets for the Emperor.

But even in the Guard there was trouble. Guardsmen who had served the king were looked down upon by the Elba battalions who had chosen exile with the Emperor. There were shouting matches and fist fights, and there might even have been a secret duel or two. But for Imperial Guardsmen such affairs were a risky business—not because of wounds or death on the field of honor, but because of Napoleon's wrath if he chanced to find out about them. The penalty for dueling was often immediate dismissal from the Guard forever, and that was worse than death for these old soldiers. But there were other ways to fight. A whispering campaign started in some of the regiments that other Guardsmen were seen in the company of *les chattes*. This, too, was enough to expel a Guardsman from the corps. The Emperor set high moral standards for the Imperial Guard. He had often delivered lectures to his officers on the necessity of morality for the elite regiments. He once said, "If I wished only intrepid men, I could take at hazard the first soldiers in the army I came to, but I desire more, I want good conduct, morality and obedience, and this I find difficult." [1]

In the line regiments, discipline was always a problem. But now the common soldier made himself the king of Paris. Had not the officers allied themselves with Louis? If it had not been for the privates and the non-commissioned officers, *le petit corporal* would be dead, or still in Elba. This was the thinking of the men, and in many regiments officers lost control of their troops. Many of the grand officers of France, the marshals and the generals, were despised. They had sworn allegiance to the king, and then turned their coats. The rank and file never had. They had always been for the Emperor. In the Palais Royale with its cafés and bars, its shows and *chattes,* the men caroused, sometimes without leave. In the barracks they collapsed drinking toasts to the Emperor. They thronged into Café du Nain Juane, Café de l'Empire in the Palais Royale, Café Godeau in the Garden of the Tuileries, and the excellent restaurants on the Boulevards du Temple and Saint Germain and Rue Dauphine. After gargantuan meals the soldiers and their *chattes* would chant merrily and

drunkenly, "let the marshals pay." But it was not long before
Napoleon re-established discipline, although he never looked after
the morals of his line regiments the way he did the Imperial
Guard. Frequent assemblies, marches and daily heavy training
began to mold a tough army.

As the weeks passed the Emperor knew there was little chance
for peace. He would have to fight for his life. On April 9 and 10
the National Guard was mobilized. Its use was restricted to garrison duty, but it could relieve line regiments for the front. Paris
became a fortress and a factory. Despite the grind and churn of
the machines of war, most Frenchmen still held hope for peace.
But by the middle of the month Napoleon's foreign minister,
Caulaincourt, had confessed his failure to win peace to the newspapers. A collision couldn't be avoided. Stocks plummeted. Shares
in the Bank of France were selling at 730 francs on April 15. Just
five weeks before they had been quoted at 1,200 francs. Five percent bonds dropped to 55 francs on April 25.

Every shop that could tailor a uniform or mold a bullet was
now at work. Across France orders moved from Paris for everything an army needs, for horses and forage, for knapsacks and
beef. Artillery, the Emperor's specialty, was in short supply. The
allies had spiked cannon or trotted them off. Herculean efforts
resulted in masses of sparkling new pieces of artillery and the
things needed to place and serve them—harness, caissons, ramrods,
buckets, ammunition and more ammunition. Anybody with any
authority at all signed orders and requisition slips. Chattering
French factory owners and shopkeepers were assured they would
get their money. Sometimes they did, in cash, but often they received only a receipt, and they were never to collect a sou. Later,
with emotions running amuck, they were to bill the dead, the
enemy, and even each other.

The number of marshals for the coming campaign was, like
everything else, in short supply. Murat had acted the fool and
Napoleon wouldn't have him. Macdonald's loyalty remained with
the king, along with others, and he had left Paris. Berthier, who
had served brilliantly as Napoleon's chief of staff, was neither in
physical or mental condition to return to war. He finally retired
to Bamberg, and either jumped to his death or fell accidentally
from a window. Davout could not be released as Minister of War

because Napoleon needed someone he could trust in Paris. Suchet couldn't be spared from his command in the Alps. Junot, along with so many others, was dead. As preparations for war continued, Napoleon had but a few marshals for his campaign. They were Ney, Soult and Grouchy, who was promoted to marshal after successfully suppressing the royalist rebellion which had spread to Lyons.

The supply of good generals was better. There were d'Erlon, Reille, Gérard, Rapp, Vandamme, Lobau and a host of others. They had all proven themselves many times on the field. Most of them were eager for combat. As preparations continued, Napoleon formed six corps. D'Erlon had charge of the 1st Corps near Lille; Reille, the 2nd in the Valenciennes region; Vandamme, the 3rd, near Maubeuge. The 4th was in command of Gérard in the Metz area, the 5th in the hands of Rapp at Strasbourg, and the 6th under Lobau near Paris. They could move quickly for a blow in Belgium where the British and Prussian armies had begun to concentrate.

On April 13 Napoleon had asked for detailed reports on the conditions of the canals and rivers in Belgium. He also asked for a study to determine the number of pontoons necessary to move approximately 100,000 men and 400 guns. Since the last days of March some of his lieutenants had been urging a swift move into Brussels. At that time, the allies had not built up their armies, and it seemed that success would be easy. Belgium would fall, and Dutch and Belgian troops could be drafted into the French army. It was argued that their numbers would be necessary to deal with the huge foreign armies which soon would be pouring into France. But Napoleon cast aside the idea. It took time to build a proper French army and besides he wanted to make a try for peace. But now that all the attempts for peace had failed, he felt he had to move fast.

Although Napoleon did not know the allied plans in detail, he surmised that they would try to choke him with huge masses of troops converging from almost every direction. When their offensive was mounted he felt he would be outnumbered everywhere. He was right. The allies planned to use five armies against him. By April 4 the Duke of Wellington had reached Brussels to take command of a mixed force of British, Belgian, Dutch and

German soldiers. His army built up slowly to nearly 95,000 men. The Prussian army under Blücher, which planned to join Wellington, totaled nearly 120,000. Moving to cross the middle Rhine would be a Russian force of 150,000. Two Austrian armies would march. A force of 210,000 would cross the upper Rhine and advance in the direction of Paris in support of Wellington and Blücher. Seventy-five thousand troops would move up from Italy with Lyons as their objective. France would have to repel a massive invasion of 650,000 men.

As the day for action drew near, Napoleon had little more than 180,000 soldiers he could use in the field. With these, he not only had to guard the Spanish frontier where another attack might come at any moment, but he had to quell revolts and throw up something in the way of the Russians and the Austrians. He used over 50,000 men for these purposes. This left him a striking force of around 130,000. He could not wait with his army for the onslaught. To do so would be suicide. There was just one slim chance to defeat Europe. His first step: beat Wellington and Blücher. By late May his spies had reported that the allied cantonments spread out for miles in Belgium. If his army could fly swiftly and silently as an arrow, he could plunge into the allied lines in force before Wellington or Blücher had a chance to concentrate their armies or to join them. Then he could leave a small army group to hinder one allied army as it rushed to assemble. At the same time he could tear the other one to pieces by using the bulk of his troops. After victory No. 1, he would gather all of his battalions to deal with the other army. Such tactics would permit him to outnumber the enemy where it counted—on the battlefield.

Success in Belgium just might bring down the allies like a stack of cards, the Emperor believed. With victory, Belgium would become his ally. With Wellington crushed, the British government might fall. This could mean that a peace party would take over England, and Britain could be out of the military picture for months to come. Blücher, if he lived, would straggle back to Prussia. Then with the forces the French had picked up in Belgium, Napoleon would move against the Russian and Austrian armies. Most of the troops he had left on the French frontiers would be part of his victorious army. There would be reinforcements from garrisons and new trainees. He could destroy the Russians and pin down the Austrians by threatening Vienna. Finally, with only the Austrians on the field, total victory would be his.

The days flew. It was now June. The army was as ready as it would ever be. Napoleon would have high hopes for it, and then would sink into depression. One day he would burst with energy, the next he would be ill. Stomach pains and a persistent cough bothered him. The past tormented him, especially when he returned to Malmaison to recapture his memories of Josephine. Fear of the future plagued him. What would happen to his son, the King of Rome? At times he felt his star was fading. His pride suffered. He had been in France for three months, and still he was not her master. The old days had passed forever. His advisers, his friends, even his brother Lucien openly begged him to abdicate. It was the only way to peace, they argued. It was the way to save France. Only his old soldiers were loyal, he felt. On the march to Paris he had called for a festival to mark the new constitution, the new reign and the coronation of the Empress Marie Louise and the King of Rome. Marie Louise had forsaken him but the festival would be celebrated just the same.

The ceremony, called the *Champ de Mai*, was delayed until June 1. It was a thundering panorama of blasting artillery, marching troops, beating drums, waving pennants, a dazzling parade and the celebration of a High Mass. On a great elevated stand in the *Champ de Mars* near the Ecole Militaire, homage was paid to the constitution and to Napoleon. The Emperor spoke to the hundreds of dignitaries from church and state, the thousands of soldiers and Parisians. He said he had returned to France as a "guardian" of "the rights of the people." He said he had hoped for peace, but that "foreign kings" were bent on aggression. Victory, however, would come if France remained steadfast. Later, legions of the Old Guard received the eagles and colors they would soon carry into battle. The cries of *"Vive l'Empereur!"* rang and rang.

But there was something about the great event which didn't quite come off. Perhaps Napoleon had been thinking too much about the past. The imperial pomp and ceremony seemed strangely out of place. Even his old soldiers were embarrassed when the Emperor arrived. It was his clothing that shocked them. He had given up his uniform and notorious hat. He wore "a gold-embroidered violet velvet mantle of state, crimson velvet tunic, a velvet toque and white plume, white satin vest and breeches, white satin shoes with diamond buckles; grand cross of the Legion of Honour in diamonds and rubies, and diamond-hilted sword." [2] He forced his brothers to dress in similar costumes, although their clothing was less grand.

All over France the violets were wilting. The season for them was ending. Children who had pressed bouquets of violets, still damp with morning dew, into Napoleon's hands could find them no more. Artificial violets were manufactured. The violet was still the sign of Napoleon. Suddenly it was the second week of June. Early in the morning of June 12 Napoleon left Paris to take command of his army.

Chapter Five

Of Men and Arms

BEFORE the French Revolution many battles in continental Europe were conducted by professional armies which were maneuvered like chess pieces. When a general saw that his antagonist had outsmarted him, and he was cut off from his base of supplies or had been trapped by a river or a forest, he would surrender more often than not. Seldom would he fight a pitched battle if he thought the odds were heavily against him. On occasion, he might show his mettle and engage in a token action before running up the white flag. But generally he would not allow a bloodletting to continue for very long. Surrender would be preceded by numerous truces to secure the best conditions possible. Often they were generously granted by the victor who on a previous occasion could very well have been a loser himself. The surrender ceremony was a splendid affair, and often it was difficult to tell the losing army from the winning one, so immaculate were the uniforms and so spirited were the men and horses on both sides.

There were often large contingents of mercenaries on the battlefield. Practically every European army had them in the eighteenth century. There were Swiss, Germans, Scottish, Irish, men of almost every origin who would fight for any flag if the pay was enough. They did not have the political power which they had wielded during the days before centralized governments, but their professional approach to war often was an influence in national armies. With the trained eye of any good professional, the mercenary could quickly calculate the odds against him. If the odds seemed overwhelming, it seemed better to stop and try again later.

But with "the shot heard around the world" by America's Minutemen in 1775 things began to change. Ideas, principles and beliefs marched along with American soldiers going into action. Civilians who wanted to fight for a cause enlisted.* These armies puzzled the professional. Sometimes civilian soldiers would fly like chaff at the opening boom of a cannon, but very often the cause they were fighting for would sustain them and they would fight much too well. Untutored in the skill of professionals, they would not know when they were beaten. Often they could be surrounded or out of supplies and still dispute the issue on the battlefield. Their surprised foes would back off, or have to rally and crush them completely. The British professional soldier, considered the best in the world in the late eighteenth century, learned much about the dangerous properties of civilian armies in America, and so did their allies, the Hessian mercenaries.

France answered the shot heard around the world with the avalanche of the French Revolution. In the wars that immediately followed, Frenchmen fought for a cause, "liberty, equality and fraternity," and they fought very successfully. Civilians were enlisted. Masses of civilians were later conscripted and indoctrinated with the principles of the Revolution. The day of huge armies of civilians in uniform had arrived, and Napoleon was to make the most of it. He thought so much of the amateur soldier who had outfoxed the British that when he heard of George Washington's death in 1799 he ordered his regimental flags to be draped in black for ten days. But Napoleon was a professional artillery officer, and to shore up zealous but often unpredictable civilian armies he was to establish a corps of professionals which was second to none. As a young general and then as First Consul, he organized a guard to protect him on the battlefield. Later, from this small beginning, was to emerge the Imperial Guard, one of the most dependable corps of professionals ever to wear a uniform.

In addition to the Guard's professional qualities of military

* This, of course, was true in religious wars throughout the ages, but the American Revolution introduced a new phase in wars based on principle.

craftsmanship, it had a devotion for its leader which would sustain it in battle long after most valorous professionals or civilian soldiers had given up. The Guard's cause was Napoleon, and for these soldiers this cause was more sacred than any patriotic or revolutionary slogan. Hence Napoleon, as he destroyed one army after another through Europe, was the first national leader to use huge masses of amateur soldiers along with a small hard core of professionals as a regular method of waging war—a system which almost every nation was to adopt.

Napoleon made fearful use of both kinds of soldiers, and in exploiting the modern conscript system the battlefield became a bloodbath. Duels between small professional armies had disappeared into history. To use his amateurs quickly and effectively Napoleon modified the rules of warfare. In his heyday he had manpower to spare, and he massed the amateur soldiers for attack in simple formations—deployment which was less professional, easier to learn, but often much more costly. He backed up his troops with masses of artillery. As the battle raged, his professionals, the Imperial Guard, always a reserve, were left in the rear. They would not be called unless a desperate defensive situation arose, or unless their weight was needed to carry the day. Sometimes they would not be used at all. His line regiments occasionally could win on their own.

The amateurs who survived to reenlist became professionals in their own right as their years of service increased. Through the years many fine regiments of the line developed, with their officers often coming from the ranks of the Imperial Guard. As the Napoleonic wars continued, the Emperor's enemies were forced to build huge civilian armies. England, however, preferred to support the war against Napoleon with its magnificent navy and with pounds sterling rather than manpower. Her small highly professional army fought successfully, however, against Napoleon's forces, although not against Napoleon himself, in Portugal and Spain. Under Wellington, the British army's strength lay in firepower rather than masses, and its soldiers were among the most stubborn in the world.

The regiments had a loyalty to their own colors which seemed stronger than their loyalty to the Union Jack, although their patriotism could not be underestimated.

As the tide began to turn against the Emperor before his first abdication, it was his own system, however, that of using masses of civilians along with an elite professional corps, that was beating him. He was outnumbered everywhere. Now it seemed there were not enough men left in France to wage successfully the kind of battles he had fought in the past. Those who fell in costly charges could not be replaced with fresh conscripts. Yet, when Napoleon moved against Wellington at Waterloo, his tactics were the same ones that had been so successful during his years of triumph as Emperor—heavy artillery barrages, assaults with massed battalions three columns deep, and then, if necessary, a final charge by the Imperial Guard.

A nineteenth century battlefield was an uncomfortable place to be. Artillery was devastating. Rapid technical strides had been made in this arm at the beginning of the century and some of the techniques and devices used at Waterloo, although greatly improved later, lingered on through World War II. The British used horse-drawn artillery which was very similar in appearance to batteries used in some armies twenty years ago. Cannoneers were mounted on horses pulling caisson and gun, and could swing into action, unlimber and fire in minutes. Although the guns themselves bore no resemblance to those used at Waterloo, horse batteries were employed in the German and Russian armies through World War II.

Shrapnel is no longer stockpiled in any large quantities by modern armies for their artillery, but it was a terrifying weapon at Waterloo and in World War I. At Waterloo shrapnel was called canister, although the inventor of the shrapnel shell * was Henry Shrapnel, an officer in the British army, in 1815. Shrapnel shells are nothing more than cylinders filled with lead balls which are timed with a burning fuse to explode over the heads of troops. In the early nineteenth century the velocity of the propelling charge was thought to have enough force to turn the pellets into deadly missiles, and it did. But later, charges within the shells would increase the velocity of the balls or pellets, and French seventy-fives of World War I would kill thousands of Germans

* The words shell and shelling as they refer to artillery are generally thought of as modern terms, but some British officers referring to their experiences at Waterloo noted that they had been shelled by the enemy.

with the weapon. But shrapnel or canister used during the Waterloo period was bad enough as it was. The French had one type which sprayed 42 large balls, and another shell which carried up to 100 small pellets.[1]

By World War II artillery shrapnel was obsolete, and armies concentrated on the manufacture of high explosive shells. The charges would splinter the casings of shells into hundreds of razor sharp pieces. But the term shrapnel persisted, and a soldier wounded by a shell fragment would generally report that he had been hit by shrapnel.*

Grape, large iron spheres which spewed from cannons like huge shotgun charges, was used at Waterloo, but had to be fired at close range to be effective. For distance the armies used a solid iron ball which would knock down men as pins are toppled in a bowling alley. Effective ranges varied between 1,000 and 2,000 yards, but some unlucky soldiers were killed at up to 4,000 yards. Such extreme ranges depended on the density of the air and the powder charge. Calibres of the guns were generally listed according to the weight of the missiles fired, with the 12-pounder being the largest piece which could be maneuvered conveniently. There were also 8-pounders and 4-pounders. Howitzers and mortars, which would lob bursts at high angles, were also used. The British, who seemed to have a mania for rockets during the period, had a troop at Waterloo which fired rockets from tripods at the enemy. They would sizzle through the air for over 3,000 yards, and explode magnificently. But they were no more effective against the French at Waterloo than were the British naval rockets against Fort McHenry in the War of 1812.**

Incendiaries were fired in the form of a hollow iron casing or ball filled with inflammables. Set afire by the flash of the propelling charge, they were used against wooden buildings, ammunition dumps and supplies. Although precise survey instruments were seldom used in laying or setting up batteries, the same basic

---

* The Germans, however, did use an anti-personnel mine called the Bouncing Betty which sprayed shrapnel from a height of three to five feet. Buried in the ground, it crashed through the earth to explode when it was activated by a soldier's foot or other object.

** "The rockets' red glare," from the Star Spangled Banner, written by Francis Scott Key after watching British men-of-war bombard Fort McHenry, Baltimore, Md., on September 13, 1814.

principles of mathematics which govern artillery today were used. Range and deflection of artillery could be quickly determined by firing two or three shots, and the forward observation methods of World War II and the Korean War were not widely different from those used on the Napoleonic battlefield. One thing, however, was painful to artillerymen. After each round the gun had to be laid anew. There was no such thing as a mechanism which would absorb the recoil, or the backward movement of the gun which resulted during firing. But skilled artillerymen could fire, clean the muzzle, reload, and reset the gun in thirty seconds.

Location of artillery was crude compared with placement in modern warfare. Batteries often had to be massed, and fairly close to the enemy lines, if they were to be effective. Artillery often accompanied the infantry in attacks. Napoleon was a master at directing flying horse artillery of the Guard, and small batteries which would be pulled by soldiers along with advancing troops. These tactics persisted through both world wars. German infantry pulled 37 millimeter guns along with them in World War I. Small artillery pieces accompanied Russian infantry into action during World War II.

On many a battlefield a well-placed battery turned the tide for Napoleon. Artilleryman Napoleon once wrote, "The better the infantry, the more one must husband it and support it with good batteries . . . the invention of powder has changed the nature of war. Missile weapons have now become the principal ones . . ." [2]

But as in most battles through history it was the infantryman who finally had to settle the issue, and he had to depend on his ten- to fourteen-pound flintlock to do it. Although the percussion cap had been invented in 1814, its use at Waterloo was restricted to side arms. Muskets in all three armies which clashed there were substantially the same, unimproved smoothbores which were a carry-over from the previous century. The length averaged about fifty-five inches, with the bayonet adding another fifteen inches when it was fitted in a socket outside the barrel. Loading was a tedious operation, and one can imagine the emotions of a soldier as he carried out the thirty- to forty-second operation while the enemy bore in. Each army had its own established procedure for loading and firing, but essentially they were all the same. The agonizing ritual of muzzleloading was performed with these materials: powder wrapped in thin but very tough paper, a lead ball, weighing about eight ounces, a ramrod of approximately forty inches in length, and a small piece of flint which was always in place before loading.

The soldier would balance his unwieldy musket while he pulled out a cartridge from a little case at his side. He would tear it open, generally with his teeth, and then sprinkle a small portion of powder into what was known as the firing pan. Too much and he might get a nasty powder burn on firing. Too little and the gun was sure to misfire when he pulled the trigger. Next he had to make sure that the hammer was closed or the powder would spill out as he finished loading. He would then shove the butt backward, forward or sideways so he could get at the muzzle. Inserting the powder, a ball, and the rest of the cartridge paper (which he had shaped into a wad) into the barrel, he would ram it home. Sometimes the ramrod would stick and precious seconds would be wasted as he fought desperately to pull it out. Charging infantry in its final dash could be coming seventeen feet closer every second, cavalry over two to three times faster. Finally he would cock the piece and aim. When he pulled the trigger, if everything went well for him, the flint would spark against steel. The powder he had sprinkled in the pan would ignite the main charge through a vent. But on an average, even when an infantryman had calmly followed the ritual of loading meticulously, his weapon would misfire three to four times out of every twenty-five loadings. After fifty to one hundred loadings it would be useless unless he had carefully cleaned out the vent, swabbed the barrel, and inserted new flints. And during the battle he had to make sure that the firing pan and his cartridges were kept absolutely dry. Humidity, sweat or rain would spoil everything. A clogged vent meant only "a flash in the pan," an expression handed down from early musketeers.

Despite these time-consuming and complex procedures, the musket, which had an effective range of 50 to 100 yards, was deadly in the hands of experts. Some rifles were also used at Waterloo. Although they were more accurate and could be fired at longer ranges, their rate of fire was even slower than the musket. The task of forcing powder, wad and shot down a grooved bore, which built up with powder residue after every firing, was an exasperating one.

At least a handful of British officers, after the horrifying experience at Waterloo, had the idea that it might be well to have some archers attached to infantry regiments. Perhaps they had had the painful experience of watching young Dutch-Belgian soldiers trying to load and fire during a French cavalry charge. It was next to impossible for a nervous infantryman to load a musket properly. He spilled the powder, knocked comrades in the head with his long musket, dropped the lead balls, and permitted his perspiration to reach the firing pan. Often he would forget to unseat the ramrod before firing. The ramrod might impale a charging enemy, but if the nervous soldier couldn't retrieve the ramrod or find another, his weapon was useless. Then there seemed to be nothing to do but run to the rear, and that was what frequently happened. However, when hysterical soldiers deserted the line it was often a break for their companions. In the heat of battle many men would mechanically load and reload after misfires, piling charge on top of charge. Sometimes the musket would finally fire. There would be a shattering explosion. The musket would be torn asunder and so would the soldier who had fired it and his nearby companions.*

It is evident that the suggestion, perhaps half serious, that archers should be attached to British field forces was never accepted. But some of the officers serving under Wellington had considerable respect for the power of the bow and were members of the Royal Toxophilite ** Society in London. The Prince Regent was its patron, and one of his lasting contributions to posterity was to establish the values of 9, 7, 5, 3 and 1 for target rings. A nineteenth century arrow could pass completely through the body of a deer unless it struck bone. At ranges of less than 100 yards, where a great deal of fighting was done at Waterloo, archery could have been devastating. A good bowman in one of the nineteenth century archery clubs could get away thirty accurate shots a minute at 50 yards. The British officers who talked about the prospect

---

* Some muskets recovered from American Civil War battlefields were found to hold as many as 12 charges.
** A devotee of archery.

of giving archery another chance in warfare were dead many years before civilized armies were to turn to it again. In World War II special forces were to use the bow and arrow to silently pick off German sentries.

Cavalry was the most glamorous arm, and the elite of every nation generally preferred to make this their branch. Napoleon used hordes of it for observation, communication, to screen his advances, for pursuit, and to crush infantry which had been softened by artillery and foot soldiers. There were all kinds of cavalry, dragoons, lancers, hussars and the French cuirassiers. For shock action it was the heavy cavalry, dragoons and cuirassiers. The cuirassiers were so named because of breast plates or cuirasses they wore in action. The mounts, some of almost draft horse proportions, carrying their heavily-armed riders, could generally ride roughshod over lighter cavalry. The hussars and lancers, the light cavalry, were the eyes and ears of the armies, with the British mounted on swift hunters. They were also deadly against artillery and infantry when they were used properly. The lance was carried by some regiments on the theory that it would be easier to deal with infantrymen, since the lance was longer than a musket, even after the bayonet was attached, but often the lance was a disadvantage against another light cavalry regiment equipped with sabres. Various kinds of swords were used. Some were slightly curved and had cutting edges as well as a dagger point. The French heavy cavalry, however, preferred a long straight heavy sword designed for thrusting rather than cutting. The swords of the British and Prussians were somewhat lighter. All cavalrymen carried one or more pistols, while some units were equipped with carbines. This weapon, however, was good for about one shot during a hot action. To reload it required the same manipulations as loading the musket. To do this from horseback while in combat must have been virtually impossible.

The cavalry's greatest danger lay in infantry properly assembled to receive it. And one of the infantry's greatest dangers lay in a surprise attack by the cavalry. Safety for the infantry when fighting cavalry meant the square. Soldiers were trained to form a four-sided bulwark. Depending on the size of the unit being attacked, lines could be two or three deep in square, with reinforcements in the center ready to take the place of fallen comrades. The British units formed the square into two lines deep with the first line kneeling. The second line would fire over the first line at will. Officers would direct the action from the center. Every side of the square had to be properly fortified with bodies, bayonets and muskets, or the cavalrymen, who would continue to move around the defense, would plunge into a weak spot with charging horses. Swinging sabres, they would move into the core of the square, and the formation would be overwhelmed from the inside. But this rarely happened with resolute infantrymen. Bayonets would be driven into horses, and at such range few soldiers could miss cavalrymen with their flintlocks.

But infantrymen were slaughtered if cavalry closed with them when they weren't in square. Horsemen would move through them, over them, and then wheel to attack from the rear and flanks. It took a compact mass of infantrymen covered on all sides to deal with the cavalry. Foot soldiers, however, quickly had to break their squares as soon as a cavalry attack was driven off. To remain for long in such solid formations was disastrous. Artillery was the worst enemy of the square. A heavy barrage would chew one to pieces. Attacking infantry also was deadly since three-quarters of the square's strength was faced in neutral directions.

An infantry battalion could be in and out of squares all day long in a hotly contested battle. Feints by cavalry would send infantry into a square. The enemy artillery would then blast away. To save itself, the infantry would then dissolve the square, and again the cavalry would be back. It was a deadly game that was played on the battlefield, and if a commander wasn't fast enough in deploying his troops to meet the right threat or combination of threats, his entire unit would melt away before his eyes. If a major breach could be opened in the enemy's line, victory would be close. Cavalry and infantry would storm through to roll up the ruptured flanks on both sides. Additional units would pour in to hit the rear, and the main line would begin a general advance. The days of the noble victor were mostly past in Europe except for the British who would accept a broken enemy's sword with some kindness.

Victorious continental armies, on the other hand, would hack a retreating foe to pieces with their cavalry. Many prisoners were shot. The wounded were often shown no mercy. Women accom-

panying the losing army would be raped. The worst antagonists
were the French and Prussians. Both sides would scream "no
quarter" when they rushed into battle.

To be an effective soldier in any European army required courage, fortitude, and plenty of stamina. Size, it seemed, was only
important in the Imperial Guard, with the Emperor preferring
large men for his crack battalions. The men in some units averaged
close to six feet tall. But soldiers who were as tough as anything
the French could throw against them were the much shorter Scottish Highlanders. With fierce pride in their land, themselves and
their regiments, they gloried in battle. The average height of the
Gordon Highlanders who fought at Waterloo was around 5 feet
6 inches. Statistics on the height of the rank and file of the regiment show the following: [3]

6 ft. 2 in. and upwards	0
6 ft.	11
5 ft. 11 in.	11
5 ft. 10 in.	30
5 ft. 9 in.	71
5 ft. 8 in.	70
5 ft. 7 in.	77
5 ft. 6 in.	110
5 ft. 5 in.	77
Under	94

Their ages ranged from eighteen to over fifty and their service
from less than a year to over twenty-five:

AGE		SERVICE	
50 and upwards	3	25 yrs. and upwards	1
45	7	21	15
40	26	18	22
35	59	14	54
30	95	12	60
25	105	10	73
20	110	8	53
18	48	7	27
Under	4	6	17
		5	60
		4	25
		3	25
		2	16
		1	3
		Under	56

The Gordons cannot be considered typical of the home-troop regiments who served under Wellington since every regiment had its own unique characteristics. Nevertheless, it is safe to say that the size of the Gordon men and their length of service were not too far from the averages in the British army, particularly the Scottish regiments. The height of the average French, Prussian, Belgian and Dutch soldier was a little more. Length of service, except for the Imperial Guard, would on the average be shorter, however, since the Gordons were professionals.

Discipline was severe in all the armies, with the British meting out cruel floggings for minor infractions. One thousand strokes for robbery was not uncommon. Occasionally, a soldier guilty of a major crime could receive 3,000 lashes over a period of time, with such brutal treatment resulting in long periods of hospitalization. The French, however, were shocked at the whole idea of corporal punishment and Napoleon managed to control his army without it, but on the whole discipline was more lax. Looting was part of the French soldier's trade. In the British army it was punishable by death. The Prussian soldier not only looted, but often destroyed or defaced what he could not carry away.

All armies had adequate if not efficient wagon trains. The British probably had the best system in its Royal Waggon Train, a forerunner of the Transport Service, although it, too, left much to be desired. The Royal Waggon Train received its start sixteen years before Waterloo with a War Office letter of August 8, 1799, addressed to about thirty regiments calling for volunteers. The letter requested "men nearly worn out in the service, or whose appearance does not correspond with the body of the regiment." [5] The Royal Waggon Train not only had to scrape the barrel for men, but the only horses available to it were cavalry castoffs, mavericks and swaybacks. Nevertheless, the organization managed to secure better officers, men and horses as time went on. At Waterloo, most of its equipment was used for ambulances, with supplies carried in civilian wagons. Although the ambulances had springs, the wounded often would refuse to ride in the jolting contraptions, which carried two stretcher cases or eight sitting wounded.[6]

One of Napoleon's problems before Waterloo was to secure

enough ambulances and to recruit enough doctors. Medicine, of course, was not the accomplished science it is today, and it just might be possible that some of the gravely wounded who survived Waterloo did so because there was a shortage of physicians. Sometimes a doctor's decision on attending a wounded man who had lost considerable blood would be to bleed him afresh. The soldier, already near death from loss of blood, would often succumb during treatment. The agony of the severely wounded was indescribable. Ether and chloroform were over thirty years away in 1815. The only pain killer available was large doses of intoxicants. But there never seemed to be enough alcohol around at the right time. The British did get a daily rum or gin ration, but it was downed in a hurry. Some Britishers, especially the officers, carried private stocks of gin and whiskey. The French had their cognac and wine. The Prussians, wine and schnapps.

British soldiers had the bad habit of eating and drinking all their rations as soon as they received them. "Rations were issued in the evening, usually for three days at a time, one day's being issued to the men, the other two being with the regiment, but often enough the men had to carry the whole, with the result that they were short after the first day. Corn for three days was issued to the artillery and was carried in their wagons. Bread was baked in the villages, and meat was obtained from the cattle accompanying the troops." [7]

French soldiers were more frugal with their rations, which they got mostly from foraging. They seemed always to have something in their knapsacks, and it was incredible the dishes they could concoct on the march. A smart soldier would often organize a team to scour the neighborhood for food. One man would be responsible for meat, another for vegetables, and one would even be assigned to search for condiments. Sometimes the results would rival those of a superb Paris restaurant. Soups and stews were eaten often. Endless variations of *pot-au-feu,* with soup stock carried in canteens, and soup bones wrapped in cloth and shoved in knapsacks could be prepared on short notice. At camp in the evenings, a *marmite,* which soldiers took turns lugging, or which had been stored on a supply wagon, would be hung over an open fire. The troops belonging to the little eating club would empty their canteens and knapsacks into the pot. Water and fresh supplies would be added, along with some wine. Then with bread which had been issued, and perhaps a stolen chicken, duck or goose, which would be carefully roasted and basted, the soldiers would have a feast. Improvisation would turn out some exciting dishes. The story is often told about how *poulet sauté à la Marengo* got its start. "At the time of the battle of Marengo in 1800, so the story goes, Napoleon's chef was unable to obtain butter for dinner. So he sautéed his chicken in olive oil and added whatever else was at hand. Napoleon was delighted and so have been the French ever since. Veal Marengo is a pleasing variation." [8]

Two very hearty, if not very exciting dishes were vegetable soup, and olive oil and bread soup. The first recipe called for the following ingredients to be placed in boiling water—bacon, potatoes, carrots, salt and beans. After cooking, meat was added to simmer for ten minutes. The second recipe called for adding olive oil, meat, vegetables and salt to boiling water. After cooking, unbreakable army bread was added and stirred.

But often the meals were very bad, although they seemed delicious at the time. When the French were at grips with the enemy, there was little time for *pot-au-feu*, and to hungry and exhausted soldiers anything seemed good. The story is told that some years after Waterloo, a group of Napoleon's former officers held a reunion and decided that they would have the same lunch they had had during the battle. Most of them recalled it as one of the tastiest meals they had ever eaten. One of the old soldiers still had a list of the ingredients. Somehow the recipe had never been revealed to his companions. He turned it over to his cook. The meal appeared. The odor was outlandish and the dishes completely repugnant—a yellowish juice made from boiled plants, water and salt, horse ribs and crows grilled in horse fat.

Traveling with the French regiments were the *cantinières* (canteen women) who wore not unflattering uniforms. With civilian drivers, they managed wagons stocked with tobacco, cognac, wine and other luxuries or necessities. There were also *blanchisseuses* (washerwomen) who moved with the troops. Often the wives of soldiers, these *cantinières* and *blanchisseuses* doubled as nurses, doing what they could to clean wounds and comfort the dying.

Les chattes often managed to move with the troops, and it was not an uncommon sight to see a handsome baroque filled with prostitutes following the rear guard. Napoleon would have their carriages overturned if he chanced to see them so they had to keep a respectful distance away from headquarters. But evidently they managed a profitable trade even under these hazards. Often the women were as courageous as the men, advancing right with them into action. There is the story of *le Bréton-Double,* wife of one of Napoleon's young officers, who vowed she would follow her husband everywhere. So heroic was she that even Napoleon was won over and he presented her with the *Légion d'Honneur.* She managed to live for ninety-three years, although she left two legs and one arm on the battlefield.

British women were as magnificent in battle as anyone could be, and although Wellington detested the idea of wives following their husbands on campaign, he couldn't do much to stop them. Troops would be out of the country for years, and if women had been kept out of the army altogether, few men would have enlisted. Some English women, although severely wounded themselves, rescued their injured husbands at Waterloo. The Prussians, too, had their women, and some of them rode double on horseback "looking as warlike as the soldiers." [9]

If for nothing else a woman's touch was needed to help keep uniforms presentable, for the armies who marched to war in the Napoleonic period were among the most fashion-conscious ever assembled. Often women in British, French or Prussian camps were kept busy, along with other tasks, sewing and mending. There were the intricate jackets of the Hungarian hussars, which all armies seemed to favor. There were tight pants, embroidered stripes, buttons galore, and every color in the rainbow. There were epaulettes, sabretaches, pelisses, busbys, shakos, czapkas, flapped cuffs and spangles. So taken were the British with the uniforms of the French cuirassiers, their burnished helmets with long flowing horsehair tails, that they copied them extensively for the King's Household cavalry. The uniform is still in vogue. Fashionable units in Latin America to this day wear Napoleonic uniforms on parade. The West Point cadet's marching uniform topped off with the big black shako goes back to the period. It is similar in many respects to the British line uniform of 1815. Modern drum majors seen in any American parade on Main Street probably would be welcomed as needed reinforcements at Waterloo if somehow they could board the proper time machine.

Some of the uniforms of the period were so similar in their complexities that sometimes foe couldn't be told from friend until the last minute. The smoke of battle, which often became so dense that one couldn't see for a hundred yards, added to the confusion. For this reason the shrill note of a trumpet or the whine of a bagpipe were of extreme importance for communication. So were the colors, flags and pennants, which every regiment carried. Great importance was attached to capturing an enemy regiment's colors. It left the troops no rallying point and desperately shook the unit's morale. Napoleon made his Imperial Guardsmen swear to die before allowing their colors, topped with a metal eagle, to be captured. Napoleon would say, "Soldiers, I confide to you the French eagle; I commit it to your valor and patriotism. It will be your guide and rallying point. You swear never to abandon it. You swear to prefer death to the dishonor of seeing it torn from your hands. You swear it." [10] "The last words were pronounced with sudden energy, and in a moment the swords of the officers shook in the air, and 'yes, yes, we swear it,' rolled in one prolonged shout along the lines. The bands of music then struck in and *"Vive l'Empereur!"* was repeated in frenzied accents over the field." [11]

Martial music was also important, even as it is today. Regimental bands would play stirring tunes during rest periods and at meal time. Musicians would also play as soldiers trotted by to form for a charge with trumpeters and drummers accompanying units into action. Scottish bagpipers attached to every Highland regiment played almost incessantly in battle. A piper never seemed to lose his composure. He marched and piped with charging soldiers, or in the center of a vast melee of frenzied fighters from both sides, he would stand undaunted, playing "Johnny Cope, are ye waukin' yet?" The pipes managed to pierce the heaviest din of battle. To enemy ears it was a constant barrage on the nervous system, with a reminder that death marched with the piper. To friendly ears it was reassurance that formidable comrades still stood. In World War I German soldiers sometimes surrendered en masse after a night of listening to the pipes across "no man's land." In Korea American soldiers said the din of Scottish regiments, including those of the Gordons and the Argyle-Sutherland Highlanders, "was the most beautiful sound in the world."

Numerous nationalities were represented at Waterloo. Besides the contingents from the British Isles, there were French, Germans, Prussians, Belgians and Dutch, and a few native-born Canadians. There were observers from Austria, Portugal, Spain and Russia.

Among the forces Wellington could depend on was a foreign corps serving the British army, the King's German Legion. By the time of Waterloo the Legion was made up of a mixture of nationalities serving under German and British officers. "The Legion's ranks became filled with Poles, Illyrians, Hungarians and Russians as well as Danes, Swedes, Dutchmen and Germans of all sorts." [12] The Legion had been formed ". . . as a depository for men of all the nations of Europe—except France, Italy and Spain—willing to fight in the war against Napoleon." [13] It offered commissions to Britishers who wanted an army career, but who didn't have the money to purchase their ranks in British units.*

There were Negroes in the British army, but just how many of them were at Waterloo has not been determined.** As early as 1750 Negro musicians were employed to serve in cavalry bands. The first Negro to be regularly enlisted was accepted by the Third Guards in 1806. "In 1813 a Negro, John Baptist, enlisted into the Royal Waggon Train . . ." He was transferred to the Third Guards in 1818 to play the cymbals.[15]

Included in Napoleon's forces were soldiers of fortune from various countries. There were Polish lancers in the body of the Imperial Guard who were sympathetic to the Emperor because of

* The purchase system was a unique British institution, the theory being that if men of position and wealth were officers then the established government had nothing to fear from the military. Wellington was a staunch backer of the system which sold rank to gentlemen of position for enormous sums— from ensign right on up. It was not until 1870 that the purchase system "was substantially abolished . . ." [14] The British who served in the King's German Legion were not regarded as gentlemen, but Wellington liked their reputation as fighters.

** Maj.-Gen. Sir Hussey Vivian, a British cavalry commander, was served by a Negro trumpeter at Waterloo.

his wars with their enemies and because Napoleon had reconstituted a Poland of sorts. There were the Mamelukes attached to Napoleon's bodyguard. Including whites and Negroes, some of them had been recruited in Egypt during Napoleon's campaign there sixteen years before. They wore turbans, decorated tunics, baggy trousers and carried light curved swords.

Chapter Six

Objective Brussels

NAPOLEON arrived at Avesnes on June 13 to catch up with his army. It had started its march and concentration several days before. The Emperor's objective was Brussels. The glittering city, seventy miles north of Avesnes, was still, in a way, celebrating his abdication of the previous year. The news of his escape from Elba had arrived on March 10, and had caused some consternation, but with the arrival of Wellington the following month and the build-up of British and Prussian forces near Brussels, the city breathed a sigh of relief and went on with its gay carnival, which had started with the arrival of the first British tourist after the Emperor's first fall from power.

When Napoleon was dispatched to Elba, all of Europe had celebrated. During the Napoleonic wars even the resolute British tourist had been stopped from making his excursions across the channel. After twenty years of Brighton, the English seaside resort, he permitted no dallying whatsoever, and headed for the Continent at once. It was his way of celebrating. Brussels was a must on the itinerary.

From every corner of England the best families crossed the Channel to arrive in Ostend and then carriage the seventy miles to Brussels. It seemed that almost everybody of any consequence in British society had visited the city in 1814 or was going there in 1815. British gentlemen found excuses to go, and carefully made arrangements for their mistresses at the finest hotels. Ladies,

74

disenchanted with their husbands, sought escape in the city. Young lovers, the target of outraged parents, rendezvoused there. Attractive young girls, the daughters of vacationing parents, the governesses of spoiled children, the domestics of tottering tourists poured into the city in droves.

It was an enchanting place to be. In the evening the Grand Place with its ornate Hôtel de Ville, the tall tower capped by the golden copper figure of St. Michael, and the Maison du Roi, was filled with visitors. The concerts at the Guinguette Tivoli were among the finest in Europe, and it was always difficult to get a seat although the attractions of the city were varied. There were huge balls at the Concert Noble, the Grand Concert, the Salle de la Monnaie, at Vaux-Hall and even on occasion at the Hôtel de Ville. It seemed that everyone wanted to dance. Couples whirled under glittering chandeliers in waltzes and quadrilles. There were parties at the Tivoli and the Chien Verte, and tempting treats at all the famous restaurants, which were on a par with those of Paris. In the theaters there were French comedies, gypsies, acrobats, fencing demonstrations. Some showmen catered directly to the British taste and presented Shakespeare. Opera stars made frequent appearances and some of them were brought to Brussels directly from Covent Garden. Every night all the famous places were alive with smart young women dressed in the latest fashions.

Brussels was a paradise for the soldiers, especially the aristocratic young officers of Wellington's army who were invited everywhere. In England, they had welcomed the news of Napoleon's escape with shouts of glee. Lt. Frederick Mainwaring of the 51st Foot was in Portsmouth when the news broke. A newspaper had been casually laid on the mess table by a noncommissioned officer and someone glanced at it just as casually and after a moment of being dumbstruck shouted out the news. "In an instant we were all wild—'Nap's in France again' spread like wildfire through the barracks—the men turned out and cheered. . . ." [1] That night nearly everyone got drunk celebrating the news.

Lieutenant William Hay was in Dorchester with the 12th Dragoons, waiting for marching orders to London because of disturbances over the high price of bread. He was about to dine at an inn with brother officers when the mail arrived, and with it the news that "old Bonny has broken out again and got to Paris." [2]

Hay and his companions were astonished and for a moment thought the news was a mistake. But there was an immediate order for the dragoons to proceed to Dover for embarkation to Ostend. The troops were delirious with joy. The news was disregarded as rumor for close to two days by Lt. Basil Jackson and his regiment, the 72nd Foot, but finally it was confirmed, "and soon troops of all arms began to reach Ostend...." [3] Captain Cavalié Mercer, commander of 'G' Troop, Royal Horse Artillery, was at Colchester. The order to march was "received with unfeigned joy by officers and men, all eager to plunge into danger and bloodshed, all hoping to obtain glory and distinction." [4]

The women in Brussels were quite struck by those young gallants. Some of them were hopeful of marriage, especially to those coming from noble families, and relentlessly waged a campaign of seduction. The Belgian men were just as anxious to trap British women into affairs, and Brussels, although feeling quite secure from actual war, was the scene of numerous engagements being conducted in the ball room, the parks, the drawing rooms and boudoirs. The Duke himself was seen one day in a remote section of a park with an attractive woman. The woman's mother, apparently solicitous for her daughter's welfare, had followed in a hired carriage, and was spying from a safe distance. Miss Capel, on holiday in Brussels, was shocked at Wellington's behavior, and wrote about it: "The Duke of W— has not improved the morality of our society, as he has given several things and makes a point of asking all the ladies of loose character..." [5]

Young Belgian women were very curious about the swinging kilts of the Scottish Highlanders. But in some places embarrassed ladies would only look at the Scots through their fans. In some of the Belgian villages the young girls were shut up when a Highland regiment encamped. Occasionally a Highlander would discover a group of young women peeking at him through a window, or bold enough to raise the flap of a tent. He would snap on his kilt and with a shout of "Hoot mon," which is not just a fictional exclamation, would stampede after them in mock anger. Many young Scots found their dress not an encumbrance when they courted the young ladies of Belgium. Even then there seemed to be unusual interest in what a Scot might wear under his kilt.

The British officers brought their sports and games with them.

They played cricket, held horse races and tried repeatedly to conduct fox hunts. "The hunting, however, was a great failure; in the first place the Belgian foxes had no idea that they were to run before the hounds, not being trained, I presume, to do from their birth like our own; moreover, the farmers could not see the propriety of our riding over the land. Indeed, the prince * had to pay a considerable sum as indemnification for alleged injury to the crops. This drove us to hunt in the forest of Soignies, but, as the stupid foxes would not run, hunting had to be given up." [6]

But there were other things to do. Picnics often gave young cavalrymen a chance to exercise their horses. One outing at Grammont, a pleasant village near Brussels, turned into a wild orgy on horseback, with drunken British officers swinging sabres and chasing Belgian peasants to the cry of *"Vive Napoléon!"* Not accustomed to British humor, the dumbfounded peasants, hiding behind trees and diving into bushes, must have thought that the whole British army had gone mad. The affair started innocently enough. Various Belgian officials and British gentlemen, including Lord Edward Somerset, sponsored the event. There was to be horseracing, and then a pleasant dinner. The Earl of Uxbridge, Lieutenant General, and commander of Wellington's cavalry, offered a prize of fifty guineas to the winner. Hundreds were invited, and the roads from Brussels were jammed with carriages carrying members of British society. After the racing, which included a comic event of ponies racing against mules, a champagne party was held to honor the winning horsemen. It was very gay, and after much drinking and singing, some officers, quite drunk, made for their horses and rode all over the place. They charged the peasants, their fellow officers, carriages filled with screaming women. One British officer, however, preferred to remain in a dining room. He stood on a table and methodically broke dishes, bottles and glasses with a stick.

The party was not an unusual one, and almost every night there were drinking sessions, with sauterne, claret and champagne sending officers reeling. With much more money than they knew what to do with, British officers wrote to London for every conceivable item, additional equipment, and cases of port and barrels of ale, which they especially preferred. Stories were even told of one

* The Prince of Orange.

officer ordering his favorite London restaurant to prepare him a side of mutton. A specially chartered vessel was said to have brought it to Ostend. Cavalry officers seemed the most reckless and the most extravagant of the lot. "A considerable portion of the officers were careless young fellows, brought up in luxury, and unused to anything bordering on serious application; they seemed to entertain the mistaken notion that all a dragoon had to do was to make a dashing appearance, and to charge while his horse could carry him." [7]

The pleasures of Brussels did not soften the army. It may, if anything, have toughened it. It was mind over matter for young officers who plunged at dawn into vigorous military duties after carousing half the night. Sometimes with crashing hangovers they would arise to maneuver with their regiments or to assemble for a military review. The bulk of Wellington's army was encamped in villages outside the city, and only a few of the officers were in town every night. But a long horseback ride often added to the discomfort of those who visited Brussels from a distant camp. Not infrequently a group of officers would return from a night in Brussels just in time for morning drill. For a review they might have to sit a saddle for hours. The stamina developed during these arduous days of play and preparation may have helped some of them to get through Waterloo. The noncommissioned officers and the rank and file, of course, were not given nearly as much freedom, although several regiments were stationed in Brussels itself.

The days slipped by, with both Wellington and Blücher having the mistaken notion that it was they who would carry out an offensive against Napoleon. They prepared their move leisurely. Wellington had many difficulties, of course, including the job of acquainting himself with the Belgian and Dutch regiments under his command, and building up supplies. He found it especially difficult to secure enough horses. Blücher had a supply problem with materials for his army flowing all the way from Prussia. But neither man knew enough about Napoleon's character to guess his design. As late as June 3, Blücher had written his wife that the invasion of France would soon begin because Napoleon would never dare to attack them. Ten days later Wellington was telling friends that the allied strength in Belgium precluded any idea of a French attack. Two days later, on June 15, the Duke wrote a letter to the czar stating that he hoped to take the offensive at the end of June. He didn't mention it in his letter but he planned to give a grand ball on June 21 before the advance.

Napoleon did everything possible to make his enemies believe that he would wait at the borders of France for their assault. He had his engineers throw up dummy fortifications, dig shallow trenches, and he massed some of his troops around border strong points. But if his enemies couldn't be convinced of this then they might accept the idea that he would try to cut off Wellington's communications to the Channel. False information was spread by Napoleon's agents that if he should decide to march he would try to seize Channel ports and separate Wellington's army from the Royal Navy. This pinched a nerve, and right until the last shot at Waterloo, Wellington kept a reserve many miles from the battlefield to cope with such a thrust. Finally, on June 7, Napoleon closed the Franco-Belgian border, and all ships in French ports that could possibly sail into Belgium were ordered to remain anchored. Meanwhile false information was fed to the Belgians by the French, and much of it flowed into Wellington's headquarters and Blücher's post at Namur, thirty-five miles southeast of Brussels.

Wellington had his own spies out. Colonel Colquohoun Grant, a dashing officer, whose own spying consisted of daring reconnaissances in uniform, was in charge of intelligence. He had selected a man and wife team as his agents in France. Reportedly close to the Emperor, they would soon have some interesting news for the Colonel. Wellington, however, worried constantly about his right flank which led to the Channel and his escape route. He had fought with his back and his flanks to the sea before, in Portugal, and to be encircled or to lose one's supply line would not only jeopardize a battle but a whole army. Besides the quality of his army worried him. Many of his Peninsular veterans were in America. Among the casualties at New Orleans was his brother-in-law, Gen. Sir Edward Pakenham, who had been the Duke's adjutant general. He had been killed while leading the charge against General Jackson. Only about a third of the forces under Wellington's command were British, and the bulk of them had not been under fire. The rest of his army was made up of Dutch-

Belgians, many of whom had once served under Napoleon, and there were a number of Germans in his ranks.

Wellington's forces, along with Blücher's, were spread over an area of 2,700 square miles, with the front running nearly ninety miles and the depth around thirty miles. This farflung dispersion was considered necessary for numerous reasons. It caused no serious drain on food for the men and forage for the horses in any one area of Flanders. The cantonments and camps could be emptied in an orderly way when the advance began toward France. Troops could be brought up quickly to guard Wellington's link to the sea. Blücher's supply lines to the East could also be guarded. But generally the whole arrangement hung on the proposition that Napoleon would either wait for the allies to attack in France or would attempt an abortive attack in the west in the Channel area.

Wellington's army of 106,000 men was divided into two corps, a reserve, cavalry and artillery forces, and garrison troops. He had a total strength of 82,000 infantry, 14,000 cavalry, 8,000 artillerymen, various service troops and over 200 guns.

All of his forces were integrated units, with each corps and the reserve a composite of nationalities. The First Corps, commanded by the Prince of Orange, consisted of four divisions. The 1st division was commanded by Major-General George Cooke, and was mostly British. Its main strength lay in the regiments of the Guards. There was no second British division in the First Corps, but there was one called the 3rd, commanded by Lt. Gen. Count Sir Charles Alten. It was a mixture of British, King's German Legion and Hanoverian units. The other two divisions were the 2nd Dutch-Belgian division commanded by Lt. Gen. Baron de Perponcher and the 3rd Dutch-Belgian division commanded by Lt. Gen. Baron Chassé.

The Second Corps, commanded by Lt. Gen. Lord Hill, was made up of three divisions. There was the 2nd British division commanded by Lt. Gen. Sir Henry Clinton, the 4th British commanded by Lt. Gen. Sir Charles Colville, and the troops under Prince Frederick of the Netherlands which included the 1st Dutch-Belgian division under Lieutenant General Stedman.

Wellington was in direct command of the reserve. It consisted of the 5th British division headed by Lt. Gen. Sir Thomas Picton, the 6th British under Lt. Gen. the Hon. Sir Lowry Cole and contingents commanded by the Duke of Brunswick and General von Kruse. It was close to corps strength, and was fortified with extra artillery. Uxbridge was in over-all command of the cavalry. He had close to twelve brigades, including British, German, and Dutch-Belgian units, and six troops of British Horse Artillery.

First Corps headquarters was at Braine le Compte, fifteen miles southwest of Brussels, with the Prince of Orange's divisions quartered in dozens of villages. Hill's Second Corps was dispersed around Grammont on the Dender river. Most of the artillery was about Ghent, twenty-five miles northwest of Brussels. The cavalry was bivouacked up and down the Dender. So dispersed was the army under Wellington's command that even he who took so much pride in knowing everything about his troops didn't know exactly where all his units were. Inept staff work compounded the difficulties.

Wellington's staff included Col. Sir William Howe de Lancey who bore the title of chief of the staff. De Lancey, however, was not a chief of staff as the title is normally understood. He was not directly concerned with tactics or strategy. Wellington had an adjutant-general, Maj. Gen. Sir E. Barnes; an artillery commander, and an engineer commander. Major General Baron von Muffling was the Prussian liaison officer attached to the Duke's headquarters. There were dozens of young officers in the headquarter's command who carried messages, either oral or written, to field commanders. Their job was to accompany Wellington wherever he went. Also in his train was a large delegation of foreign observers.

Lightly touching the British left was the Prussian army. Blücher had 125,000 men, including service troops, and nearly 300 guns. The army was divided into four corps, with three of them at almost equal strength of approximately 31,000 men each. The weakest corps was the Third with 24,000 men, which was commanded by Lieutenant General von Thielemann and headquartered at Ciney. The First Corps, in contact with the British left, was commanded by Lieutenant General von Ziethen, with headquarters at Charleroi. Marchienne was headquarters for the Second Corps commanded by Major General von Pirch I. The Fourth was at Liège. Its commander was Gen. Count Bülow von Dennewitz. Blücher at Namur met often with the Duke in Brussels

to plan the offensive. His staff included General Count von Gneisenau, quartermaster general and chief of the staff, and General
von Grölmann, chief of the general staff. They had command
functions to perform, with Gneisenau second in command and
Grölmann next in line. The corps were divided into brigades
rather than divisions, with each unit supported by corps artillery
and cavalry.

Moving toward this broad ribbon of Anglo-German forces was
the French army, which Napoleon called the "Armée du Nord."
The army was divided into five corps, the Imperial Guard, and
the reserve cavalry, with a total strength of 125,000 men and 350
guns. The corps varied widely in strength, with the Second Corps
of 25,000 men, commanded by Lieutenant General Count Reille,
the largest, and the Sixth Corps,* of 11,000 men, led by Lieutenant General Count Lobau, the smallest. The First Corps of 21,000
men was under Lt. Gen. Count Drouet d'Erlon, the Third Corps
of 18,000 under Lieutenant General Count Vandamme, and the
Fourth Corps of 15,000 was in the hands of Lieutenant General
Count Gérard. The Imperial Guard, 21,000 strong, which had
been commanded by Marshal Mortier, was led by Lieutenant
General Count Drouot when Mortier became ill. The reserve
cavalry of 13,000 was under Marshal Count de Grouchy.

Napoleon's corps were divided into divisions. The French division, smaller than the British unit, was about the size of a
Prussian brigade, or about 4,000 men. The Emperor's headquarters staff consisted of his Chief of Staff, Marshal Soult, and chief
commanders of artillery, engineers and supply. Numerous officers
were always available for messenger service, but they generally
took their dispatches from Soult who had the job of translating
Napoleon's orders into action. The Emperor's forces originally
had been spread out on a 175-mile front, which ran from Lille to
Metz, but in his orders of march Napoleon converged them into
a front of twenty miles. The front had continued to narrow as
the concentration continued. The army moved in three main
forces on three parallel routes of march. On the French left, which
was to the west and nearest the Channel coast, came the First and
Second Corps. In the center marched the Third and Sixth Corps
and the Imperial Guard.

* There was no Fifth Corps in the "Armée du Nord."

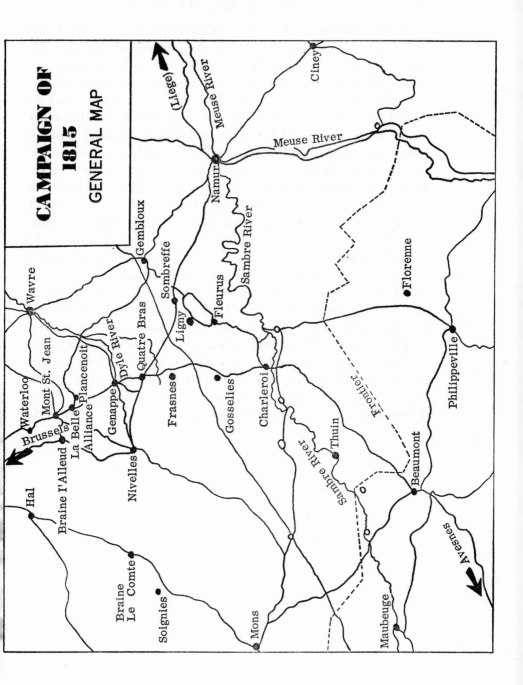

CAMPAIGN OF
1815
GENERAL MAP

(Liège)

Meuse River

Meuse River

Ciney

Namur

Gembloux

Sombreffe

Wavre

Ligny

Fleurus

Sambre River

Florenne

Quatre Bras

Dyle River

Mont St. Jean

Waterloo

Genappe

La Belle
Alliance
Plancenoit

Brussels

Braine l'Alleud

Frasnes

Gosselies

Charleroi

Philippeville

Nivelles

Hal

Thuin

Beaumont

Frontier

Sambre River

Avesnes

Braine
Le Comte

Soignies

Mons

Maubeuge

To the east on the French right flank came the Fourth Corps and hordes of cavalry. Napoleon's plans remained the same. He would move into the widely dispersed ranks of his enemies, and deal with them piecemeal. He would chew up one army and contain the other as it assembled. Then after the first army was defeated he would turn on the other with the full fury of his whole force. As he approached battle he would divide his army into two wings and a reserve, all of about equal strength. One wing could be used to hold off an assembling army. The second wing and the reserve would deal with the other. In the process he might be able to borrow extra troops from his first wing so weak would be the opposing army madly trying to concentrate its troops from vast distances. The attack would depend on the situation as he found it. It mattered not which army he destroyed first. But under no circumstances could he engage the full strength of both armies on the same day since his forces were not powerful enough. A death stroke could be given to Wellington's or Blücher's army on one day, and a day or two later the other army could be destroyed.

The element of surprise remained with Napoleon. On the night of June 14 Prussian sentries at outposts near Charleroi noticed a strange sight in the sky. Clouds to the south seemed to be ablaze. The reflection of a thousand campfires along the Franco-Belgian frontier was caught in the clouds. It was the "Armée du Nord."

Chapter Seven

Like a Juggernaut

I N an anxious moment a young officer could have glanced at an unoriented map to get his bearings. If he had looked at it from west to east for a few seconds before righting it, he might have noticed that the boundary lines between France and Belgium looked very much like the profile of an awe-struck, long-necked peasant with a huge Adam's apple. In the vicinity of the Emperor's advance the frontier dipped and protruded on the map like a meandering stream, and the features of an open-mouthed peasant seemed apparent.* Cutting at a slant through the neck of the "peasant," who was facing almost directly north, was the Avesnes-Charleroi road. The road was an artery for Napoleon's troops. It ran to the northeast. Piercing the "peasant's" Adam's apple was the Sambre River. Napoleon's plans called for the bulk of his forces to cross the river after he had moved into Belgium, since a crossing in France would take him too far west for the strategy he had in mind, that of splitting the Allied armies. His first target was the Belgian village of Charleroi. Northward from Charleroi on the banks of the Sambre, shaded by poplar trees where young boys fished for tench, bream and pike, were scores of hamlets, villages and towns. Three-quarters of a mile directly north of this pleasant village, which was sympathetic to the French, a road forked almost directly east and then curved northeast to the villages of Fleurus, Le Point du Jour and Gem-

* See map on page 83.

bloux. The north road bore a little to the west through Jumet and Gosselies, then jutted northeast, and then ran north to Quatre Bras. This village, little more than a cluster of farm houses, was so named because it was intersected by four roads. There was the road running south to Charleroi. There was the one connecting it which came down from Brussels. The Brussels road passed through Waterloo, Mont St. Jean, La Belle Alliance and Genappe before reaching Quatre Bras. At the intersection in Quatre Bras a road led to Nivelles in the northwest, and one led to Le Point du Jour in the southeast. The forked roads running out of Charleroi formed a triangle with Quatre Bras and Le Point du Jour as the other two corners. In this triangle were numerous hamlets: Ransart, Wangnies, Heppignies, St. Amand, Mellet, Wagnelée, Ligny, Brye and Sombreffe.*

On the night of the 14th, French soldiers brought out their *marmites,* and most of the little eating clubs decided to prepare enough for two meals. There wouldn't be time to cook breakfast in the morning for word had filtered out that the advance would begin early, even before daybreak. French officers estimated the dawn at 3:38 A.M.—the split second when the top rim of the sun could be seen in the east. But they were on Paris time, French marching time. The dawn that June 15 morning would be at 3:46 A.M. in the area where they were bivouacked.

In the camps that stretched out along the frontier, veteran soldiers held young recruits spellbound with descriptions of the attractions in Belgium, particularly in Brussels. Some anxious young soldiers, although enthralled by the conversation, slipped away to sharpen their swords and bayonets. On other occasions they had been horrified by tales from grisly veterans of what happened to good men who were not properly prepared for battle. One veteran campaigner who liked to tease young recruits was Pvt. Johann Gaertner. He had marched with Napoleon for years. He had seen men die in a score of campaigns, and among his worst experiences was the long retreat from Moscow. Private Gaertner tried not to think of death. He joked about it to drive away the thoughts. But his mother thought of it. Since he had marched away as a young soldier he was remembered in her prayers constantly. Now on the eve of the campaign she fervently

* See maps on pages 83 and 141.

begged that his life be spared. Finally, in a moment of desperation, she knelt in a little French shrine and promised that if he lived, somehow she would see that a church was erected in honor of St. Anthony.

In camp the night was cool, and the moon, which was in its first quarter, was half black, half silver.* The Emperor seemed more assured. He had moved his troops up swiftly, and now he was preparing for the deathstroke against his enemies. The hours passed. Tired sentries looked toward Belgium. Old Guardsmen, the veterans of so many campaigns, slept as soundly as worn out children.

One of them was Bartholomew Ribault. Like so many of his comrades in the famous corps, he had seen everything there is to see in war. Since 1805 he had marched with Napoleon. His corps had guarded the Emperor in the Alps, and in the long Russian winter. On a dozen fields his square had sheltered the "little Corsican" in battle and in camp. Lieutenant Colonel Gruchet was worn out. He had been with Napoleon since the Italian campaign, but he couldn't remember a more difficult march. Occasionally there was the bark of a dog, and the troublesome neighing of a nervous horse. In a hayloft somewhere a young girl giggled. A *chatte* had found a soldier.

It was a little after 2:00 A.M. on June 15 when Lieutenant General Pajol, at the head of the center column of the Emperor's army, was awakened by an aide. He moved quickly to get his cavalry in motion. Within a half hour he had eaten breakfast, assembled his troops and started his march to cross the frontier. A little later, Napoleon himself was up. He downed a quick breakfast and by 3:00 A.M. was on his horse, Désirée, to direct the invasion. The juggernaut moving against Belgium consisted of three huge columns. To the west, on the French left, Lieutenant General Reille began his movement of the Second Corps at 3:00 A.M. Up and down his column, camps were broken at half-hour intervals as more and more regiments fell into the line of march. In the center marched Napoleon with the line and the Imperial

* Through the years even the size of the moon during the Waterloo campaign became a subject for debate. Modern scientific calculations show that the moon was a half moon on the night of June 14. The moon became progressively larger on the nights of the 15th, 16th, 17th until on the night of the 18th it was nearly a full moon.

Guard. On the right toward the east the movement was delayed. In the night a courier carrying Napoleon's order of march to Lieutenant General Vandamme's Third Corps fell from his horse. In a desolate spot he lay in agony with a broken thigh. Vandamme's troops did not stir until they were aroused by soldiers from other commands who were moving up.

Each unit as it assembled to march heard a message from the Emperor. The troops eyed their commander proudly when they heard these words: "Soldiers! This day is the anniversary of Marengo and of Friedland, which twice decided the destiny of Europe . . . Soldiers! We have forced marches to make, battles to fight, dangers to encounter; but, with steadiness, victory will be ours—the rights, the honour, the happiness of the country will be re-conquered! To every Frenchman of spirit, the moment has come to conquer or to perish."

Across the frontier many young Prussian volunteers had found it difficult to sleep. Most of them had never been in combat before. Nervous sentries at lonely outposts had fired at shadows during the night. At 3:00 A.M. cannons boomed in some of the camps as a warning that the French movement had started. In Brussels gay parties were breaking up, but more parties were planned for the following night. War still seemed improbable to the gay city.

General Grouchy moved out his cavalry at five, six and seven. Napoleon's army was now an arrow flying to a target between the British and Prussian armies. The allied forces were still unconcentrated. Success was just a matter of time, or so it seemed to the Emperor and his generals. Their confidence inspired the soldiers as they marched through the early morning fog. When the sun came out, its sparkle gave them even more confidence. The sun danced on the clear streams, blazed the bronze eagles of the color guards and made everything fresh and clean. The soldiers joked, laughed and sang.

At 7:00 A.M. something very disturbing happened. Lieutenant General de Bourmont, the commander of the Fourth Corps' 14th Division, rode a little ahead of his troops. Several of his staff officers galloped up to his side. For a moment they all moved along slowly together. Then the general and his staff spurred their horses and broke into a dead run for the enemy lines. In a moment the desertion was known to the men. A courier returned to the division from de Bourmont with a note. He and his officers were joining King Louis at Ghent. The news of de Bourmont's treachery raced up and down the columns of the 14th Division. Regiment after regiment halted. The soldiers threw themselves to the side of the road, refusing to move. A storm of cursing against all commanders in general and de Bourmont in particular broke out everywhere. "Could any marshal or general be trusted?" the soldiers asked. *"Le petit corporal* is doomed because of treachery."* General Hulot, the second in command, was shaken by the news. He ordered his junior officers to swear their loyalty to the Emperor, and he rode back and forth before his troops with drawn sabre, pledging his fidelity. An aide of Hulot's was rushed to Lieutenant General Gérard, the Fourth Corps commander. Gérard answered the message by galloping from regiment to regiment urging the men to move forward. The men rose to their feet, fell in for the march, and although still grumbling, finally began to shout their approval of Gérard and Hulot. "Was this a bad omen?" the soldiers asked themselves. "Did the traitor carry the Emperor's plans with him?" they wondered.

Forward elements of Prussians from Lieutenant General Ziethen's First Corps were now being encountered here and there across the frontier. But since Napoleon had stolen a march on his enemies, cantonments were still spread far and wide. In fields of rye and wheat there were small isolated struggles between cavalry units. A Prussian courier riding swiftly down a road would slump in the saddle as a shot rang out from a clump of trees or a cottage window. Advancing French infantry would occasionally stumble over the body of one of their own.

Small but sharp actions began. Prussian outposts, although driven across the Sambre, fought stubbornly. They fortified the bridges and repelled several attacks, but by noon Charleroi had fallen to the French, and the enemy was retreating to the northeast.

That morning in Brussels in an apartment on Rue Royale across from the park, Colonel de Lancey and his bride of two months, the former Miss Magdalene Hall, continued their honeymoon. Mrs. de Lancey was to recall it as the "happiest day" of her life.[1] At Soignies, thirty miles southwest of Brussels, rumors of a French advance reached Maj. Gen. Sir Colin Halkett who commanded a brigade in the First Corps' third division. Within minutes, talk of possible action buzzed through his command.

At a house near the hamlet of La Belle Alliance, Monsieur Decouster worked at his chores, occasionally glancing at horsemen who trotted along the Brussels road. In Gosselies, a young bride worried about all the Prussian soldiers who were pouring into the village. She was Jeanne Thérèse Ghiselain, who had married Joseph Théophile Pieux just five days before. In the same village kind thoughts for Maria Lebonne by her old friends were interrupted by fear of what might happen if a battle developed. Maria had died at sixty-seven on June 11. Eighteen miles to the northwest, at Braine l'Alleud, there was another Marie. She was just a few days old, and her parents, the Delvals, had taken her to the church to be baptized on June 11.

Joachim Laroque lived on the road from Charleroi to Ligny. So did Jean-Baptiste Amand. They, like so many others, were wondering where they could hide if there was a battle. Father Jean-Baptiste Bouvrie, at Waterloo, some miles away, may have been thinking of the coming Sunday, June 18. There was no daily Mass, and the celebration of Mass was an occasion for him. As always, he planned two Masses, one at 7:30 A.M., the other at 10:00 A.M. In most of the little villages near Waterloo that Thursday children were still allowed to play outdoors, yet as more military traffic built up on the roads, mothers grew more apprehensive and called their children from their games. They played blindman's buff and prisoner's bar, and marbles, checkers, hopscotch and hide-and-seek. But their favorite was *boule*. Little pins were lined up and knocked down by small balls.

Thirty miles northwest of Brussels, at Ghent, exile headquarters for Bourbon royalty, King Louis had his usual huge breakfast of lamp chops. The Inniskillings,* an Irish regiment just returned from the United States, were quartered there to guard him. The officers and men, many of them still weary from their long trip, found it difficult to keep children from peering at the king during meal time. The children found it as exciting to watch him eat as had the French peasants who trooped around the royal table in Paris on special occasions.

---

* The name of the regiment comes from the ancient parish of Enniskillen in Northern Ireland.

The bells of St. Christopher tolled at noon in Charleroi. The townspeople who had hidden in their church, in cellars, and in the shops and cottages poured into the streets. *"C'est Napoléon!"* echoed through the town. The Emperor was acclaimed as he rode through the streets with his troops and the welcome was reminiscent of those he had received on his march to Paris. At the small Belle-Vue inn a member of the Emperor's staff informed the proprietor that Napoleon would stop for lunch. The manager and his wife scurried to make their place presentable. Kitchen maids went to work furiously, and when the Emperor dismounted with members of his staff, the inn was sparkling. Napoleon did not tarry over table. By 12:30 P.M. he had eaten and had dispatched numerous orders. He got up, walked outside and ordered a chair brought to him from the inn. It was placed at the side of the road so he could watch his advancing troops who were moving up to clear Prussian outposts from the numerous villages that lay north of Charleroi.

On seeing Napoleon the marching troops roared their salute of *"Vive l'Empereur!"* Some men dashed from the ranks to stroke his horse which was tethered nearby. Mass after mass of marching men honored him. For a while the Emperor returned their salutes with a smile and expressions of pleasure to nearby aides. But finally his head slumped and he fell into a deep sleep. The deafening cheers continued as rank after rank caught sight of him, but Napoleon did not stir.* It wasn't until after 2:00 P.M. that he awoke. A flood of dispatches was ready for him. He tackled them with a new freshness. Gosselies, a village four miles north of Charleroi, had been reinforced with Prussian troops, he was told. The Emperor ordered an attack, sending a dispatch to Reille on his left who had crossed the Sambre four miles from Charleroi. Cavalry was ordered from Charleroi to assist in the action. The Emperor also heard that some of his troops were far behind their marching schedule.

Meanwhile, a Prussian courier was on the outskirts of Brussels after a long ride from Namur, thirty-five miles away.** He was

---

* Many historians feel that his drowsiness was due to illness, not exhaustion. By 12:30 P.M. on June 15, however, the Emperor had been on horseback for nine hours.

** Wellington, however, said the distance was thirty miles.

a huge, heavy man. His tired horse moved slowly, and the rider seemed not displeased with his average speed of one mile an hour. In his sabertache which swung back and forth like a pendulum was a message from Gneisenau, Blücher's chief of staff, to Muffling, the Prussian liaison officer attached to Wellington's headquarters. The message told of the French advance. Moving at more speed toward Brussels was the Prince of Orange, the commander of Wellington's First Corps. He was returning to Wellington's head-quarters from army outposts, and he knew that the French had crossed the frontier and were attacking.

A rider was urging his horse on to Charleroi. He sped past units of Napoleon's army which were moving up. The horseman was well known to every French soldier. Cheers rang up and down the marching columns when he was recognized. "There is Redhead, there is Redhead!" they shouted. It was Marshal Ney, who had come to report to his old chief. The fiery marshal's presence with the army compounded the soldier's confidence. For *Rougeot* was "the bravest of the brave."

At 3:00 P.M. Marshal Blücher, riding furiously on his stallion, Prince, was only an hour out of Sombreffe. The village, just ten miles northeast of Charleroi, was the concentration point for his army. At this hour the rotund Prussian officer with his message from Gneisenau arrived in Brussels and was asking directions to Muffling's headquarters. The Prince of Orange had also arrived and interrupted the Duke at an early dinner to announce that the French were advancing on Brussels. The Duke took the news calmly, finished his meal, and wondered aloud and to himself if Napoleon's movement was only a feint. The idea that the Em-peror's real intention was to spring his main attack further west, so the British forces would be cut off from the sea, stuck in his mind like a barge on a beach. Finally, the Prussian courier car-ried out his mission and presented his message to Muffling. When the Duke found out about the delayed message and the Prussian courier's girth, he became annoyed, but kept his temper in check. He was later to tell a friend, "It would not have done for me to proclaim to the world that the Prussians had picked the fattest man in their army to bring such a message; nor that he had taken thirty hours to ride thirty miles." [2]

At 3:00 P.M. Ney arrived at Charleroi to find the Emperor.

Would there be a place for him in the army? Would Napoleon forgive him for his past loyalties to Louis? What would happen to him? No arrangements had been made for him to accompany the army. He had had to make his own way to Charleroi. But the army had cheered him. That was a good sign. In a moment he was in the presence of the Emperor. Napoleon greeted him warmly. There was a command for him, and it was a big one. Ney was to take over immediately the left wing of the army. His orders: sweep up the road to Brussels, drive in the Prussian outposts, seize any villages and roads that have strategic value.*

Before him lay Gosselies, four miles away, and then Frasnes four miles more, and finally, after three more miles, the village with the important crossroads, Quatre Bras. Units of Ney's new command were already advancing on Gosselies. He hurried after them with an aide-de-camp. As he galloped away he had a hundred questions in mind. The meeting with the Emperor had been so brief. The whole affair had been handled in such a pell-mell way. The command was given to him so quickly. He didn't know his troops. He didn't know his junior officers. The dust had barely settled at Charleroi from the scurrying hooves of Ney's horse when Marshal Grouchy, who had arrived from the right wing, started to confer with Napoleon.

In Brussels there was a constant chatter in the great hall at No. 9, Rue des Centres off Boulevard Botanique. A former coach showroom near the Porte de Cogne, the place could be used for the mammoth affairs so popular in the city. It had been reserved for some days by the Duchess of Richmond for a grand ball on the 15th. One hundred and seventy-five invitations had gone out to Brussels society, visiting dignitaries, and many of the young officers of the Duke's regiments. The Duke himself had promised to come. In the late afternoon, there was the usual clatter of preparation. Servants were checking the silver and crystal, charwomen were cleaning and dusting, and workmen were making one last check of the woodwork and the trellis and rose-patterned wallpaper. In the excellent hotels—the Hôtel Wellington on Rue Ducale, the Hôtel d'Angleterre on Rue de la Madeleine, the Hôtel de New York on Rue Neuve and so many others—ladies made their prepa-

---

* Historians are divided on Ney's orders. Ney's defenders insist that Napoleon did not order Ney to seize Quatre Bras.

rations for the evening, allowing time for a nap and an elaborate toilet before going to the ball.

At the camp of the Cameron Highlanders on the outskirts of Brussels a few soldiers practiced their sword dance. Some of them and the pipers had been asked by the Duchess to entertain at the ball. The orchestra selected to provide music for the dancing had scheduled an early rehearsal.

Back at Charleroi, Grouchy gave Napoleon a situation report on what was happening on the right flank. But the Emperor decided to see for himself. In a moment, he and Grouchy were mounted for a ride to the fork north of town. They took the road which branched to the northeast for Gilly, a hamlet less than three miles from Charleroi. Here and there lay dead Prussian soldiers. Discarded knapsacks, broken swords littered some of the fields. Some disheveled prisoners stood on the side of the road. They were ordered to be paraded before the advancing French army. This infused even more spirt in the Emperor's corps. As Napoleon, Grouchy and their aides alternately galloped and trotted on their way to Gilly, Prussian units dispersed to forests and hills north of the village.

Over nine miles northeast of Gilly was Sombreffe. Blücher and his staff swept into the town like a gale at 4:00 P.M. Arriving from Namur, the old marshal was determined to crush Napoleon. He issued scores of orders, received reports from his widely separated corps who were converging on the area. By now rumors of the French attack were spreading rapidly through all of Belgium. At Soignies, a British outpost eighteen miles west of the junction, Quatre Bras, Ensign Edward Nevil Macready was standing in the town square with a group of fellow officers. They were speculating on what would happen now that a rumor was afloat that the French had crossed the border. At that moment, Lieutenant General Halkett dashed through the town to pull his horse up at the square. "Are any light infantry officers among you?" he asked. "Yes, sir," replied Ensign Macready. "Parade your company in ten minutes' time on this spot," Halkett ordered.[3] Within seconds the peaceful village had been turned into a turmoil of shouting officers, rolling drums and blaring bugles. Some miles away at the regimental camp of the 73rd, officers and men were playing handball. A dragoon arrived from General Halkett's headquarters promptly at 4:00 P.M. with orders to march at once to Soignies. Although the men were everywhere, with some strolling casually in the countryside, others resting and playing in camp, the assembly sounded by drum and bugle brought them running. Sgt. Thomas Morris, like most of the men in the 73rd, felt that the "tone of the bugles" [4] seemed more demanding than usual. The news had not yet reached the British cantonment at Mons. There Ens. James Grant Kennedy, only fifteen years old and the youngest British officer in Belgium, wondered if he would ever see action. He was regimental color guard for the 3rd battalion of the Royal Scots.

In Brussels Mrs. Thomas Deacon knew that her time was near. Would her husband be on campaign when her baby was born?

The Duke was still at table with his officers, and had started making a number of notes preparatory to concentrating his troops. Muffling, the Prussian liaison officer, had arrived. He wondered when the Duke would decide to march in support of Blücher, knowing that the two officers had an agreement—if one army was attacked, the other would come to its assistance. Wellington, however, still pondered the situation. If Napoleon's movement was only a feint then the entire right flank of the British army would be in jeopardy.

At 4:00 P.M., Ney was approaching the spearhead of his new command. He would flush the Prussians out of Gosselies, four miles north of Charleroi on the Brussels road. He would drive the enemy out of Frasnes, another four miles north. *"Voilà Rougeot!"* his soldiers shouted. In the fields east of the Brussels road, the Prussian wounded stumbled to the northeast. Occasionally a horrified Belgian peasant would hear a piercing scream as a dazed Prussian took a bayonet thrust through the back.

Major Norman of the Royal British Artillery had command of a handful of Nassau infantry and a Dutch artillery battery. His outpost was at Frasnes on the Brussels road. Late in the afternoon he and his troops had heard firing in the south and the southeast. The major seemed left out on a limb. He had no orders, and his small unit was at the extreme left of Wellington's string of forward outposts. Nobody could remember when the first sound of shot was heard. But with the decision that the firing was real and not just someone's imagination, the major and his men worked feverishly to strengthen their position. Soon a unit of cavalry from Ney's left wing appeared. Major Norman and his men made a spirited stand. The cavalry found the fire so hot and the artillery so accurate that they fell back. A hurried call for French infantry was sent down the road by the cavalry commander. In the meantime, the decision was made for some cavalry units to bypass Major Norman's command and explore the road north of him which led to Quatre Bras. At this very minute, north of Quatre Bras, units of Dutch-Belgians under Prince Bernard of Saxe-Weimar were marching to the front, moving south from Genappe to Quatre Bras.

Napoleon inspected the right flank at Gilly. He ordered Grouchy to attack and drive the Prussians northeast to Sombreffe. It was at Sombreffe where the fiery Blücher had just arrived. After his inspection at Gilly, the Emperor began his ride back to Charleroi.

To many, time didn't seem to have much meaning. To some, it stood still. To others, the hours flew at many times their normal rate. For many, three and even four days would be telescoped into one. Two soldiers in the same place at the same time found later that what one remembered as noon was recalled as early evening by the other. But Mrs. de Lancey remembered. The evening of June 15 was one of the few times since their Brussels honeymoon that her husband was forced to leave her side. Sir William felt that it was impossible to refuse a dinner invitation from the Spanish Ambassador. He didn't really want to go, and had lingered until the last minute before getting ready. It was nearly 6:00 P.M. when Mrs. de Lancey fastened the last medal on his dress uniform, and he turned back at the door and smiled at her just before he left. She went to a window, watching him until he was out of sight.

A stately clock in a white wood case, handmade by the Vandercam family in Waterloo and the only valuable possession of Jean-Pierre Maurage, struck the hour with precision. Outside the door of his little cottage on the Brussels road, the tramp, rumble and pounding of marching men, artillery caissons and trotting horses contrasted strangely with the soft movement of the clock. As its hands made their almost imperceptible turn around the dial, so much was happening. Major Norman, feeling that he would soon be surrounded, decided to retreat from Frasnes to Quatre Bras.

A Polish unit of Ney's cavalry had circled his position to reconnoiter Quatre Bras and found it unoccupied by the enemy. It
wheeled around to report back to headquarters. North of Quatre
Bras, and almost within shouting distance of the Polish lancers
who didn't see them, came 4,500 Dutch-Belgian infantry and a
battery of six guns. Napoleon was riding back to Charleroi from
Grouchy's right wing. Ney continued up the Brussels road to
Quatre Bras. When he arrived there with aides and cavalry he
found it occupied by the enemy, which the Polish lancers had not
seen arriving from the north. There, also, was Major Norman's
small unit. Not quite seven miles southeast of Quatre Bras, Blücher was making plans to fight a pitched battle at Ligny. The little village was only a mile and a quarter southwest of the Prussian's headquarters at Sombreffe. Ligny was just one of the many
villages in the triangle whose three points were Charleroi, Quatre
Bras and Le Point du Jour.

Sometime earlier the Duke had decided to concentrate his
troops. Now he needed de Lancey, to write many of the necessary
orders. They would have to be hurriedly transmitted over a hundred roads. A corps of couriers had horses saddled and ready.
Wellington decided on a cautious approach. He had prearranged
mustering orders which were developed to stop a push towards
Mons. Mons was twenty-three miles almost directly west of Charleroi. This meant that the concentration point was twenty-three
miles closer to the English Channel and the Royal Navy. Wellington wasn't ready to gamble. Nor was he ready to rush to Blücher's
side. The prearranged concentration orders would have to do for
now. But Wellington made it known in his orders that his troops
should be prepared to concentrate elsewhere at a moment's notice.

Mrs. de Lancey had remained at her window for almost an hour
reflecting on her love and respect for her husband. It was almost
seven when an aide sent by the Duke arrived, asking for Sir William. She told him where he could be found, and then returned
to the window, disturbed by the note of urgency in the soldier's
inquiry. In a few minutes she watched her husband race on horseback past their apartment to 54, Rue Royale, the Duke's residence,
which was only a few doors away. Sir William sprang from his
horse and ran inside. Wellington greeted him cheerfully and in
a few minutes briefed him on what had happened and what must

be done. The Duke continued to confer with his staff officers and to study his maps.

De Lancey immediately began to assemble his own staff. Lt. Basil Jackson, who was now serving with the Royal Staff Corps, was among those summoned. He would have much to do. Some twenty miles south of Brussels, Col. John Jacob Lehmanowsky congratulated himself. The sun would set in a few hours and he had gotten through the day without injury. He was one of the Emperor's oldest soldiers. This was his twenty-third year of service. He could not know it then, but he would see ghosts for the rest of his life. Pvt. Henry Davis of the 42nd British regiment marched to the front fortified by the fact that he had plenty to eat in his knapsack. A whole ham had arrived from his mother. He had carefully wrapped it and stored it way. He could eat some of it later.

Meanwhile more reinforcements had moved into Quatre Bras. Some officers of the allied army acted without orders from the Duke, deciding that the best thing to do was to guard the important crossroads of Quatre Bras. With this village in allied hands, communication between the British and Prussian armies had a better chance of being maintained. When Ney looked over the enemy position around 7:00 P.M. he saw the village bristling with bayonets and guns. Within immediate call Ney had 1,700 cavalry and a lone battalion of infantry.[5] This was not enough to throw against the enemy barricaded in the cottages and positioned in the fields, Ney concluded. But he could rush up additional troops moving up from the south. In all, his command totaled 50,000 men. But less than a third of these could be brought into action before nightfall. Yet, that should be enough. The sun hung in the west. The day was fading away. The decision had to be made and it had to be made now. Perhaps it was the long shadow of an elm tree that made the marshal feel that it was too late to attack. Perhaps it was the haggard faces of the weary men around him. Ney made his decision. He would attack the next morning. He started the ride back to Gosselies to spend the night. It was over seven miles down the Brussels road.

At this same minute, Napoleon was still returning to Charleroi. He had done what he could to push his right flank north. He was dead tired. Almost sixteen hours in the saddle and he still had another hour of riding ahead of him. For hours now, Lieutenant General de Bourmont had been detained by suspicious Prussian officers who did not believe his story that he and his aides had deserted Napoleon because they were loyal to the king. De Bourmont demanded to see Blücher, insisting he knew all the details of Napoleon's plans of attack. The French general had his operational order from Napoleon, but it didn't add much to what Blücher already knew. When de Bourmont finally was escorted to the Prussian marshal's headquarters, old Blücher, who hated Napoleon, showed that he despised traitors even more. Reminded that de Bourmont was wearing the white cockade of Louis, Blücher snorted out, "Cockade be hanged! A cur (Hundsfott) is always a cur!" [6]

Night was approaching. The walking wounded tried to hurry a little faster so they could find safety with their units. Messengers spurred their horses. Travel at night on the strange roads was difficult. Volunteer Henri Niemann of the 6th Prussian Black Hussar Regiment had seen some action.[7] His heart had beat faster, but in the fighting he had forgotten that he might be shot. Now, late in the day, he found that he had become extremely thirsty. But there was no water nearby. He stretched out that night on the bare ground with his throat parched. His bivouac was near a mill, just a mile west of Ligny, where Blücher was ready to fight the next morning.

In Brussels the news of the French attack managed to escape many. Captains William Verner and Standish O'Grady of the 7th British Hussars had taken a room at the Hôtel la Reine de Suède on 29, Rue de l'Evêque prior to going to the Duchess of Richmond's ball.[8] They had brought their dress uniforms from camp with them so they could change in their room and be fresh when they set out for the gay night ahead. The ball really wouldn't get underway until around ten so they had plenty of time to kill. They enjoyed a leisurely dinner. The time passed slowly for them, but elsewhere it was flying. Lieutenant Jackson, who had been summoned by de Lancey, was one of a group of staff officers writing out assembly orders. The minutes flew by. It seemed impossible to get everything finished. Fnally it was eight. The sun began to set at 8:13. Just before its final plunge it fired the underside of a range of massive clouds in the west and made them look like glowing embers. Mrs. de Lancey heard a knock on the door at sunset. It was her husband, Sir William. He told her there would be fighting tomorrow and that she must be ready to leave for Antwerp early. He tried to calm her anxiety, but asked her to say nothing about leaving Brussels since it might cause alarm. Sir William had many more orders to write to get the army moving, and estimated that it would take him most of the night. Mrs. de Lancey left him to his work. But she could be useful by brewing large amounts of strong green tea. Messengers were in and out of the apartment.

By 9:00 p.m. Ney had returned to Gosselies. Napoleon had gone to bed at Charleroi. Some of Grouchy's troops on the French right were still on the march. Blücher at Sombreffe was exuding confidence. He had had a little gin in the evening. Wellington was still in his quarters, considering his next move.

At Acren, another village where Wellington's troops were stationed, Ens. George Thomas Keppel, third battalion, 14th regiment, was having a nightcap with fellow officers. They were seated around a table at the local inn. A Belgian peasant entered the door, sputtering in French. None of the officers paid much attention to him, but he came to their table and finally made himself understood. Napoleon was in Belgium! The officers were stunned. At Hal, seven and a quarter miles directly west of Waterloo, officers and men of the Royal Welch Fusiliers were wondering what was in store for them. Wellington had inspected their position several times in the last few weeks. He seemed to have an unusual interest in them. The cantonment at Hal constituted part of the Duke's right flank. In a lonely field of thick corn nearly twenty-five miles southeast of Hal, a squadron of Westphalian Landwehr was bivouacking for the night. The men, mostly young Germans who had volunteered for a chance at adventure, knew that there would be heavy fighting the next day. "Their gay songs and chatter died steadily away." [9] Many of the soldiers started scribbling letters to wives and sweethearts. Their captain laid a sheet of paper on the saddle of his horse and started composing a letter to his fiancée. Sgt. Hippolyte de Mauduit of the Imperial Guard was one of the six hundred men assigned to guard Napoleon's headquarters.[10] Stationed near a château on the banks of the Sambre at Charleroi, he was in the courtyard helping his comrades cook.

For the last eighteen hours, his regiment had had no time to prepare food.

Wellington had decided to issue a second set of orders. At 10:00 P.M., after much consideration, he seemed more convinced than ever that this thrust by Napoleon was just a feint. Now, on the heels of his first orders which had not yet been delivered to scores of his regiments, he sent out messages demanding that roads on the army's right be covered from Mons to Ath to Brussels. At the same time he had all of his units in Brussels alerted. They were to be ready to march on a moment's notice. One of the couriers carrying a message through the night was Lieutenant Jackson, who had earlier helped Sir William compile the orders of march. He was dashing to Ninove. His message would set all of Wellington's cavalry in motion.

Wellington's outposts and cantonments all over Flanders were now being alerted by the first orders dispatched in the early evening. Frightened peasants ran to their windows at the roll of the drums and the screams of the pipes. It was 11:00 P.M. when Wellington's concentration orders arrived at the Prince of Orange's headquarters at Genappe, which was fifteen miles south of Brussels and three miles north of Quatre Bras. The Prince was not there. He had left hours earlier to report to the Duke at Brussels on the French attack, and was now at the Duchess of Richmond's ball where Wellington was expected momentarily. The message was delivered in Genappe to the Prince of Orange's chief of staff, Lieutenant General Rebecque. He quickly signed a receipt for it, jotted down the time of arrival, and tore open the message. It seemed impossible! Wellington had ordered the Prince's troops to march to Nivelles. Nivelles was five miles west of Genappe. Rebecque had fully expected the orders to dispatch the remainder of the troops to Quatre Bras. But here he was being told that the entire command of the Prince must move in a different direction. To follow the orders to the letter would be to recall units from Quatre Bras which were looking into the very eye of the French attack. Dazed, he handed the message to Lieutenant General Baron de Perponcher, commander of the 2nd Dutch-Belgian division. Many of Perponcher's men were at Quatre Bras waiting to grapple with the enemy in the morning. Perponcher read the message slowly, and then again. To comply would be disastrous.

The orders must be disregarded. They were. Quatre Bras would be reinforced. Nivelles would be forgotten. At that very moment on the road which runs from Mons to Brussels a messenger was urging his horse on to Wellington's headquarters.

Private Gaertner had had many brushes with death that day, but now it was dark. The fighting had stopped. He had gotten through another day. His mother had said her prayers that night, and again he was remembered. Imperial Guardsman Ribault gathered around the *marmite* with his comrades. It was a late supper. A young girl slipped out of her dress in the dark. She might have thought that this was the last affair her new lover would ever have. Perhaps it was. Lieutenant General de Bourmont had a supper given to him by the enemy. He had been treated with a strange coolness by the Prussians. He was marked a traitor. Mrs. de Lancey's love went out to her husband. He was working so hard. She didn't want to bother him. Monsieur Decouster had gone to bed. The turmoil outside his cottage increased throughout the night. The Brussels road was a busy place.

Monsieur Maurage's fine clock could be heard ticking in his cottage through the night, but occasionally sounds on the road near Quatre Bras would drown it out. The young married couple at Gosselies had seen some of the soldiers who had been killed in the skirmishes. Perhaps they wished they had taken their friends' advice and gone into Brussels for their honeymoon. It was peaceful in Braine-l'Alleud, and little Maria Delval must have been sleeping soundly. On the road from Charleroi to Ligny, peasants watched wounded Prussian soldiers still moving along the road. Monsieur Laroque and Monsieur Amand were afraid of looting. Father Bouvrie must have wondered if his little village of Waterloo would be safe. People were saying that there might be a big battle.

King Louis had had a big dinner. He was now contemplating breakfast. Ensign Macready had been ready for combat since late afternoon, but his unit hadn't marched a step. Young Ensign Kennedy knew now that his dream of action would soon come true.

Sergeant Morris marched south with his regiment. For him the night was pitch black. A big cloud hid the moon from the view of the 73rd. But on other roads the moon could be seen, and many soldiers remembered it. Mrs. Deacon was spending the night with her husband, but it now looked like he would be away when their baby was born. Major Norman had inspected his position at Quatre Bras. Many of the men dreaded the sharp fighting which they knew would come in the morning. Colonel Lehmanowsky went to sleep as soon as he could. He slept soundly. The ghosts which he would see did not visit him that night. Pvt. Henry Davis still hadn't touched any of the ham his mother had sent him. It was a reminder of home and after all it could be eaten anytime. Lieutenant Colonel Gruchet might have wondered if this would be his last campaign for the Emperor. He had been through so many. Pvt. Henri Niemann couldn't get his mind off his thirst. He would have paid a high price for a few drops of water, but there was none. He must have thought of the sparkling streams he had forded, of the times his horse had arched its graceful neck to drink its fill in the middle of a creek. Lieutenant Jackson rode on through the night. On a hundred different roads messengers from the three armies galloped to headquarters, cantonments, outposts, supply columns and ammunition dumps.

French couriers were in and out of Ney's headquarters at Gosselies. He was still up and at 11:00 P.M. was writing a message to Napoleon. The marshal detailed his plans, but noted that he had encountered a strong force at Quatre Bras. Then it occurred to him that it might be better if he contacted the Emperor personally. It meant a four-mile ride through the darkness to Charleroi, but it might be better.

At No. 9, Rue des Centres in Brussels, young ladies and their escorts in handsome regimentals found it difficult to work their way through the maze of carriages. The Duchess of Richmond's ball had started some hours ago, but there were many late arrivals. The place was all aglow. A profusion of gay sounds was echoed everywhere—the murmur of a hundred conversations, light laughter, the tinkling of glasses and the rhapsodies of talented violinists. And now a fascinating ingredient, adventure, made its appearance. Rumors that the exciting young officers who whirled around the room with their pretty partners would soon be called into action had begun to tantalize some of the guests. Some officers who knew what was afoot may have reveled in their secret, using it as a kind of romantic fulcrum to force a parting kiss, or a promise. It was approaching midnight when the Duke himself

arrived. Many of his lieutenants who knew of the swift movement of the French confided that their leader had kept his promise to attend the ball so as not to alarm the ladies. On his arrival,
Lady Georgiana Lennox, the daughter of the Duke and Duchess
of Richmond, was dancing. She excused herself and went immediately to the Duke's side to ask him if the rumors were true. He
confirmed them, noting that the army would move "tomorrow."
The word that action was imminent now spread quickly to all the
guests. But the Duke did not leave the ball. It became his headquarters. Some officers immediately left to return to their regiments. Seventeen-year-old Ensign, James, Lord Hay of the First
Foot Guards, could not hide his delight that he would soon be in
action. Some of the young ladies were worried by his bravado.
Others congratulated him on a regimental horse race he had won
two days before. Messengers were being received by the Duke.
High-ranking officers gathered up their staffs. It was just a minute
before midnight when the messenger who had ridden from Mons
bounded up the steps of the entrance to the ballroom. He had a
message of great importance for the commander. The Duke now
had confirmation that Napoleon's troops were not attacking his
right flank. Everything in front of Mons was clear. The army must
hurry to Quatre Bras.

Chapter Eight

Humbugged, by God!

JUNE 16 was only minutes old when reveille was sounded throughout Brussels. Drummers, buglers, pipers were routed out of quarters by hundreds of sentries alerted by their officers. They dressed hurriedly and ran to assembly points to sound the call of arms. The roll of the drums, the strident notes of the trumpets, and the piercing cry of the pipes enveloped the whole city. The warmth of a thousand beds which lovers shared was chilled by the cold demands of the regiment.

The Duke still remained at the ball. He alternately discussed frivolities with his host and hostess and their guests, and gave orders to his lieutenants. The orchestra still played and young women continued to dance when they could find partners. But partners were becoming scarce. At the first alarm that the French were attacking, many young officers had kissed the hands of their dancing partners and had hurried away. Some had lingered on until receiving definite orders from their regiments. The romance of the moment had not been lost upon them. A departure from a brilliant party crowded with dazzling women straight to the battlefield should be savored.

Twenty-eight miles south of Brussels, Napoleon was awake. At midnight, he was aroused by Ney who had ridden from Gosselies, four miles away. The two men were left alone to discuss the tactics which would be put into operation at dawn. The strategy still remained the same. Crush one of the armies, contain the other.

Then strike with everything for complete victory. The campaign still depended on fresh developments. To win depended on well-coordinated reactions to situations as they developed. Only general plans could be outlined now. The minutes passed slowly in the courtyard outside the château where Napoleon and his marshal discussed their plans. Sentries were rotated often so all could get some sleep. But some men stayed awake. They smoked and looked at the moon and wondered what the sun would bring.

Ten miles northeast, at Sombreffe, old Blücher was in bed. But before retiring he had done all he could to put his large army in motion. Village clocks had struck twelve, and now giant hands were reaching for another hour as his messengers galloped to the northeast to hurry the concentration. At Quatre Bras to the northwest, the fragment of Wellington's army, which was barricaded there, waited for the dawn. Would reinforcements arrive, or would they be overwhelmed by a vicious French attack, which they knew was coming?

Brussels was now in ferment. Townspeople were at their windows. Some dressed to hurry to the streets. "What could it be?" they asked one another. Pvt. Harry Lewis of the 95th was aroused by the clatter. Sergeants were everywhere ordering the soldiers to get their gear and assemble. Somebody shouted, "We have just an hour before we march." [1] The details of what was happening melted like sugar in tea as reports on the situation dribbled through the echelon of command to the private soldiers. Private Lewis rushed to get ready. His comrades tore at their stockings, pulled at their breeches, while trying to guess what was at hand. "The French," a soldier shouted, "was making different movements on our left." [2]

Caught in a mélange of assembling soldiers, inquiring Bruxellois,* and chattering party-goers was a train of peasants' carts bringing to market cabbages, green peas, potatoes, onions, turnips, string beans, strawberries and other produce. As usual, the country people started arriving shortly after midnight so they could get their merchandise ready for sale in the best market places on the outskirts of the Grand Place. As their husbands in red nightcaps and blue smocks [3] led the huge cart horses, old Flemish women who sat atop their piles of vegetables, dug and pulled from

* Citizens of Brussels.

the earth only hours before, managed a kind of homely dignity.

To some of the young women in their splendid dresses who had deserted parties to follow the excitement, the old women looked somewhat comical. But the old country people belonged in the market place at this hour. They and their ancestors had been feeding Brussels for a thousand years. Their precinct was being overrun by men in gaudy uniforms and women who had no business there. The confusion appeared even more ridiculous to the country people. Officers fresh from the ball strode in dancing pumps, ordering their men to arms. Harried valets and batmen appeared from nowhere, carrying boots for their masters. Dispatch riders wove in and out of the crowds. Soldiers sat on the cobblestones pulling on shoes. Rising above the din was the occasional shrill laughter of women so intoxicated by the excitement of the moment that they didn't know what else to do.

Candles were lighted in almost every home in Brussels since there was hardly a place where one or two soldiers weren't quartered. All over the city soldiers poured into the streets. The wives and children of officers and men rushed with them to assembly points for a last good-bye. Artillery caissons and supply wagons rumbled everywhere and infants, awakened by the strange sounds, bellowed. Some of the citizens of the city who had developed a fondness for the soldiers assigned to their homes tried in various ways to show their affection. Attempts were made to cook an early breakfast. Here and there a talisman or a religious medal was pressed into a soldier's hands. Some young girls scampered into gardens to pick bouquets, their shyness preventing them from giving the roses and poppies away until the very last minute. Women wept softly while they packed an officer's kit or touched a soldier's hand. Parents of many Belgian soldiers walked with them to the mustering place. Fear was on their faces. They passed young boys chattering in delight while they watched prancing stallions and waving pennants.

The Duke took a late supper which had been arranged at the ball for the honored guests. The fear that Napoleon meant to separate his army from the English Channel and the British fleet subsided somewhat. Nevertheless, the Duke felt that some of his forces should still be retained on his right flank in case the Emperor changed his mind. Most of his troops at Hal, seven miles southwest of Brussels, were ordered to stay where they were. Suddenly many realized that some of the gaiety had left with departing young officers. The realization of what lay ahead in the dawn made its sting felt. Napoleon was bearing down on Brussels like an avalanche. To many of the titled Belgians present the Emperor was invincible. The clatter throughout Brussels continued. Ambulances and ration carts poured through the streets from supply centers. The new day followed its inevitable course. It was 1:00 A.M. and then another hour began to fly. At the glittering table, the Duke was in hushed conversation with the Prince of Orange, and then a piece of their conversation was heard by all. Wellington said he had no fresh orders, and that the Prince should get some sleep. Some minutes later the Duke said, "I think it is time for me to go to bed likewise."

Wellington stood to thank his host and hostess. All eyes were on him as he started to make his way out of the dining room. There was a whisper to his host, the Duke of Richmond. Was there a good map in the house? The Duke led Wellington to a small adjacent room. The door was shut, and Wellington for a brief moment dropped his reserve. The burden of the hour was heavy and his responsibilities grave. The destiny of Europe rested on his orders, and now with a major battle coming nearer and nearer, his soldier's mind knew that the odds at the moment were tilted in favor of his enemy. Perhaps it gave the Duke relief to say, "Napoleon has humbugged me, by God! He has gained twenty-four hours march on me." "What do you intend doing?" Richmond asked. Wellington eyed the map which had been given him. It was stretched out and his thumb moved over it. "I have ordered the army to concentrate at Quatre Bras; but we shall not stop him there, and if so, I must fight him here." Richmond looked at the map. Wellington's thumb was resting on a village called Waterloo. Wellington then said his last good-bye of the evening and left for his quarters through a side door.

Colonel de Lancey had returned to his apartment sometime earlier. His wife was waiting for him. She had more hot tea ready and hoped that it would lift some of the weariness from his face. Most of the dispatches had been written, but de Lancey could not sleep. Around 2:00 A.M. the Colonel walked to Wellington's quarters to see if anything more was wanted of him. He found that the Duke had returned from the ball and was sleeping soundly. De Lancey did not disturb him and returned to his wife and the few hours they had left together.

At that moment, men were marching throughout Flanders— troops from Wellington's scattered outposts, Prussian soldiers moving from the northeast to concentrate near Ligny, some scattered French units who had been delayed by insufficient orders or who had tarried too long for supper.

Napoleon and Ney ended their meeting at 2:00 A.M. The Emperor went immediately to bed, with Ney returning the four miles to Gosselies. The road was fairly quiet now as Ney rode slowly with a few of his lieutenants. The half moon was in and out of the clouds, and the night was very dark. Occasionally a fatigued courier would pass Ney's small party. The croaking frogs announced each small stream that trickled through the meadows and the fields.

Near Soignies, headquarters of Sir Charles Alten's third division, which was nineteen miles almost due west of Quatre Bras, Ensign Macready was sleeping much too soundly. After he had been alerted at 4:00 P.M., he had been ordered on picket duty at Naast, three miles from Soignies. The sun had set, and he had received no further orders. Now it was 2:00 A.M., and the whole division was marching to war, with the exception of Macready and his company.

In Brussels, some units had been ready to march for over an hour. Orders to fall out were given various companies and the men stretched out on the cobblestones to talk or sleep. Lieutenant John Kincaid of the 95th Rifles tried to take a catnap, but every time he managed to fall asleep, milling civilians, "ladies as well as gentlemen," would wake him to get a report on the news.[4] He begged them to go home to bed, and again would try to nap, but in a moment another worried civilian would be tugging at his collar.

Three-day rations of beef and bread had been issued to troops as they waited to leave Brussels. Already soldiers were wolfing down a whole day's rations in minutes. Those who were fortunate enough to be near market carts found the expensive strawberries especially tempting. A few even risked a flogging to steal some. But pears were cheap. Even a soldier could afford them. Apples were dear, even the stunted ones. Peaches were a deluxe item, expensive and hard to find. June had been too cold for Flanders to produce good fruit. The sun hadn't been out enough to ripen fruit, although the field crops were good. The grapes were bad, and 1815 was a bad year for wine. The average noon temperature for June was 62.96 degrees Fahrenheit.[5]

Finally the orders came to leave Brussels. The first contingents were on their way to Quatre Bras. But all night long the din was heard as additional regiments assembled. It was 2:30 A.M. in the Hôtel de Flandre when Miss Charlotte Waldie, her brother and sisters, who had come to Brussels on vacation, heard a banging on their door. Awakened earlier by the noise outside, they felt for a minute that the French had arrived. But it was an old friend, Major Richard Llewellyn of the 28th Foot, who had come to say good-bye. The Waldies dressed hurriedly. A candle was lighted in the boy's room, and they all gathered around the major. The incident seemed like a dream to Charlotte. She looked into the major's face for a long time "as if to retain a lasting remembrance ... should we ... be destined to meet no more." [6] Outside in the courtyard she heard the major's charger "neighing and pawing the ground." [7]

At 3:00 A.M. in Volsel, thirteen miles west of Brussels, Lieutenant Hay of the 12th Dragoons heard someone in his room. It was his servant, and Hay, half asleep, found it difficult to believe that it was time for morning drill. "Is it so near the time for marching already?" [8] The servant, at that moment packing the lieutenant's kit, answered: "We are going to march in earnest; the field-day is countermanded and the colonel, who has this moment arrived from Brussels, wishes to see you at his house immediately." [9] Hay sprang out of bed. He quickly dressed and hurried to Lieutenant Colonel Ponsonby's quarters.* The colonel greeted him. "You were lucky not to go to the ball. I am quite knocked up. The French are coming on in great numbers, and yesterday attacked and drove the Prussians back!" [10] The colonel then gave Hay his first orders of the campaign: "Tell the sergeant to give orders immediately for three days' rations and forage to be served imme-

---

* Lt. Col. Frederick Cavendish Ponsonby, commanding officer of the 12th Dragoons, is not to be confused with Maj. Gen. the Hon. Sir William Ponsonby, a cavalry brigade commander.

diately; and as soon as that is done, the order is to be given for the regiment to march." [11] Hay saluted, but before being dismissed the colonel told his lieutenant that he would like to be left alone "as long as possible, to get some rest." [12]

Dawn was approaching. Marching southward to reinforce Quatre Bras were additional troops from Perponcher's Dutch-Belgian battalions. At the crossroads village, allied soldiers maintained their vigil, some feeling that the French would attack with the first light. The veterans were less anxious, noting that the French always liked a leisurely breakfast first. Some miles northeast of Ligny the roads streamed with Prussians. Old Blücher's concentration seemed to be working smoothly. Along the French lines, some young officers slept fitfully. Their responsibilities for moving their troops into action seemed to magnify by the hour.

It was nearing 4:00 A.M. when Lieutenant Jackson of Colonel de Lancey's staff was returning from Ninove, where he had delivered a dispatch. He rode along the Rue de la Madeleine in Brussels. The clamor of troops readying for the march in the park adjacent to the Palais Royale was heard and he reined in his horse to watch. Lieutenant General Picton, commander of the 5th division, was dashing back and forth on horseback inspecting his troops. The lieutenant considered Picton's 5th "a splendid division" [13] and was impressed by the sight. He heard the orders echo up and down the park for the division to form into marching units. And then he heard "quick march."

The young officer then moved to a new vantage point, a place in front of the Hôtel de Belle-Vue on the Palais Royale, to watch the troops march past. There were the 95th Rifles, "dressed in dark green, and with black accoutrements." [14] Then came the 28th Regiment, with the 42nd Highlanders right behind. Jackson watched the sable plumes of the Highlanders' bonnets. He noticed that they scarcely vibrated because the men were marching "so steadily." [15] He also watched the 79th and 92nd Scottish regiments. The division would be leaving Brussels by the Porte de Namur for Quatre Bras.

Miss Waldie watched from her hotel window. She, her sisters and her brother had visited with Major Llewellyn, and now after a good-bye to a dear friend who was riding into action, she could not take her eyes off a soldier and his family who stood in the

courtyard below her. The soldier's wife had arrived with her child
to say good-bye. The soldier "turned back again and again" to his
wife and to take the baby "once more in his arms." [16] Finally, she
saw him "hastily brush away a tear with the sleeve of his coat" as
he gave his wife the child "for the last time." [17] He then "wrung"
his wife's hand, and ran after his company.[18]

Captain Mercer, commander of "G" Troop, Royal Horse Artillery, was bivouacked at Strytem. The exact minute when his servant rushed into his quarters to wake him was forgotten, but the
captain realized that the hour was very unreasonable. His orders
were to march "with utmost diligence" to Enghien.[19] As he stumbled out of bed, the captain realized that he had some problems.
Most of his officers had gone to the ball in Brussels. His supply
wagons were widely dispersed. One-third of his artillery was
quartered some miles away at Yseringen.

"Send the sergeant-major here," the captain bellowed to his
servant as he pulled on his stockings.[20] Then as he slipped into his
trousers he called for his supply officer, Mr. Coates. And as he
buttoned up, he gave his servant a third order, "William, make
haste and get breakfast." [21]

The sergeant arrived first and was told to turn out the troop
instantly with three days' rations, and to send a messenger for
the men at Yseringen. Within seconds, "the fine martial clang of
'boot and saddle' resounded through the village and courts of the
château, making the woods ring again, and even the frogs stop
to listen." [22]

Mr. Coates arrived on the double. "What! are we off, sir?" [23]
"Yes, without delay; and you must collect your wagons as quickly
as possible." [24] The job would take time, the captain knew, so he
decided there and then that he would move off with his guns as
soon as the force arrived from Yseringen. The supply wagons
could catch up late. The decision was to give him some anxious
moments. In the meantime he found that most of his officers had
heard of the battle plans in Brussels, and had returned at once.
While he waited for his guns from Yseringen the captain had a
hearty breakfast. Everybody in the troop who wanted to could
have a double portion of eggs.

Napoleon had been up since 4:00 A.M. He was confident. A
march had been stolen against his enemies, and now all he had

to do was attack. A swift, terrible victory and he would be the master of Europe once more. A quick breakfast, a greeting to his Old Guardsmen who had guarded him throughout the night, a swift look at dispatches that had come in, consultation with his lieutenants and orders for Soult. At the moment it looked like Wellington would be his first victim. He would crush the British and then turn on the Prussians. An hour passed. On the French right Grouchy had been receiving a flood of reports of a massive Prussian buildup. At 5:00 A.M., he dispatched a message to the Emperor, in which he noted that the Ligny area was swarming with Prussians. Grouchy's courier was on his way to Napoleon's headquarters shortly after 5:00 A.M. In the meantime, Napoleon had worked out these tactics: he would order Grouchy to attack what he thought was a limited number of Prussians around Sombreffe. After the French right had flushed the Prussians out of Sombreffe and had reached Gembloux, a little over four miles more to the northeast, he would lead his reserves to join Ney. Together they would crush Wellington.

Old Blücher had also risen early. He went over reports on his concentration. He would have 85,000 men that day to throw against the French. He would seize the initiative, he figured. Then Wellington could hit Napoleon with his whole army, and Napoleon would be finished.

A little after 5:00 A.M., the sun was bathing all of Flanders in the light of a beautiful morning. On the Brussels road, Perponcher's reinforcements filed into Quatre Bras. Ney, with his headquarters at Gosselies, a little over six miles south of the crossroads, had not yet begun his preparations for attack. Large numbers of his troops were still miles from action.

At this hour Brussels rocked with marching men, and the jumble of artillery, cavalry, wagons and ambulances. The din was deafening. Wellington, however, was still sleeping soundly. He had gone to bed around 2:00 A.M. and would arise at 6:00 A.M. for the twenty-mile ride to Quatre Bras.

Chapter Nine

The Sun and the Forest

IT would be a hot day, a day when the sun seemed anxious to scorch the earth. Clouds could not interfere for they had retreated somewhere during the night, and now in early morning there was nothing to stop the sun except the shade of the forests. The brilliance of the sun made the morning hours seem much later than they were.

Armies were mobilizing to fight, and their divisions moved down scores of roads like raging streams storming toward a swollen river. In the great forests there was another concentration. Little animals that foraged the meadows were startled by cavalry, by the clamor on the nearby roads. They fled to the wilderness, preferring danger from animals that preyed upon them to the unpredictable nature of men at war.

Startled red deer, and roe-buck, their ears pricking at the thunderous cavalcade, darted for the trees. Foxes, rabbits and squirrels streaked across ditches. Singing sparrows, brown nightingales and fawn-colored warblers gathered on the fringes of the forests. Black and white swallows, yellow orioles, green woodpeckers and brown and blue kingfishers sheltered in the trees. Quail were flushed from the meadows and quivered near hedges, sedge and brushwood.

Deep in the forests other animals sensed an uneasiness. They roamed to more inaccessible places. Wolves and wildcats sought the darker recesses, where the burning sun was fought to a cool standstill by the broad branches of oak, birch, beech, white wood and fir. Vipers slithered from rocky sunny oases into dank recesses which were unnatural to them.

Only wild boars seemed not sufficiently afraid to run. They paid dearly for their bravery. They could not know that cowardly men can kill easily, sometimes more easily than stronger men. When they saw a human, they charged. Deserters who sensed death in battle or who knew that they could not stand against the enemy when the time came had slipped away from their units. They fled to the center of the forests. There were not many, but their movement and the snap of dead branches under their feet alerted the animals. The deserters were desperate. Death was sure if they were caught. They jumped at every noise. They could kill a charging boar, an animal that often unnerved a courageous hunter.

Fear had wrapped itself around some men like the early morning fog of Flanders. Deserters had chosen dishonor for a chance at life, but there were others who tried to hold on to safety without the risk of desertion. They were seldom successful. Pvt. James Gibbons of the 33rd Regiment dreaded the action that he knew was ahead. He had discarded the idea of desertion, but perhaps there was a way out. In the last few weeks he had been practicing his civilian trade more than soldiering. A barber before enlisting, he added to his army pay by shaving officers and cutting their hair. Now he was a soldier again. He was with his company on the road. Every step was taking him closer to the French lines.

At 6.00 A.M. Napoleon sent orders to Ney and Grouchy. The plan he had considered the previous night and the early morning was the one he had settled on. Wellington would be beaten first. Grouchy's courier who carried word of a massive Prussian buildup was hurrying to the Emperor's headquarters in Charleroi. He still had twelve miles ahead of him. On the French right Grouchy now had even more evidence that old Blücher was pouring in everything he could. He decided to dispatch a second messenger with the additional information. It was a little after 6:00 A.M. when the second messenger galloped for Charleroi.

At Quatre Bras allied soldiers looked southward toward the French lines. There was no action. Did they face Napoleon? young soldiers wondered. Veterans didn't think so. It was some other general, they figured. "Old 'Boney' would have been at us by now," said one of them. They faced Ney's army, and the marshal seemed to be taking a lot of time that morning.

In Brussels, Wellington was up. He, too, did not seem to be in a rush. He put on a freshly laundered white shirt, white riding breeches, a waistcoat to match, and slipped into half boots.* He chose a dark short coat. Minutes later, he was consulting with his staff over breakfast. Hanging nearby was a blue surtout coat and his marshal's hat decorated with badges from Spain, Portugal and Prussia.

The hours, the minutes were running out for many. It was around 7:00 A.M. when Wellington mounted his horse, Copenhagen, for the ride to Quatre Bras. His staff rode with him, a glittering assemblage of British and allied officers. Colonel de Lancey was at his side. He had said good-bye to Mrs. de Lancey sometime earlier. From her window she could watch the whole procession. There were many young staff officers in Wellington's train. Among them was Capt. Arthur Hill. At Eton his companions had nicknamed him "Fatty" or called him "Fat" Hill. Since leaving school he had taken on even more weight, and for him a huge horse was a necessity. The two of them would make a gigantic target for the French, "Fat" Hill's comrades surmised. The Duke, as he glanced at Hill, must have wondered on occasion how he had managed to inherit such a fat officer.

The way to the village was familiar to Wellington. As he rode at a brisk gait, he would have found it hard not to remember the early mornings when he had trotted over the same ground. It had been more than thirty years earlier when his mother had taken him to Brussels to live. He hadn't shown much promise at Eton, and for economic reasons she had pulled him out for a sojourn in Flanders, where living costs were lower. He had often rented a horse to ride to the Forest of Soignies outside Brussels. His rides had taken him to Waterloo, Mont St. Jean, and down the road which intersects the farms of Hougoumont and La Haye Sainte. Quatre Bras was only nine miles farther south.

Some weeks before this bright Friday of June 16, he had reconnoitered the area. He knew the land well—its slight rises, the forests, the nearby villages, the roads and streams. Landmarks familiar to him when he was a youth forced their attention upon him.

* Boots which later came to be called Wellington boots.

On his reconnaissance he had mentally placed his troops as he studied reverse slopes, hedge rows and sunken roads. Perhaps he had imagined himself a general during those rides so many years ago, and had played at arranging imaginary soldiers even then. During this ride he may have recalled the incidents and inwardly smiled at his early ineptness.

Time is most precious in war. But its value did not seem to be really appreciated by any of the commanders except old Blücher. He spent the minutes bargaining for their worth by urging every unit forward. The seventh and eighth hours of the new day slipped away. The Prince of Orange had reached Quatre Bras. His troops were in good order, but the long wait for the French attack by Ney was unnerving some of them. At 8:00 A.M., Napoleon had received Grouchy's report of the big Prussian concentration on the French right. If this is so, he thought, then his plan to defeat Wellington first would have to be abandoned. He would beat the old man today and then turn on the British. It mattered not since his plans were elastic enough to cope with a major change in tactics. But he wanted to see for himself. He would be leaving shortly for the French right.

At the same time, some twenty miles northwest of Napoleon's headquarters, Ensign Macready, who had been assigned to picket duty with his infantry company, rode into Soignies for supplies. But where was his regiment? There was an unearthly silence in the village—no soldiers, no cavalry, no artillery. His regiment and ten thousand other men had disappeared.

He remembered that the breath left his body "as if extracted by an air pump." [1] He ran into the first house he could, and learned that the troops had moved toward the front at 2:00 A.M. Macready fought a balky horse back to his picket, where he had a short conference with other young officers. To remain where they were was to follow orders. Their commissions would be safe. But to stay would risk missing the battle. The small unit set out hurriedly to pick up the trail of their regiment. The British fifth division en route to Quatre Bras from Brussels paused for a brief rest outside Brussels at the Forest of Soignies. The heat was stifling for early morning, and dust was thick from the road. A quick snack was eaten: boiled beef, a bit of ham, some dry biscuits. Peasants provided water and milk. But the rest was a

short one. Officers had not had time to prepare tea before the
bugles sounded. Captain Harry Ross-Lewin of the 32nd Regiment was standing near another captain when the order to fall
in was given. "That is my death warrant," the captain said to no
one in particular.[2] Ross-Lewin couldn't drive the captain's statement from his mind.

Soldiers talked about death as they marched under the hot sun.
Some sought release from their preoccupation with it by making
weak jokes, or appearing entirely too nonchalant. Others with
unfathomable logic sought to guarantee their own safety with
half-serious predictions of death for their comrades. Lt. James
Hart of the 33rd regiment told his friend, Lt. Fred Hope Pattison, "Pat, you will be going to grass with your teeth uppermost
before night." [3] This was a disturbing thing to say to a comrade.
The remark came out of the blue. It was a strange way to word
a prediction of death. But Lieutenant Pattison only replied, "Take
care of yourself, Jamie." [4] Lieutenant Hay of the 12th Dragoons
had somehow torn his trousers. A fellow officer said unexpectedly,
"I know who expects to be killed today." [5] To whom was he referring? The officer pointed to Lieutenant Hay's torn trousers
and laughed.

The certainty of combat sometimes gives a man a glimpse into
the future. For some inexplicable reason he knows in advance
whether he will live or die. But as the sun rose higher and higher
into the sky most men moved forward, fortified by the soldier's
creed, "Every bullet has its billet." If a man was meant to die,
a bullet had his name on it, and there was nothing he could do to
save himself. But if his death bullet hadn't been molded, then he
could stand unscratched in a hail of fire.

On the French right, Napoleon's Imperial Guardsmen knew
that they would soon be moving up. But in the meantime they
had made themselves as comfortable as possible. They had stacked
their arms, and then stretched handkerchiefs and pieces of can-
vas over the muzzles. Each musket stack provided a shelter against
the sun for two or three men. Their camps always had more
serenity and more comfort than those of the line regiments. There
was less anxiety, less tension among the officers and the men.
They, too, accepted the soldier's creed. But they had extra armor
as well. Death was a comfort if they knew they had performed

their duty. They talked less about death than some of the others.

It was 9:00 A.M. when the Guard's drums beat assembly. They marched north behind line infantry regiments and cuirassiers.

A half hour later, a messenger arrived at Napoleon's headquarters at Charleroi to report that enemy troops at Quatre Bras were barring the way to Brussels. The Emperor hastily dictated a note for Ney, ordering him to destroy these forces. He noted in his message that it appeared that old Blücher was too far to the French right to send help. The Emperor then mounted his horse for the ride to Fleurus, a little over six miles to the northeast. If Grouchy was only correct in his assessment of the Prussian buildup then old Blücher was playing right into his hands. He would strike him with Grouchy's forces. Then he could borrow troops from Ney who was facing only fragments of Wellington's army. When the time came he could throw in the reserves, which were under his direct command. That would be the end of Blücher. Wellington's disaster would come the next day or the day after that. The English would be heavily outnumbered after the Prussians were defeated.

It was 10:00 A.M. when Wellington reached Quatre Bras. There he could see that the position was held by a thread of troops, most of whom were there in direct disobedience to his orders. He left well enough alone. He neither complimented the Dutch-Belgian commanders for their audacity in countermanding his orders nor did he reprimand them. To reprimand them would be ridiculous. They had done the right thing. To compliment them would be to acknowledge that he had misinterpreted the reports of Napoleon's attack. The situation was so clear now. Quatre Bras must be held at all costs if communication with Blücher was to be maintained. He inspected the defenses and wrote a number of dispatches to hurry his divisions forward. Many of his commanders were completely confused. Miles away, they weren't quite clear on the marching orders and hurried couriers to brother officers in distant camps to learn where they were to go. Several regiments had headed their troops for Nivelles, acting on Wellington's first orders, and were chased by frantic messengers hoping to direct them to Quatre Bras. Wellington at this time had 6,000 men at the crossroads village. He was short on artillery and had practically no cavalry. It would take hours for his forces to build up to a respectable size but he decided to risk leaving the small defenses and ride to Prussian headquarters to confer with Blücher.

It was shortly before 11:00 A.M. when Napoleon reached Fleurus on the French right to see if old Blücher had assembled his army. At the sight of the Emperor, Grouchy's troops sent up tumultuous cheers. A group of liaison officers greeted him, and he hurried to the northern outskirts of the village. He was led to a mill which towered above his assembling regiments. A sergeant took a squad of sappers and they climbed up the mill's creaky steps. Working with pride in their corps and with zeal for their Emperor, they punched a hole in the mill's roof and set to work building an observation platform for Napoleon and his officers. The work was accomplished in a few minutes while Napoleon paced back and forth, seething because he had learned that Gérard's corps, part of Grouchy's forces, was lagging behind and wouldn't be in position for at least two more hours. The minutes were now turning to gold. Just a little before they had been silver. The work was finished. The platform was ready, Napoleon was told. He went up the steps. There was a smell of damp grain. Somewhere a farmer would agonize over the ruptured roof. Napoleon was at the top. He grasped his spy glass and turned it on the north. There they were! In the distance was the grandeur of an assembling army—hordes of infantry, cavalry and artillery with the sun skipping on burnished sabre, harness and gun and occasionally exploding in a blinding burst on some remote piece of military hardware. Napoleon studied the formations as they wheeled into position. Perhaps he mentally congratulated himself on the plan he had devised weeks before in Paris. He would smite one assembling army, while containing the other in the first day of battle. Old Blücher was making it easier for him than he had ever imagined.

Napoleon studied the area carefully. He saw the Ligne River sparkling in the distance, carefully tended acres of wheat and rye, neat farm houses, and a string of villages—Brye, Ligny, St. Amand and a half dozen others. He could see Blücher's troops assembled in and between the hamlets.

At 11:00 A.M., Napoleon's six o'clock message was received on the French left by Ney. The dispatch was a long one. It detailed the Emperor's ideas for using two wings and a reserve to crush the allies. It precisely detailed the way Ney should disperse his troops. The orders also stressed that elements of the marshal's command should be arranged so that they could be available to reinforce the right if circumstances dictated. It was specified that one of Ney's divisions should be well north of Quatre Bras by the evening of the 16th so that Brussels could be taken the following morning. The theme of the message, however, underlined the elasticity of the Emperor's plans. When the dispatch was written, Napoleon reasoned that Wellington would be his first victim and that the main assault would be on the French left. But he had also made provisions to hit Blücher first if the opportunity presented itself. This was exactly what was happening now. Blücher's rush to assemble his forces made the Prussians Napoleon's No. 1 target. The fluidity of the situation was underlined in this sentence, "According to circumstances, I may reduce one or other wing to augment my reserve." The reserve would be used as always. Led by the Emperor, it would be held in hand until the *coup de grâce* was to be delivered. As matters stood it could be used on either the right or the left.

The message was read hurriedly by Ney and then again more slowly. It was passed around to his staff officers. Perhaps Ney regretted that he had not summoned the last resources of energy the night before to take Quatre Bras. Perhaps the swift passage of the new day mocked him for the tasks he had left unfinished the night before. His army strung out for miles. To comply with Napoleon's orders would take hours. With the official order of movement from the Emperor now at hand, Ney issued a flood of dispatches to his divisions. The sun was reaching for its summit.

In a thousand cottages across the Flanders fields, peasants gathered around their tables to eat their soup. At Quatre Bras in a corner house a man sat at his table as he had done for years. As he satisfied his hunger he might have noticed how still and peaceful it was. Almost everywhere outside his cottage, soldiers were waiting for battle, but the sounds they made were muffled by the stout walls. And, too, when soldiers wait for an assault they often whisper to each other—there is the feeling that the enemy can hear across distant fields. The skylark could not be heard by the man in the corner cottage. It had flown away.

On the road which runs southeast from Quatre Bras to Sombreffe, Wellington and a number of his aides were hurrying to confer with old Blücher. The Prussian commander had made a windmill his headquarters. It provided a fine observation tower, standing at Bussy between the villages of Ligny and Brye which faced Napoleon's right wing. Blücher exuded confidence. He received and dispatched his couriers with zest and fire. His confidence inspired his lieutenants, and optimism swept through his army. Could it be that Napoleon would be dangling from the end of a rope before the day was out? The rough old soldier was forever entertaining the idea, turning it slowly in his mind, perhaps as slowly as a gallow's corpse swings before a gentle breeze.

Just two and a half miles to the southwest, Napoleon waited at Fleurus. He should attack now. He should do it at once. But the 4th Corps, Gérard's corps, had not come up. He would need it badly since he could not tell how many Prussians lay ahead of him. He could not tell what plans the old man had made with Wellington. Courier after courier had been sent to spur Gérard's arrival. Sloppy staff work, the confusion when de Bourmont had deserted all figured in the delay.

Southwest of Fleurus, Gérard's divisions were suffering all the agonies of a forced march. The burning sun made some of the men shed their tunics. Exhausted soldiers began to discard their beloved *marmites*. Knapsacks were abandoned. Officers rode up and down the struggling columns shouting that their Emperor needed them desperately.

It was nearing 1:00 P.M. when Wellington and his staff approached the Bussy windmill. Lt. Col. Sir Henry Hardinge, a British liaison officer at Prussian headquarters, saw them in the distance. He had no idea that Wellington was among them, but felt that the men were British because of the "cut tails" of the horses. But Hardinge wasn't sure. They could be French, he thought. He decided to gallop towards them, feeling that if they were the enemy he could dart away on his swift hunter. He discovered that he was approaching the British commander in chief. In a moment, Wellington was welcomed by Prussian staff officers and old Blücher himself.

The position allowed both commanders to survey the entire enemy line. They swept the field with their glasses from atop the windmill.

Before them was the glittering panorama of Napoleon's army. They saw phalanxes of infantry formed to advance. Units of the Imperial Guard, which Napoleon had brought up from Charleroi, stood sweltering in fields south of Ligny. In the distance the movement of Gérard's corps could be seen as it raced for a rendezvous with the assembled right wing. In fact, a few advance elements of Gérard's were already being directed to places in the line. Much closer to old Blücher's mill another enemy unit was picked up by the glasses. Napoleon was in that group. He had moved forward with a headquarters staff to make an inspection. For a brief moment it seemed that Wellington and Blücher had spotted the Emperor. Other officers who surveyed the field from the Prussian lines saw him clearly. To Lt. Col. Ludwig von Reiche, a Prussian staff officer who was present at the mill "... Napoleon was clearly distinguishable ..." [6]

Wellington was as interested in the positioning of Blücher's army as in that of Napoleon's. He figured the main thrust would be aimed at the Prussians and he wondered if they could hold. He did not like what he saw. The old man had deployed his troops on the exposed slopes. The main villages he was attempting to defend, Ligny and Brye, seemed to be too far apart. They were not within musket range of one another, the Duke guessed. Consequently, old Blücher's units in and around the two villages could only support one another with artillery fire. Blücher was violating the Duke's ideas of how to handle an army on the battlefield— interlock fields of fire, and, "by God," use every hillock, every tree, wall, ridge and slope for cover. Cheat the enemy's artillery, make it as difficult for their cavalry and infantry as possible. He had fought that way in Spain and Portugal, and if he had anything to do with it that would be the way his ally, Blücher, would fight here. Discussing the situation with Blücher, Wellington was blunt. "Everybody knows their own army best; but if I were to fight with mine here, I should expect to be beat," he said. The old man swung a verbal mace in reply, stating that his men were assembled that way because they liked to see the enemy. The meeting lasted for nearly an hour.

Besides the blunt conversation on the deployment of the Prussian army, Wellington insisted that the forthcoming attack would be Napoleon's main effort. He also said that he would come to

Blücher's assistance if circumstances permitted it. He said that such assistance would have to wait for the buildup of his army before Quatre Bras. Then, if possible, he could advance southward. This would permit him, he reported, to operate on the French left and rear, and would create a diversion which would siphon off the French strength which lay before Ligny and the Prussians. But now it was getting late in the afternoon. Wellington was anxious to return to Quatre Bras and his own army. The slender thread of men he had left there could be broken in a dozen places under furious French attacks. As the commanders parted they probably knew in their own minds that they would have to get through the day on their own. Wellington mounted Copenhagen. Prussian officers admired the Duke's horse and the equipment which it carried. A valise was strapped to the saddle with a change of clothing, paper, pen and ink. The baggage had replaced the pistol holster which was generally part of a horseman's equipage.[7] Some minutes out on the elm-lined road to Quatre Bras, Wellington and his staff heard artillery fire. It was coming from Quatre Bras.

Chapter Ten

Quatre Bras and Ligny

ARTILLERYMEN never forget the smell of exploding powder. It lingers and lingers, rasping nostrils and lungs and
stimulating the emotions. It is an aroma that reminds a cannoneer
of power, death, adventure and success. Success is very important
since the first whiff of smoke is a signal that everything has gone
well. The gun has fired properly. Before the first shot there is
always the feeling that there could be a muzzle burst. A premature
explosion in the barrel and all is over for the cannoneer. This
depressing thought flies away with the first projectile. From then
on, success means hitting the target. Destroying it brings elation.
Thoughts of power and death recede after the first few smoke
rings, but adventure is always there, an indefinable feeling which
intoxicates.

Cannoneers serving the "Armée du Nord's" left wing signaled
the attack on Quatre Bras. It was nearly 2:00 P.M. when Reille's
Second Corps was ordered by Ney to launch the first attack. The
thin Dutch-Belgian line of skirmishers which extended for almost
two miles stiffened. The long-awaited assault by the French was
coming.

The right of the allied line was anchored in the forest of Bossu.
From there it extended almost directly eastward, with its left
curving around the road which runs southeast to the Ligny area
where Blücher had concentrated the bulk of his army. The left

flank of the allies at Quatre Bras was eight miles from the Prussians.

Ney had brought his troops up the Brussels road which extends almost directly north and south. The road intersected both the attacking and defending armies. The marshal had no idea of the strength or weakness that lay ahead of him. At the moment he could throw in almost 20,000 French infantry and 3,000 cavalrymen.[1] They were backed up by sixty guns.[2] The Prince of Orange was outnumbered almost three-to-one. His Dutch-Belgian command consisted of 7,800 infantry, a handful of horsemen and a dozen guns.

French skirmishers dispersed and the crackling of musket fire spread along the line. Now that the tension of waiting was over, soldiers on both sides experienced a sense of relief. Heavy smoke began to drift slowly over fields of rye and wheat as the firing became more intense. But the assault was not as massive as it could have been. Only a portion of Ney's power was put to use. Ney was convinced by his attacking general, Reille, that the heavy cover of luxuriant crops and the trees could shield the bulk of Wellington's army. Reille had felt Wellington's battlefield sting in Spain and implored Ney to be cautious.

Nevertheless, things were going well for the French. Reille struck the allied right flank. It began to quiver. French artillerymen were now hitting their targets. Cheers of Reille's infantry terrorized young Dutch-Belgians. To some, these screams seemed worse than the artillery which was now mangling whole companies. But the forest was a fort. The first shots flushed thousands of birds who had sheltered there. They darkened the sun for an instant. The lost second of surprise at the massive fluttering of so many wings could have been the difference between life and death for a hundred men—a pause with fingers frozen on triggers, a pause in the open as targets. Seconds later the allies began to pour in a heavy fire from behind tall firs and clumps of bushes. Ney ordered Reille to throw in more troops against the allied right flank and some minutes later the Dutch-Belgians began to fall back slowly through the trees.

A messenger was now on his way with a new dispatch for Ney. At 2:00 P.M., Napoleon asked Soult to emphasize again to Ney what he expected of the left wing.

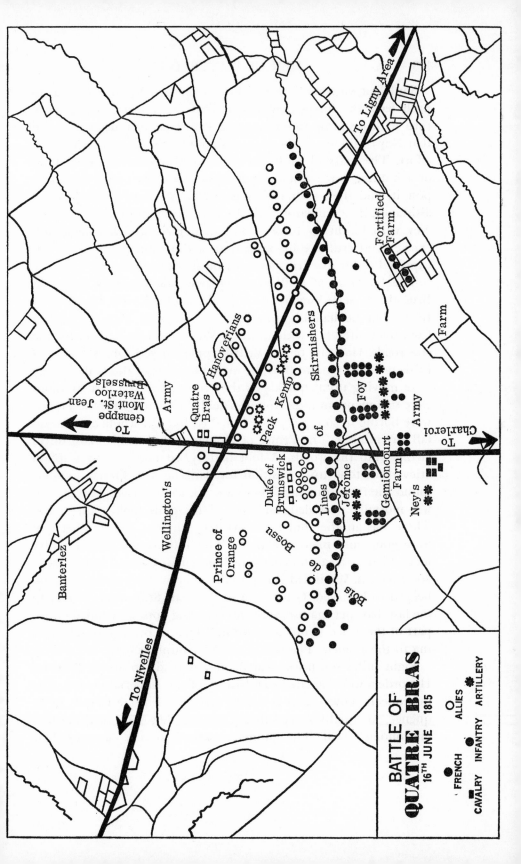

BATTLE OF:
QUATRE BRAS
16TH JUNE 1815

FRENCH   ALLIES
CAVALRY   INFANTRY   ARTILLERY

To Nivelles

Banterlez

Wellington's

Prince of Orange

Bossu

Duke of Brunswick

Lines

de

Bois

To Genappe
Mont St. Jean
Waterloo
Brussels

Quatre Bras

Army

Hanoverians

Pack Kemp

Skirmishers

of

Jérôme

Gemioncourt Farm

Foy

Army

Ney's

To Charleroi

Farm

Fortified Farm

To Ligny Area

Soult got off a message which told the marshal that he was to push back the forces that lay in front of him and then was to turn with his army to envelop the Prussians. Napoleon reasoned that Ney could secure the crossroads of Quatre Bras without much effort. The marshal could then use his discretion on what kind of a holding force would be needed there. He could detach it, post it, and then rush with the rest of his army to Napoleon's assistance. The Emperor with the right wing and the reserve and Ney with his heavy forces could then place Blücher in a nutcracker and crumble his army into a thousand pieces. Ney was expected to hit the Prussian army on its right flank and rear.

The booming of artillery in Quatre Bras could be heard in Brussels. It seized many with panic. Old Blücher heard it at Bussy, but he had his own battle to contend with. Returning from his conference with Blücher, Wellington pressed on for the crossroads. Had any of the British come up yet? On the maze of roads north of Quatre Bras the main elements of the Duke's army were moving up as quickly as they could. But the first divisions were still many minutes from the field. At Quatre Bras the French were boring in so rapidly that it looked like the whole area would fall any minute. The Prince of Orange withdrew his main forces farther into the woods. A foot battery, commanded by Captain Stievenaar, took up a position for flanking fire. French gunners found the range quickly. There was a blinding flash. The captain was mortally wounded, and one of his guns took a direct hit. There was another burst. An artillery carriage and another gun were gone, and men with them. The 17th Dutch light infantry melted before a cavalry charge of Lieutenant General Baron Piré's 2nd division. Wounded Dutch soldiers threw down their arms and begged to be saved. Others ran to the rear. Still others fought to the last, bayonet against sabre and charging horses. Fortified farms, part of the allied strongholds around Quatre Bras, were now falling to the French. The action was fifty minutes old.

Eight miles southeast, Napoleon was ready to attack Blücher. His orders were signaled to a battery of the Imperial Guard. The cannoneers moved with precision and got off three rounds in sequence, so equally spaced that it seemed they were working to a metronome's beat. The gunners watched for the effect of their artillery. Although the firing was only meant to announce the attack, an Old Guardsman preferred to waste nothing.

Napoleon was confident. He, too, did not know Blücher's strength, but he had 68,000 men and 260 guns before Ligny. Grouchy could hold the right flank, pin down the Prussian left, while he kept smashing at the center. The old man was sure to keep throwing in his reserves until the last of them were ground to pieces. The Prussian would be sure to weaken his right flank to strengthen his center. Pressure would be maintained against this flank also, and then at the proper moment Napoleon would strike with the Imperial Guard in the old man's middle. At the same time Ney would arrive to roll up the Prussian right and rear. Attack, attack, attack! This was Napoleon's formula for victory. It was costly. It required steel-nerved lieutenants to lead the assaults, but he had them, and they could do it for him. The whole campaign could be over in forty-eight hours.

Blücher was confident, too. His whole army was on the field except for Bülow's corps which couldn't come up in time. But he had over 85,000 men and 225 guns. He liked his position. There were strings of villages, châteaux and farm houses he could use for fortifications.

The smoke of the Imperial Guard battery which signaled the attack rose slowly in the still air. Before it had disappeared, Lieutenant General Count Vandamme launched an assault on St. Amand, a hamlet only a musket shot from the village of Ligny. This was the first thrust to the center.

It was Lt. Gen. Baron Lefol's division of Vandamme's corps which had the honor of striking first for the Emperor. The men cheered. A band, its instruments reflecting the sun, seemed to sparkle optimism. Then from the Prussian lines came a heavy barrage. The French were coming through the fields slowly. Angry bursts ripped their battalions. As they came closer a curtain of musket fire descended over them. They came on. They began to run faster and faster toward the enemy who fired and fired from cottage windows, stone walls and hedges. And now came another charge from the French lines. It, too, was directed at the Prussian center. Gérard, who had been so late in arriving on the field, threw 10,000 men at Ligny which was a little to the northeast of St. Amand. French artillery began firing all along the line.

Wellington had arrived at Quatre Bras just seconds after three o'clock. The situation was desperate. He surveyed a field of broken Dutch-Belgian battalions. But somehow the allies were still holding on, although to several British staff officers it looked like the whole force was streaming to the rear.

Wellington was doing what he could to form a more solid defense. The Prince of Orange looked anxiously to the north. When would help come? The whole line was about to disintegrate. The fortified farm of Gemioncourt was still holding, however, and now a Dutch-Belgian cavalry brigade had arrived from Nivelles. But what was a brigade against so many? Perhaps one general charge against the trembling allied line by Reille's corps would have swept the field. But a general advance was not ordered. A cloud of dust could now be seen to the north. It was coming very close. Red coats of British infantry could be clearly seen. Picton's 5th division!—Part of Wellington's reserve which had been in Brussels the night before! Regiments of Scottish Highlanders in the vanguard began quickening their pace as they neared the field. The pipes began to skirl. The French saw them and opened up with their biggest barrage so far. Some of the Scots were caught in fields of rye and wheat. With the crops five and six feet tall, many of them died without getting a glance at the enemy. It was 3:30 P.M.

Somewhere behind the lines rode Lieutenant Jackson, the staff officer who had been so impressed when Picton's division had paraded that morning. When he neared Quatre Bras he saw "... a remarkable group of human beings, clustered upon some sort of wheel carriage, that turned out to be a Dutch 12-pounder gun ..." [3] They clung together—"a dozen or more of wounded men, bloody and dirty, with head or limb bound up, and among them two or three females." [4]

Napoleon and Blücher had been locked in combat for forty-five minutes. There had been numerous charges and counter-charges. The whole line was on fire. Villages were burning. The screams of the wounded could be heard above the roar of cannon and musket. The sun hung naked in the sky.

At 3:15 P.M., Napoleon had dispatched another message to Ney. The marshal was "to maneuver immediately" to hit the Prussian's right and rear. To spur him on Napoleon had instructed his chief of staff to tell Ney that "The fate of France is in your hands." Napoleon's first message, which had been sent at two o'clock, an hour and fifteen minutes before, still had not reached the marshal.[5]

French units were being cut to pieces by the stubborn Prussian resistance. Captain Charles François of the 30th regiment of the line became so angry at his superiors as well as the Prussians that he didn't care whether he lived or died. His regiment had helped storm Ligny. He led his men over felled trees and barricades of farm implements and wagons which had been thrown up by the Prussians. His command had been caught in a hell of artillery and musket fire. But there were still some men left to advance. Finally they reached the village church, but there the advance was halted by a stream. Fire swept them from the front and on the flank. Major Hervieux, regimental commander, and two of his battalion commanders were killed.[6]

There seemed to be nowhere to go except back to the French lines. The retreat went off badly. The wounded were left behind. Captain François and his friend, Captain Christophe, tried to rally what was left of the regiment when they reached their artillery. Their regiment was part of General Rome's first brigade. In minutes the brigade had suffered 726 casualties, most of them killed. No sooner had the two young captains formed what was left of their regiment than they were ordered to charge again. They were again driven out. Finally after four more charges they gained a foothold in the village. Captain François was still alive. Death had struck all around him, but he had not even been wounded. He found that he was bruised on his thighs and right leg.[7]

The French artillery was taking a terrific toll. It played everywhere—along the lines, into Prussian reserves which were massing. It challenged Prussian batteries to individual duels. Captain von Reuter, an artillery commander in support of a Prussian corps situated near St. Amand, watched a French battery drop bursts with amazing accuracy on his gun crews.[8] He directed his guns to silence it. He must stick to his post even though a large number of casualties were piling up. Blücher wouldn't have accepted less. He was everywhere urging his men on. He would have sited every artillery piece if he could have.

It was just minutes after Napoleon sent the 3:15 P.M. order to Ney when the Emperor received a message that his marshal was facing 20,000 of the enemy at Quatre Bras. The word came from Lieutenant General Lobau who commanded the Sixth Corps.[9] "My God!" a French staff officer could have moaned when he learned the news. Such a heavy force in front of Ney was taken in stride. But Lobau! At this very minute he was serenely situated in Charleroi—10,000 French soldiers in his corps nine miles southwest of the Ligny battlefield. And he had no marching orders! At this minute the weight of his corps would have been welcomed by the French on either field, Quatre Bras or Ligny. Lobau's corps was a forgotten army. A courier was now dispatched by Napoleon to Lobau. The general was to bring up his corps at once to Fleurus, which was directly to the rear of the French lines on the Ligny battlefield. But after such a long march, Lobau's forces could be expected to play no part in the action this day. Ney had his hands full, Napoleon surmised, but the action at Quatre Bras was secondary. Ney could certainly hold his own at Quatre Bras with what he had at the front. Napoleon decided that he would detach one of Ney's corps which had not yet been engaged at Quatre Bras. This corps, d'Erlon's, 20,000 strong, could do the job he had expected of Ney.[10] It could crash in on the Prussian right and rear. The Emperor called to one of his aides and directed him to take a penciled note, which he was now scrawling, to d'Erlon. After d'Erlon had been given his orders to swing his columns in the direction of St. Amand instead of Quatre Bras, Napoleon's aide was instructed to gallop on to Ney and tell him what had been done.

At Quatre Bras, fresh allied troops were deployed by Wellington personally. Through a storm of musket fire he directed English and Scottish regiments along the road which runs southeast out of Quatre Bras. The French cannonade seemed to increase with every second. A cannonball very neatly removed the bonnet of a young Highlander who was marching with his 92nd regiment. "Did you see that, sir?"[11] he asked his company commander. The Duke ordered the men as they took their positions to lie down in ditches and behind the road bank. He did the same. Some of the men now had a chance to live. Artillery shot streaked over their heads. They were glad that their commander was fighting as he had always fought, using every available twist and wrinkle in the landscape to save their lives.

Sergeant James Anton of the 42nd Highlanders, 3rd battalion, found himself advancing against the enemy as soon as he hit the field. His men "plowed" through rye up to their heads and then found themselves on an uncultivated patch of land.[12] Pausing for a second, breathing hard, they watched terrified Belgian skirmishers running toward them. Hot on their heels were French infantrymen boring in with bayonets. The Belgians didn't stop, but tore through Scottish ranks to the rear. The French, surprised by the sight of fresh troops, paused and then withdrew. But in a minute Sergeant Anton caught sight of a force of lancers bearing in. The Scots mistook them for Brunswickers pursuing the retreating French who a moment before had been chasing the Belgians.

From somewhere a German orderly raced up on horseback screaming "Franchee, Franchee!" and pointed to the lancers. "Form square! Form square!" was the firm command heard over the whine of bullets and canister. Companies wheeled and formed their masses to take the impact of the charge. The long shafts of the lances darted in from charging horsemen, plunging into arms, shoulders, stomachs. The Scots threw up a withering fire, and finally the charge was broken. Lt. Col. Sir Robert Macara, their commander, had suffered an agonizing death. A lance had been thrust through his chin "with the point screwing upward into the brain." [13]

It was nearing 4:00 P.M. A courier, his horse bathed in sweat and caked in dust, had arrived from the French right wing. Ney was found and the message handed to him. This was Napoleon's 2:00 P.M. order. The feelings of "Old Red Head" as he read the message can be imagined. The orders were clear. He was to sweep the enemy back and then march seven miles to take the Prussians on the flank. And now at this very moment fresh allied troops were pouring into Wellington's lines. And more were on the way. But perhaps it could be done. The marshal ordered an attack all along the line.

The assault was born of desperation. The allied line now was strengthened by solid British regiments and a force of Hanoverians. But the push broke the Brunswick infantry. To save his countrymen the Duke of Brunswick led his black-garbed hussars with the glistening silver skulls on their caps against French cavalry. French infantrymen intervened to raise their muskets and pour volley after volley into the Brunswick hussars. The charge staggered and disintegrated. The French cavalry then charged the Black Hussars who were now fleeing to the rear. Their commander had been mortally wounded. Many of the Hussar officers were dead or dying. The melee which thundered across the field—spirited French cavalrymen slashing right and left against the defeated Black Hussars as they desperately sought safety—almost trapped Wellington. Only Copenhagen's speed saved him from death or capture.

The French cavalry, intoxicated with their success, plunged toward the 92nd Highlanders. The Scots waited until the final moment and shattered the charge with a well-directed volley. The entire front was swept away. The rear retreated. The flanks carried on into the village. One young French officer, Captain Burgoine, reined in his exhausted horse behind a line of British soldiers. He was only trying to escape, but it looked like he was attempting to kill Wellington. There were shouts to stop him. Mounted British officers charged toward him. He fought them off with his sword, and again escaped. Highlanders started firing at him. His horse was killed, and a ball tore through both of Burgoine's feet. He was finally captured and removed to the rear.

Ney saw his general attack fail. The British regiments were taking punishment, but they were holding. Many of the Dutch-Belgian regiments were doing better now. Wellington's reinforcements had given them hope. French casualties were heavy and mounting. The marshal hoped, however, that as soon as d'Erlon's corps arrived he just might be able to comply with the Emperor's orders. And now advance elements of d'Erlon's corps were approaching the field. But Napoleon's aide had contacted officers of the main column some miles from Quatre Bras. The Emperor's penciled message ordering them to the Ligny field had been given to d'Erlon's deputy since d'Erlon had ridden ahead with a reconnaissance troop to Quatre Bras. The marching orders for Quatre Bras were canceled and the troops began their movement to Napoleon's left. D'Erlon was apprised of the situation as soon as he returned from his reconnaisance. He immediately sent his chief of staff to inform Ney of events and continued with his soldiers toward the Ligny battlefield.

The Ligny field had become an inferno. Cries of "no quarter" came from the attacker and the defender. Prussians and Frenchmen tore at one another in burning buildings. Disarmed in the swarming melee, they would fight with their hands, tearing and clawing as charred roofs gave way to trap them in screaming, burning agony. Units were surrounded and cut down to a man. Prisoners were slaughtered. Soldiers ran to the tops of churches, mills and haylofts to escape their pursuers. Then they would pour a deadly fire through trap doors and into the streets of the villages. Torches, incendiaries from the artillery would ignite the buildings and the defenders would be trapped. The wounded were helpless as flames crept toward them. Their screams nearly drove men insane. Villages had been captured and recaptured. Hand-to-hand fighting erupted almost everywhere—in streams, in rye fields, in the streets. Napoleon was keeping up pressure all along the line. On his right Grouchy had bedeviled old Blücher with his cavalry. In the center the pressure of artillery and infantry had been relentless. On his left Napoleon had made good advances which threatened to outflank the Prussians. Blücher, however, was determined to take these positions back, and beyond that he was determined to crumble up the Emperor's left himself.

Both commanders found the western side of the shifting battlefield extremely sensitive. A turned flank here for either one meant that communications were cut off with friendly forces at Quatre Bras.

Blücher gathered up troops for one of the movements against Napoleon's left. He had rallied a number of battalions. Their bayonets bristled. He galloped up to the forward units. The attack must succeed! *"Kinder, haltet Euch brav! lasst die Nation nicht wieder Herr über Euch werden! Vorwärts—vorwärts in Gottes Nahmen!"* * the old man shouted.[14] The troops cheered. *"Vorwärts, vorwärts!"* Napoleon had picked up the massing of Prussian troops on his left in his telescope. He immediately dispatched some reinforcements to that side of the line. Another holocaust at Ligny!

* "Now, lads, behave well! don't suffer the '*grande nation*' again to rule over you! Forward! In God's name—forward!"

It was nearing five o'clock. More and more British troops were approaching Quatre Bras. Among them was Maj. Gen. Sir Colin Halkett's brigade consisting of battalions of the 30th, 69th and 73rd regiments, and the 33rd regiment in strength. Action was close. Lieutenant Pattison's company had stopped to load. Private Gibbons of the 33rd, who had dreaded this moment, saluted his lieutenant and asked to be sent to the rear because of illness.[15] Lieutenant Pattison, about to lead his men into action, was understandably disturbed, but he called up the company surgeon to have a look at Gibbons. The doctor found nothing wrong with him, and Gibbons was forced to go into battle. If his comrades found out what he had done he would be better off dead. The 33rd was on its way into combat and so was Gibbons. As part of Halkett's brigade the 33rd was used by Wellington to shore up a part of the line which was under constant pressure from the troops of Lt. Gen. Jérôme Bonaparte, the Emperor's brother.

Sergeant Morris's company, part of the 73rd British regiment, was ordered to charge the French as soon as it entered the field. On his left, Pvt. Sam Shortly was keeping up with him stride for stride. They ran into heavy fire. Shortly was dead. A bullet had crashed through his temple. "Who is that, Morris?" the sergeant's officer asked.[16] Sergeant Morris called out, "Sam Shortly," and then pointed to his officer's arm.[17] "You are wounded, sir."[18] In the heat of battle, Ens. Thomas Deacon had not noticed his wound. A ball had passed through his arm. "God bless me! So I am," he said, as he fell out and hurried to the rear to get the wound dressed.[19] If the young ensign seemed pleased because he was wounded, it was because he was worried about his pregnant wife. Their child was due. Mrs. Deacon accompanied the troops, and was at this moment somewhere behind the lines. As soon as the ensign's arm was bandaged he started looking for her.

The 33rd British regiment had not been in line long when it started to die under the pounding of artillery. The position became untenable, but before re-deploying, Lieutenant Pattison's friend, Lieutenant Boyce, was killed. Just minutes before, Lieutenant Boyce had said, "Pat, I feel certain I shall be killed."[20] He was dead now, but Pattison remembered rebuking him "for indulging such a feeling," and had said that he should drive such thoughts from his mind.[21] Pattison also remembered saying, "No doubt some of us will be killed, but you have the same chance as others." [22] The shelling was intense. Lieutenant Pattison saw another friend go down. Lt. James Furlong staggered and leaned on his sword for support. A noncommissioned officer carried the wounded man to the rear.

Ney was informed that heavy British reinforcements had just arrived. He still did not know how many men Wellington had, but now for the first time during the long day Ney was outnumbered. He had thrown attack after attack against the British. These assaults had accomplished nothing. Now there were more British. The pressure began to mount. Where was d'Erlon? It was while the British units poured into the line that General Delcambre, d'Erlon's chief of staff, arrived to break the news. He had been delayed in the traffic of ambulances and walking wounded that choked the roads to the rear.

The report that his First Corps had been taken from him struck Ney like a thunderclap. The smoke of battle drifted slowly from the field. The constant clamor of battle continued unrelentingly. The dying groaned. Ney, his uniform stained with perspiration, began to seethe. His anger was a fuse that began to burn. In another moment it exploded away all reason. The final pressure had been thrust upon him. For at this moment Napoleon's message of 3:15 P.M. arrived.[23] These words stood out like braille—even to a man blinded by anger: "The fate of France is in your hands."

Ney became a wild man. He shouted to Delcambre that he was to find d'Erlon's corps at once and bring it to Quatre Bras. Never mind Napoleon's order! By now, however, the troops were well on their way to the Ligny battlefield. As Ney spotted more allied soldiers coming into the line he shouted for Lieutenant General Kellermann. Kellermann, a skillful cavalry commander, had four brigades, but three of them had not been brought up. They had been stationed in the rear as a reserve on orders by Ney. The cavalry commander had less than a thousand men on immediate call. The marshal had thrown everything within sight into the struggle with the exception of Kellermann's command, and Cavalry of the Guard which was now at Frasnes, two miles behind the lines. Napoleon had cautioned Ney to use the Cavalry of the Guard sparingly, but now the marshal completely forgot about it.

Kellermann was told that he must break the British with what he had. The officer considered the order insane, and as tactfully as he could pointed out the overwhelming odds against him. Ney raved that it must be done, and that Kellermann would get as much support as possible. "The fate of France is in your hands!" "The fate of France is in your hands!" These words of Napoleon's and Ney's bombastic orders to Kellermann left both men with nothing but raging emotions. Kellermann sprang on his charger and galloped to his cuirassiers. They had not been touched by battle. Their silver breastplates glistened. Their long swords were unstained. Moving swiftly, before his heavy cavalrymen could reflect on the dangers ahead, Kellermann ordered his men into line. He dashed several yards in front of them to take up a leading position. There was a second's pause, and then the command to charge. Swords were unsheathed, and Kellermann's 1,000 thundered forward. Their charge was aimed a little southeast of the Quatre Bras crossroads, about the center of the British line. The brigade, made up mostly of crack professionals, rode at terrific speed.

Major General Sir Dennis Pack's brigade had been under heavy strain for two hours, and ammunition was running low. With the arrival of fresh troops the second battalion of the 69th Welsh regiment was turned over to his command. The 69th had not been on the field long before Kellermann charged. The troops were now in line, ready to receive infantry. "Cavalry! cavalry! form square!" was heard when the cuirassiers were seen. The 69th began to form square. The Prince of Orange, not seeing the cavalry, countermanded the order, and cursing soldiers obeyed. Now they were in line again when the cuirassiers appeared only a few yards away.

"Form square, form square!" was again heard. The cavalry was close and coming at full speed. But the regiment might make it. Companies wheeled. But two of them were ordered to swing around and fire. The square had not been made. An accurate volley dropped some horses and cuirassiers. But now the soldiers were naked against cavalry. The impact of the storming cuirassiers overwhelmed the 69th. Two full companies were destroyed. The rest were broken. Ensign Duncan Keith, carrying the King's color, was ridden down by cuirassier Lami who rode back to display the flag before thousands of cheering French infantrymen. Volunteer Christopher Clarke, carrying the regimental flag, killed three cuirassiers in its defense. His body was a mass of wounds when he finally found cover. He still was grasping the colors of the 69th. The regiment had been ground into squads of men who took refuge under the bayonets of the Highlanders.

The third battalion of 42nd Highlanders watched the massacre. They got in shots when they could at the cuirassiers. The battalion had been hit badly by artillery and cavalry. Since Macara's cruel death, Sergeant Anton had seen two of the succeeding commanders wounded, one mortally. Brevet Major John Campbell was now leading the Scots who had bayoneted scores of "the old grey-headed devils!" [24] The cursing French horsemen often preferred death to surrender, fighting with pistol and sword when they were dismounted. Wounded and dying Frenchmen littered the inside of the 42nd's squares. A British officer seeing the French charge said they advanced "like motes in the sun." [25]

Kellermann's onslaught roared on. The cuirassiers tried to break a square of British infantry, the 30th, glanced to its flank, and overran an artillery battery. Dazed cannoneers tried to fight back with ramming rods and short swords, but were mercilessly cut down. Soldiers who had not found the shelter of a square were impaled by the cuirassiers' long swords. Onward they rode. A square of Brunswickers was broken. The French artillery roared, making massive gaps in the British regiments which had formed squares to repel the cuirassiers. Ney threw in what support he could. Pressure was mounted against the British right. A French infantry charge hit the extreme left of the line and for a minute threatened to turn it. The cuirassiers were now on the road leading to the village. They flashed past the 92nd Highlanders, taking a cruel blow from carefully aimed muskets. Now they were at the crossroads. They had penetrated to the very heart of Wellington's defenses. But now fire from everywhere poured into them. The support Ney had tried to give them was not enough. It was running down like a weakly-wound clock. The efforts on both flanks were being defeated. The cuirassiers were left to get back to their lines the best way they could. For a moment, there had been a ray of hope for Ney, but now there was only darkness. It was darker for the cuirassiers. Artillery was turned on them. Kellermann's horse was killed. He stood in a hurricane of fire, trying to reorganize his command.

He could do nothing. It was every man for himself. The way back was worse. Every regiment was now alerted to bring down the cavalrymen. The remaining cuirassiers spurred their horses and rode through a withering fire for the French lines. Some French infantry units, seeing the desperate retreat of their cavalry, fell back also. For Ney it was no longer a question of taking Quatre Bras, it was a question of holding Wellington at bay. More allied units were pouring into the British lines. Ney watched his retreating infantrymen. Enraged, he ran after them, and with sword in hand, rallied them and led one more attack.

On the Ligny field the attack that Blücher personally led swept back the French. But another Prussian attack in conjunction with it failed. And then the French counterattacked against the troops Blücher had so dashingly led. The action on the western side of the field became a nightmare of indecision for both sides. No real triumph had been gained by either army on the whole trembling battlefield, which "... resembled for a time some violent convulsion of nature, rather than a human conflict—as if the valley had been rent asunder, and Ligny had become the focus of a burning crater." [26]

"The combat was supported on both sides with equal valour: it is impossible to give an idea of the fury which animated the soldiers..., the one against the other; it seemed as if each of them had a personal injury to revenge, and had found, in his adversary, his most implacable enemy. The French would give no quarter, as they said the Prussians had vowed to put to death every Frenchman who fell into their hands; ... they had addressed this menace particularly to the Guard, against whom they seemed greatly exasperated. In short, on both sides, the carnage was prodigious." [27]

It was after five o'clock. Napoleon's calculations were proving correct. The old man had thrown in most of his reserves while Napoleon had hoarded his Imperial Guard. From his reserves only a division of the Young Guard had been sent into action. The Emperor had given up on Ney, but d'Erlon's corps striking the Prussian right and rear when the Imperial Guard plunged through

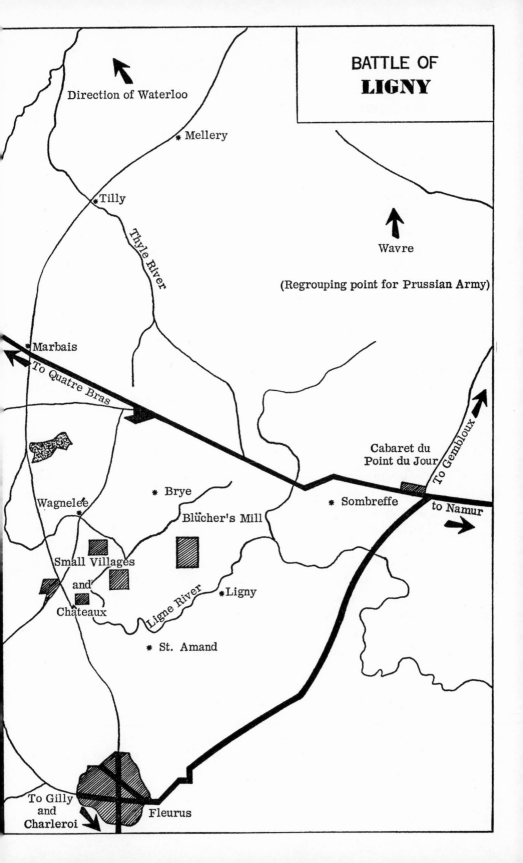

BATTLE OF
LIGNY

Direction of Waterloo

* Mellery

* Tilly

Thyle River

Wavre

(Regrouping point for Prussian Army)

* Marbais

To Quatre Bras

Cabaret du
Point du Jour

To Gembloux

* Brye

Wagnelee

Blücher's Mill

* Sombreffe

to Namur

Small Villages

and

Chateaux

Ligne River

* Ligny

* St. Amand

To Gilly
and
Charleroi

Fleurus

the center should carry the day. It would be enough to destroy the old man's army.

Napoleon's reserves had been carefully sheltered behind the lines all day near the mill at Fleurus. Occasionally Prussian artillery had overfired and reached their position, but there had hardly been a casualty. The Guardsmen had played one of their favorite games, a lottery in which men bought chances on the exact time *le petit corporal* would require their services. They had been alerted earlier in the afternoon, and for some time now had been maneuvered close to their line of departure for the final assault. Napoleon had carefully screened their advance—to hide his intentions from the old man, and to shelter them from the Prussian batteries. But now the Emperor was confronted with a crisis. A messenger arrived from the left flank with word that an enemy column was approaching from the west to the French rear. Had Ney been defeated? Was it a column from Wellington's army? These questions must have entered Napoleon's mind for a moment. But he couldn't believe it. The column must be d'Erlon's, but then again, there must be proof. In any event he must act quickly. The morale of his whole left flank was collapsing. General Lefol was forced to turn his own artillery on his hysterical men who were deserting the line.

There were proposals from Napoleon's officers for abandoning some of the vital posts for which his army had fought tenaciously all day long. Napoleon acted swiftly. He dispatched a troop to make a reconnaissance of the mysterious column. He delayed his attack against the center and reinforced the left with some of the Imperial Guard. In the meantime Blücher had seen the disturbance on the French left. He had also caught sight of some of the Imperial Guard moving behind the lines. From Blücher's position it looked like a retreat. It looked like the French had had enough. He would mount another heavy attack on Napoleon's left wing. He threw in every available battalion of Colonel Langen's 8th brigade. They collided with the Guard which had arrived just in time and were violently repulsed.

Ney had had two horses shot out from under him. No attack had succeeded. He was heavily outnumbered. D'Erlon was miles away. Wellington began taking advantage of French weakness, but Ney was everywhere urging his tired troops to hold on. Every

British gain was hotly disputed. But as the long shadows began to fall the French were being pushed back all along the line.

A wounded soldier baking under the burning sun of Ligny probably was the first one to notice the light northwest breeze. It brought with it thunderclouds, and for the first time during the day there was a shield against the sun which had burned with the intensity of the two battles beneath it. At six o'clock, the battle for Ligny raged without any respite. At seven, the fury was still unabated. Napoleon had learned that the mysterious column was French, but when it seemed on the verge of joining his line it had disappeared. In any event the threat to his left was over. Blücher had been fought to a standstill. He was without reserves. It was now the time to strike. The death thrust of the Imperial Guard! At 7:30 P.M., a concentrated bombardment of over 200 guns opened up on the Prussian center. Fifteen minutes later the Guard, 6,000 strong, struck as it had always struck, with disciplined fury. Lightning flashed in the skies as the storm broke. Thousands of cavalry, cuirassiers, lancers and hussars accompanied "the old bear skins" on their flanks and in the rear.

A barrage of shouts of *"Vive l'Empereur!"* mixed with thunder, artillery fire and the roar of musketry as the Guard moved faster and faster through the downpour. Swirling in the flood of sound were military bands and shrill trumpets. Battered battalions from all three of Blücher's army corps stood in the way. They fought desperately. The 21st Prussian regiment charged against the advancing Guard. But the cuirassiers darted in to smash the Guard's assailants. Two squadrons of the 1st Westphalian Landwehr Cavalry charged the Guard. Musket fire from twenty yards scattered them. The Prussians were forced out of Ligny. On every side they were threatened by the advancing French. The tide had turned. Hardly had the retreat begun when the rain stopped and the clouds receded to reveal a brilliant sunset. A good omen to the Guard. Blücher had heard of the advance while he was organizing one more attack against the French left. He flew to the breach. Scraping together every man he could, he was determined to plug up the opening. He picked up three understrength regiments of cavalry, including the 6th Uhlans. Lieutenant Colonel Lützow must have had desperate thoughts similar to Kellermann's as he led his 400 against the heavy battalions of the Guard.

The Guard, with professional skill, maneuvered into squares and met the charge with a precise volley. Lützow fell wounded. Around him 13 officers and 70 men were smashed to the ground. The remainder were forced to retreat. Another Prussian attack was ordered—this time with two regiments of Prussian cavalry. For a moment it seemed that even the squares of the Old Guard were wavering, but on the flank came the cuirassiers. The impact was tremendous as the heavy French cavalry struck. The Prussians reeled and were broken. From somewhere Blücher appeared with twenty-one squadrons of Landwehr cavalry. They, too, charged, but they could not penetrate the firm squares of the Guard. And the cuirassiers were everywhere, thrusting and slashing. The sun was sinking. The French must be stopped before nightfall. Again the old man scraped together a force for one last effort. He rallied the broken, bleeding regiments and squadrons that had gone up against the Guard. He found a handful of stragglers. He placed himself at the head of them and led the charge himself. It was as before. The Guard was not to be broken. The same heavy curtain of musketry. The same thrust of the bayonets. Not a square had been dented. Blücher withdrew with his force. They would rally and charge again. But now as they galloped away to re-form, the cuirassiers swarmed after them. A shot rang out and Blücher's grey charger broke stride and fell. The old man stuck in the saddle and his dying horse rolled on top of him. The Prussian commander was unconscious.

Blücher's aide-de-camp, Lieutenant Colonel Nostiz, who had been at the marshal's side all day, dismounted and with sword in hand prepared to defend his commander as best he could. There were bodies and fallen horses all over the slopes behind Ligny. Nostiz remained motionless behind his horse as the cuirassiers flashed past. The disorder on the field, the speed of the charge and the twilight had saved Blücher, at least for the moment. Again there was the thunder of charging cavalry. The Prussians had rallied and had turned on their tormentors, the cuirassiers. The cuirassiers swept past in retreat. As soon as they had gone, Nostiz managed to flag down Sergeant Schneider of the 6th Uhlans. A squad of Prussian cavalrymen lifted the heavy charger and freed their commander. Another French attack was at hand. Nostiz and the cavalrymen placed the old man, who was now coming around, on Schneider's horse, and they all made off for the shelter of the nearest Prussian infantry, with the cuirassiers not far behind.

En route to Quatre Bras in the dusk came British horse artillery and British cavalry. Wellington's army had been so widely dispersed that although he outnumbered Ney on the field in mid-afternoon, he had had to depend throughout the day on non-British artillery and cavalry.

More than 40,000 of his troops were quartered over twenty-five miles from Quatre Bras. They could not reach the field in time to be of any use.[28]

Captain Mercer, the artillery officer who had found it so difficult to get out of bed at Strytem that morning, was now nearing Quatre Bras with "G" troop. The noise of battle sounded like "a distant water-mill" to him.[29] He was in the backwash of the battlefield. He saw wounded Dutch-Belgians staggering with blood streaming from them. He watched priests administering the last sacrament to the dying. The captain became disgusted with the Dutch-Belgians. He remembered that some wounded had "ten or even more attendants." [30] Again and again he heard that Wellington had been beaten. *Monsieur, tout est perdu!* [31] He wouldn't believe it. Besides, he hadn't seen a Britisher yet. Then he spotted one, a wounded Scot who was all alone. Mercer asked him about conditions up front. Was it true that Wellington had been beaten? "Na, na, Sir, it's aw a damned lee ... " [32] But the Scot did concede that "it's a bludy business..." [33] He reported: "Ooor ragiment was nigh clean swapt off, and oor Colonel kilt jist as I cam awa." [34] The wounded soldier was referring to Lt. Col. John Cameron. He had suffered a painful wound in the groin and had lost control of his horse. The animal had returned to the colonel's groom and the officer fell from the saddle unconscious. He was taken to Waterloo, where he died. His regiment, the 92nd Highlanders, had been charging two columns of French infantry. Maj. James Mitchell succeeded Cameron, was wounded, and Maj. Donald MacDonald took command. The French retreated to a heavily fortified house. The Scots came on, with the pipes screaming the "Camerons' Gathering." The men, furious over the loss of their colonel, took to the bayonet. As they advanced, the officer carrying the regimental colors was killed, the flag staff shattered. Musketry was intense from the house, but the Scots made it and a fierce hand-to-hand struggle ensued. The French were driven out. But the Scots had no sooner taken the place when they were besieged by the French. Attack after attack was launched against them, but they held. As one of the Highlanders said of the French, ". . . they were driven oot, an' keepit oot." [35] The losses were severe. About half of the 92nd's six hundred were killed or wounded.

Just moments before Cameron fell, he had congratulated a major of the 42nd because he had fought so bravely. One of a troop of cuirassiers killing wounded Scots came upon the major who had been badly hurt. Just before the death blow which was intended for him, the major grappled with the cuirassier, pulling him from his horse to the ground. A French lancer came to the cuirassier's aid and thrust with his lance. The major wrestled the Frenchman in front of the thrust and it was the cavalryman who was killed. Highlanders rushed to the major's aid, dispatching the lancer. When they reached the major they found that he had been wounded sixteen times. [36]

The fighting was now subsiding. Mercer's tired horses stumbled over corpses as his guns and wagons entered the field. A few final French shells lumbered overhead to explode behind them. But for all practical purposes the battle was over. Mercer had arrived too late to fire a single round.

Wellington had pushed hard against the French during the final hours of the battle, but without his regular cavalry and artillery and because of the lateness of the day he had not launched any crushing assaults. He did, however, have nearly 40,000 men on call by nightfall. [37] The allies had lost 4,800 killed and wounded. [38] Ney's losses were about 800 less. [39] As darkness came at 9:00 P.M., the firing ended, with Ney's troops about where they had been when the first French attacks were launched. To the rear of the lines he took a light meal with Jérôme Bonaparte and staff officers, and went to bed in a cottage which had been set aside for him. Three miles away, at Genappe, Wellington dined on cold meat and had his usual wine, one glass of port.

The Prussians had been beaten, but it was not until the center had been pierced that the retreat began, with Prussian rearguards fighting back to help stem the tide. The night made operations impractical.

Captain von Reuter, who had kept his artillery in action throughout the day, had moved to take a new position when his guns were about to be overrun and then finally had joined the retreat.[40] All around him streamed the infantry. The heat of the day and the exertion of battle had produced oceans of perspiration. Smoke and dust had clung to every face, and a brownish mud coated the skin. Every uniform was split and torn. Blood was soaking through old bandages. Many of the soldiers had discarded everything: knapsacks, shakos, pouches, belts and coats. Most, however, still clung to their muskets.

Blücher had been carried to a cottage several miles behind the lines. He was undressed, given an alcohol rub and put to bed. Before going to sleep, however, he managed to down a good amount of Dutch gin which an officer had found for him. He was badly shaken, still dazed, and was unable to retain command. Some miles away at Brye, a little over a mile northwest of Ligny, his chief of staff, Gneisenau, who had no idea what had happened to him, felt that perhaps he was dead or had been captured, and took over the responsibility of conducting the retreat. A defeated army can get out of hand quickly. Already over eight thousand young soldiers had found they had had enough of war and had made up their minds to return to Prussia. They were fleeing eastward, moving in the general direction of Namur, more than thirteen miles from the Ligny battlefield. Other troops still under control of their officers, but without firm orders because of the disorder on the field, also fell back to the east. Some rearguards were ordered to hold out until morning. The bulk of the army, however, retreated to Sombreffe, nearly two miles northeast of Ligny. Firm orders for rallying the army and then conducting it to a good defensive position were needed at once. Although only the center had been broken, the whole army could quickly dissolve in the confusion.

The dark night, the poor maps, the spectre of defeat all abetted the turmoil. Gneisenau studied a map under a flickering oil lamp. Should he fall back on his supply lines to the east? Should he move north? He had no idea what Wellington planned. In fact, he couldn't care less about the English. He distrusted them, and he wasn't convinced of their fighting qualities. His eyes fell on Wavre, a village fourteen miles due north of Ligny. The roads were good. The village was situated on a stream, which could be a defensive factor. It was a little stream, only six to twelve feet wide and about five feet deep, but it would be an ocean to soldiers who had to cross it under fire. The orders went out. Wavre!

The last of d'Erlon's corps had been bivouacked for some time now behind Ney's lines. The general had received the orders from Ney to return to Quatre Bras when he was within sight of the Ligny battlefield. He had complied at once, wheeling his troops around to traverse the ground he had just covered. His 20,000 troops had spent a good part of the afternoon, evening and night marching between the two battlefields. His column was the mysterious force that had frightened the left wing of the French army before Ligny. His corps had approached the field from the wrong direction because Napoleon's message had been misread. He did not know it, but his troops as they neared Ligny field also had shaken Blücher. The Prussian had seen them and thought the worst, "French reinforcements," but d'Erlon's compliance with Ney's orders had taken the corps back to Quatre Bras.

It was nearing 10:00 P.M. when Napoleon left the battlefield to return to Fleurus for the night. He was very tired and was not feeling well. Aside from routine orders which he issued, he did nothing to follow up his thrust through the Prussian center, although his officers specifically asked him if he had orders for the pursuit of the enemy. He would issue orders in the morning, he said. The night was dangerous for maneuvering. Besides, hadn't the old man been beaten?

At Ligny the Prussian army had suffered over 16,000 casualties; the French about 12,000.*

* These include dead, wounded and prisoners. Many prisoners were killed. There are no completely accurate totals of the losses.

Chapter Eleven

To Mont St. Jean!

A BATTLEFIELD at night is strange, weird, unreal. There is often the feeling that men who lie so still are only sleeping, that they have not been killed, but have only slumped to the ground because of exhaustion. A flickering campfire offers strange presentments. A man seen for a fleeting moment passing by on a personal or military duty takes on the appearance of a friend killed in action. There is a feeling, a cheerful feeling, that the friend lives after all, and that the news of his death or the sight of him falling isn't true. There is a strange urge to cry out his name. There is the urge to help the wounded and the dying, but finally there is relief that the seemingly ceaseless cries in the night are ending. The dying have died, the wounded have been carried to the rear. Or often they have not, and their cries are just as violent as ever, but the living do not hear them as well as before. There are such necessities as eating and drinking and sleeping, and these things must be done if the army is to fight again.

Private Davis was dead. His friends had seen him die. His body lay on the field somewhere—just where no one could say because there had been so much movement that afternoon. But someone by this time had probably emptied his knapsack. That was the usual thing to do. They had found the whole ham his mother had sent him. He had not taken any of it. He had been proud of it, and talked about it. He had carried it as a kind of talisman.

Ensign Kennedy had died. Men wanted to forget the fighting, just for a while, but they talked about him now. They were sure that few people would believe them back home. He was, they said, the youngest officer on the field, only fifteen. Carrying a flag in advance of the third battalion of the Royal Scots, which was attached to the 28th British regiment, he was wounded in the arm. He continued to advance along with his comrades through a galling fire. He was hit again. This time he had suffered a fatal wound. A sergeant seeing him stagger attempted to take the color staff. The young ensign, however, refused to release it. A hail of shot hit around them. The young man was dying, but his fingers could not be pried away from his flag. The sergeant then picked up the officer, placed him on his shoulder, and continued the advance. Moments later the firing subsided around them, although it continued with intensity against other parts of the advancing battalion. It was as though the sergeant and his young officer, who still clung to his flag, were encased in invisible armor. The French officer in command of the defending battalion had seen their acts of heroism. Through his chivalrous intercession his men had stopped firing at the sergeant and the young officer who was now dead.

Lieutenant Pattison was just one of hundreds of young officers going over casualty lists. Private Gibbons, who had tried so desperately to get permission to go to the rear just before the 33rd regiment had gone into action, was dead. Had he died bravely after all? No one seemed to know. Walking through the area where the 69th had been slaughtered by the cuirassiers were Lieutenant Hay and the 12th Dragoons' commanding officer, Lieutenant Colonel Ponsonby. The colonel was interested in seeing if the cuirassiers' breast plates were bullet proof. Lieutenant Hay stood where the desperate action had raged. He was "speechless with wonder." [1] The colonel's voice stunned him. He had called Hay to show him a breastplate he had removed from a French corpse. It had been shot through three times. Hay, his thoughts now back with the colonel's, spotted several other bullet-riddled breast plates still clinging to the dead French which he showed to his commanding officer. Some distance away, the 92nd had done all it could for its wounded and was now cooking supper. The Highlanders had found that the breast plates made good stew kettles, although if one was not careful he could lose some of the gravy through a bullet hole. A British officer stumbling on their camp in the darkness came away a little pale. The idea appalled him. The word spread to various English regiments. "Ghastly barbarians, that's whot they ere," was a sentence that was often repeated that night, but few said it in the presence of the fierce Highlanders. The Belgians were much more shaken than the English. Somehow some of them got the idea that the Scots were cannibals.

The soldiers tried to get as comfortable as possible. It would be a short night. Captain Mercer and his troop bedded down in a wheat field. The company doctor turned up with a meat pie which was divided among the officers. Later, someone produced cigars. It wasn't too bad. But Genappe, three miles north of the lines, was the best place to be. Wellington had set up his headquarters there. Lieutenant Jackson was taken in by a shoemaker and his wife. Furthermore, they saw to it that he was properly fed, boiling a chicken and frying an omelette. But the lieutenant knew that as comfortable as he was it would be difficult to sleep. There was "... the incessant clatter of hoofs, joggling of steel scabbards, and rattle of artillery ..." as the rest of Wellington's army moved up.[2] Private John Marshall of the British 10th Hussars had ridden about fifty miles that day. His cavalry unit was among the first to reach Quatre Bras. Exhausted as he was, he would be awake for guard duty most of the night. It would have been of small consolation to know that his unit had arrived early enough not to disturb Lieutenant Jackson.

Colonel de Lancey had been with Wellington most of the day. The night had given comfort to some men, but not to him. He was now writing numerous orders which the Duke had given him before retiring. His thoughts must have turned to his courageous wife who had been so helpful the night before. "Fat" Hill had amazed his friends. He and his huge horse had been in the Duke's company all day long, often where the fighting was the hottest. There had been casualties everywhere around them, but the captain and his huge horse, such excellent targets, had not been scratched. Ensign Macready had caught up with his regiment just fifteen minutes after it marched on the battlefield. Looking desperately for his unit, he had taken his company through and around the formations of irate British officers without too much regard for the heavy enemy fire which splashed dirt over his whole company. He arrived while his regiment, the 30th, was under attack, and immediately went into action. A high point of his day had been the laughing and joking in the square after the regiment had beaten off the enemy. It was so loud, even over the roar of the battle, that it brought down the fury of a British general who questioned if the unit had any officers present.

It was cold. The men huddled in their cloaks. Some slept. Some had horrible nightmares, living the whole day through again. Some could only think of water, scrambling everywhere in search of it. Some thought of the wounded, crammed into every nearby church and cottage. With nothing but alcohol to relieve them, they were suffering the tortures of the damned. Somewhere a piper was playing for the dead. Now the sound was mournful. A few hours before it had been so fierce.

A night breeze, varying from the north to northwest, carried the sound to French outposts at Quatre Bras. There was even less cheer in their camp this night. Before trying to get some sleep many soldiers had had to scour the neighborhood for food. Although a *marmite* glowed here and there, many had been discarded along the route of march with knapsacks, canteens and soup stock. But here and there soldiers brought in supplies: turnips, green beans and pears. Lieutenant Colonel Lehmanowsky had no time to search for food. He made a meal of ration bread. He had been at Ney's elbow as a staff officer most of the day. He could not forget the agony in his commander's face when the attacks, one after another, failed. Small groups of men huddled together to whisper that some of the generals had betrayed Napoleon. That was why the army had failed, they said. The news of Lieutenant General de Bourmont's treachery had reached Ney's divisions and now the extent of the damage was being exaggerated a thousand times. Others insisted the desertion of the general and his staff from the 14th division was an isolated case, but this failed to quiet the camp gossips. Behind the French lines, at Ligny, the atmosphere was a little different. Blücher had been beaten. Besides, the food was in better supply. It always was in the wing that marched with Napoleon and the Imperial Guard. Camp fires dotted the whole area—thousands of *marmites* simmering stews and soups. Soldiers were cheered as they emerged from the shadows carrying armfuls of vegetables which they dropped into the steaming kettles. Private Gaertner remembered that he had not eaten since dawn. He was ravenous. Perhaps he thought of his mother after he had dipped a cup into the *marmite* for his share of soup and had taken it somewhere to relax. What was the name of the saint she kept praying to for his safety? Oh yes, St. Anthony. So many were dead. Imperial Guardsman Ribault had seen his comrades fall on both sides of him. Somehow, though, he had come through untouched. The cavalry attacks never seemed to stop. But soon, perhaps, the whole thing would be finished. Sergeant de Mauduit was still alive.[3] So was the bruised Captain François, but it seemed that all his friends were dead—Hervieux, Richard, Lafolie, a litany of names.[4]

The Prussians had retreated, but under heavy rear guards they prepared to camp around Sombreffe until morning. The retreat to Wavre was to be continued at dawn. Captain von Reuter must have counted his losses over and over again—cannoneers, horses and one of his guns. He may or may not have appreciated it, but his artillery battery had had the distinction of engaging every arm at close quarters—artillery, infantry and cavalry.[5]

How was it possible for Pvt. Franz Lieber to stop thinking of the first man he had killed? He had been in Ligny and had stepped around the corner of a house. There in front of him, not fifteen paces away, stood a French grenadier with rifle aimed directly at him. Franz pulled up his musket to fire. The Frenchman fired. Franz felt the grenadier's shot graze his hair. He fired back, seeing the effect of his shot. It had exploded in his opponent's face. His foe was dying.[6] Probably Sergeant Schneider was the proudest man in the Prussian army. He would always have a story for anyone who would care to listen. If it had not been for him and his horse perhaps the marshal would be dead. Perhaps the fate of the whole war hung on the rescue of Old Blücher. Gneisenau had found his commanding officer at Mellery, six miles behind the Ligny battlefield. He was resting quite comfortably. The chief of staff spent most of the night readying the army for the march to Wavre, conferring with his generals and receiving massive casualty reports. In an anteroom outside Blücher's quarters lay Lieutenant Colonel Hardinge on a straw bed. The British liaison officer's amputated arm was in the room with him.

As long as the schnapps held out there was a celebration every time a missing soldier found his regiment. The army had been beaten, but its morale was still good.

In the late evening, Brussels still hadn't heard how the battles had gone. Firing from both fields had been heard in the city, and of course there had been some apprehension but there had been no panic. Panic was now about to storm the city, sweep through its streets and paralyze its citizens and tourists. It came with the soldiers who had cracked under the storming of the French at Quatre Bras. They swarmed down the main road which leads through Genappe, La Belle Alliance, Mont St. Jean and Waterloo to Brussels. Broken regiments of Dutch-Belgian cavalry clattered through the center of the city at 12:30 A.M. They created a gigantic traffic jam, mingling with supply wagons and troops marching through the city on the way to the front. The night before had been bedlam, but at least the city was filled with a powerful army. Now defeated cavalrymen, dirty, disheveled, some hemorrhaging from serious wounds, were back, beaten and shouting that the British had been broken and that Napoleon was on his way to the city. Windows and doors flew open. The word that the allies had been crushed reached every home. It was bedlam again, but this time with despair. Crowds gathered in the streets. British gentlemen, their ladies and women, porters, maids, merchants were racing everywhere. Some ran to pack to flee the city at once. Others started hiding their jewelry and whatever they considered precious enough to keep from the eyes of the French.

On their way to add to the turmoil were mobs of shaken Dutch-Belgian infantry coming down the roads into Brussels. Moving along with them were carts filled with dead and wounded. The exodus from the battlefield was impeding the progress of Wellington's cavalry and artillery which had been so badly missed during the action. Everywhere dispirited soldiers shouted that it was no use to continue on to Quatre Bras since Wellington's men were marching to their death. There were cries of "Save yourself, save yourself!" Somewhere in the turmoil was Ensign Deacon, the wounded British officer whose wife was about to have her child. Somehow he had missed her behind the lines.

This night through Flanders there seemed to be movement on every road. The fields and meadows and forests were alive with terrified peasants and deserters. Soldiers on reconnaissance could never know until it was too late whether shadowy figures darting over roads, dashing into forests, were peasants or the enemy. Reconnoitering to the east of Ligny was Lieutenant General Count Pajol, Grouchy's First Corps cavalry commander. Pajol had been ordered by Grouchy to find out Blücher's main line of retreat. It was after one o'clock, and Pajol, with his strong force of cavalry, could see a trail of Prussian dead and wounded leading to Namur.

In Waterloo, a way-stop from the field of Quatre Bras to the security of Brussels, the inns remained open. Pierre Bodenghien was afraid to close the bar while hundreds of soldiers were still demanding service. He figured they might tear down his inn, *La Joye*, or burn it. Catherine Bodenghien's inn, the biggest one in Waterloo, was doing a huge business. Catherine's late husband, Antoine, was Pierre's brother. Too bad Antoine wasn't alive to see it. Maybe the soldiers couldn't fight well, but they certainly could drink. The hours passed for many weary Dutch-Belgian soldiers over glasses of Louvain's white beer and brandy.

The movement of cavalry and artillery into the line continued. At Genappe, Wellington was sleeping well, but he had given orders that he should be ready to move out by three in the morning. It would be necessary for him to get to Quatre Bras early. The last word he had had from Ligny was that Blücher was still holding out, although he was sorely pressed. If Blücher had been defeated, then the British army would be in jeopardy. Napoleon would be free to move like lightning along the road that runs northwestward to Quatre Bras and hit the allies on the flank. The situation was rather sticky, that is, if Old Blücher had been defeated.

The idea that the big guns explode the clouds and make it rain probably got its start after some forgotten battle centuries before. It had not rained yet, but the heavens were in ferment, with huge black clouds traveling across the sky and hiding the stars. It was almost 3:00 A.M. An aide approached Wellington to wake him.

Another long day was about to begin—a quick breakfast and the three-mile ride to Quatre Bras was the start of it for Wellington. By 3:30 A.M., he and his staff, many of them still not quite awake, had crossed the river Dyle which flows serenely south of the little village. At 3:46 A.M., the rim of the rising sun could be seen. Night was fleeing and it would not be long before the sights of the Quatre Bras and Ligny battlefields would sicken whole battalions.

In Brussels, some of the dying Belgian soldiers were making one final effort to get home. Some of them could do no more than crawl over the last cobblestones to their doorsteps. An anguished wife or parent would embrace them just before they died. Some of the terror-stricken tourists and townspeople were already trying to reach Antwerp, forty miles closer to the coast than Brussels. Many of the British, however, couldn't believe Wellington's army had been destroyed, and had refused to budge until they received official word. It was 4:00 A.M. when Miss Waldie decided to get up. With all the noise, it was impossible to sleep anyway. The city had become a madhouse. The streets were filled with hysterical men and women. The traffic jam had become worse. Carts, coaches, wagons and limbers were stuck in a Babel of bellowing Bruxellois, tourists and soldiers who could make no headway in any direction.

It all seemed very clear to General Pajol. The Prussian army must be falling back on its supply line. It was moving to the east directly away from Wellington's forces. He and his cavalrymen had caught up with a great mob of Prussian soldiers, all streaming toward Namur. Furthermore, the soldiers he saw were in panic. They were traveling as fast as they could. They were abandoning their wounded. The general sent a dispatch to Napoleon in Fleurus, stating that he had caught up with the Prussians and that they were retreating in panic to the east. He dated the message 4:00 A.M., June 17.

All was quiet at Napoleon's headquarters. The Emperor was asleep. He was not feeling well, and yesterday's action had worn him out. He needed this rest, and everybody had done what he could to assure him some peace, even to moving some of the wounded out of earshot. But at Quatre Bras, action had flared up when nervous pickets started firing across the lines. The firing woke up sleeping soldiers from both sides. Officers aroused their commanders, and quick surveys were made by both British and French to see if the firing signaled an attack. But the firing died down quickly. Now there were only a couple of orange flashes along the line, now one, now nothing. Some soldiers decided that since it was past four, they might as well get on with the business of making breakfast. For many, rations issued in the early morning hours of the 16th were still holding out. The march had been so rapid that British soldiers hadn't been able to eat up all of their biscuits and salt beef. By 5:00 A.M., Wellington had arrived at Quatre Bras. His arrival was signaled rapidly up and down the line. A troop of generals assembled to give him their reports. Had there been any word from Blücher? This was what he wanted to know at once. There had been nothing. Some miles away a Prussian officer lay dead. In his sabretache was a dispatch from the Prussians, explaining the defeat at Ligny. Another Prussian officer was at this minute riding through the darkness with another message. He did not know the fate of his brother officer, but he was conscious of the gauntlet of French cavalry and pickets who had killed him.

Wellington ordered a cavalry reconnaissance of the Ligny field. He told Maj. Gen. Sir Hussey Vivian, a brigade commander, to send a strong patrol down the Namur road to find out what had happened to Blücher. The force had to be strong enough to fight its way back, and it had to return with specific details on the Prussian success or failure. In either case it must bring back Blücher's plans. Vivian sent a troop of one of his regiments, the 10th Hussars, under the command of Capt. John Grey. Lieutenant Colonel Alexander Gordon, a Wellington aide, was instructed to accompany the command.

In Mellery, Blücher, his body stinging with pain, began stirring. He was going to get out of bed. Besides that, he was going to mount the best horse he could find and lead the retreat. And beyond that he had some other ideas, too. He was going to meet Napoleon again and crush him once and for all. The order of the day which he insisted had to be read to all of his battalions was: "I shall immediately lead you against the enemy;—we shall beat him, because it is our duty to do so." There must have been a barrage of protests from his staff when the old man insisted on leading his army, but he was up, and in a few minutes was cheer-fully greeting Lieutenant Colonel Hardinge, the British liaison officer. He called the one-armed Hardinge *Lieber Freund* and em-braced him.[7] The old man smelled "most strongly of gin and of rhubarb." [8] *"Ich stinke etwas,"* the old man said as he grinned, noting that he had had to take a little medicine because of the events of yesterday.[9]

Then he said that he would be very happy if he and Welling-ton could grapple with their "old enemy" and defeat him.[10] Hardinge also learned that the sick Blücher was adamant about remaining in touch with Wellington instead of falling back on the Prussian supply lines.

The sun was now warming the soldiers. The clouds had disap-peared, at least for a while, and it looked like a fine day. Soldiers watched in amazement as their marshal rode along with them, making jokes and bantering with them. The retreat to Wavre was moving with precision.

At Quatre Bras, British soldiers argued about what Wellington would do. With most of the artillery and cavalry up, an attack seemed assured. There were all the sounds of an army in the field meeting a new day—the clatter of cooking utensils, the end-less soldier talk, loud and raucous, only subsiding when a burial party moved past. In a nearby field a shallow grave was being dug. Finally it was finished. "On the ground lay a tall form, en-veloped in a military cloak, around which were standing, bare-headed, three or four officers; two soldiers were leaning on their spades..." [11] "... Ralph Gore stood motionless as a statue, with eyes fixed on the cloaked mass at his feet; young Haigh, a boy of eighteen, was crying like a child; even the hardy soldiers seemed powerfully affected." [12] The burial service was read. When it was finished the men looked at Haigh. He stooped down and "with-drew from the corpse a portion of its covering..." [13] They gazed into "the remarkably handsome features of Arthur Gore." They were all from the 33rd.

At 6:00 A.M., Napoleon was up. At breakfast, Pajol's message of 4:00 A.M. was delivered to him. He read the report carefully. It had worked. The Prussian army was falling back on its supply lines. Every minute was taking Blücher farther away from Wel-lington. Certainly the Prussian's army wouldn't be able to fight today. By tomorrow, if the retreat continued, it would be so far away from Wellington that it would not matter. By that time the French would have Wellington in a vise, and could crush him at their leisure. It was too bad that Ney could not have joined him yesterday. There would be no Prussian army left. Nevertheless Blücher was broken, Wellington held at bay. Now the whole French army could move against the Englishman. Blücher, it appeared, was no longer a threat.

Wellington surveyed the field of Quatre Bras with his telescope. He could not be sure of anything. If Blücher had been beaten, it was quite possible that Napoleon had moved some of his troops to join Ney during the night. Even now there might be French troops pouring down the Namur road to engage his flank. The news from Captain Grey's troop was needed desperately. As he waited, Wellington made a number of moves to strengthen his line with the artillery and cavalry which had come up during the night.

Miss Waldie continued to watch the drama of panic-stricken Brussels from her hotel window. From the courtyard came a stream of cursing in French, English and Flemish as servants turned on their masters, coachmen upped their prices, and furious women assailed their husbands and lovers for bringing them to Brussels in the first place. Some British gentlemen boxed unruly servants with their walking sticks when the "blighters" refused to move mounds of luggage until they received double wages. Some stubborn coachmen couldn't be hired at any price. Gentlemen exchanged blows among themselves when they couldn't settle on who had hired a coach first. Purchasers of fashionable Brussels coaches couldn't find horses for them.* Piled with luggage and sagging under the weight of ladies, children, nannies and maids, they were as transportable as houses. Through the streets to plunge into the traffic jams came more disorganized Belgian cavalry. And now livestock began to plow through the crowds. Keepers of the army's beef supply, which traveled on the hoof, had lost control of the animals. The British commissary had hopefully believed that the cattle could be brought up behind the army. They could then be slaughtered and the troops could have fresh meat. The idea had worked well in Spain, but it wasn't working here.

* Brussels was a center for fine coaches.

Meanwhile Miss Waldie noticed her room maid. "The poor *fille-de-chambre*, nearly frightened out of her wits, was standing wringing her hands, unable to articulate anything but '*Les François! les François!*'—while the *cuisinière* exclaimed with more dignity, '*Nous sommes tous perdus!*' " * [14] It was now approaching 7:00 A.M.

The cavalry patrol sent out by Wellington to reconnoiter the Ligny area was hurrying to Quatre Bras. It had made contact with both French and Prussians, and had evidence that Blücher was falling back on Wavre. Furthermore the evidence seemed clear that Napoleon had done nothing as yet to follow up his victory and was not hastening to engage Wellington.

As Wellington studied the French lines he became aware of a great stillness. It was the kind of stillness that often precedes a major retreat. Wellington felt that the most logical assumption was that Ney was planning to pull out. Of course it all depended on what had happened at Ligny. But the French marshal had been driven back yesterday. He had suffered heavy losses. The allied army was getting stronger all the time, and Ney must know it. A half hour before, Ney had ordered one of his generals, Flahaut, to ride to Napoleon's headquarters. The general was instructed to report on the action at Quatre Bras, secure a detailed report of the action at Ligny and bring back what orders he could. Meanwhile, Ney decided to wait for fresh dispatches from Napoleon, or the return of his general. The situation had changed from yesterday morning. The British were before him in strength. He could get nowhere against them yesterday as their army built up. Now they were even stronger.

At 7:30 A.M., the British cavalry patrol had returned to Quatre Bras. Although it bore bad news, the defeat of Blücher, Wellington was pleased to have some firm word on events so he could make his plans. With the Prussians retreating, his army was in peril. It would be suicidal to hold the hard-won field of Quatre Bras. Ney could push from the front. Napoleon could engulf him on the flank and even in the rear. The orders would be hard to give to his men who had fought so well yesterday, but if he were to save his army and eventually cooperate with Blücher again he must withdraw. London wouldn't like it. The newspapers

* "We are all lost."

would say he had been beaten. Nevertheless, it had to be done. But there was a little time, or so it seemed since there was no evidence that Napoleon had yet started to bear down on the British. There would be enough time for those who had not had breakfast to do so. Arms could be cleaned, the rest of the wounded cared for, and most of the burying completed. Wellington decided that withdrawal should begin at 10:00 A.M. New orders were to be rushed to units which had not yet reached Quatre Bras. The army would concentrate on the heights a little south of Waterloo.

Napoleon had taken his time at breakfast. He went over dispatches and reports from Paris, and conferred with Flahaut, who had made a swift ride to Fleurus. After considering Ney's requests for details on Ligny and for fresh orders, the Emperor conferred with Soult who wrote a long message to Ney. At Napoleon's order, Ney was given a short lecture. Soult wrote: "His Majesty was grieved to learn that you did not succeed yesterday; the divisions acted in isolation and you therefore sustained losses. If the corps of Counts Reille and d'Erlon had been together, not a soldier of the English corps that came to attack you would have escaped; if Count d'Erlon had executed the movement on St. Amand ordered by the Emperor, the Prussian army would have been totally destroyed and we should perhaps have taken 30,000 prisoners." It was pointed out that the Prussians had been routed in the direction of Namur and were under pursuit by Pajol.

Next, it was explained that the Emperor's position allowed him to attack the British on the flank if Wellington dared to act against the French position at Quatre Bras. Ney was told to carry out his orders of yesterday. This included taking Quatre Bras and moving beyond it. It suggested that if Ney got in trouble all he had to do was send a message and Napoleon would move with his whole force down the Quatre Bras road to his rescue and Wellington's destruction. Finally, Ney was specifically ordered to attack any rearguard before him.

Blücher and his troops were well on the way to Wavre. His optimism refreshed the whole army. They were not really beaten, they said. They would assemble and fight Napoleon again. Pajol was still following broken battalions eastward, feeling that he was in the wake of a completely routed Prussian army. It was now approaching 8:30 A.M. Many of the Emperor's soldiers at Ligny had been up since dawn. As exhausted as they had been the night before, they had not been able to sleep in the early morning hours. They were accustomed to long marches. But the orders had not come. Napoleon knew best, of course, but it would have seemed better if orders had been given to chase the Prussians or move against the English. Besides, the smell of death was everywhere. Small knots of soldiers gathered to discuss the situation. Perhaps the Prussians had been so badly beaten that there was no need to pursue them. Perhaps they were all headed back to their homeland. But some of the Old Guardsmen remembered Napoleon at Moscow. Time seemed to stand still for him then. Guardsman Bidault recalled that the city had been set on fire, and that the flames were threatening what military stores the French had, and finally were creeping toward Napoleon's headquarters. Yet no orders came. For agonizingly long minutes it had seemed that the Emperor would never again give an order. He seemed to be in a trance. His Imperial Guard stood with him, and finally, when it seemed that they would all die in the flames, Napoleon became the man they had all known. He snapped out of his trance, issued a flood of orders and began the movement out of Moscow. It would be so again, the old soldiers reasoned. Napoleon was about ready to leave his headquarters at Fleurus. As yet, he had no general orders for his forces at Ligny, but he had just ordered a reconnaissance of Wellington's defenses by his own cavalry, and he had ordered an infantry division to assist Pajol. But his officers, like the men who stood around some of the smoldering campfires which hours ago had heated their breakfasts, wondered about the delay of moving the vast French force that had beaten Blücher. But there he was now! One of the Emperor's coaches had drawn up in front of headquarters. Shortly before 9:00 A.M., Napoleon emerged to spring into the coach and set out for the Ligny battlefield to visit his troops. Later, he changed to a horse and everywhere he rode his men cheered him —so resoundingly that even some of the retreating Prussians could hear it miles away.

A little after 9:00 A.M., Ney received his orders from Napoleon. The sermon from Soult did not go over well with him. The burning anger of yesterday was still smoldering. It may have seemed obvious to Napoleon that the orders clearly called for an attack on Wellington that morning. But if they were clear to Ney, then he decided to ignore them either because of his anger or because of the situation in front of him. He studied the British lines. There was no evidence of attack or withdrawal. The French were heavily outnumbered. Ney decided to do nothing.

The news spread swiftly among the British at Quatre Bras that the Prussians had been defeated. Until now it looked like a major victory might be scored against Ney. Until now there had been some elation despite the bloodstained cottage walls, the littered battlefield and the sight of wounded toppling off their horses as they tried to ride to the rear. Word of the Prussian defeat left officers and men guessing what Wellington would do. But a little later there were rumors that he would withdraw, and then the rumors were confirmed. Lieutenant General Picton, the division commander who had arrived in the heat of battle yesterday to throw back the French, was angered by the order. His division had lost heavily. To withdraw would mean another huge battle in the next day or so. The French would have time to maneuver, time to patch up their wounded battalions. Wellington had given Picton his orders in a face-to-face meeting, and Picton made his feelings clear to his commander. "Very well, sir," he had finally said, but the short sentence had been dipped in acid and ice. In fact, no one knew it, Wellington did not know it, but his division commander had been badly wounded. A ball had crushed three ribs during yesterday's battle, and Picton had retired a short distance behind his troops. He found a sheltered area where he could be alone. There he treated his own wound as best he could. He returned to the line and told no one.

When Wellington arrived at Quatre Bras, the 92nd had kindled a fire for him in front of a little hut made from tree boughs. The hut was now his headquarters, and after receiving the news of the defeat he had remained inside, conferring with his officers, issuing orders and studying maps of the area. Finally he came out, and for what seemed like a very long time walked alone back and forth in front of the hut. Staff officers gathered in small groups and were careful not to interrupt him except when important dispatches were received. He carried a small switch and as he walked he frequently chewed on the end of it, seemingly unconscious of what he was doing. Later he stretched out on the ground to nap. A parcel of newspapers had arrived from London, and he took one of them and spread it over his face. Later he was up to mount his horse and ride along the lines surveying the French positions. It was still very quiet. An aide reported that a Prussian officer had ridden into the lines with a report on Blücher's retreat. Wellington immediately conferred with him. He detailed his plans and asked the officer to inform Blücher that he would fight Napoleon at Mont St. Jean, but that he must be supported by at least a corps of the Prussian army. If he could not be assured of this support then he would have no alternative but to give up Brussels and retreat, he said. It was nearing 10:00 A.M. The withdrawal to the ridge south of Waterloo was about to begin.

There had been a chill in the air that morning, but now it was warming up. There was no wind. As he looked toward the French lines about 10:00 A.M. Lieutenant Pattison noticed "two very remarkable little clouds, rising from the horizon ... in the rear of the French army." [15] He remembered a Biblical reference to a cloud which "was no larger than a man's hand." [16] He noticed that the clouds were getting larger. But at this moment few of Wellington's soldiers had time to study the clouds. The retreat began promptly at 10:00 A.M. Cavalry had moved in slowly to build a screen around the retreating infantry.

As some units headed for the Brussels road they passed wounded cuirassiers. Although some of them could barely move, they struggled to be heard. Some cursed the British. Others, with unshakable faith that they would be revenged, shouted, "The Emperor is coming, you will see him soon!"

Napoleon seemed convinced that the Prussians were no longer an immediate threat. He took his time inspecting his troops, complimenting various line officers, visiting the wounded. He even saw that some of the battered Prussian prisoners were given brandy. Followed by a train of staff officers and commanders, including Marshal Grouchy, who desperately awaited their orders, he taxed their impatience time and time again. Walking from one regiment to the next, with every stop seeming endless, he came to Col. Fantin des Odoards, commander of the 22nd line regiment. Napoleon stopped again, his hands behind his back. A hint of a smile crossed his face. "I know you. You used to be in my Guard, didn't you?" [17] Des Odoards, who had saluted briskly with his sword, replied that he had, and that he owed every promotion to his Emperor. Napoleon asked about the regiment's strength and learned that 220 men had been lost yesterday. He noted that he had watched the regiment in action and was very pleased with the men and its commanders. He wanted to know what was being done with the hundreds of muskets which had been left on the field by the retreating Prussians. He learned that they were being destroyed, and then stated that this was "wrong" since he had given orders that they should be collected and sent to France. Des Odoards replied that he had not received such orders.[18]

Turning to staff officers, Napoleon said, "Do you hear that? An order of this importance not yet known. Have this set right as soon as possible. Good-bye, colonel. I am pleased with you and your regiment." [19] Soldiers and muskets, it seemed, were increasing in value. Finally, as predicted, orders came like a deluge. It was nearing 11:00 A.M. A strong force, including the Imperial Guard, was to march at once on the road to Quatre Bras. It could halt within striking distance of the crossroads village, at Marbais, just three and a half miles away. Napoleon would follow with thousands. Wellington was to be trapped if possible. If not, he would be pursued until he had to fight. Grouchy was given a separate command, thirty-three thousand men, and ordered to follow the Prussians. Blücher had been badly beaten, the Emperor figured. It seemed impossible that he would be ready to fight soon but when he was, Grouchy should be able to prevent him from cooperating with Wellington. Grouchy was to locate the Prussian army and keep track of it. Judging from Pajol's reports it was fleeing eastward. Yet other dispatches were reporting that strong elements were also in the north. The final orders for Grouchy called for him to march to Gembloux. Six miles northeast of Ligny, the village would be a reconnoitering point for the north as well as the east. Gembloux is ten miles east of Quatre Bras.

Wellington's retreat was going well. It had been underway now for an hour, and nothing had been done to interfere with it. Ney had had Napoleon's orders since 9:00 A.M., but seemed stricken with the same disease which earlier had paralyzed Napoleon. The whole French force before Quatre Bras wallowed in lethargy. Old Blücher led his men on to Wavre. Tired soldiers who fell from exhaustion were driven on by their officers, or so humiliated by jeering comrades that they struggled to their feet. In Brussels there was a temporary respite from panic. Many wounded British officers had now reached the city. Surrounded by inquiring tourists and townspeople, they said that Wellington had won yesterday's battle. Official messages arriving from the field stated that there was no disaster, that the British army was still holding out. City officials began to plan for the wounded. Calls would have to go out to the people for clothing, beds, bandages. Hospitals would have to be set up in private homes. It was noon. Through Brussels came a reassuring sound—Irish troops tramping along to drums as they headed for the front. It was the first battalion of Royal Inniskilling Fusiliers, part of Maj. Gen. Sir John Lambert's 10th British Infantry Brigade. With them marched the 4th and the 40th regiments.

The men looked formidable and morale shot up in Brussels. As the Inniskillings marched along they considered the unpredictable fortunes of war. Some months before they had been fighting Americans along the Canadian border. Later, they had shipped to Louisiana but had arrived after peace between Britain and the United States had been declared, and weren't even allowed to come ashore. Then it was a stormy crossing to Bermuda and England, and just a few days later Belgium. From Ostend they had moved to Ghent to guard King Louis, who on the morning of June 15, when the Inniskillings were ordered into action, had had his usual mutton-chop breakfast. Some of the soldiers, although they were as good at fighting as they looked, experienced occasional attacks of nausea. Most of them traced their illnesses to long periods of sea sickness, but a few may have felt that the sight of all those mutton-chops had had something to do with it. Private Haughton was one of the drummers. He was only a boy, and just weeks before had been a civilian. This time he would have some deeds of his own to talk about, and would not have to depend on his uncle, a sergeant in the 27th regiment, for war stories. The Inniskillings had been about to sail from England to Belgium when young Haughton managed to stow away. During the voyage he was discovered, and it looked like his dream had ended, but a drummer became ill and young Haughton was permitted to take his place. He was now proudly wearing the Castle insignia of the Inniskillings.[20]

Napoleon dictated a note for Ney, informing him that troops were on the way to join him, and again ordered the marshal to attack. The Emperor then climbed into a coach and hurried toward Quatre Bras. The whole French army, with the exception of Grouchy's force, was concentrating against Wellington. Time seemed so precious now. Scarcely anything moved fast enough for the Emperor—coaches, cavalry, marching men. It seemed that the day was disappearing much too swiftly, it would soon be 1:00 P.M. A sky boiling with massive black clouds exaggerated the lateness of the hour. Lieutenant Pattison had left Quatre Bras with his company, but when he looked back he saw that a huge cloud floated over Ney's lines. Blücher's columns could see lightning in the direction of Brussels. A severe storm broke there at one o'clock. First there was heavy thunder and lightning, and then rain in torrents. Miss Waldie watched it. It looked to her "... exactly as if pitchers of water were pouring down." [21]

The storm was moving southward from Brussels at about eighteen miles an hour. It could reach Quatre Bras a little after two if the winds held. Captain Mercer, whose battery was part of the rearguard, wondered about the inactivity in the French lines. Here it was after 1:00 P.M. and nothing could be seen but smoke from their campfires. The French were preparing to eat. Napoleon arrived in Marbais, two miles closer to Quatre Bras. He paused for a quick lunch, and picked up the force he had sent there earlier, which included the Imperial Guard. It seemed that the little village trembled with the cheering. Napoleon was his old self again, the soldiers said, as they watched him rush on to Quatre Bras.

Mercer continued to watch the French lines. As he stood next to his guns, he was joined by Lord Uxbridge, the cavalry commander, and an aide-de-camp. They all seated themselves on the ground to study the enemy's positions, with Uxbridge sweeping the lines with his spyglass. A little later a staff officer galloped up to say that a heavy force of cavalry was advancing from the east. They all looked in that direction, and a moment later, Uxbridge was on his feet gleefully exclaiming, "By the Lord, they are Prussians!" [22] The general leaped on his horse and "dashed off like a whirlwind to meet them." [23] His aide swept after him.

Lieutenant Hay, whose squadron of British hussars was part of the rearguard screen, saw the cavalry movement. First there were clouds of dust, and then cuirassiers, lancers and brass-helmeted dragoons. They were French, unmistakably French. They were advance elements of Napoleon's cavalry riding frim Ligny. The lieutenant noted a "dead silence" as his troopers "anxiously" watched the enemy.[24] ". . . Even the horses were more still than usual, no champing of bits, no clattering of swords." [25]

Lord Uxbridge and his aides rode on toward the cavalry. And then someone recognized the horsemen as French. An abrupt halt, a wheeling around. The rearguard would have a major job if Wellington's retreating infantry were to remain unscratched. It was just before 2:00 P.M. when Napoleon jumped from his coach a mile from Quatre Bras to mount his horse, Désirée. Along the way he had listened for Ney's guns, but he had not heard them. Ney, however, was moving his troops. Captain Mercer had watched Uxbridge gallop away, ". . . wondering how the Prussians came there." [26] He then turned his eyes toward the French lines and saw ". . . their whole army descending . . . in three or four dark masses . . ." [27] The Emperor was a whirlwind now. He sent forces to establish contact with Ney. With elements of Lieutenant General Milhaud's Fourth Corps cavalry, he dashed on to Quatre Bras. Troops swept behind him and on the flanks. It was a little after 2:00 P.M. when he met d'Erlon who had marched back and forth across Flanders the previous day. "France has been ruined," Napoleon shouted to d'Erlon in disgust. The Emperor had hoped to trap Wellington's whole army, and here there was nothing but a rearguard. But he would try to bring the Englishman to bay. He still had time, he thought. Ordering d'Erlon to charge and pursue, Napoleon rode ahead to organize other units. Sharp skirmishing was erupting along the line. The sky was getting even darker.

Minutes before, at Gembloux, ten miles east of Quatre Bras, Grouchy had written a dispatch for Napoleon. The marshal wasn't sure where the masses of the Prussian army were concentrating, but he had learned from his scouts that at least one column was marching toward Wavre. He looked at his map, and it was clear that if the Prussian army or parts of it were concentrating there, Blücher would be in a position to cooperate with Wellington if the British commander fell back toward Brussels. He included this danger signal in his message: "Perhaps it may be inferred that one portion is going to join Wellington..." He then stated that if he found that "the masses of the Prussian army" were moving to Wavre, he would follow "... to separate them from Wellington."

Mercer, seeing that he was about to be overwhelmed, had limbered up and galloped his artillery to a new position. But now he encountered a storming cavalry officer, Maj. Gen. Sir John Vandeleur, who commanded the 11th, 12th and 16th Light Dragoons. He flayed Mercer with: "What are you doing here, sir? You encumber my front, and we shall not be able to charge. Take your guns away, sir; instantly, I say—take them away!" [28] Mercer attempted to explain his situation, but it was useless and he was preparing to move when Lord Uxbridge rode up. "Captain Mercer, are you loaded?" "Yes, my lord." "Then give them a round as they rise the hill, and retire as quickly as possible." [29] Uxbridge then gave some orders to Vandeleur, and artilleryman Mercer could congratulate himself that he had bested three regiments of cavalry, even though they were British.

Napoleon, riding his small, wiry horse, darted to cavalry commands and artillery batteries, issuing orders, and then began to gallop toward the British rearguard. Mercer, waiting for the order to fire, saw him. He saw "... a single horseman, immediately followed by several others..." mount the plateau where he and Uxbridge had studied the French lines.[30] Napoleon and his aides "pulled up" for an instant to survey the British cavalry and Mercer's battery, and seconds later squadrons of French cavalry came up rapidly.[31] "Fire—fire!" Uxbridge commanded.[32] Mercer's guns thundered, and it seemed that they "burst the clouds." [33] For immediately after there was a crash of thunder, blinding lightning and a torrential downpour. It seemed that no one could remember such a heavy rain. Even British veterans who had campaigned in India and had seen the monsoon seasons come and go could not recall such a cloudburst. Wellington had taken lunch in Genappe, three miles north of Quatre Bras along the line of retreat. As he watched the downpour he was thankful he had retreated when he did. It would still be a struggle to get all the troops into position by nightfall, but Napoleon would find it difficult to maneuver if the rain continued. If the British had stayed a little longer, the whole army could have been trapped in the mud.

Mercer could not study the effect of his bursts. He had to limber up and get out or the French would be on him. They came through the storm at a furious clip. The guns were now ready to roll, and off they went with Uxbridge urging Mercer on. The French cavalrymen were gaining with every step.

It seemed they were about to be taken when the French cavalry pulled up; they had all seen patrols of British hussars. But the whole area, it seemed, would soon be enveloped by the French. Uxbridge saw a narrow garden lane and cried, ". . . follow me . . ." [34] Mercer did, but grew increasingly apprehensive because there was barely room for the gun carriages. They were moving as fast as they could when to their front, at the end of the lane, appeared a body of French cavalry. Mercer thought he heard Uxbridge say, "By God! we are all prisoners," and then saw him spur his horse over a garden bank.[35] The little unit was left to get out of the scrape as best it could, Mercer thought. He immediately ordered the guns unlimbered so they could execute the difficult job of reversing their direction in the narrow lane. Guns were pushed as far to the side as they would go, the horses slipped past, and then the guns wheeled around to be hooked up again. As the complex procedure progressed, Mercer occasionally glanced toward the French at the end of the lane. For some reason they did nothing and Mercer charged it up to the "blunder and confusion" of the day.[36] Finally out of their perilous position, Mercer ran into Uxbridge who was organizing a rescue party of British hussars.

The whole area around Quatre Bras became a mélange of cavalry duels, of flying horse artillery limbering and unlimbering, of pursuing French infantry slithering through the mud. Napoleon, bitterly stung by the fact that Wellington had slipped away, conferred with Ney, but was too busy organizing the pursuit to really reprimand him.[37] Napoleon saw no reason why Ney had not captured Quatre Bras. Ney felt it was suicide to have moved ear-

lier than he had. But the whole French army with the exception
of Grouchy's forces was moving against the British rearguard as
rapidly as it could through the downpour. The meaning of time
seemed to dissolve in the storm. The French would gain contact
with British cavalry. A British commander would see the French
gaining and would counter-attack with more horsemen. Batteries
from both sides would pause to fire and then relimber, the British
to retreat, the French to pursue. The fighting surged up and
around the road to Genappe, the little village where Wellington
had lunched. Napoleon was everywhere urging his men on. He
galloped up to place a battery of flying horse artillery, he organized a cavalry attack and then another, and another. The
French were moving quickly even in the rain, but the fields became soaked, the ground would absorb no more water, and the
churned earth became gumbo and clung to every artillery wheel
and horse and man. Only the good roads, the roads paved with
small square stones fitted so precisely that the surface was smooth,
would support the masses of troops.

The road to Genappe was such a road, and there was no choice
but to keep most of the men on it as the pursuit continued. The
French advance guard would surge forward to engage the enemy
hussars. The fight would spread to the sides of the road, and struggling cavalrymen from both sides would flounder in the gumbo,
with horses sometimes sinking to their girths. Into Genappe rode
Lieutenant O'Grady of the 7th Hussars. Perhaps he had a second
to think of the leisurely dinner he had had in Brussels the night
of the Duchess of Richmond's ball. But perhaps he didn't. Major
General William Dörnberg, in command of rearguard skirmishers, was speaking to him. O'Grady was ordered to take his troop
along the road and delay the advancing French until units of the
rearguard cavalry were safely on their way to the other side of
the village. Dörnberg grasped his hand just before O'Grady left to
rally his troop and take charge of a detachment of skirmishers.
The lieutenant didn't know it, but Dörnberg never expected to
see him alive. Dörnberg galloped away with retreating cavalry
and O'Grady with his men behind him hurled down the road
toward the advancing French. His boldness saved him. The French
stopped and wheeled around, probably convinced they were faced

with a whole squadron. O'Grady followed for a short distance and stopped. He decided to play a game. He would rush them one minute and retreat the next. While executing this action, O'Grady kept a sharp lookout on the units he was ordered to protect. When the last of them was safe, he ordered his men to walk their horses to the rear. But occasionally the lieutenant would halt and have his men turn around to pause before the enemy. This series of maneuvers continued until O'Grady felt they could safely make a run for it, and they raced through Genappe to join their regiment.[38]

The rain still poured down. Napoleon would not stop. North of Genappe, Uxbridge decided that a stand would have to be made. It was clear that the enemy was coming entirely too close to some of Wellington's retreating infantry. There is a ridge north of Genappe, and here Uxbridge assembled his heavy cavalry. Elements of light cavalry, including the 7th Hussars, were also in the rear of Genappe. Squadrons of French horsemen poured into the other side of the village, followed by flying horse artillery and infantry columns.

The British waited. In a few minutes there was a furious clatter as a small group of French cavalrymen came charging out of the village. They plunged headlong into a leading squadron of the 7th Hussars commanded by Maj. Edward Hodge. They were quickly captured. It was found that these horsemen had been drinking heavily. The British cavalry lines were dressed, and in minutes the leading French squadrons appeared with troops of lancers in the vanguard. Seeing the British, they stopped. With no order to halt, the long columns behind them continued to press forward until in a few minutes the narrow road through Genappe was choked with soldiers. The lancers could not retreat because of the traffic jam behind them. To their flanks were houses. Uxbridge seized what he thought was an opportunity and ordered the 7th Hussars to charge. Major Hodge led his squadron in first. This was the moment hundreds of young men had been waiting for. Each officer and trooper would show the rest of the British cavalry what the 7th could do. The 7th swept forward. The charge seemed magnificent. But the French stood with cool determination under the reassuring commands of a gallant officer.

Lances were lowered, and the French cavalry became "a complete *chevaux de frise.*" [39] Riding fleet light chargers, the British hussars could not muster the impact that was needed to overwhelm the French lancers. Scores of young Englishmen riding in the forefront were impaled, and their screams could be heard above the tumult of clashing swords, cursing soldiers and crazed horses. Other hussars bore in, chopping, thrusting with their swords. Major Hodge died. So did the French commander. A French artillery battery came to the aid of the French from outside the village. It dealt with support elements of the 7th, chewing great gaps in the orderly ranks of men and horses. The lancers drove back the hussars. The hussars rallied, and the action surged back and forth until it was clear to Uxbridge that heavier cavalry was needed. The 7th was ordered to withdraw. The French, elated with their victory, galloped after them and charged past the last houses of the village to advance up a slight rise. Before them were light cavalry, the 23rd Light Dragoons. Uxbridge, however, had ordered units of the Life Guards to repulse the lancers. The 23rd opened its rank for them as they thundered down the hill. The impact was shattering. ". . . although the French met the attack with firmness, they were utterly unable to hold their ground a single moment, were overthrown with great slaughter, and literally ridden down in such a manner that the road was instantaneously covered with men and horses, scattered in all directions." [40]

The huge traffic jam of the French columns in Genappe was cause for alarm. A heavy bombardment would have been disastrous, and French commanders took steps to correct the situation. French cavalry became more cautious after the lancers had been overwhelmed. The pursuit continued, but not at such a furious clip. Rockets were fired when British artillery ammunition ran low, but the rockets, although appearing very formidable, seldom hit a target and had little effect in stemming French pressure, although there were one or two lucky hits. After clearing Genappe, French cavalry attempted to strike the flanks of the retiring British columns, but with British regiments, including the Royals, Greys and Inniskillings, constantly maneuvering against them, they had no success.

For four hours Napoleon had pressed the British with all his energy. It was now after 6:00 P.M., and despite all his efforts the day was dying with Wellington slipping away. Blücher had arrived at Wavre some hours before. The long ride exhausted him, and after giving some final orders to his lieutenants and staff officers he had gone to bed. He could do no more this day. It seemed that no one could.

Chapter Twelve

The Eleventh Hour

THE château had been built many years before. In addition to the well constructed brick dwelling, there were several other buildings in the compound: a farmer's house, a gardener's cottage, a barn, storehouses, cattle pens, a dovecot, and a charming little chapel with a well proportioned miniature tower. Framed within a rectangle of stout brick walls were the buildings, a garden, a courtyard and carriage parks. A road lined by tall elms ran northwest some yards to a highway which connected Mont St. Jean with Nivelles. The place was called Hougoumont and it was situated about 500 yards south of the area where Wellington had decided to form his lines. No military commander could ride past it without seeing its value as an outpost. Wellington decided that it should be manned since it would be a formidable obstacle in front of the attacking French. Again he studied the buildings, the land, the trees. He knew of the reputation of French artillery. He would cheat it of every man he could.

Some days before, there had been a *petite événement* * at Hougoumont. One of the château's cats had delivered a litter. There is no question that she had scores of hiding places in the maze of buildings. But some animal instinct told her that Hougoumont was no place for her family, even in the secure nooks she had always known. Perhaps it was during a short lull in the storm, around 6:30 P.M., when she began her evacuation. Nevertheless,

* Small incident.

175

there was a retreat. She made a half dozen round trips to save her kittens, carrying them northwest to the highway, crossing it, and moving west several yards and then north to a rye field.

Most of Wellington's troops, completely soaked, had maneuvered into defensive positions. They were strung out on the northern heights at Mont St. Jean above a shallow valley which sloped gently toward the south. Wellington, looking in the direction of the advancing French, assumed that Napoleon would establish his positions on the south side of the little valley, taking advantage of a slight ridge roughly parallel to the British line. Part of the rearguard which had been slushing through the mud, in and out of scores of deadly contests with the French, was now moving into Wellington's line. Captain Mercer, at this point, wasn't sure how far he had retreated. It had been close to ten miles, and he found that his battery had spread havoc among retreating Brunswick soldiers, part of Wellington's command. Thinking Mercer's battery was French, they tossed their "... arms and knapsacks in all directions..." with "a general race" ensuing when he caught up with them outside of La Belle Alliance, which is a little less than two miles from Mont St. Jean.[1] Although he didn't realize it, he was now within a stone's throw of the whole British army. He found a gravel pit which had shed some of the rain and unlimbered. Glancing across the valley, he could see British cavalry units moving steadily toward him in retreat. The French were at their heels.

Mercer opened fire at the biggest mass of French he could find, at a range across the shallow valley of about 1,200 yards. Prepared to move out instantly since the last of the British cavalry was the only thing that remained between his battery and death or capture, he heard a heavy cannonade commence from behind a ridge which was directly to the rear of his guns. The firing "rolled along the rising ground" and the truth "flashed" through Mercer's mind.[2] He had rejoined his army. The captain found it "impossible to describe the pleasing sense of security" he felt "at now having the support of something more staunch than cavalry."[3]

Napoleon had plunged into La Belle Alliance. For the moment he felt that the British were still retreating, but when a division of his cavalry was heavily shelled, it appeared that the British had formed their lines. To make sure, he ordered his artillery to open

The general conception of Wellington is
that he was an old man at the time of
Waterloo. He was a vigorous 46.

The Duke of Wellington.
Courtesy of Victoria and
Albert Museum.

The sweet life in Paris softened the Emperor
through the years. By the time of his first
abdication he lacked the energy of his younger days.

Napoleon (engraver
unknown, after a painting
by Delaroche). Courtesy of
Library of Congress.

Blücher's tenacity paid off at Waterloo. If the Prussian army had been in the hands of a commander with less drive, the results of the battle could have been reversed.

Gebhardt Leberecht Von Blücher, by Furst v. Wahlstatt. Courtesy of Ullstein Bilderdienst.

King Louis XVIII had little faith in the loyalty of the Emperor's former soldiers. As soon as he heard of Napoleon's escape from Elba he knew he would have to leave Paris.

Louis XVIII, by F. H. Drouais. Courtesy of Château de Versailles.

Napoleon constantly reviewed his troops. After his return from Elba to Paris, he began to mold a new army.

La Revue, etching by A. Boulard after painting by F. Hamerg.

A scene Napoleon's soldiers carried to their graves — the Emperor on horseback, leading his battalions into one more battle.

Napoleon at Jena, by Meissonier. Courtesy of Library of Congress.

On Napoleon's battlefields the Imperial
Guard always marched with the Emperor.

L'Apogee, etching by
Coppier after painting
by Meissonier. Courtesy
of Library of Congress.

After Blücher was injured, Chief of Staff
August von Gneisenau took command of the
Prussian army. He ordered the retreat to Wavre.
His new defensive position permitted cooperation
with Wellington and sealed Napoleon's fate.

The Battle of Ligny.
Courtesy of Historisches
Museum Schloss Rastatt.

The day after the battle of Quatre Bras, Wellington ordered a withdrawal. Some of his officers questioned the decision but it saved the army from entrapment.

Wellington withdraws from Quatre Bras, by E. Crofts. Courtesy of Sheffield Corporation Art Galleries Collection.

The Charge of the Scots Greys, by Lady Butler. Courtesy of the collections of Leeds City Art Gallery and Temple Newsam House.

The British cavalry's thirst for glory was forever worrying Wellington. He saw the Scots Greys cut to pieces at Waterloo when they charged the French guns.

Struggles for British and French banners
went on throughout the battle. A regiment
that lost its colors was dishonored.

*"The Capture of the
Eagle . . . ,"* painting
by W. Wollen. Courtesy
of The Scottish United
Services Museum,
Edinburgh.

Some of Napoleon's light cavalry units carried
short, curved swords, but the heavy cavalry used
long, straight swords for thrusting at the enemy.

Vive l'Empereur,
mezzotint by Varin
after painting by
E. Detaille. Courtesy
of Library of Congress.

British squares smashed a succession
of French charges.

Vive l'Empereur,
etching by A. Boulard
after painting by
F. Hamerg. Courtesy
of Library of Congress.

Blücher rushed his troops into the fighting as
soon as he could. But even with the additional
strength, Wellington desperately needed
help on his immediate left.

*The Arrival of the
Prussians.* Courtesy of
Ullstein Bilderdienst.

The Defense of Le Haye-Sainte, by A. Northern. Courtesy of Landesgalerie Hannover.

La Haye Sainte punished the attacking French all day. When it finally fell to Napoleon, the way seemed open for the destruction of the British line.

The Imperial Guard moved into action against the British center. They were Napoleon's last hope.

1815 (Napoleon's Old Guard at Waterloo), etching by J. Jacquet. Courtesy of Library of Congress.

The Imperial Guard was repulsed. To French soldiers it seemed unbelievable. Panic began to crumble Napoleon's army. The British attacked with cavalry and then with their entire army.

Wellington at Waterloo. Courtesy of Historisches Museum Schloss Rastatt.

Battalion after battalion of Napoleon's last reserve of Imperial Guardsmen was overwhelmed.

The Last Square at Waterloo, by Bellangé. Courtesy of Musée de Picardie, Amiens.

The Battle of Belle-Alliance. Courtesy of Historisches Museum Schloss Rastatt.

General Cambronne of the Imperial Guard refused to surrender. He was shot in the head, but survived.

Plancenoit, a village to the right rear of the Emperor's main attacks had been under pressure since the first Prussian troops reached the field.

The Battle of Belle-Alliance. Courtesy of Historisches Museum Schloss Rastatt.

The Prussians Storm Planchenois, 1815, by A. Northern. Courtesy of Hamburger Kunsthalle.

Resistance at Plancenoit collapsed. Everywhere there were cries of defeat.

The Imperial Guard defended Napoleon to the end. Finding his coach too slow for escape, the Emperor mounted his horse.

On the Evening of the Battle of Waterloo, by E. Crofts. Courtesy of Walker Art Gallery, Liverpool.

Execution of Marshall Ney at Luxembourgh, by J. L. Gerome. Courtesy of Sheffield Corporation Art Galleries Collection.

Did Ney feign death before a mock firing squad? A legend says that he did.

Funeral of Napoleon, by Guiaud.
Courtesy of Château de Versailles,
Cliché des Musées Nationaux.

When Napoleon's body was shipped from St. Helena to Paris for reburial, many old soldiers took the last march with their Emperor.

up on the crest which rose above the misty valley toward the north. The British announced that they were there to stay by replying with another heavy bombardment. The battleground had been chosen. Napoleon felt that it was too late to attack. The French army strung out for miles. Besides, the weather was atrocious. D'Erlon, whose corps had spearheaded the chase, conferred with Napoleon. "Have all the troops take up positions and we will see what happens tomorrow," Napoleon said.[4]

Wellington set up headquarters in Waterloo three miles behind the British lines at Catherine Bodenghien's inn which had done such a land-office business the previous day during the flight of Dutch-Belgian units from Quatre Bras. The rain had started again, and its steady fall indicated an all-night drenching. Even the bustle of couriers dashing in and out and the crackling of a good fire could not drown the constant sound of the downpour as it filled gutters and splashed windows. No message had yet arrived from old Blücher. If the Prussian wasn't able to come up in support, then it seemed that there was no choice but to order another withdrawal, Wellington felt. He believed he faced Napoleon's whole army since he had received no intelligence that the Emperor had withdrawn 33,000 men from his army to pursue Blücher. In and around Mont St. Jean, Wellington had nearly 68,000 men and 156 guns.[5] He could also call on 17,000 additional soldiers and thirty guns commanded by Prince Frederick of the Netherlands.[6] The Prince's forces had been left near Hal which was a little over seven miles directly west of Waterloo. Although there was every indication that Napoleon would not now attempt to outflank the British to cut Wellington off from the Channel, the Duke kept Frederick's forces where they were to check such a move. A successful maneuver by Napoleon on the right would be disastrous. The whole British army could be destroyed. Wellington was still nagged by this worry which had caused the delay in committing his troops in the first place.

Napoleon's headquarters were being readied at Le Caillou, a comfortable farmhouse on the Brussels road; the same road that ran to Waterloo and past the inn that Wellington had taken over. The farm and the inn were six miles apart, a pleasant journey under normal circumstances. The road to Waterloo ran northwest past Le Caillou, and then struck almost due north just be-

fore reaching a farm called Rossomme. It passed a farm on the
right where Monsieur Decoster on the 15th had watched the
buildup of the struggle. Next came La Belle Alliance, also on
the right, where Captain Mercer had frightened the retreating
soldiers. From there, the road, still running almost due north,
came to La Haye Sainte on the left. The La Haye Sainte farmhouse, as stoutly built as Hougoumont, but somewhat smaller,
had not been overlooked by Wellington as an outpost. It, too,
could be a hindrance to any French attack. Near it was the gravel
pit where Mercer had fired the last rounds of his rearguard action. Just a quarter of a mile north of La Haye Sainte was a crossroads, with the west road running to Braine-l'Alleud, a little over
two and three-quarters miles away, and then to Hal. The east
road connected with Wavre, nine miles away, where Blücher had
decided to concentrate his defeated army. The Brussels highway
dissected Wellington's lines. It jutted a little to the northwest to
pass the farm of Mont St. Jean on the right and to move through
the village of Mont St. Jean. From there it still ran northwest,
and finally to Waterloo, past Wellington's doorstep and on to
Brussels. Along the Brussels highway from Le Caillou to the inn,
roads and pathways seemed to be everywhere. Near the Rossomme
farm a road led northwest from the Brussels highway to the road
that connected Nivelles with Mont St. Jean. From the Brussels
highway eastward were pathways and roads leading to numerous villages and farms. Among them were the hamlet of Plancenoit
and the farms of Papelotte, La Haye * and the Château de
Flochermont.

It was 7:00 P.M., then 8:00 P.M., and as the rain continued, Napoleon reconnoitered the area and French troops slowly arrived
to fill out their lines. Their right was anchored in the east near
the village of Plancenoit, their left in the west at the farm of
Mon Plaisir. The farm was nestled next to the road running from
Nivelles to Mont St. Jean, the road which the cat from Hougoumont had crossed. Somehow the new mother had selected her
position with military precision. She had nearly outflanked both
the French and British lines.

Few soldiers could remember a more miserable night. Most of
the French were still moving up. Many infantry regiments had

* La Haye is not to be confused with La Haye Sainte.

to march in the flooded fields so that cavalry and artillery could be brought up on the roads. They slipped, slid, struggled and cursed. Units became hopelessly lost. Sergeant de Mauduit of the Guard, slogging along with his company to reach Napoleon's headquarters, was miles away.[7] His soldiers were losing their shoes in the thick gumbo, and had to continue the march barefooted. Ensign Deacon had never found his pregnant wife. Yesterday he had looked for her everywhere, and finally had been hospitalized in Brussels. His wife, hearing that he had been wounded, went in search of him. She had learned that he had been taken to Brussels, and now as the rain poured down she was attempting to walk to the capital from Waterloo.

At Genappe, scene of the cavalry actions earlier in the day, Lt. Gen. Jérôme Bonaparte had arrived at an inn called the Roi d'Espagne with a group of officers for dinner. The harried cooks and waiters had served Wellington and his staff the previous night, and were attempting to give the impression that they much preferred their present company. One waiter was especially talkative. As Jérôme and his companions relaxed at table, dry and comfortable for the first time in hours, the waiter noted that one of the Duke's aides the previous evening had said that the British would wait for the Prussians to join them against Napoleon. He also reported that he had heard that the Prussians had taken the road to Wavre. This intelligence provoked immediate interest among Jérôme's companions. If this were so, then the French army would be moving against the combined forces of Wellington and Blücher. Jérôme decided that he would tell his brother about the conversation in the morning.

It was around 9:00 P.M. when Napoleon arrived at his headquarters, soaked to the skin. Everything was ready for him. Aides-de-camp were waiting for orders in a room especially set aside for their purposes. On the ground floor a room had been selected for Napoleon's bedroom, a fire built, and his camp bed already erected. In the kitchen, a meal was being cooked, and in the dining room, tables had been pulled together for his maps. Upstairs quarters were being made ready for his staff, and in the orchard, some companies of the Guard had arrived to protect him. Henri Boucqueau, the farm's owner, had long since fled. The Emperor dried off, then ate, and began attacking a pile of dispatches. There were several from Paris and Napoleon dictated a stream of messages dealing with civilian affairs before he tackled military dispatches. There was information that Prussian cavalry had been seen heading in the direction of Wavre. Napoleon gave the intelligence no consideration. Blücher had been severely beaten. He could not possibly rally his wounded army in time to help the British. Tomorrow the French would attack the English army and destroy it. The Emperor huddled with a group of staff officers to pore over his maps. He meticulously dictated his battle orders by candlelight which reflected against a wall crucifix, and then went to bed.

Soldiers on both sides of the lines craved food and warmth. Rations were running out, and forage parties searched every house for something to eat and something to burn. Hogs and chickens were bayoneted, cattle were shot. Doors were unhinged, shutters pulled down for firewood. Furniture was carted out of the houses, with tables, chairs, pictures, and the carefully made white wood clock cases of the Vandercams' factory in Waterloo all going on the fires. The British had been in line longer, and had had a better chance than the French to get fires started. Along their lines thousands of fires began to sparkle. Some had been drowned out by the heavy rain, but in some positions with a heavy supply of furniture to feed them, they began to burn furiously. But even with the fires it was impossible to keep dry. Some soldiers erected small tents. But inside, the bed seemed as wet as if it were at the bottom of a lake. Some filled up trenches with straw, but the water slowly rose around them as if they were in a sinking boat. For many the only comfort was cigars or pipes.

Private Matthew Clay's company of the 3rd Guards had taken up a position at Hougoumont. The company tried to get some rest in a ditch next to a high hedgerow. Added to the drip, drip, drip of the rain were other sounds coming from a short distance on the other side of the hedgerow. It must be the enemy. It was. The French were taking up positions close to the château.

Near another Wellington strong point, La Haye Sainte, Capt. John Kincaid of the 95th Rifles was bedded down for the night. It seemed that there would be a major battle in the morning. Would there be time for breakfast, and what would it be? Ensign Leeke of the 52nd Foot huddled with a friend under a cloak.

Horses were picketed near them, and somehow managed to get loose. Now added to the young officers' misery was the threat of being trampled to death. The horses galloped toward Hougoumont, and then thundered back, and Leeke and his friend had to jump up to scare them off a dozen times that night. Lieutenant James Hope found himself "in a newly-ploughed field, well soaked with six hours' heavy rain . . ." [8] His feet sank into the mire. The thin blanket he had did nothing to shed the rain. He was tired, "cold, wet, and hungry, without a fire." [9] Sergeant Major Edward Cotton of the 7th Hussars was near the farm of Mont St. Jean. It seemed ridiculous to try to lie down since streams of water were flowing beneath him. He finally found bundles of bean stalks from the farm for himself and his friend, Robert Fishers, to sit on. Some officers and men decided to spend the night on their feet. They walked back and forth along the ridge. The long night wore tediously away.

Despite the heavy rain, the soldiers found it impossible to quench their thirst. As streams of water poured down, some of them were tormented by the thought of a cold drink of water. Some cupped their hands, others found utensils, but they never seemed to get enough. They grouped around wells, and in their eagerness to pull up buckets of water they often broke the frayed ropes. Down the buckets would plunge, and there would be no way to retrieve them. Peasants, fearing a water famine, cut the draw ropes to wells and cisterns when they could. Cursing soldiers swore revenge.

Behind the French lines, the roads were choked with Napoleon's army. Behind the British lines, in Waterloo, the village shook with preparedness and confusion. Soldiers seemed to be in every room, in every corner. The road running from Waterloo right into Brussels was loaded with supply wagons, baggage carts and servants attempting to bring up their officers' gear aboard horses, donkeys and mules. Peasants were hired to haul supplies to the front. Then suddenly there was a cry that the French were attacking. Servants streamed to the rear. In the hubbub they lost control of their animals or fled without giving them a second thought. Pack animals loaded with pistols, ammunition, brandy, wine, dress swords, extra uniforms, books, packets of letters from home and all the other impedimenta which gentlemen officers

carry into war, went berserk. They bucked and rolled and tumbled to loosen their loads, and stampeded. Peasants cut the traces
of the harnesses and tried to flee with their horses, leaving overturned wagons and carts behind. The road became so strewn
with litter that it looked like the battle had already been fought.

Tupper Carey, the commissary officer of the 2nd Division, had
ridden through the morass of confusion along the Brussels road
on his way to the capital to check on supplies. During the tumult
he had tried to leave the road, but found it impossible to make
any progress because of the mud, fences and trees, and had at
last taken to the road again where he was forced to move at
a snail's pace. As he rode along, he looked at a brother officer
who had joined him. The man, still in the dress uniform he had
sported in stylish Brussels two nights before, was a sight. His
smart jacket decorated with golden epaulettes and his "white duck
pantaloons" were completely unprotected against the downpour.
Carey's thoughts went out to him.[10] The "poor man" didn't even
have a cloak.[11]

In Brussels, panic was becoming a steady diet. When the last
of the Inniskillings had trooped out of the city on their way to
the front, word spread swiftly that only a handful of British troops
remained, and that most of those were attached to the supply
corps. Now, with nothing more forceful than the local gendarmerie to protect the capital, Brussels began to rock with panic
once more. But many of the detached British, fortified by reports
that Wellington was standing fast, wondered why the Belgians
were so frightened. They argued among themselves that Brussels
had been under Napoleon's heel before and had survived.

Unknown to many of them were rumors that the Belgians had
heard. Napoleon wanted revenge, and in order to buy his victory
he had promised his men twenty-four hours of looting when they
captured the city. The French could have anything they wanted.
They would race through the streets unmolested by their officers who would be as bad as the rank and file. Soldiers would
gorge their sexual appetites, trapping Belgian girls in the streets,
on balconies, anywhere and everywhere. Rigid discipline, long
marches, the battles had not permitted many of them to spend
their lust. It would now flow all through Brussels like burning
lava. No woman would be safe. Lovely women, their men dead

or dying, would cringe before a pack of dirty, drunken soldiers. These were some of the thoughts that terrified the Belgians. Panic was fed by those who always exaggerate. Along with it came thoughts of burning houses, stolen wealth and death. The rumors had no foundation. Throughout the day Napoleon had been thinking of the best way of incorporating Belgian troops in his command. He would need them in later battles against the Russians and the Austrians. Destroying their city and raping their women would be a poor start at recruiting.

At 10 o'clock, Blücher's troops were fully concentrated at Wavre, nine miles east of the British position. The day had been a long, hard one for the old man. He had personally led his army, and now, after more gin and rhubarb, was sleeping. He had informed his chief of staff, Gneisenau, that he fully intended to cooperate with Wellington in the morning. There were some arguments against going to the Duke's assistance. If the Prussians arrived too late, then the British might be beaten and the French would be ready to fall on the Prussians. Nevertheless, Blücher had made up his mind. He had stubbornly led his men in retreat. He would just as stubbornly lead them to the support of Wellington.

Grouchy, whose troops had been pursuing fragments of the Prussian army, was confused. Had the bulk of the Prussian army retreated safely to Wavre? Or had it moved elsewhere? Although he had cavalry units seeking out the enemy, Grouchy and his main force were at Gembloux. The town was almost ten miles due east of Quatre Bras, where Napoleon had been hours before. Wavre, Blücher's headquarters, was eleven miles north and a little west of Gembloux. The Prussian army was actually closer to Napoleon's forces than to Grouchy, and it was the marshal who had been charged with pursuing the old man.

Grouchy scribbled a message for the Emperor at 10:00 P.M. He wrote that he had occupied Gembloux and that it appeared the Prussians had divided into three columns. He noted that one of them must have taken the road to Wavre, but indicated that he wasn't clear yet on where the bulk of the Prussian forces was moving. The marshal did say, however, that if he found that the "masses" were retiring on Wavre he would follow them. He would then act "to prevent their reaching Brussels and separate them from Wellington." The message was given to a cavalry officer, and as lightning flashed across the sky and the seemingly never-ending rain poured down, he raced for Quatre Bras, where he thought he would find Napoleon.

To those on the roads and meadows leading north to the French lines the next two hours seemed like a lifetime as they struggled to reach their positions. They moved in complete darkness. They could not stop. There was no rest. There was nothing to eat. Their thirst was made even more bitter by the deluge of water that was falling all around them. Private Gaertner's pack seemed to weigh a ton. Men had fallen, and great packs of mud clung to them. Some could take no more. They fell into the ooze and slithered into a hedge or crawled into a forest. The rain pelted them, but they slept. Some dreamed horrible dreams. They raced toward the muzzles of a thousand cannons—faster, faster, and then a blinding, violent explosion, and they would be awake again. They would roll in the mud, and sleep would come again, blissful sleep until another dream. Sergeant de Mauduit could never stop. Nor could Old Guardsman Rebo. They were Imperial Guardsmen, but they could grumble. Napoleon himself called the Guard his "Old Grumblers." The Guardsmen cursed their generals, the weather, the fences, the trees, the streams, the mud. They were lost, they were found. There were shouts of "treason!" But at midnight, "despite everything," de Mauduit's regiment had arrived, their greatcoats and trousers "caked with several pounds of mud." [12] Their bivouac: the grounds of Le Caillou.[13]

Six miles north at Wellington's headquarters, the Duke was growing impatient. It had been hours since he dispatched messengers to Blücher detailing his plans and stating unequivocally that he would have to have help or it would be necessary for him to retreat once more. It was almost too late to retreat now. A retrograde movement amidst all the confusion on the roads would be next to impossible. The movement would be agonizingly slow. The troops would be exhausted in the morning, and if a morning sun dried the meadows, Napoleon could be on the British in a flash, and new-found defensive positions probably wouldn't be as good as those at Mont St. Jean. At this moment a Prussian officer, a sealed dispatch from the old man in his sabretache, was moving toward Waterloo as fast as the slippery roads would permit. He was still two hours away from Wellington's headquarters.

It was now a little past midnight, the 18th of June. It was finally 1:00 A.M. Napoleon couldn't sleep; he got up, dressed, and put on his light grey cloak. Sentries who had relaxed somewhat after Napoleon had retired snapped to attention and watched their leader as he walked out into the rain.

The emperor decided to examine his position, and with a few aides who were quickly aroused he began an inspection of the whole area. The night was very dark and occasionally there were flashes of lightning in the sky. To the north where Wellington had selected his positions on the ridge, Napoleon could see thousands of flickering campfires. To him the forest of Soignies looked as if it were on fire. The utter silence was nerve-wracking. Finally Napoleon heard movement. He was at a position very close to the woods which fronted Hougoumont on the south. It was a column of British troops on the march. The Emperor wondered, were the British retreating after all? Were reinforcements arriving in the line? The noise faded as quickly as it had begun and Napoleon was now satisfied that the British were ready for action the next morning.

North of Waterloo on the road to Brussels the turmoil continued. Mrs. Deacon, clothed in only a light gown, continued her long walk to Brussels in search of her wounded husband. There were times when she felt that she could never continue, but her love for her husband would not let her surrender. She walked past drunken soldiers, frightened peasants, and carts filled with wounded and dying soldiers. Young Tupper Carey found the road so difficult that he didn't arrive in Brussels until 2:00 A.M. The rain continued to fall, and the commissary officer, completely exhausted by his long ride, went at once to an inn. It was so crowded that even floor space for a pallet was scarce. But he did find a small space and immediately went to sleep.

Back at Waterloo, there was a stir in front of Wellington's headquarters. The Prussian officer who had been delayed for so long by the tortuous road had arrived from Wavre. When he told the sentries of his mission he was led to an officer who immediately contacted Wellington. The message from Blücher was here. Wellington tore open the dispatch. It was good news. Bülow's corps, the only major unit which had not been engaged at Ligny, would soon march for Mont St. Jean. In fact, it would be on its way in support of Wellington in only a matter of hours, since the dispatch stated that it would begin to move at daybreak. Wellington also found that he was getting more support than he had ever imagined, for the message said: "The First and Second Corps will also be ready to proceed toward you. The exhaustion of the troops, part of which have not yet arrived, does not allow my commencing my movement earlier." The issue of whether Waterloo would become a battlefield was settled once and for all. The Duke was determined to hold on and to fight until Blücher would join him to overwhelm Napoleon.

On both sides of the line, soldiers tried to get what rest they could. At some of the British outposts, the French could be heard moving into the line. At Hougoumont the noise never stopped. The place was being fortified. Platforms were being erected so that riflemen would have positions to fire from the wall tops. Loopholes were being forced through the tough brick and stone. Ammunition was being stockpiled, gates reinforced, hedgerows and bushes uprooted for fields of fire.

Wellington, relieved by the communication from Blücher, worked with new confidence on dispatches to various units in his command and on communications to his supply center in Brussels. He even found time to write a letter to a lady friend who was staying in the capital. To Lady Frances Wedderburn Webster he mentioned the "desperate battle on Friday" which he had fought "successfully." He told her that he had accomplished his victory although he had "but very few troops." He said he had been forced to retreat because the Prussians had been "roughly handled" by the French. The Duke was frank with Lady Webster, saying that Brussels might be left uncovered and he recommended that the lady and her parents, the Earl and Countess of Mount Norris, "should be prepared to move to Antwerp at a moment's notice." He closed the letter by saying that he would warn her of any danger that might put her in jeopardy.

Although for the soldiers lying in the mud the night seemed endless, it was hastening away for the two busy commanders now in the process of making dozens of decisions. At 3:30 A.M. Napoleon heard from officers returning from reconnaisance, and from secret agents who had skirted the enemy lines, that the British army was sure to accept battle from the position it now held.

Nine miles east of Mont St. Jean, Bülow's corps was now preparing to move. All the endless details needed for an advancing army were accomplished. Supply and ammunition wagons were loaded, regiments inspected, and at about 4:00 A.M. the whole corps began its march to the side of Wellington. Reconnaisance parties who had ridden ahead to survey the roads returned to headquarters, reporting that the march would be difficult. The torrents had washed away parts of the road, and the infantry would find it almost impossible to move through the fields. The spirit of the men was good. None of them had yet fought the French in this campaign and they envied their comrades from the other corps and regiments who had battled Napoleon two days before. Most of the units had been camped a little east of Wavre and it would be necessary to march through the city in order to take the west road.

It seemed now that Napoleon was awake for good. At 4:00 A.M. dispatch riders arrived at the Emperor's headquarters with a peasant who had guided an English cavalry brigade some hours before. From him the Emperor learned that Wellington had stationed several units of cavalry near the village of Ohain, which is a little east of Mont St. Jean on the road to Wavre. Two Belgian deserters had slipped away from their regiment and passed safely into the French lines. They tried to court Napoleon by giving him as much information as they could on the British position. They confirmed the Emperor's belief that the British would stay and fight. The two Belgians, glowing with the artificial pleasure of men who try to please too well, said that Belgium was praying for the Emperor's success, and that Napoleon was looked upon as a savior of their country because the British and the Prussians were despised. The Emperor consulted his staff. When did they think it was possible for the French to attack? The rain had not stopped. The whole area seemed a giant quagmire. Most of the officers felt that it might well be impossible to maneuver the artillery and cavalry until the following day. Some estimated that it would take twelve hours of good weather before the ground would be hard enough to sustain the numerous assaults which they knew Napoleon planned.

It was now nearing 5:00 A.M. No one who was there could forget the chill of that morning. Perhaps it was more than the coolness of the dawn that chilled the soldiers on both sides of the line. It seemed that everyone from drummer to supreme commander now knew that there would be no turning back and that a heavily contested battle would be fought. A few men had hoarded away supplies of cognac and gin for just such an occasion. Private Le Roux, who had a position just a few hundred yards in front of the British redoubt of Hougoumont, reached into his pack for the small flask of cognac he had saved. The temptation to take it had been with him for hours, but he was glad that he had saved it until now. He had heard that there would be a ration of cognac before battle, but a smart soldier could never really depend on that. He knew, too, that most of the supply wagons had been left at Charleroi, miles behind the line. Much less than a mile away, Lt. William Turner of the 13th Hussars pulled out a bottle of gin. Although he hadn't had the slightest inkling that it would be possible to buy a bottle, some hours before a peasant had broken out some good gin, and Turner bought it with a quick greediness that sometimes comes to a buyer who thinks the seller may change his mind. The stout, raw, hot Holland gin sent life flowing all through his aching body.

At Napoleon's headquarters, Soult had dispatched orders to all of Napoleon's divisional commanders that they should have their troops in line and ready for battle by 9:00 A.M. The Emperor's chief of staff knew that it would be impossible to obey these orders since many French units were still far away from the field. But Soult hoped that the order would force commanders to squeeze the last measure of energy from their exhausted troops.

Napoleon now noticed that the sun was sending a few feeble rays through the dark clouds. Sometimes a man wishes that the day was through. It seems that the events he is about to face are too much. Napoleon now must have had this thought. For when he looked at the sun he tried to imagine the end of the day with the brilliant glow of sunset complimenting a victorious French army. Would the setting sun light up the defeat of the English?

Decoster, the farmer and tavern keeper who had watched soldiers from both armies hurrying down the Brussels road for the past three days, was seized by French soldiers and taken to Napoleon. Decoster had lived in the area all his life and would make a good guide. The poor peasant, however, had no idea what his fate would be. He shook with fear and finally was approached by Napoleon at the Rossomme farm. There in a small room amidst a large number of Napoleon's staff, the Emperor questioned Decoster carefully about the countryside, urging him to be as frank as if he were with his children.

The men who had spent the night on the sodden field were now getting ready for the day. William Gibboney, assistant surgeon of the 15th Hussars, found himself sitting in water up to his hips. Bits of straw were hanging all about him, and he remembered feeling ridiculous when he rose to his feet. Around him horses and men were shaking with the cold. All along the British line soldiers were looking for fresh wood to rekindle the fires which had gone out during the night. Ensign George Keppel of the 14th Foot had received orders to see that his company cleaned and dried their muskets. The same orders the young ensign received were repeated up and down the line. Troops everywhere began to dry the firelocks of their weapons. They secured new flints, and began to take practice shots after swabbing the muzzles of their muskets. The French did the same, and in some portions of the battlefield it sounded as though a sharp skirmish had begun.

Some of the British troops were lucky. A few supply wagons had somehow managed to reach their regiments and some bread and meat was issued. Private Matthew Clay, whose outpost was at Hougoumont, found that his company sergeant had given orders for some of the men to butcher a pig. Clay's share was a "portion of the head in its rough state." [14] He put it on a fire which someone had kindled and after a few minutes tried to eat, but after a couple of bites he found it "too raw and unsavoury" and put the remainder in his knapsack.[15] Capt. John Kincaid, stationed near the Brussels road, learned that his men had made a roaring fire next to a cottage wall. A massive camp kettle had been found and filled with a mixture of tea, milk and sugar. For cold and tired soldiers, whether private or general, the piping hot "soup" was a delight. The captain found that practically everyone was dipping into the kettle with his tin cup. During the night the Gordon Highlanders had tried to keep warm by sleeping four to a bed. Four men would spread two blankets over the mud, stretch out together, and then pull the remaining two blankets over them. When they faced the morning, however, they seemed as cold as the rest. An issue of gin was given to each man. Sergeant Duncan Robertson asked one of the privates what he thought of it. The soldier, smiling and exceedingly comfortable for the first time in hours, replied, "If mother's milk was so good, I would be sucking yet!" [16]

It was 6 o'clock when the orders which Wellington had carefully detailed for each division started going into operation. Although the line had been manned during the night, many of the regiments had camped several hundred yards from the positions which Wellington now wanted them to take up. Wellington, on Copenhagen, had left his headquarters sometime before. He had trotted down the Brussels road to Mont St. Jean and was now riding along the line which extended for a little over three miles. When the troops saw him, they would start to cheer, but often Wellington would put a finger to his lips and silence them. The Duke was more interested in the roll and swell of the land than in the cheers. He even took time to post companies, and made sure that every hillock, hedgerow and copse was used to advantage in shielding his troops. Wellington visited two of his major outposts, Hougoumont and La Haye Sainte. He offered suggestions to the commanders on their fields of fire and pointed out weaknesses in their preparations. Nervous Belgian troops posted near Hougoumont discharged some of their weapons when they saw the supreme commander inspecting them. Wellington gave them a stern look as balls whizzed past his head, and he must have wondered how the green troops would react in battle if they were so excited at seeing a general on horseback.

Although the battleground was a small one, Wellington knew that he couldn't be strong everywhere. Still feeling that Napoleon might attempt to fight around or through his right flank, he built up the west end of his line. His center and his left center were also strengthened. It was on the far left side of his line where he felt he could take a risk. This extremity was not nearly as well posted. Wellington, knowing now that Blücher would join him from this direction, was relying on the Prussians to fill up the gap on this part of the battlefield. With his trained military eye, Wellington peered through his telescope toward Wavre and could see elements of Bülow's advance guard in the distance.

As preparations for the coming battle continued on both sides of the line, nine miles to the east the Prussians were hurrying to Mont St. Jean as quickly as conditions would permit. But sometime after 7:00 A.M. a fire broke out in Wavre. No one is quite sure how it started. It could have been an overheated fireplace or a carelessly tossed smoldering cigar. But for a while it looked as if the whole village would go up in flames. Bülow's troops, on their way to Mont St. Jean, were streaming through the village when the fire started. It seemed that they were hopelessly delayed. Before they could resume their march they had to take time to put out the fire which was on the verge of getting out of control. Wellington had no way of knowing about the delay.

A little before 8:00 A.M. Napoleon returned to Le Caillou to breakfast with his chief of staff. A number of other generals were present. As the meal progressed, it was clear that Napoleon was very optimistic. He joked with his staff and finally started discussing the chances of victory. Although Napoleon's officers preferred not to antagonize their superior, they had many lingering doubts about the upcoming battle and when Napoleon asked them for their thoughts they offered guarded judgments. Many of the officers present had battled Wellington in Spain, and they talked about the difficulty of beating him. They underlined the toughness of the British infantry and pointed out the dangers of a direct attack against the enemy. Napoleon's disposition now took a turn for the worse. He criticized his officers and insisted that "the English are bad troops, and that this affair is nothing more serious than eating one's breakfast." Jérôme had now arrived, and he attempted to tell his brother about the conversation with the waiter who had served his meal at the Roi d'Espagne in Genappe the evening before, but Napoleon refused to believe that old Blücher could join Wellington at Mont St. Jean.

By this time the Emperor had had numerous warnings that Blücher was not as badly defeated as he thought, but he discarded every one of them. Although Wellington could see Bülow's advance guard which had passed through Wavre before the fire, the distance obscured these troops from Napoleon.

It was close to 9:00 A.M. when the rain finally stopped. The huge dark clouds had moved away and the sun was now shining brilliantly and the long job of drying the muddy ground had begun. French units were pouring into the line, but it would still take some hours before all of the regiments would arrive. After breakfast Napoleon made another inspection of the French line, and then arrived at the Rossomme farm. Napoleon's officers noticed that the Emperor did not ride Désirée, Marengo and his other horses nearly as much now. Everywhere he went, a detail of soldiers followed him with a camp table and chair. When he dismounted at Rossomme, the soldiers hurriedly set up the table and chair for him. It was 10:00 A.M. when Napoleon decided to send a dispatch to Grouchy. The marshal's messenger had been delayed in contacting the Emperor. The message Napoleon was answering was the one which Grouchy had sent from Gembloux the night before. Napoleon dictated his answer to Soult. Grouchy was told that the French were about to attack the British army which had taken up positions near the Forest of Soignies. The marshal was instructed to continue toward Wavre as quickly as possible. He was also instructed to keep in close communication with Napoleon.

It was now very quiet on both sides of the line. Napoleon was waiting for the earth to dry and Wellington was waiting for Napoleon to make his first move. The morning disappeared slowly. After writing Grouchy, Napoleon left the farm to review his troops. From Wellington's lines every eye seemed to be on the French regiments as they deployed for action. As Wellington's infantry clutched their weapons and checked them again and again, they watched the light French regiments in their brilliant green uniforms, the cuirassiers in their gleaming breastplates and burnished helmets, the heavy French infantry in dark blue, and the dash of the artillery as it took up position. Toward the rear they could see the Imperial Guard in white and blue, and the awesome bearskin shakos which made them all look nine feet tall.

Napoleon's plan was simple. He would try to create a diversion on Wellington's right, hoping the Englishman would weaken his center, and then he would strike with a frontal assault against the British left center and left. He had disregarded the advice of all of his lieutenants. They had argued that he should try to outmaneuver Wellington on one of the flanks. Napoleon, however, decided that there would not be time for such tactics, and that the ground itself would not be firm enough to permit them. Besides, Napoleon had lost his zest for flanking movements. Some-

where a long time ago he had begun to depend more and more
on the heavy frontal assault. These tactics had certainly worked
against Blücher at Ligny, although the price had been heavy. By
11 A.M., Napoleon had completed his inspection. The ground had
had a little more time to dry. In that hour Wellington's troops
heard the Emperor cheered almost every minute. On Napoleon's
left, Reille had assembled his corps. The diversion would be conducted by one of his divisions. It was commanded by Jérôme.

Chapter Thirteen

The Battle Begins

NAPOLEON watched from an elevated position at Rossomme, a little more than a mile southeast from the woods of Hougoumont. He took pinches of snuff, frequently consulted with his staff and eyed a huge map which had been spread out on the table before him. A little earlier he had ordered Ney to prepare for a grand assault against the British left center. But the immediate, the first action would be just a diversion. It could very well trap Wellington into weakening his center.

Reille had the responsibility for the diversionary attack on Hougoumont, and he had three divisions in position on that part of the field. It had been Reille who had earlier cautioned Napoleon in his movement against the British. Perhaps this was the reason he had chosen Jérôme's division to lead the assault. If Napoleon's brother botched the job, the blame would not be Reille's. In issuing his orders to Jérôme, Reille emphasized that the movement was only a diversion, nothing more.

It was a little after 11:30 A.M. when Wellington's thousands saw a column of French infantry advance rapidly toward the Hougoumont wood and then quickly spread out into a formidable line of skirmishers. In one of the units which would soon move out was Lieutenant Legros, a giant of a man. He was nicknamed "l'enfonceur" by his comrades because of his strength and daring.

Mademoiselle Givron, barely twenty, had had a burning curiosity all morning to find out what was going on. Finally she ran away from her parents, who had their home nearby, and wandered to the woods near Hougoumont.

Posted in Hougoumont along with a strong command was Sgt. James Graham of the light company of the Coldstream Guards. There, too, was Pvt. Matthew Clay of the 3rd Foot Guard who had had such an unappetizing breakfast that morning. They must have asked themselves the question: Would the Germans from Nassau and Hanover who had been posted in the woods by Wellington be able to hold out? Hougoumont would come under severe attack if the woods were cleared by the French.

The French seemed confident. They moved toward Hougoumont with precision and from all along the British line soldiers watched their flowing pennants and heard the bugles sound the attack. The British artillery was waiting, and as the troops moved closer to the woods a barrage opened up and within the first few shots the range was found. Screaming shells seemed to bury the skirmishers in geysers of smoke and mud, but by now the French had gained the woods and they seemed so determined that the battalions of Germans recoiled and moved through the forest. From the trees, the Germans began a well-sustained fire. But the French did not stop. They countered with heavy musketry of their own. In spots there was bayonet fighting as the French continued to advance, determined, it seemed, as though the whole battle depended upon their success.

Wellington had posted himself directly behind Hougoumont and then seemed to be everywhere directing his artillery. The fire was devastating and occasionally almost a score of French soldiers would crumple when a shell exploded. Jérôme, watching the action intently, moved fresh troops into the woods to reinforce his skirmishers.

The sound of the attack around Hougoumont drifted across the lines. It moved to the east, finally leaving the two clashing armies and then faintly whispering and dying several miles away. Slightly more than fourteen miles to the southeast, at the village of Walhain, near the road to Wavre, Grouchy was at lunch in a pleasant summerhouse. He was topping off a hearty meal with a plate of strawberries when one of his officers ran in to say that firing could be heard from the garden.[1] It was hard to determine where the firing was originating. In fact the sounds were so faint that some officers could not trust their ears and believed that perhaps the campaign was feeding their imaginations. Soldiers dropped and placed their ears to the grass-covered ground that surrounded the garden. There was no question, it was the sound of gunfire.

Peasants who had gathered when the marshal arrived now pointed to the horizon. It the distance faint wisps of smoke could be seen. Grouchy asked a terrified peasant where the sound and smoke were coming from. He conferred with his friend and they exclaimed "Mont St. Jean." There was no doubt, a major action was taking place between Napoleon and Wellington. There was a quick conference and Grouchy was urged by Gérard and General Valazé, an engineer officer, to march at once to the sound of the guns. Some officers argued that it would be impossible to reach the battlefield because of the difficult march across rain-swollen terrain. Grouchy himself was not quite sure what he should do, although he remembered that Napoleon had told him that it was his intention to attack the British and that he had been ordered to follow the Prussians. Finally a heated argument developed on what should be done. The marshal, disturbed that his lieutenants would question his judgment, became more stubborn with each petition that he should dash to Napoleon's support. He refused, and said that it was his job to pursue Blücher.

At Waterloo, the fight for the forest continued. Wellington studied the attack carefully. Except for outbreaks of skirmishing along the lines there was no movement. Wellington swept the line with his spyglass. This could not be the main thrust. Where would it come? Would it be on the right, the left, or in the center? Wellington kept his troops in their original positions. He had not weakened his line in order to reinforce Hougoumont. Along the ridge British troops waited patiently for the next move.

It was 12:30 P.M. when the Hougoumont woods were cleared of allied troops. The French, after bitter fighting, had driven them out, and were now in possession. Both sides had lost heavily, and the French, well situated, could direct sniper fire at Hougoumont and the British line. The thrust, however, had not accomplished what Napoleon had planned. The gambit had not worked. Wellington still refused to rise to the bait and weaken his line. Jérôme now ordered a direct assault on Hougoumont itself. He refused to listen to his superior, Reille, that the movement was to end, that it had only been intended as a diversion in the first place. It had failed, but the French had won the woods. Was that not enough?

Perhaps Jérôme's thoughts went back to the Russian campaign of 1812. That summer Napoleon had tried to give him some responsibility as a Bonaparte, a challenge which he had always refused. The Emperor probably knew better, but in that summer he placed Jérôme in command of the right wing of the Grande Armée. He commanded four corps, and after a minor victory over the Russians became enraptured with the pleasures of a captured town, and allowed the enemy to escape. Napoleon, hotly angered, turned over Jérôme's command to Marshal Davaut. Jérôme was to serve under the marshal who hitherto had been in his command. Young Jérôme erupted in a fit of wounded pride, promptly resigned and returned to a life of luxury while the Grande Armée went on to fight and die in the Russian winter. The Emperor considered Jérôme's act desertion and never forgave him.[2] Now Jérôme in a humbler role at the Battle of Waterloo seemed possessed with the idea of taking Hougoumont. As he called on more and more of his men to attack the heavily fortified château, was Jérôme driven by the idea of proving to his brother that he knew how to fight?

The order was received by the leading elements in the woods. The attack by the French through the woods had not stopped. They had plunged through a hedge directly in front of them and with confidence increasing with every step ran toward Hougoumont. There was a shattering volley as murderous fire came from loopholes and gun platforms which the British had constructed the night before along the masonry walls which surrounded the château. The fire was thirty yards from the hedgerow and the whole first line of the French charge was almost consumed. Survivors retreated back to the forest, and now were told that they must capture the deadly fortress. More French infantry pushed forward to join them. There was another heavy barrage of artillery and French batteries came into play and a violent artillery duel developed. More troops were thrown into the conflict and the storming of Hougoumont began.

Orders for a major attack by Napoleon were well underway.

Wellington's attention was focused on La Belle Alliance. Through his glass he could see artillery men making final preparations for a heavy barrage. Marshal Ney, who had been given the responsibility for preparing and leading the attack, had brought up eighty guns in and around La Belle Alliance which was just to the right of the Brussels road which intersected both the French and the British lines. Everything was ready at one o'clock. Napoleon, still at Rossomme, walked back and forth in front of his table, his arms locked behind his back. Just before he was about to give the order for the bombardment, he faced the British lines and decided to make one final sweep of the area with his spyglass. In a moment the heavy cannonade would shroud Wellington's ridge in smoke. He could have easily missed it, but in the northeast, in the direction of the village of Chapelle-Saint-Lambert, he saw what looked like a black cloud hugging the outskirts of the forest. Napoleon was six miles from that "cloud" but he knew what it was. On other battlefields at other times he had seen the same sight. It was troops! The Emperor's staff gathered around him. Some insisted that it was nothing but a cloud after all. Others agreed with Napoleon that there were masses of soldiers emerging from the forest. Was it Grouchy? Could it be Blücher? The attack was postponed, a cavalry reconnaissance was ordered, and the debate on what the French were seeing resumed. But just minutes later, a captured Prussian officer was brought to Napoleon and the truth was known. The officer carried a letter from Bülow to Wellington. When questioned, the Prussian officer admitted that the "cloud" was Prussian troops and that the whole Prussian army had camped at Wavre the previous night. Napoleon had no way of knowing, but Blücher himself had left Wavre on his way to Mont St. Jean at 11:00 A.M. The going was rough—the fire, bad roads, the traffic jam of the hurrying army—but the Prussian marshal urged his men forward, telling generals as well as drummers that they could not have him break his word to Wellington.

The battle for Hougoumont grew in intensity. The cloud of Prussians could still be seen. It was now 1:30 P.M. and time for the grand assault. There was a battle to be fought here and now. Ney reported that all was in readiness, and the barrage began. The British watched and waited. Officers with their spyglasses could see the magnificent precision of the cannoneers and for anyone who had undergone a French barrage the feeling was one of resignation intermixed with a great turbulence of terror. Resignation, because professional soldiers knew there was absolutely nothing they could do about it, terror, because they knew the devastation and agony of the bursting shells.

Wellington had, as he had often done in the past, posted some of his weakest troops in frontal positions. They could sustain the first shock and in their wavering pitiful efforts delay the immediate blow. Then whether they stood or fled would make little difference to the hard, tough, battle-proven troops which were sheltered behind them.

It was Bylandt's brigade of Dutch-Belgians who were the ones to absorb most of this barrage. They stood in terror on the forward slope of Wellington's positions near the Brussels road a little to the left of the center of Wellington's line. The barrage hit their lines, killed their officers, mangled, disemboweled and disjointed their masses of men and horses. They were pounded into garbage and the living stood for an eternity of eternities, wondering and hoping that the agony would cease. They stood in an eruption of blood and in a cyclone of screams.

To their right and behind them was Picton's 5th division, regiments of Scots and English and Germans. They had been ordered by their officers to stretch out on the ground and for them the barrage was not too bad, but here and there a soldier would look to his right or left and see that his friends were dead.

At Rossomme, Napoleon watched the effect of his artillery. He continued to walk back and forth. Sometimes he crossed his arms in front of him. Other times he clasped his hands behind his back, and then he would thrust his thumbs into the pockets of his grey greatcoat. Artilleryman Napoleon hoped that his *petites belles,* as he referred to the guns, would decimate the enemy who stood before the divisions that were about to advance. The guns were devouring a whole brigade. The range was not more than 800 yards.

The men in d'Erlon's corps knew they would be among the first troops in heavy action that day. They had known it for the past two days. They had missed two battles, marching from Quatre Bras to Ligny and then back again. They had heard the firing on both fields but had never tasted action that long day. Now it would be their turn. At the start of the French barrage, Wellington's artillery had not waited. They threw a shower of ball and shrapnel at the French lines. D'Erlon's divisions, before they ever jumped off for the attack, received a heavy taste of the British artillery.

The rain of French artillery continued for over half an hour. It was about two o'clock when d'Erlon's four divisions, commanded by Allix, Donzelot, Marcognet and Durutte, about 16,000 men, moved down the ridge held by the French and began, at first, a slow walk toward the British line. Ney, still simmering with anger because of his inability to drive the British from their positions on the 16th, was in overall command. He dashed to the front of the advancing troops.

In a little cottage near the intersection of the Brussels and Wavre roads, a woman had climbed to the attic. Sometime before she had had a heated argument with her husband about whether they should leave or stay. She had insisted that their little cottage and their livestock—a cow, pigs and a dozen or two of geese and chickens—were all they had and that someone had to stay to protect them. Her husband did not agree and, after repeated attempts to convince his wife that she should join him, set off in the direction of Brussels. But she was there to stay. She gathered her livestock together, shooed them into the cottage, bolted the door and retired to the attic. She could now hear the pounding of Napoleon's and Wellington's artillery. Some of it was crashing around her cottage. Now, some of it was hitting the cottage.

Unseen by prone soldiers in Wellington's line, who were hoping that they could live through the barrage, was a small boy crouched in an elm tree slightly to the rear of Wellington's forward line. His parents were unaware that the fourteen-year-old, after repeated requests to approach the battlefield were denied by his father, had finally decided that this was too big to miss and had found what he considered a safe and excellent observation post. From his position he could see it all, including the disciplined regiments of d'Erlon coming ever closer to the British positions. He could see their flags and eagles, hear their trumpets and drums.

The direction of the French attack was almost due north. The charging thousands were compressed along a front of about a mile and a quarter. The left side of the attack had as its boundary the Brussels road which ran directly north and the fortified post of La Haye Sainte which was on the left side of the road. The right boundary was near the château de Flochermont with the fortified posts of the farms of Papelotte and La Haye as their objectives. Ahead of the massed columns, compressed into drill field formations, skirmishers spread out, running toward the British lines, and beginning a sustained harassing fire. La Haye Sainte was hit by an attacking brigade. British artillery began to plow huge furrows in the French masses. French artillery was now firing over the heads of the attacking soldiers. Wellington watched closely but showed no sign of nervousness except continually to collapse his telescope and then extend it again. He noticed that French reserves were being brought into position so that the attack could be exploited if it were successful.

Captain Duthilt of the 45th French Regiment had heard the frenzied shouts of *"Vive l'Empereur!"* and as he looked toward the British lines realized that on a good day when a person wanted to take a little stroll it would only take "five or six minutes to cover the ground..." [3] But it was taking longer today. The soldiers found it difficult advancing over rain-soaked earth and through the tall rye. The British had time to get the range. The French were getting closer now and Duthilt heard the drummers beat the charge and the pace "quickened." [4] The shouts of *"Vive l'Empereur!"* could be heard over the sound of battle.

The valley was filled with smoke. The attack was pressed so eagerly that companies of the 95th British regiment who had taken positions in the gravel pit which Mercer had used as an artillery platform the night before were driven back. Bylandt's brigade could take no more. They broke, almost as a mirror breaks when it is dropped—suddenly, totally, and shattering all in one instant. The fragments flew through Picton's division, with howling Scots and cursing English challenging their manhood and so incensed at what they considered cowardice, that their officers found it difficult to keep them from firing at the fleeing soldiers. The officers of the Dutch-Belgian troops vainly tried to rally them. Two horses were shot dead under General Perponcher. His lieutenants were cut down by enemy fire as they tried to rally their men. General Picton, who had watched the nervous

Dutch-Belgians at the very beginning of the onslaught, had told an aide that he felt the 5th division would have to handle the French on their own. Picton's two brigades which stood in front of the cheering French included no more than 3,000 men. Almost 12,000 French soldiers were streaming towards them. By now the French barrage ended. The assault was almost upon the ridge. Then the British who had been half hidden by hedges and the reverse slope of the ridge stood and fired at close range. In some places along the line of attack it seemed that the French had succeeded. Through the smoke Napoleon's officers felt that this first assault was victory in itself. There was a swirling of banners, bayonets and closely pressed bodies which from a distance resembled angry waves. Napoleon saw that on his right some of the fortified areas were giving way, but on his left the defenders of La Haye Sainte grimly hung on. The point of victory for the assault, however, lay on the smoky crest where Picton's division was receiving the major impact. Picton ordered a volley and in some places with the range less than forty yards, the musketry was completely destructive. As the blow struck, there was a moment's hesitation in the charge. Picton seized upon the opportunity and cried for his troops to advance. The command had barely left his lips when a bullet crashed into his temple and he died without uttering a sound. But his troops had heard his command and they surged down the ridge.

A forest of bayonets borne by British regiments and Scottish Highlanders tore into the dazed French who were just now recovering from the shattering volley. But to the aid of the French now came heavy cavalry support and it looked like the British would be forced into squares and that heavy volleys from the pressing French infantry would cut them to pieces. But at this moment, roaring down the slopes came the British cavalry under the command of Uxbridge who had been waiting for this opportunity since the battle had started. A mass of British infantry and British cavalry were storming through French infantry.

Captain Duthilt of the 45th French Regiment was attempting to achieve some order in the ranks when he saw one of his men fall at his feet from a sabre slash. That was the first time that he realized English cavalry was plowing through the French ranks. His men tried vainly to bayonet the horsemen but had no success.

Officers, privates, drummers and fifers were being slaughtered. The captain swung his sword mechanically, feeling that death would come at any instant.

The Scottish Greys, fierce cavalrymen riding huge dapple grey horses, had charged at Uxbridge's command. Gordon Highlanders, the 92nd Infantry, joined them, with infantrymen grabbing the stirrups and shouting "Scotland forever!" It could have been the torment and anguish of the last two days of fighting and retreat. Or it could have been the patient waiting during the fierce French barrage, but all of Picton's charging troops and all of the supporting British cavalry seemed half mad. The French were reeling, breaking and trying to struggle back some way to the French line. Only on the French right of the assault was there a semblance of order as the French, who had been on the verge of taking and holding Papelotte, were retreating in order.

Corporal John Dickson of the Greys found that his horse, Rattler, was responding beautifully, and as he experienced "a strange thrill" because of the charge, believed that his horse shared the same intoxication because she uttered "loud neighings and snortings..." [5] The sight of the charge was splendid and to some those split seconds seemed elastic. They streched and stretched into long lazy intervals, allowing time for reflection. Dickson saw his officers wave their hats and swords in the air. He watched the graceful horses as they soared over hedges. He was aware of the "terrific speed" of the charge and the sound of the trumpeters and the Highland pipers.[6]

Some of the French infantry was so closely packed together that they could only wait for the slashing sabres and the plunge of bayonets. In some areas where troops had broken in complete rout, British cavalrymen were seen in a swirl of infantrymen trying to capture regimental flags. Bursts from French artillery dropped into the swarming masses, killing both French and British.

Napoleon saw that the grand assault had failed. Everywhere the French were now streaming back toward their lines. The French cavalry, which had been sent in support of the infantry, had arrived too late to help. Squadrons of cuirassiers were charged by Maj. Gen. Lord Edward Somerset with his brigade of the 1st and 2nd Life Guards, the Royal Horse Guards Blues, and the 1st

Dragoon Guards. The clash could be heard all over the field and it was a rare fight in wartime, with both sides about equally matched—the heavy French troopers, their burnished armorplate shining, and the agile British swordsmen looking for openings for quick thrusts. Individual duels developed across the field, and infantrymen from both sides cheered their own cavalrymen. The British, however, had hit the cavalry while charging down a slope and the French began to give way. The collision exploded near the Brussels road. Sharpshooters from the ridges crowning the British position attempted to help their comrades and poured fire into the cuirassiers, and occasionally a shot went astray to kill a British cavalryman as he fought hand-to-hand with a Frenchman.

Napoleon, hoping somehow that the French would rally, saw that this was impossible. Furthermore, the British cavalry were not stopping. They were going to charge the French lines. Uxbridge was desperately trying to halt them. Trumpeters were ordered to sound recall and the threat to Wellington's lines was over for the moment. The British infantry regiments were moving back to the previous positions after the French assault, but now a great force of cavalry was plunging towards Napoleon's positions. It was the British cavalry facing Napoleon's right who seemed to be throwing caution away. Major General Sir William Ponsonby, commanding a brigade made up of the First Royal Dragoons, the 6th Inniskilling Dragoons and the Greys, was galloping toward the enemy. Some said Ponsonby had heard the recall and was trying to stop his men. No one is quite sure. There seemed to be but one goal, the French guns. The pace grew faster. No one, it seemed, could now hear the pleading notes of the bugles as recall was sounded. Or perhaps the intoxication of the moment was too much and the cavalry did not care to hear. Troops, sections, solitary horsemen and clusters of horsemen from numerous British cavalry units, including the Life Guards, were charging. There might never be another opportunity like this. They thundered through the little valley which separated the two armies. They shouted, cheered and screamed as they approached the French lines. Officers stood in their stirrups, waved their swords, and shouted over and over again, "Charge the guns, charge the guns!" Some startled French infantry in position near the French lines could only look on in horror and were too paralyzed with fright to fire their muskets. More disciplined units, however, poured volleys into the advancing cavalry and the effect was devastating. Some artillery pieces also had time to fire and their bursts ripped the charging cavalry.

This, then, was the charge of the heavy brigade. Wasn't this what young officers and troops were trained for—all the drills in London, the long days in the saddle in parks and squares, and the meticulous maneuvers in Flanders? The moment was electric. The wind howled. Stragglers from the broken French regiments fell to the ground to be pulverized by lightning hooves. Those still on their feet were quickly sabred. The cavalrymen drank in the glory around them. The seconds were still elastic and there was time to hear the cheers of the British infantry urging them on. There was time to hear muted martial music, and the clamor, commands, cursing, hoofbeats and all the varieties of thunder from guns big and small being fired from everywhere. They saw their comrades fall, the horses tumble, but this was part of the game. Risk is necessary if there is to be glory, but no one seemed to think of risk. It was a stampede now. The French guns were just ahead. General Ponsonby was in front of some of his cavalrymen, and finally it appeared that he was trying to stop the attack, but it was so late now. He found himself bogged down in a freshly-plowed field near the French lines. He urged his horse but here came enemy lancers—and as the Greys, who had slashed their way through entire regiments, tried to rescue him, he was pinioned to the ground, dying in agony. British cavalrymen had crossed the valley, had ridden up the French ridge and were storming the positions. By the time some troops had made contact there were only sections, only squads, often just two or three men fighting their way into points along the French lines.

On few fields had a cavalry attack been so violent. Up and down the lines the British rode, with Napoeon's artillery the main target. Gunners scrambled under their guns to escape, but scores died under swinging sabres or from thrusts which caused men to emit "a long-drawn hiss through their teeth." [7] Horses were stabbed, traces cut, ramrods broken. Nearby units of French infantrymen cried *"Diable!"* and tried to escape to the rear. Others calmly stood their ground and began to drop the British from their saddles with well-aimed musket and pistol shots.

During the cavalry charge, artillery and heavy musket fire could have killed many of the valiant officers and troopers who had seized the eagle standards from Napoleon's infantry regiments. But often their bravery had been rewarded by orders to return to the lines. Before the hasty valorous charge across the valley, Private Fry of the 28th Regiment had seized a French eagle. A young captain of the British Blues fought a winning duel with a French officer in his attempt to wrestle an eagle standard from his hands. Sergeant Eward slashed at every Frenchman within sight as he fought for a French eagle. At the very beginning, when the Greys swept at d'Erlon's corps, Eward made a bee-line for a French standard-bearer. Before reaching the flag he killed at least three men, and a British commander seeing the action ordered that he take his prize to the rear.

It was the Greys who had suffered most severely in the fighting. As they ranged the French lines it was quite clear that they would have a desperate time returning across the valley. Their horses were winded and many of them were spouting blood from half a dozen wounds. Some horses could still bear a rider but they were in so much pain from their wounds that they stumbled when ascending slight inclines or when stepping on knapsacks and muskets strewn on the ground.

Wellington saw his cavalry's plight. He had been standing near an elm tree behind La Haye Sainte at the start of d'Erlon's assault. He had been forced to return to the main lines when the attack was pushed so aggressively. He was always worried about his cavalry and here they had over-extended themselves again. He knew that Napoleon would not allow this affront to go unpunished and he saw hordes of fresh French cavalry racing to finish up the remnants of the attacking horsemen. French lancers lowered their deadly arms and cuirassiers galloped wildly, hoping to trap the British on the flank. Some were caught already and they fought back with all their remaining energy. The horse would often give in first, sliding to the ground on his haunches and sitting as a dog would sit. There would be no mobility for the doomed cavalryman and he would fall while his wounded and exhausted animal tried desperately to rise again.

Lieutenant Hay was stationed on the left side of Wellington's line. Commanding a half-troop of the 12th Dragoons, he had watched the battle develop and worried about what he would do with his dog, "Poor Dash." [8] Earlier, he had instructed his groom to keep Dash safely behind the lines, but the dog had escaped and somehow among all those thousands he had found his master and had given him the friendliest kind of dog greeting. When it became necessary for the 12th to move out, Dash had followed, and now with Ponsonby's heavy brigade being massacred, Lieutenant Hay's regiment and the 16th Dragoons of Vandeleur's brigade charged to aid the stricken Greys and other British horsemen. Dash charged, too, accompanying his master and his "favorite companion," the lieutenant's charger.[9] Off tore the 12th on its rescue mission, "sweeping past" muskets of French infantrymen who had been part of a unit withdrawing from the field in order.[10] One French soldier ran at Hay and shoved a musket to his head and fired, but the movement was so swift that the ball whizzed past harmlessly. In seconds, the 12th was engaged in hand-to-hand combat. Forced to deal with fresh antagonists, the French now ignored the retreating remnants of the heavy brigade and the other cavalrymen who had charged. The Greys and the rest of their companions headed for Wellington's line and safety. The 12th and 16th Dragoons broke off action as quickly as possible, but when Hay looked for "Poor Dash" he was told that the dog had been killed during the charge.[11]

The first threat to Wellington had been stopped, but it had been costly. During those few minutes which had seemed to stand still when the British charged across the little valley, Wellington had lost a quarter of his cavalry. Twenty-five hundred of his horsemen were either dead, wounded or captured. Bylandt's Belgian-Dutch brigade of over 3,000 men had been slaughtered and the survivors were useless as fighters. What was left of the brigade had been pulled back behind the British lines as a reserve, but the men were so broken in spirit that it was impossible for any commander to depend on them.

The French had lost heavily, with d'Erlon's corps suffering over 5,000 casualties. About 3,000 of them lived, but they had been captured and were now milling behind the lines guarded by British bayonets. Neither Napoleon nor Wellington knew how many had been killed or wounded in the line, but the casualties from artillery had been heavy.

While remnants of British cavalry returned to their line, the battle seemed to be suspended. But it was a matter of contrasts. Both lines had been afire for some minutes, and the heavy action had drowned out the struggle at Hougoumont. It had never ceased, and although the struggle there seemed small to the action touched off by Napoleon's grand assault, it was becoming even more deadly. Both the French and the British fought as though it were an isolated battle. Assault after assault had been launched against the stout walls.

Often it seemed that the French would sweep into Hougoumont itself. Gates were blocked with whatever could be found —farm implements, ladders, wheelbarrows, and at one point a giant tree was rushed in to shore up a gate that was about to fall. Officers took on the duties of privates, grabbing muskets and firing, and rushing up with tree trunks to reinforce the position. At one point when French infantry was about to push through a gate, Lt. Col. James Macdonell, Capt. Henry Windham, Ensigns Henry Gooch and James Hervey and Sergeant Graham, all of the Coldstream Guards, had pushed a crashing gate into the very faces of the attackers. At times the French infantry after repeated assaults had managed to enter the courtyard. Under galling fire from every direction they would fall screaming from hideous wounds. Some British soldiers had felt themselves trapped in the garden just outside the walls. Private Clay was one of them. As he ran toward an open gate with Pvt. R. Gann, an old soldier and his companion, he somehow had time to notice the gate and walls, pock-marked by shot and shell. He saw the dead, the valiant French, whose bodies lay where they had fallen at the entrance. They looked as though they had been "very much trodden upon" and "covered with mud." [12] The men in Hougoumont knew that it was a question of defending the position to the last man. One officer stood at the entrance of a room in the château from where a number of sharpshooters picked off advancing Frenchmen. A young drummer boy found himself all alone for a moment in a part of Hougoumont. A more experienced soldier discovered him and pushed him into a shed. Time was a stranger now and no one could think of minutes or hours. During the severe struggle Jérôme's troops blew a rear gate open and mingled in hand-to-hand combat with the British in one room after another. A

British officer and some infantrymen retreated to a parlor, smashed the windows and fired fusillades at the French in the courtyard.

Jérôme, who had directed the attack from a position some yards to the south of Hougoumont, was struck by a spent ball. When the Emperor heard about it he ordered Jérôme to his side and sent a message to Reille that howitzers must open fire on the fortress. As the shells plunged in, the defenders in the château felt that the floors would crash to the ground, trapping them all. Almost everything combustible at Hougoumont started to burn —straw, hay, drying wood which had been covered from the heavy rain. It was like Ligny now. Flames crackled as they inched toward wounded soldiers, both British and French, who had been carried into barns and outhouses. Through the smoke the infantry still poured forward, trying to dislodge Wellington's troops who still stuck to their posts. Ensign George Standen of the 3rd Foot Guards saw some officers' horses who had been quartered in a barn rush out of the fire and then, after finding safety, return to the inferno to writhe in agony.

Wellington saw the fire and sent a note to Hougoumont's commander, Lieutenant Colonel Macdonell. The Duke noted that he could see that the roof of the château was afire, but stressed that Macdonell could not desert the area. He cautioned him, however, to make sure that no men were lost by crashing roofs or floors. The French continued to throw troops against Hougoumont. The British continued to defend every foot of Wellington's strong point.

Across the field, across the little valley between the two armies, some wounded could be seen trying to stagger back to safety. One officer of the Greys recovered consciousness. There was a terrific booming in his ears. No smash on the head, it seemed, could be that bad. He found that some French soldiers had propped him up just below the muzzle of a booming French cannon. If he moved he would be forced to go to the rear with other British prisoners that he saw being herded back. He decided to stay where he was. A British officer noticed the slender form of a French Hussar who had died near the British lines. It was the body of a girl whom a young French officer, thought such a fool by his comrades, had taken to a military tailor in Paris so she could stay with him on campaign. Her loveliness couldn't be concealed by the tight uniform, but at least the disguise had been good enough to keep her with her lover from Paris to the muddy field of Waterloo where she now lay. On examination the British found that there were several other dead women on the field in uniforms similar to those worn by the French soldiers. They, too, had marched to the very mouths of the British guns.

Lieutenant Hay learned that his commanding officer was missing. Hay, like numerous other officers, wondered what had happened to the commander of the 12th Light Dragoons. Lieutenant Colonel Ponsonby had received wounds in both arms. He had lost command of his horse and was carried into the French position. There he received a sabre cut, was knocked senseless and had been left for dead on the field. Some time later he had come to. In trying to raise himself to look around he was struck by a lance from a French cavalryman. A little later he was robbed by a French infantryman. At last he found a little help and was given some brandy by an officer who was on his way into action. He was alone now and it appeared that death could come any minute.

At Brussels there were no accurate dispatches on what was happening at Waterloo. Ignorance of events and fear of Napoleon were dry kindling to be set aflame every time a wounded soldier or a dazed peasant told of the merciless sweep of Napoleon's army through Flanders. British ladies and gentlemen missed their three-hour luncheons in the Grand Café on Rue des Eperonniers. Some had arrived promptly despite the turmoil. But when they entered the lavish surroundings where attentive servants and troops of velvet-coated lackies had attended to every wish, they found nothing. The servants, the cooks, and even the maître d'hôtel had fled. The coolness of the damp day seemed to be intensified by the unexpected vacancies. Other exquisite cafés and restaurants were closed—l'Amitée, which featured some of the best ice cream in the city, and La Monnsie, a magnificent house for roast duck and Flanders dumplings. Today was not a day to dine in Brussels.

Rumors circulated that the banks would not open on Monday. This raised problems for those who planned to buy their way to the coast. Huge sums of money seemed to be needed for everything, food, servants, horses. The mayor of Brussels had allocated all the horses for the military. One man had spent 10 guineas for a team to go as far as Antwerp, twenty miles to the west. But he

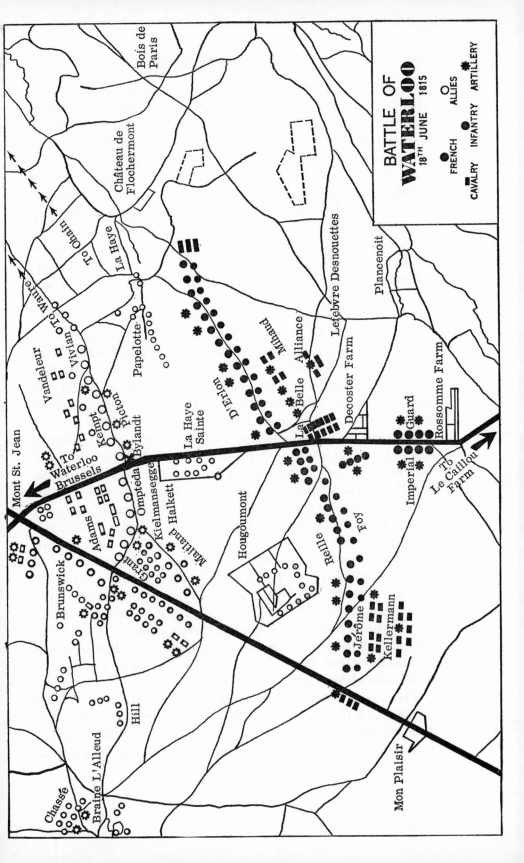

BATTLE OF
WATERLOO
18TH JUNE 1815

FRENCH ○ ALLIES
● INFANTRY ARTILLERY
CAVALRY

had special connections. Few could secure horses at any price. Miss Waldie, with her sister and brother, had managed to travel to Antwerp on the 17th. She found that "aggravated reports of disaster and dismay continually succeeded each other: the despair and lamentations of the Belgians, the anxiety of the English to learn the fate of their friends who had been in battle the preceding day; the dreadful spectacle of the wagon-loads of wounded coming in, and the terrified fugitives flying out in momentary expectation of the arrival of the French: the streets, the roads, the canals covered with boats, carriages, wagons, horses, and crowds of unfortunate people, flying from the scene of horror and danger, formed altogether a combination of tumult, terror, and misery which cannot be described." [13]

The sound of the pounding at Waterloo had traveled for miles. François René de Chateaubriand, minister of the interior to King Louis XVIII, was near Ghent, thirty-five miles northwest of Mont St. Jean. It was around noon when he took a slow walk, reading Caesar's *Commentaries* with complete concentration. Finally he was conscious of "a dull rumbling." [14] Thinking that he was about to be caught in a shower, he looked at the sky "which was heavy with clouds, and debated whether to go on or to return towards Ghent in case of a storm." [15] He listened again but now he could hear nothing "except the call of a waterfowl in the reeds and the sound of a village clock striking." [16] He decided to continue his walk but had only taken a few steps when "the rumbling began again." [17] Shortly it became clear that the sound was artillery, and "a southerly wind" which "had sprung up" brought it sharp and clear.[18] Nearby there were some women in the fields, "peacefully hoeing rows of vegetables." [19] They seemed "oblivious of the sound." [20] At this moment a courier came galloping down the road. François flagged him down and heard the alarming story that Napoleon had entered Brussels, that another battle was being fought, and that the allies had been beaten and that a retreat had been ordered. François hurried as swiftly as he could to be at the side of his King.

The way to Mont St. Jean from Wavre was the most difficult forced march the soldiers in Blücher's army could ever remember. Even the retreat from Ligny and those dizzy moments when they were surprised by French cavalry on the rear and on the flank was nothing compared to this. They were not being hit by the enemy now, but the race through the mud was completely exhausting. Under other circumstances soldiers would, despite all discipline, have thrown themselves to the ground for a moment's rest. But with Blücher urging them on and insisting that his honor and their honor all depended on reaching Wellington in time, they could do nothing but force themselves on and on.

The shelling had seemed to stop for a moment, but the woman who had chosen to remain in her cottage at Mont St. Jean still cowered in the attic.

Mademoiselle Givron who had left her parents to wander on the battlefield was terrified. She had found herself right in the center of a French attack. She had tried to hide and then was afraid to move. Finally, she tried to flee to Hougoumont itself, but was horrified by the sight of so much blood. Somehow she ran across dangerous fields to another forest, where she again hid. From the tree where the young boy perched, the view had been more exciting than he had ever expected. The young boy probably didn't even notice, but his tree had been battered with shot along its trunk and in almost every limb. But his thoughts were not on the splinters which had been gouged from his tree. He was wondering what the French would do next. So was Wellington.

Chapter Fourteen

"Tom, Tom, Here Comes the Cavalry!"

ON the British right, Hougoumont was a mass of flame. The eruption continued, with the French persisting and the British, their hot muskets singeing their hands, shouting over and over, "Here they come again!" Wellington had chosen a kind of a pathway behind the lines where he felt he would be needed most. He rode Copenhagen in back of Hougoumont and then occasionally dashed eastward, stopping here and there to issue explicit directions to artillery batteries, infantry companies and troops of cavalry. His eastern boundary seemed to be the great road which led into Brussels. He hadn't crossed it yet. Perhaps he had made up his mind not to worry too much about the east which represented the left flank of the British army, for it was on this side where Blücher was expected. At 3 P.M., the situation, although not desperate, was not as tidy as the Duke had hoped. His cavalry had been mauled. There were weaknesses showing up in the line. Some Dutch-Belgians were streaming toward the rear. Several of his high-ranking officers had been killed or wounded. It was at this hour that Wellington ordered a staff officer to ride to General Bülow with instructions to ask once more when the Prussians could be expected to come up. The Prussians were close now and in a very short time the officer was back with the report that Bülow would strike around 4:00 P.M. Wellington welcomed the news, but Bülow was optimistic about his time of arrival. His troops were fighting their way through a deep morass which was the road from Wavre. On each flank of the infantry, cavalry tried to move through marsh-like fields. The desperate journey was agonizingly slow.

Napoleon was impatient. His officers watched him as he walked back and forth at Rossomme. At times he appeared in ill temper. At other times he exhibited great kindness to his officers and his guide, Decoster. It was a typical mood of desperation which one so often sees in a person face to face with great risk. Anger rises like a fierce flame and then subsides to calmness with kind thoughts as a damper. Decoster had felt the bite of Napoleon's anger and frequently also the bite of Napoleon's snuff which the Emperor offered him. When the shot and shell flew thick and fast, Decoster, mounted on horseback with his hands tied behind his back, had cowered in the saddle. Napoleon was a whiplash, castigating Decoster for his cowardice.

Hougoumont was a fortress, a great obstacle that stood in the way of a whole corps. But the French attack there had only been intended as a diversion. Hougoumont could be bypassed. It was not the key to the battle. La Haye Sainte, another great fortified farm, was really more important as a Wellington outpost. Situated near the center of the Duke's line, it was a horror for the French. It must fall, Napoleon decided.

Ney, who had not taken Quatre Bras, who had not been able to break Wellington's line in the grand assault, was now ordered to capture La Haye Sainte. He was told that he could call upon Reille's and d'Erlon's infantry. It was part of Reille's corps which was being cut to pieces at Hougoumont. It was all of d'Erlon's corps which had been thrown back with heavy casualties from the crest of the British position. More artillery was brought up and a new bombardment began. Few soldiers had lived through such a mass of fire. Any person who wandered near the lip of the British ridge was inviting death. Heavy balls, exploding shot and canister swept down on most of the British lines. A feint was made by some of Napoleon's light cavalry against the English right. This tricked the British, and Uxbridge, the cavalry commander, shifted some of his horsemen to meet the attack. Ney himself led a brigade against the withering fire of La Haye Sainte but Major

Baring, who was in charge of the defense, laid down a shower of lead balls that clipped and cut and killed charging French masses. The bombardment continued. It smashed into British regiments and pulverized Dutch-Belgians, Hanoverians, units of the King's German Legion, and all the various contingents under Wellington's command. As death danced all along the British heights, Wellington ordered his troops to take cover on the reverse slopes, in the ditches, behind knolls. Wellington's infantry moved back. From the eyes of French soldiers it looked like a retreat. Perhaps they only wished it so, but there through the heavy smoke tough British infantry could be seen deploying to the rear. The idea of retreat stuck in some French commanders' minds. Their military training told them that it could not be true. But as they looked they could see swarms of wounded, swarms of defeated Dutch-Belgians, and thousands of French prisoners whom they could not identify, all milling, turning and wheeling like a vast mob. Seemingly, the whole British army was disintegrating. Perhaps this was the moment. Perhaps this was the time when one final heavy assault would end it all.

Ney had been given the responsibility for driving home a successful attack. Napoleon was in overall command. A cataclysmic moment was at hand. The whole plan of attack which the Emperor had envisioned at the very beginning was to fight one army at a time. The whole military gamble depended on lightning thrusts which would somehow keep the two great forces apart. Here Wellington stood, his army not yet broken. Only miles away were the Prussian hordes. Wellington must be smashed and driven from the field before the Prussians could interfere.

Commands rang for Napoleon's cavalry to form for a dash into the British right center. At 3:30 P.M., Napoleon received a message from Grouchy. It had been sent at 11:30 A.M. from Walhain, nine miles from Wavre, Blücher's headquarters of the night before. Napoleon must have realized now that Grouchy was too far away to help him. The urgency of the hour was great. Urgency was turning into desperation. Napoleon must destroy Wellington with what he had and then be prepared to defend against the thrusts of the Prussians. He must not only blunt their attacks but destroy them if his second empire was to live.

Ensign William Leeke of the British 52nd regiment had lived

through the cannonade. He stood not far from Hougoumont. He and his men watched as enemy artillery and their own screamed over their heads. At one point, fearful of a cavalry charge, his regiment stood in square. The young officer watched the bloody gaps as French artillery bursts ripped through their line. There was nothing to do but stand and take it. The ensign tried to follow the round shot which passed over his head from the British artillery. He found it easier to see than those shots which came from the French artillery. But "a gleam of sunlight" fell on some French artillery and attracted the officer's attention "to some brass guns" directly in the 52nd's front.[1] It was like watching a hangman tie the final knot. The officer observed the artillerymen "go through the whole process" of preparing their guns.[2] He could see that the mouth of one of the pieces was pointed directly at him. He saw the flash and he could see the ball. Those elastic seconds measured time again, and Leeke could see the ball coming directly toward him. He thought to himself: "Shall I move? No!"[3] He gathered himself up, with the regiment's color in his right hand. It seemed perhaps "two seconds elapsed" for the ball's flight.[4] It hit. It struck four men a little to the front and to the right of Leeke. It ricocheted and whizzed within inches of the color staff. One of the wounded cried in agony and an officer spoke "kindly to him" to silence his outcry.[5] The wounded man "recollected himself and was quiet."[6]

Nine miles to the east, Grouchy's forces had made contact with part of Blücher's army. It was Vandamme's corps that struck for the French. A sharp fire echoed all through the town, and if the deadly contest at Mont St. Jean had not exploded, the firing could have been heard by Napoleon and Wellington. The French hit hard and the Prussians fell back slowly. But this was a Prussian rearguard action. The bulk of Blücher's forces was on its way to join Wellington, and only Thielemann's corps was left in Wavre to fight the French. Grouchy was now attacking troops who had been instructed by Blücher to fight a delaying action. For the old Prussian, this battle was nothing. It was the one raging in the west that was the decisive conflict. When the Prussian marshal heard that Thielemann was engaged with Grouchy's 33,000, he told staff officers not to worry. The main fight was at Mont St. Jean!

It was nearing 4:00 P.M. Through the heavy rumbling of artillery, soldiers could hear a mass of trumpets. Orders had been relayed to squadron after squadron of French cavalry, the cuirassiers of Milhaud, the Light Cavalry of the Guard, commanded by Lefebvre-Desnouettes, among them. There were more than 5,000 arranged for the assault. Ney, who had already lost three horses to British fire, was mounted on his fourth and dashed to the front of the columns. The attack on La Haye Sainte was left to subordinate commanders. He would lead the new attack directly at the British. The target for the assault stood behind and between Hougoumont on the French left and La Haye Sainte on the right. Only 1,000 yards separated the two strong points. Through this front the cavalry was directed to charge, and officers on the flanks realized the storming troopers could pass too close to these British fortresses. They compressed the lines even more. The front on which the 5,000 would charge was narrowed to approximately 500 yards.

The squadrons started off at a slow trot. The British watched. No soldier ever had seen such an array of cavalry. Wellington ordered Alten's division and the British Guards to form squares to meet them. The British soldiers rose from their sheltered positions and maneuvered through shattering artillery fire into closely packed masses. There was no other way to stop the attack.

Wellington had anticipated the cavalry attacks. On other battlefields British gunners had stayed at their guns through that last moment when enemy cavalry descended upon them to cut and slash and slay them. A cavalry charge like this could mean defeat. Even if the first charge was beaten off, a second and a third assault could sweep a field. The big danger was to lose the artillerymen. Then the guns would be useless. The Duke ordered his artillerymen to seek shelter in the infantry squares just before the cavalry reached the crest.

Captain Mercer, who had had so many narrow escapes during the rearguard action, had been ordered to bring up his guns on the gallop before the cavalry charge. He had six guns and when he wheeled them near the center of the line to the British left of Hougoumont he could not help but watch the reaction of those in his troop who had not been under fire. In position they "breathed a new atmosphere . . ." [7] "The air was suffocatingly hot, resembling that issuing from an oven." [8] The battery was "enveloped in thick smoke, and *malgré* the incessant roar of cannon and musketry, could distinctly hear around..." (them) "...a mysterious humming noise, like that which one hears of a summer's evening proceeding from myriads of black beetles; cannon-shot, too, plow the ground in all directions, and so thick was the hail of balls and bullets that it seemed dangerous to extend the arm lest it should be torn off." [9]

The captain, although realizing the seriousness of the whole situation, could not help being amused "at the astonishment expressed by..." (the battery's) "...kind-hearted surgeon, who heard for the first time this kind of music." [10] The doctor moved up the slope with Mercer "and, hearing this infernal carillon about his ears, began staring around in the wildest and most comic manner imaginable, twisting himself from side to side..." [11]

" 'My God, Mercer, what is that? What is all this noise? How curious!—How very curious!' and then when a cannon-shot rushed hissing past, 'there!—there! What is it all?' " [12]

The doctor was listening to the music of war. Until now he had never heard a note. But here he was listening to Napoleon's greatest "symphony." Mercer begged him to retire to the rear. Finally Mercer explained how important his services would be when men were wounded. The captain told the doctor that if his talents were lost, the men would suffer unnecessarily. The surgeon finally moved to the rear. The artillery captain was flabbergasted when he looked around him. Here he found himself next to "the very boys" who "but yesterday" had thrown away "their arms" and fled "panic-stricken" from the sound of his trooper's horses.[13]

The bursting French shells were ripping the infantry's square. Officers and sergeants manhandled the scared soldiers as they plugged up the gaps, knowing that the cavalry would soon be upon them. Mercer, as he prepared his artillery for action, could not help but watch. "Today they fled not bodily," to be sure, but spiritually, for their senses seemed to have left them.[14] They seemed to stand "like so many logs" or like "wooden figures." [15] Mercer, turning over in his mind Wellington's order that he and his men should flee to the squares when the cavalry was up, decided that he would just have to forget this command. He became convinced that the terrorized infantry near him would break and run to the rear as soon as he and his men tried to leave their guns and seek "a refuge" in their square.[16]

The orders had been heard along the line: "Prepare to receive cavalry! Prepare to receive cavalry!" The squares were formed. There were two lines, with the front ranks kneeling and the bayonets formed into a bristling steel wall. Ensign Rees Howell Gronow of the 1st Foot Guards had seen Wellington near a corner of his regiment just before the charge began. The young ensign saw only one aide-de-camp with the Duke. He thought that most of the commander's staff had been killed or wounded. "Fat" Hill was one of the few aides who had not been hurt. He was riding the same huge horse. Gronow turned his eye toward the French charge. The advancing horsemen seemed to glitter "like a stormy wave of the sea when it caches the sunlight . . . the very earth seemed to vibrate beneath their thundering tramp." [17]

Sergeant Morris of the 73rd Foot watched his captain. The man was sixty and had never been in action before. As the captain looked toward the sergeant he made a declaration which was utterly evident to all, "Tom, Tom, here comes the cavalry!" [18]

The cavalry was getting close now. The French artillery still thundered and British soldiers knew that once the horsemen ascended the ridge the French artillery would stop. Although the impact of Napoleon's cavalry might be ferocious it would be a relief when the firing ended. Every square had been hurt, the dead and wounded piling up. It would not be long now. To some the cavalry seemed to advance slowly. To others it came as swift as an express. The British admired the coolness of the French as they approached. The cuirassiers "shone in burnished steel, relieved by black horse-hair crested helmets; next came the red lancers of the Guard, in their gaudy uniforms, and mounted on richly caparisoned steeds, their fluttering lance-flags heightening the brilliance of their display; while the third line, comprising the chasseurs of the Guard, in their rich costume of green and gold, with fur-trimmed pellisses *à la hussard,* and black bearskin shakos, completed the gorgeous, yet harmonious, coloring of the military spectacle." [19]

The British artillery tore at this gaudy array. To one officer who was seeing his first action, the slaughter suggested a spoiled child on a bawling rampage crushing squadrons of brightly colored toy soldiers. Lt. Edward Sumner tried to think of the men who were being maimed, but his careful aristocratic years had been devoted to horses, beautiful steeds that he had been taught to respect and love. It was the horses that he thought of most. He saw a horse's head disappear in a mash of orange and crimson when a shell struck. He watched tormented animals spin around in agony. He saw shell fragments, canister and grape slice through the sides, the backs, the hindquarters of these beautiful animals. He thought of freshly slaughtered cattle he had once seen in a London stall.

The pressure against the line was to be very severe on Halkett's brigade in Wellington's right center. Heavy casualties had already so reduced the regiments that the 30th and the 73rd formed one square and the 33rd with the 69th another. Lieutenant Macready of the 30th watched in amazement. "Hougoumont and its wood sent up a broad flame through the dark masses of smoke that over-hung the field. Beneath this cloud the French were indistinctly visible. Here a waving mass of long red feathers could be seen; there, gleams as from a sheet of steel showed that the cuirassiers were moving; 400 cannon were belching forth fire and death on every side; the roaring and shouting were indistinguishably co-mixed . . ." [20]

When the cavalry was about to collide with the squares the cuirassiers "bent their heads so that the peaks of their helmets looked like visors and they seemed cased in armor from the plume to the saddle." [21] Halkett's squares did not fire until the chargers were "within 30 yards." [22] "The effect was magical." [23] Macready could see "helmets falling, cavaliers starting from their seats with convulsive springs . . . horses plunging and rearing in the agonies of fright and pain." [24]

French batteries which had been thundering for many minutes were silenced. British gunners fired their last shots at the charge and then darted to the protection of the infantry. Captain Mercer had opened fire when leading squadrons were no more than 100 yards away. He saw his first round bring down "several men and horses." [25] Between rounds he would glance at the Brunswickers, that fearful square which he thought would break any minute. The cavalry was almost at his guns. But Mercer kept the Duke's order to retire to himself. More of his guns were now in action, "in an instant covering the ground with men and horses." [26] French cavalrymen had watched the British gunners retreat to the squares. There was hope that the battery of six guns which kept slaughtering them would eventually cease. But no, the guns kept firing. Mercer watched the carnage. The slaughtered piled up in front of his guns. He saw some of the French struggle among themselves, "using the pommels of their swords to fight their way out of the melee." [27] Some were "carried away by their horses, maddened with wounds." [28] As the cavalry swarmed around Mercer's battery, few horsemen thought to use their swords. They swept past, thinking only of escape.

But along the line the cavalry raged against the squares. Horses shied at the bayonets. Peals of fire from the determined infantry swept the horsemen from their saddles. When an infantryman fell from a swinging sabre or pistol shot, the hole would be quickly filled by a reserve soldier or the square would be dressed. Cavalrymen rode furiously around and around looking for a weakness.

At some points horses paralyzed with fright would not approach the forest of bayonets. Cavalrymen tried to back them into the squares. But these maneuvers were useless. The British fired into the backs of the cuirassiers. Other cavalrymen felt the shock of cold steel. The impact—a rearing stallion and a swift thrust, multiplied the force, and bayonets and swords plunged through cavalrymen, saddles and horses. In a whirlpool of agony a horse would spin to topple while his master screamed at the sharp steel which had transfixed his leg, or thigh to saddle and then to dying horse.

From Rossomme where the Emperor stood, some of the officers cheered, feeling that the cavalry charge had broken Wellington's infantry. But Napoleon wasn't convinced. Victory or defeat was shrouded in smoke. Practically all of Wellington's artillery for the moment was in French hands, but there were no means to retrieve the guns and in the frenzy no one thought to cripple the artillery. It would have been so easy to do—pounding nails in firing vents, smashing ramrods, exploding charges in fouled barrels. But none of this was done. The squares could not be broken by this charge. Even the weak infantry near Mercer's battery stood. It had been sustained by the captain's last-minute artillery fire and there were fewer cavalrymen moving against it.

The horsemen struggled back down the ridge. This was what

Uxbridge, the British cavalry commander, was waiting for. He now struck with regiment after regiment against the battered French cavalry that had tested the stubborn British squares. Everywhere it seemed there was a clash of steel and the French were broken and scattered. This time most of the British cavalry heard the sound of recall and moved back toward their previous positions. But again some troops ventured too far and paid for their enthusiasm in heavy losses. The British watched the French cavalry. They had been shattered, hurt, bloody, but now they were re-forming once more. And while they organized for another assault the French bombardment resumed. Again the British squares were staggered by bursting shells and clouds of canister. Sergeant William Lawrence of the 40th Regiment had just received an order which he didn't relish at all. He had been told by an officer that he was to carry the color of his regiment. He made a rough calculation and found that at least 14 sergeants had already been killed or wounded "carrying these shattered colors." [29]

Private John Lewis of the 95th Regiment looked to his right during the bombardment and saw a comrade die. Blood was streaming from his friend's stomach and back and just before he died he cried, "Lewis, I'm done." [30] Private Lewis was preparing to ram a shot down the barrel of his musket when a ball tore into the musket, bending the barrel. It was useless and could never be fired again. He was wondering where he could find another when a cannonball smashed into the square to kill his sergeant. The sergeant's musket lay there, undamaged. Private Lewis picked it up.

It was 4:20 P.M. when the first French cavalry assault was repulsed. Wellington, in the company of the 1st Foot Guard, watched the French as they were driven back and asked Lt. Col. James Stanhope of the 1st Foot Guards the time. Wellington drew in a breath of optimism, and said: "The battle is mine; and if the Prussians arrive soon, there will be an end of the war." [31] But the Duke might have made the statement for his soldiers who had undergone so much. How much could they stand? The situation was fraught with disaster. Ensign Gronow saw the Duke at this moment. He felt Wellington "appeared perfectly composed; but looked very thoughtful and pale." [32]

The French artillery had again started its destruction of the

British lines. But now British artillery was replying, sending shot after shot into re-forming French cavalry and plowing devastation into the French lines. As soon as the cavalry had been beaten off, Wellington's artillerymen dashed from the squares to their guns. Some had arrived early enough to blow up retiring cuirassiers and lancers.

The second charge began. Everything seemed to be repeated exactly as before; thundering artillery from the French guns as the cavalry approached the ridge, a fierce cannonade into the charging horsemen. The British squares re-formed. Sergeant Morris again heard his old captain say "Tom, Tom, here comes the cavalry!" [33] Captain Mercer again elected to stick by his guns. Just before the second charge he watched "a cloud of skirmishers" come up.[34] They "galled" his battery "terribly by a fire of carbines and pistols at scarcely forty yards" away.[35] The captain knew that to fire too early would be fatal. Hordes of cavalry would be on them if they fired now. To curb the impatience of his men he did a foolhardy thing. He leaped on his horse "and began a promenade up and down" the battery front.[36] This had the effect of calming his men but as he rode slowly, in complete defiance of the French skirmishers, his heart was in his mouth although he did not betray his feelings to his cannoneers. He noticed one of the Frenchmen who was very close. The cavalryman fired at him, and Mercer, still maintaining an air of calm defiance, shook a finger at him. He noticed that his antagonist grinned as he reloaded. Again the aim! Captain Mercer felt completely ridiculous at that second and realized just how foolish he had been "but was ashamed, after such bravado, to let him see it . . ." [37] The French cavalryman seemed to take forever in firing. Mercer's torment seemed eternal. He heard a shot. He heard a ball whiz near the back of his neck. The shot crashed into the forehead of Private Miller, the leading driver of one of Mercer's guns.

Minutes later the cavalry was approaching very close. In front of Mercer's guns, the assaulting troops were led "by an officer in a rich uniform, its breast covered with decorations . . ." [38] Both the advancing cavalry and the British artillerymen were studies in calm deliberation. The charge was now about 50 yards in front of Mercer's guns. " 'Fire!' The effect was terrible. Nearly the whole leading rank fell at once; and the round shot, penetrating the column, carried confusion throughout its extent. The ground, already encumbered with victims of the first struggle, became now almost impassable. Still, however, these devoted warriors struggled on ..." [39]

In front of Sergeant Morris's square the cavalry brought their own artillery support with them. Sergeant Morris had given his captain a drink of rum to sustain him. "Tom, Tom, here comes the cavalry!" [40] the captain said. But this time the horsemen paused some yards in front of them. Artillerymen leveled a cannon and fired at the square with grapeshot, "making complete lanes" through the battalion.[41] The cavalrymen then spurred their horses, trying to enter the openings. But before they could gallop through, the regiment closed its files, "throwing the dead outside, and taking the wounded inside the squares ..." [42] The cavalry was then beaten off. But they retired to the advanced artillery and again tried the same tactics.

Sergeant Morris "saw the match applied, and again the shot came as thick as hail ..." [43] The sergeant looked to his left and saw a comrade dropping, "... the blood falling from his left eye ..." [44] The "poor comrade on the right" was struck in the thigh.[45]

The situation for Sergeant Morris's battalion was desperate. A shell fell just in front of him and his men. They watched the fuse sputtering as it burned itself out and wondered how many would die. There was a tremendous blast and "about 17 men were either killed or wounded by it ..." [46] The sergeant was hit by a bean-sized piece of "rough cast-iron in the left cheek ..." [47] The blood "ran copiously down inside" his clothing.[48] But finally the cannon and the cavalry withdrew, and on all sides horsemen began streaming back toward the French line.

Napoleon watched closely. Again he had seen his beautifully trained units so fortified with their devotion for him plunge into the smoke and fire. Again many of his lietuenants felt he was on the verge of his greatest victory. But, as before, he watched dazed horsemen emerge from the crest. He saw dismounted cavalrymen scurry for their horses. He saw a disorganized mob of what had once been a great cavalry division. And then, thundering down the gentle slope, charged British cavalry, taking his cuirassiers and his lancers in the rear and on the flanks. Again he saw the deadly blossoming of artillery fire as it poured into units which were not under attack by the cavalry.

Napoleon shouted that the cavalry units had been committed too early, and he complained to the men around him that the deed had been done without serious concern for the real tempo of the battle. It had come too early, perhaps like the premature clashing of a cymbal in a great concerto, but it had been done, and if the cavalry had not broken the British lines at least it had kept the infantry in squares for the horrendous appetites of his *petites belles.* For the British had to move into squares every time the cavalry threatened and when they did the massive artillery thundered to devour hundreds. Wellington's lines were showing weaknesses, like corroded chains or frayed ropes.

Napoleon saw his infantry attacks on La Haye Sainte, fail. His soldiers had done everything, it seemed, to take the fortified farm. They had tried to crash through gates, walls, windows. At one place there was a mound of French bodies, and officers, through their glasses, could see other French dashing forward to crouch behind this hill of flesh. And then they would clamber around it and attempt to force their way into the fortress. They would stagger and die and become part of the little hill. But now this attack, too, had failed. The men could take no more, and they moved slowly toward the French lines. Many died on the way back. Shot in the back, their knees would buckle, and they paused momentarily, as though they had a handhold in the sky before falling to the ground. Many fell within earshot of Major Baring's troops from the King's German Legion at La Haye Sainte. The French raised themselves, turned their heads, looked at their enemies and shouted *"Vive l'Empereur!"*

Blücher could see the fighting. He could see the French reserves. It was around 4:30 P.M. He had made it against horrendous odds. Time and time again his men had become dispirited during their long march. Nearly collapsing from fatigue, they had murmured over and over again, "We cannot do it." But Blücher seemed to be everywhere and he told his soldiers, "I have given my word to Wellington, and you will surely not make me break it: only exert yourselves a few hours longer, and certain victory is ours." [49] Some had made it now. The 15th and 16th brigades of Bülow's corps, along with reserves of cavalry and artillery, were assembling near the extreme right flank of Napoleon's army. Other Prussian units were hurrying to join them.

Blücher had hoped that before joining the battle he could assemble a heavier force, but when he heard the tremendous bombardment he decided to attack with what he had. He thought, too, that his bombardment might be heard to announce the Prussian arrival and would flash new hope to Wellington's struggling army, which he felt might break at any minute. The two brigades moved from a little forest, known as the Wood of Paris, which was just two miles from where Napoleon watched the action. The attack was spearheaded directly at the French Army's right flank. French cavalry raced to meet the Prussian column. Prussian cavalry was thrown in against them. Artillery became engaged.

On the French left Napoleon's infantry were still feeding the furnace of Hougoumont. No one, no officer anywhere, protested the sacrifice. It seemed to be like the beckoning flame which draws a moth to disaster.

Napoleon was concerned with the British right center, and for some minutes now he had been organizing another massive cavalry assault. Although he felt the first attacks had come too early, he stood by the error. Milhaud's squadrons, which had hit the British lines twice, were ordered to renew the assault. So were the other cavalry units which had fought so hard. In addition, Napoleon ordered an aide-de-camp to relay orders that Kellermann's two divisions and all the rest of the cavalry within call were to support the assault. It seemed that now Napoleon's main fuel was emotion. The Prussians were entering the battle. Wellington's lines still held. There had been repeated failures—at Hougoumont, at La Haye Sainte, on the right and in the center. Wellington must be defeated, and it must be now. The whole British army might be on the verge of collapse.

The order, like so many orders in the heat of battle, came in a hurry and was executed in a hurry. The exact command, the exact time when it was given, the specific instructions were all lost in the clamor of battle. General Kellermann sensed disaster and would have liked to protest, but the movement of the great charge swarmed around him as the bulk of Napoleon's cavalry began to deploy. Only a small reserve was left behind at Kellermann's express orders.

The previous cavalry attacks had been great, grand assaults. But this one was supreme. Every soldier in the British line who had a moment watched in disbelief. The little boy who was still perched in his tree drank in the glamor of war. It exceeded even a boy's dreams of imaginary battle. The charge was aimed at that charred piece of crest between Hougoumont and La Haye Sainte. Before, when the 5,000 had charged, there had been hardly space enough to maneuver. But now there were double that number! The new attack was preceded by a massive cannonade. As before, the French batteries concentrated their fire upon the allied artillery and squares. "The entire space immediately in rear of the crest of the ridge that marked the front line of the Duke's right wing was again assailed with a tempest of shot and shell. Again were whole files torn away, and compact sections rent asunder." [50]

Again the squares stood, and the centers of some of them were filled with the dying and the wounded. In some of the units under more intense bombardment than others there was hardly a man who was not covered with blood, either his own or that of a fallen comrade. Blinding flashes destroyed some of the British artillery pieces which were in action. A hail of shot tore through artillery wheels, sometimes driving the splinters into the infantry. These fragments caused excruciating pain, and young soldiers clutched their weapons tighter and looked to their veteran sergeants for support. But often it was these veterans who had taken horrible wounds. Their screams made the young British soldiers doubly nervous, but they stood fast.

Wellington's corps—divisions, regiments, battalions and companies—were melting away. Squares were formed in a checkered pattern so they could deliver a heavy crossfire at the charging cavalry. But now units had lost so many men that they could not properly form a square and had combined with other battered regiments to present a defense. The curtain of fire lifted and through the smoke came Napoleon's thousands. Ney, his uniform torn, his face blackened by powder, had placed himself in front of the leading squadrons. He waved his sword and plunged ahead. Now it was the turn of the British artillery to spew bursts, grape and balls. It was a British monopoly on violence. The charge was painfully slow. Piles of dead and wounded and the mounds of dead and wounded horses were barriers to the charge. The carnage from the artillery was frightful. And from the flanks, the defenders of Hougoumont and La Haye Sainte poured in volleys of musketry. But on they came. ". . . the whole space between La Haye Sainte and Hougoumont appeared one moving, glittering mass; and, as it approached the Anglo-Allied position, undulating with the conformation of the ground, it resembled a sea in agitation . . . Its very shouts sounded on the distant ear like the ominous roar of breakers thundering on the shore. Like waves following in quick succession, the whole mass now appeared to roll over the ridge; and as the light, curling smoke arose from the fire which was opened by the squares . . . it resembled the foam and spray thrown up by the mighty waters as they dash on isolated rocks and beetling crags; and, as the mass separated and rushed in every direction, completely covering the interior slope, it bore the appearance of innumerable eddies and counter-currents, threatening to overwhelm and engulf the obstructions by which its onward course had been opposed. The storm continued to rage with the greatest violence." [51]

Some French officers had pledged that they would not come back from the assault unless it succeeded. They broke their scabbards to prove that the swords would remain unsheathed, in victory or death. Again horses were backed into the squares. Cavalrymen threw their lances as though they were spears. A few managed to close with the squares. A dying horse would, in its convulsion, toss its rider upon the bayonets, and he would be suspended for a split second as hay embedded on the end of a pitchfork. Some of the horsemen had several pistols. They fired until they were bayoneted or killed by musket shots.

Many of the horses could not be driven beyond twenty yards of the squares. There they stood, blown from the long charge, the foam dropping from their mouths. Their riders could do nothing but die with the heavy musketry pounding and penetrating the cuirassiers' breastplates. Sergeant Robertson of the Gordon Highlanders heard this sound. It was like heavy rain "on a leaded roof." [52] Some French officers were so hideously wounded that they fell on their swords or begged their enemies to kill them.

Once more most of the British artillery was in French hands, but no one had thought to bring up the necessary materials to make the guns useless. The great assault was failing. Struggling back from the British crest came the survivors. Many of them unloosened their breastplates so they could escape more speedily. Broken squadrons emerged from the smoke on their way to the French lines. Miraculously, Ney was still alive. He stood near an abandoned British gun, drunk with despair and defeat, and then a great rage seized him. Stabbing his sword at the air, he stood swelling with emotion, and then started clanging the blade again and again against the muzzle of the gun.[53] His fourth horse was dead, but somehow he managed to escape and once more he mounted a fresh horse to organize another assault.

Captain Mercer, still standing at his battery, fired at the retreating cavalry. Other British artillerymen dashed from their squares, but they barely had time to get off a few rounds before Ney and his squadrons were coming at them again. This charge failed, too, but there were more. Despite the reverses, despite the utter failure of numerous attempts, the French horsemen continued each time to re-form and charge again. They rode past the leading squares and engaged reserve units. They tried to slash their way past hundreds of bayonets. In retreating they tried to avoid the same tortuous paths they had used for the advance, and in circuitous routes they often found a quick death. The British cavalry, after each charge, would attack. Sometimes unseen British infantry would drop a complete troop of French cavalrymen. On one detour nearly 100 cuirassiers were riding at full gallop. Sergeant Wheeler's company, which was on the far right of the English line, saw them. They opened fire. By the time "the smoke had cleared away, one and only one, solitary individual was seen running over the brow" in the company's front.[54] Those who had died instantly were fortunate, for the wounded lay in a heap of struggling horses and were being kicked to death. It was 6:00 P.M.

Chapter Fifteen

"Stand Fast!"

THE cavalry horses! Lt. Charles Lenox Dickson of the 69th watched them. During the attacks many mounts had lost their riders, but they stayed with their squadrons. After an assault had failed and their riders were dead, many of them retreated back, and when a new charge was formed they, too, joined in. Many of them had been wounded, but as long as they had strength and could gallop, they returned, crowding into formation. During one awful moment British soldiers had seen a French hussar in a quick clash with a British cavalryman. A sabre blow had struck just right and the hussar's head and helmet flew to the ground. The hussar, blood gushing from his neck and dripping hot on his horse's mane, stayed erect in the saddle. The horse seemed to know that something was dreadfully wrong. It had felt the reins loosen, but with the instinct of a cavalry horse, it continued on the course which had been set by its rider. For those who watched, the headless hussar seemed to ride forever, but finally the corpse slumped, teetered and slipped to the ground. There was a long pause by the hussar's charger and it joined the unit it had known.

Some of the horses were horribly mangled. They lay all across the little valley. Many would never stand again, but when they were relieved of their pain for a few moments they fed on the grass around them. Soldiers from both sides watched in disbelief as horses with bleeding stumps for legs grazed out small semicircles of bareness where they lay.

231

There was only one consolation for the wounded men. The sun was wrapped in clouds, and the heavy smoke of battle acted as additional shade for the fallen. The day was not overly warm, but the exertion of battle and the strange smell of freshly-exploded powder mingling with sodden grass and grain produced a fantastic effect of unreality. Somehow it seemed impossible that men and beasts should find themselves in such hideous predicaments.

The battle had been raging for nearly seven hours. Darkness was not far away, and the strange disease of a battle growing late infected some of the soldiers on both sides. Soldiers confess that in the birth of battle many seem to have an understanding with Fate. Death in the early part of the struggle is more acceptable, but when a soldier has managed to survive long, difficult periods of action and the action is nearing the end, it is harder to die.

After the main cavalry attacks had failed, Ney did not stop. The marshal seized command of Napoleon's last cavalry reserve, Blanchard's *carabiniers,* which Kellermann in a last-second order had posted in the rear. Ney demolished Blanchard's pleas that this small unit would be sacrificed uselessly. Ney led them with remnants of a dozen units. Again he was repulsed. He then personally led 6,000 infantrymen against the British.[1] They climbed over the dead and wounded and tried to close with their enemies. Wellington's regiments quickly deployed into line. The artillerymen were at their guns. The attack, with every fourth man a casualty, was futile and failed almost before it had started. But the whole British line had suffered seriously from repeated assaults. Some officers were now saying it might be impossible to hold on much longer.

Meanwhile, the French had their hands full on the right flank. During the final cavalry assaults against the British lines, the Prussians continued to advance. Napoleon had thrown some troops against them. And at first the Prussians had been forced to retire, but kept up a heavy fire. The blow on the right was compromising Napoleon's position. It had to be crushed, at least dealt with in force, if Wellington was to fall. But every soldier sent against the Prussians was one who could not do the main job of attacking the British. Napoleon had ordered the Sixth Corps under Lobau to move from its reserve area near La Belle Alliance to oppose the Prussians. Blücher, seeing the movement, issued a flood of orders to counteract it. Lobau's force was inferior in numbers to the corps he faced. It would need support.

A French brigade was driven out of Plancenoit. Prussian artillery flew into the village, wheeled into position, and began blasting the right of Napoleon's lines. The Emperor's headquarters came under heavy fire. Solid long shot now fell among the units of the Imperial Guard which the Emperor had hoarded so carefully in reserve. Napoleon ordered a counter-attack with the Young Guard. The pressure must be eased and it must be done quickly. Prussian reinforcements were building up fast. Another corps was about to debouch against the French.

Perhaps during this climactic moment, thoughts of the Young Guard flashed through the Emperor's mind. To supplement his "Old Grumblers" he had organized additional regiments six years before. They were young men in their twenties, called to the tricolor to support the Old Guard who had fought so long with Napoleon. In the very ranks of these men who were now moving against the Prussians were former members of his young son's guard. Just four years before, in 1811, at the birth of his son, the King of Rome, Napoleon created a guard in his honor. In a proclamation, he established a regiment of two battalions of six companies each. The regiment was made up of children between the ages of ten and sixteen who were the sons and nephews of French soldiers killed in action. Napoleon planned for his son to command this "Baby Guard" as soon as he was old enough. Many times they had marched at celebrations within the view of the Old Imperial Guard who helped teach them the ways of war. Now, four years later, some who were old enough had graduated to Napoleon's Young Guard. They carried muskets and others carried swords as commanders, as they engaged the Prussians in the streets, in the churchyard and in the cemetery at Plancenoit.

A message reached Napoleon. The Young Guard had charged and the Prussians had been driven back. The news was like an elixir. Napoleon now directed his attention against Wellington. If La Haye Sainte could only be taken, there would be a good chance of smashing Wellington's thinning line. If artillery could be brought up in that position it could kill the wounded British regiments that hung on so grimly. Once more an order went out to Ney: take La Haye Sainte. Take La Haye Sainte. The cost didn't matter! Ney acted at the instant, collaring several battalions of French infantrymen and units of engineers who were told to bring every possible entrenching tool they had. Major Baring, who defended the fortified farm with a battered battalion of the King's German Legion and a handful of reinforcements, saw the French heading for his position. He and his men had been under repeated attack since noon. Ammunition was running low, and although he had sent one desperate plea after another to the main British lines, not one extra round had been sent to him. Some minutes before, he had checked the remaining supply of ammunition and found that his soldiers averaged three to four rounds apiece. Baring was desolate. He knew it would be a miracle if his troops held out. For a second he felt it would be better if he were dead. From his position he could see two enemy columns. He now turned to his men and begged them to make sure of every shot. They shouted they would fight and die with him. The major's feelings for the confidence of his men could never be properly expressed. He experienced a feeling of pain for their safety, pain mixed with gratitude for the honor these exhausted veterans gave him.

The French struck with an awful fury. They had been cheated out of victory each time and now they intended to have it. Baring's men tried to make each shot count. French casualties mounted and occasionally two men were seen to fall from one shot, so close together were they. Burning wads of cartridge paper flashed from muskets with the shots and seared into French uniforms. Every round fired caused Major Baring new anxiety. The attack had started at the barn which was now ablaze. Baring organized a bucket brigade and soldiers, in between sniping at the enemy, filled cooking kettles with water from a well and tried to extinguish the flames. The major made one last futile effort to replenish his ammunition supply, grabbing a private soldier and telling him to scramble to the rear with a request for more ammunition.

But ammunition was becoming a problem almost everywhere for Wellington. Battered British infantrymen cheered when fresh supplies were dumped in their squares. At Hougoumont the situation was becoming desperate until a private of the Waggon Train drove his team and tumbril down the hill through a withering fire right up to one of the château's gates. Musketry from La Haye Sainte was gradually diminishing. The small supply of ammunition would soon be completely gone. Officers and men gathered around the major, swearing their fidelity but at the same time saying that the place was impossible to defend without ammunition. There was a crashing at the gates and doors as French infantrymen stormed the position, the engineers wheeling huge axes. One of the doors collapsed and Baring's infantrymen bayoneted the French who tried to clamber inside. Outside, the French had grasped many of the muskets which extended through the loopholes.

Ney's attack was succeeding. The French infantry smashed their way into the stables. For some minutes the defenders managed to keep them from entering the courtyard. But they climbed the walls, the roofs, and began to snipe at Baring's men. Now the French seemed to be everywhere. They ran through the narrow passages, into rooms, across the courtyard. The barn fell and hordes of troops emerged through the smoke. There was hand-to-hand fighting in the courtyard and Baring finally gave the order to retreat. The French, incensed because the fort had caused the death of so many of their comrades, slaughtered prisoners before their officers could stop them.

The French had scored a major triumph. Engineers now poured into the farm. They erected firing platforms, fashioned loopholes which faced the British lines. Gates and doors were reinforced. Ney's lieutenants secured the flanks, rushed companies of infantry into every tactical area near La Haye Sainte. Artillery was quickly brought up. French infantrymen scrambled up within 75 yards of the British lines. Well protected by hedges and small knolls, they began a heavy fire. Artillery started booming.

At last they had made it! Napoleon saw success through the smoke. Victory could be close now. The French would weaken Wellington's center and this could be exploited. Troops would pour through. The rupture would cause both flanks to recoil, and what was left of the cavalry could be rushed in and Wellington's forces routed. Along the center of Wellington's line French skirmishers spread out. Strings of battalions advanced. On the British right the fury at Hougoumont continued unabated. The repeated attacks had finally forced Wellington to reinforce this position—

something which he had fought against because his line was weakening. Nearly all of Hougoumont's buildings were burning. The château's roof and top floor had caved in. It was nearing 7:00 P.M. and almost everywhere there was relentless pressure against the British. On the far left of the British line the fortified farm of Papelotte had fallen to Napoleon's troops.

The position at La Haye Sainte which had been so painful to Napoleon was now a key to the entire destruction of the British army. The shattering fire swept back two companies of the 95th British rifles which had been posted in the sandpit at the side of the Brussels road. The artillery began to destroy completely many mangled British squares. A strong body of cuirassiers had rallied to linger nearby, always ready to dash into a weak position. Counter-attacks were ordered. Colonel Baron von Ompteda of the King's German Legion knew that his charge would be suicidal. He had received orders from Lieutenant General Alten to move against French infantrymen who ringed La Haye Sainte. But he knew that cuirassiers lay in wait. He delayed his advance. The Prince of Orange dashed up and ordered Ompteda to attack at once. The colonel tried to explain that the charge was doomed because his men would be slaughtered by cuirassiers. The Prince, however, demanded that the order be carried out and shouted that no further reply was necessary from the colonel. Ompteda immediately advanced with the 5th line battalion. For a moment it looked like the charge would succeed. French infantry moved back and plunged into hedges near the garden of La Haye Sainte. But in seconds Ompteda's troops were completely engulfed by cuirassiers. Ompteda died. So did most of his men. Out of the whole battalion only a handful of officers and men straggled back to the British lines. Numerous clashes followed—charges and counter-charges—but the French held on to their gains.

The British artillery had suffered heavily. Many guns stood silent on the ridge, their gunners dead, their barrels useless from excessive heat, their ammunition exhausted. Many of Wellington's lieutenants were dead or dying. Generals Picton and Ponsonby were gone. Junior lieutenants commanded some squares. Some of the cavalry units had been reduced to nothing more than messengers and outriders. Whole brigades had been pulverized into mere companies. Desertions among the Belgians and Dutch had been heavy, and at this moment it required a squadron of British cavalry to hold some of these troops in line. The backwash of the battlefield was filled with the dying and wounded. British officers swore at some of their men who now began to escort wounded away from the line. Until now almost every Britisher had stuck by his regiment's orders that the injured must make it to the rear as best they could or have men specifically assigned to them. In the ranks some men sobbed, some screamed, some stood as dumb as manikins.

Deserters had fled to the forest near Mont St. Jean. Lieutenant Jackson, who had been sent to bring up a battery of Dutch guns, was amazed when he looked into the forest. He saw thousands hidden among the trees. They had piled their arms and were cooking. The Dutch artillery commander refused to move up his guns, saying that he had no ammunition.

Numerous brigades under Wellington's command, suffering the intense fire of the French, who had gained a terrifying advantage, began to shrink into almost nothing. Lambert's and Kemp's brigades and Pack's Royals were hurt badly. Kielmansegge's was being massacred. Alten's division was ground into a brigade. Adams' brigade had been hit so hard that it was moved back. So desperate was the situation that the colors of the 30th and 73rd regiments were sent to the rear. The tattered flag of the 30th was wrapped around a dead sergeant.

Private Haughton still bore his drum, but war was entirely different from what he had ever imagined. No stories by his uncle, who was a band sergeant, could ever capture anything like this. The young drummer may have had some second thoughts about having run away from home to enlist. He stood with the Inniskillings, the 27th Regiment, near the center of the British line. Holding a key spot at the crossroads, the 27th was forced to maintain its ground or allow a dangerous penetration into Wellington's lines. The French concentrated their fire on the 27th and all around the young drummer, men were dying. Some troops near the Inniskillings faltered but the 27th stood, and within minutes half of its men were dead or wounded.

Officers from numerous regiments were sent to Wellington to ask for reinforcements. The Duke could offer nothing. He told them to return to their units and stand to the last man. Lieuten-

ant Macready of the 30th Foot admired his coolness. At one point
he saw a shell fall near the Duke. Wellington watched the explosion kill a number of men and then without emotion of any
kind trotted on to another position. Everywhere he went, troops
were ordered to "stand to your front—here is the Duke!"

Wellington also caught the sound of other voices as he rode
along through shot and shell, ordering his men to hold on. There
would be a whisper and someone would say, "Why can't we get at
them?" There would be another soft murmur, "It would be better to take them with the bayonet." Officers would rush to the
sounds and order the soldiers to remain silent.

Officers and men noticed that Wellington was constantly looking toward the east. In the southeast he could see Blücher's units
clashing in the distance against the French far right. This, however, was not enough. What he needed now were reinforcements
on his immediate left. That's where he wanted support—enough
troops from the Prussians to shore up his line so he could reinforce the center. Dispatches were sent one after another to the
Prussians. When would they come? Meanwhile, the punishment
from the French continued.

Lieutenant Colonel John W. Fremantle, one of the Duke's
aides, was sent down the Namur road. He was to find the Prussian commander who was moving up and explain the desperate
situation. The troops were not far away and in minutes Fremantle
met them and rushed to Marshal Zieten who was in command.
Fremantle proposed that anything he could send would be useful,
but the Prussian marshal had heard that the British were about
to be routed and told the colonel that he would not break up his
corps. A hot argument exploded among Prussian officers on just
where these forces should be sent—in the direction of Bülow who
was hotly engaged with Napoleon around Plancenoit, or to the
direct aid of Wellington.

Marshal Ney could see the results of the desperate French attack. The whole British line was on fire. He looked at the center
and it seemed practically bare of troops. He could see the abandoned artillery, the turmoil of whole brigades, the thin lines of
British cavalry. He dispatched Colonel Heymès to implore Napoleon to use some of his reserves. Ney felt that if he had some of
the Old Guard, which the Emperor hung onto so tenaciously, he

could end the battle. A quick thrust now and perhaps the whole
British army could be rolled up. But he had no more men which
he could throw into the action. Every troop and company he had
was now engaged. The weight of just a few more troops was desperately needed. The colonel reached Napoleon, who had moved
his headquartes to La Belle Alliance, several hundred yards closer
to the British lines. The Emperor now seemed impatient. He took
more and more snuff. He dealt with his officers in a rush and was
constantly curt. He was angry, hurt and amazed that the British
troops had not yet been broken. He betrayed his newly-won admiration for the tough English and Scottish infantry. And now
he had just heard that his Young Guard was in a desperate situation. The Prussians had been reinforced and they were driving
back the troops which just a short time before had given him a
victory. At this moment when Ney's demand reached him, he had
fourteen battalions of the Imperial Guard which had not yet
been committed to action. "Troops!" exploded from Napoleon's
lips. "Troops! Where do you expect me to get them? Do you expect me to make them?" The Emperor had never been so cautious
with men before. But his life, his crown, his future, all the things
he knew as Emperor hinged on the results of this battle. Throughout the day, the lives of thousands had been squandered. His
tremendous squadrons of cavalry and his formidable infantry of
the line had moved and attacked, and counter-attacked and defended. The blood of France had been spent in one attack after
another. But now it seemed the French were on the verge of
victory.

Napoleon courted caution. The stakes were so high. He began
to parcel out his reserves piecemeal. Two battalions of the Old
Guard were ordered to drive the Prussians out of Plancenoit. The
situation was out of hand. The Young Guardsmen were being
overwhelmed, but the veterans of a hundred battles moved in
support coolly with fixed bayonets. The younger men gained new
strength at the sight and re-formed behind the Old Guard. Plancenoit was burning. The Prussians fought viciously, but were driven
out. The situation on Napoleon's right flank seemed secure, at
least for the moment. Guardsmen amused themselves by cutting
the throats of their prisoners.

Wellington had decided that he couldn't wait for aid on the

left before strengthening the British center. But knowing that the Prussians would be up eventually and gambling that the main blow would come in the line between Hougoumont on his right and La Haye Sainte on his left, he issued orders to strengthen this part of the line. A little earlier he had ordered the cavalry brigades commanded by Vivian and Vandeleur to move from the left to the center of the line. To further reinforce his position he brought up some German battalions and a number of Dutch-Belgian units, some of which had sheltered most of the day at Braine-l'Alleud, two miles west of his main line. Every available artillery piece was being shoved into the line. Vivian couldn't believe what he saw when he came up with his troopers behind Wellington's line. For most of the day his cavalry had been protected from the most ferocious French attacks. He was convinced that the British were about to retreat. Everything he saw suggested defeat, the thousands of wounded, the soldiers fleeing from the lines, the heaps of refuse, litter and the mounds of dead men and horses. Meeting Somerset, Vivian asked the location of his brigade. Somerset pointed to his meager command which was little more than a squadron and then pointed to the ground which was covered with the dead, the dying, the mutilated horses.

But the appearance of the relatively fresh cavalry which included the 1st, 10th, 11th, 12th, 16th and 18th regiments brought new hope to the depleted British squares who saw them.

At this moment a French officer looked across the smoke-filled valley and wondered if he could safely gallop across it. If he had fallen at Waterloo no one would have suspected how much he really detested the Emperor. His friends who had often heard him castigate Napoleon would have wondered why he had found it necessary to die at Waterloo. No one knows how often he had thought of desertion. But the time had finally come. From the French lines he sped toward the British. He was all alone and he rode directly toward the 52nd regiment. It seemed that no one would take the trouble to kill a solitary French cuirassier. As he approached he was shouting *Vive le Roi!* He approached two British officers and yelled that the line would be attacked within minutes by Napoleon's Imperial Guard. The information was rushed to Wellington and the deserter was taken to the rear by a sergeant.

It was some minutes after 7:00 P.M. It had been nearly half an

hour since Ney's request for use of some of the Guard. Napoleon
had now decided to to attack with his reserves. Victory or defeat
hung on the success of his old veterans. Imperial Guardsman
Rebo had spent the entire day in the rear of La Belle Alliance.
So many times this had happened. The battle had reached its
climax. Everyone seemed on the verge of exhaustion, and then
Napoleon would give the signal and the Old Guard would rush
to deliver the death blow. It was so now, thought the veteran and
his squad of Old Guardsmen as they deployed.

On the road that led to Brussels there was a constant stream
of the wounded. The city itself was stunned. Rumor after rumor
of disaster came into Brussels with every wave of wounded. Already there were thousands of them who had fought at Quatre
Bras on the 16th. Now added to these were the freshly wounded
from Waterloo who started pouring into the city in the early afternoon. They came on horseback, in carts, and some were carried
the last few miles by comrades. Hotels, boarding houses, private
residences, churches and the streets themselves became hospitals.
Every doctor within miles was summoned to the downtown area.
In the great square, fresh straw was brought in from the country
and soldiers were stretched out. Cries of disaster went up and
down the street. At one point a herd of French prisoners were
marched into the city by British soldiers. This was enough once
again to send the inhabitants running for the outskirts. They
thought the French were conquerors. Many British citizens had
stayed on in Brussels. Officer friends who were wounded rushed
to their homes for help. Sometimes these soldiers, literally covered with blood, would give reports that Wellington was about to
be beaten. Other times they carried messages of hope. The women
of Brussels and the British tourists began to do what they could
for the wounded. The women became nurses, the men listened to
soldiers' last requests, recorded their conversations and promised
to contact their wives and parents.

Fourteen miles southeast of Brussels, General Grouchy found
the Prussian defense very stubborn. Thielemann with his corps
was doing all he could to block Grouchy's attack. Although outnumbered almost three to one, the Prussian general had an excellent defensive position. That stream which Blücher's chief of
staff had selected as an obstacle in front of the French was indeed

proving an ocean to those who had to cross it under fire. Although the French were gradually pushing back the Prussians, the heavy fighting which he knew was continuing at Mont St. Jean disturbed Grouchy. The marshal pondered the situation. Napoleon was deeply engaged. Here he was miles away, with a battle of his own, and he must have wondered at this moment if he had been correct in refusing to march to the sound of Napoleon's guns when his officers had begged him to. He did not know how strong the Prussians were. Did he face a third, a half, or even more of Blücher's army?

He held Napoleon's latest message in his hands. It was marked 1:30 P.M., and here it was nearing evening. In the beginning the words did not seem particularly desperate. Grouchy was instructed to keep drawing nearer to Napoleon and to make sure that no Prussian corps forced itself between the two French armies. He noticed again that he was to act on his own initiative according to the orders, but it seemed clear enough that he was to attack any Prussian troops who threatened Napoleon's right flank. Then he read the postscript which was attached to the message. It pointed out that Bülow of the Prussian army was about to attack Napoleon's right flank. It went on to say that they could at 1:30 P.M. make out part of Bülow's corps and then the last sentence of the message glared at him: "Therefore, do not lose a minute to draw near to us and crush Bülow, whom you will catch in the very act."

Grouchy, after receiving the message, had sent troops to seize a bridge which was on the route to the great rumbling in the west, but it too was defended by Prussians. To wheel his entire army around, to disengage from the Prussians at this point, seemed madness. There was nothing to do but drive them back and then try to move toward Napoleon, although some units which had not yet been committed were ordered to find a way westward.

The sun which had been sheltered most of the day now broke through the clouds over the Waterloo battlefield. At 8:36 P.M. it would start its plunge behind the little village of Braine-l'Alleud. Its rays tried to pierce huge clouds of smoke that flowed like a foggy sea across the shallow valley. In this smoke, which the sun had just turned to a golden haze, Napoleon was organizing his attack by the Imperial Guard. He dashed up on his horse and the cheers of *"Vive l'Empereur!"* were wild, delirious! In the British line the warning that the Old Guard was about to attack sped to all corners of the field. "Let the bloody bastards come!" shouted the sergeants, who had seen half of their companies die. Few—only a handful—of the British had ever seen the Old Guard in action. They had fought for years in Spain and Portugal against the French but the Guard was rarely used there. It was always kept near the Emperor. Stubborn English and Scottish soldiers, despite the horrible carnage around them, welcomed the charge. It would mean that the battle would soon end one way or the other and that they, as professionals, would meet the most highly praised soldiers in the world.

As the Guard prepared to strike, the whole French line was to continue its support—the attack against the right, the envelopment of Hougoumont which again was burning furiously, and from La Haye Sainte the storm of fire was to be continued. The artillerymen were told to exert themselves to the utmost. They had fought so hard, but now it would soon end. Victory would come with the Guard. The British had strengthened the center, but there were still great patches of weakness, and the heaviest artillery assault of the day began to chew out even greater gaps.

Up and down the French lines the word spread, *"C'est le Garde! C'est le Garde!"* Every French soldier on the field knew that the climax was here. It would be five battalions of the Guard which would advance. But even now at this desperate moment Napoleon was holding back. He held the rest of the Imperial Guard in reserve, the best of his finest, the old Imperial Guard. The attacking Guard marched as if on parade, in even, disciplined ranks. They moved with professional élan, with sureness but not haste.

At this very moment, Prussian troops, Zieten's corps, were moving up on Wellington's immediate left. Southeastward, the battle on the French right flank still raged. Napoleon summoned officers to his side. He spread the word that Grouchy with his 30,000 had just arrived on the field. Napoleon reasoned this false message would give every French soldier who heard it enough confidence to carry the attack. It would not matter when the word was proved untrue after the battle, since who would wonder about it in the glory of success? Now this word echoed up and down the French lines. Ney heard it, too, and sent officers to tell the soldiers that Grouchy is here. *"Vive l'Empereur! Soldats, voilà Grouchy!"*

The Guard's band struck up. The sound was triumphant. The *Carousel* must surely be a harbinger of victory. The advance began 600 yards from the British lines. Napoleon himself was at the head of his troops. The cavalcade marched past the wounded and dead. The cries of *"Vive l'Empereur!"* were deafening as the wounded raised themselves to wave their swords and bayonets. The assault swelled as some of the wounded fell in behind the Guard. Troops of the Horse Guard were in support. Broken squadrons of cuirassiers joined in. Artillery from the Guard was brought up. Leading the advance, Napoleon stopped to correct a gun which was off target.

Ensign Leeke, Sergeant Wheeler and all who had stood so long waited for the attack. For hours now they had endured so much, and under bombardment they developed an eagerness to grapple with the enemy, to meet him face to face, to slaughter or be slaughtered in hand-to-hand combat. The Guard was now within 400 yards of the English lines. It was here that Napoleon dismounted and stepped behind a small knoll which afforded some shelter from the heavy fire. The Guard was turned over to Ney, and Napoleon began to assemble a reserve. As his men marched past they acclaimed Napoleon with their cheers, but some of them wondered why he himself was not leading them in this final assault. So many times in the twilight hour of a long battle the Emperor had dashed with them into the muzzles of the enemy's guns. He had told them many times that no bullet could be molded which could kill him. Many Guardsmen swore he could not be wounded. In the past when he had been hit, he had his wounds dressed in secret so his soldiers would not know.

Ney was leading them now, mounted on his fifth horse of the day. Few could recognize him as a marshal of France. His uniform was torn and stained. Buttons dangled from uprooted thread. The Guard was formed in two attacking columns and Ney took them on what seemed like a very long route across the broken ground encumbered by thousands of bodies. They moved more to the left. On Wellington's right wing a brigade of Dutch-Belgian guns was brought up and they began to pour a heavy fire into the advancing columns. Every gun still in service on Wellington's right began to fire. They "played into the exposed long flank of the Imperial column with double charges of round, canister, case ... the French ranks ... appeared to wave like high-standing corn blown by sudden gusts of wind ..." [2]

The British could hear the Guard's drummers. They were beating the *pas de charge*. The shouts of *"Vive l'Empereur!"* rose above the clamor. Ensign Leeke heard it. To him it sounded like "... the rum dum, the rum dum, the rum dummadum, dum, dum, *Vive l'Empereur!"* [3] He heard it over and over. Lieutenant Colonel Sir John Colborne, an officer of excellent professional reputation, heard it. At this moment he was thinking of some maneuver his 52nd regiment could make to silence the drums and kill the Guard forever. Wellington's thousands heard the beat. Wellington was now with his Foot Guards who had been brought back a little from the right wing and were lying down because of the galling fire. But he remained mounted on Copenhagen. Near him was one of the few aides who had not been killed or wounded. It was "Fat" Hill on the same huge horse.

Ney and the Guard came on. The marshal saw General Friant wounded at his side. Ney's horse stumbled. It had been struck and was dying, and the marshal was on the ground. He was untouched. He jumped to his feet, waved his sword, and led the attack on foot. Scores were dying, but the Guard's enthusiasm held. More officers went down. General Michel was killed. The main artillery support from the French lines now stopped. The Guard was getting close to the ridge. The skirmishers in the vanguard of the assault fanned out to harass the British lines. But many of them were struck by artillery fire.

The truth of these climactic moments was lost forever as part of the Imperial Guard struggled to the summit of the bloody ridge. Facts died as men died. Acts of bravery were misinterpreted as acts of cowardice. Propellants of raw, stark fear which seemed to drive men during these seconds were interpreted as gallantry. Some men were not conscious of whether they were retreating or advancing. Some soldiers were carried on by the momentum in one direction or another. The thrust was too violent, too irregular to measure. It was a bomb of inexactness. In the melee only a few splinters of truth survived.

Hope, it appeared, still stood with the Old Guard. It seemed that the charge was on the verge of momentous success. Some of the Guard's units, although severely weakened, clashed with reinforcements Wellington had scraped together from other parts of the line. It appeared that the British were collapsing. Some of the old bearskins found themselves around deserted guns, but kept their own accompanying batteries firing. British regiments maneuvered to save themselves from the Guard's artillery, or were in retreat. Their men never really knew. The movement got out of hand. There was screaming, sobbing, cursing in the ranks of the 30th and 73rd British regiments. As they moved, they collided with the 33rd and 69th regiments who were also under intense pressure by the French. For a brief moment all four units seemed like a disorganized, angry, hysterical mob. Some British officers saw Chassé's Dutch-Belgians fighting valiantly. Others saw many of these soldiers fleeing, and Vivian's and Vandeleur's cavalry swore that they had to block a headlong retreat. A British officer shook a young drummer to make him beat assembly. At another point along the line Imperial Guardsmen could see nothing but a few mounted British officers. One of them was Wellington. Had they trumphed? Many old bearskins thought they had. They were charging more swiftly now. They were at the summit. The exact words were lost. Some heard Wellington say to Maj. Gen. Peregrine Maitland, commander of a brigade of British Guards, "Now, Maitland, now is your chance!" Others swore he said, "Up Guards and at 'em!" The French were within just a few feet of where the British Guards were lying down. The British sprang to their feet and fell into a compact line. It seemed to their enemies that they had come from nowhere. For one split second the French paused. There was an angry burst from what had been open ground just a minute before. Hundreds fell.

The Guard wavered. Officers were down. Heavy volleys staggered the column. Some artillery pieces which had not been bypassed in the assault continued a steady fire of grape. The Guard seemed paralyzed, but did not retreat. Now at least 500 were dead or wounded. Officers tried to scream their commands over the fury. Some of the old bearskins heard and tried to deploy, seeking a weaker front in which to advance. But they were caught in a crossfire. More and more fell. Some of the Guardsmen fired over the heads of their comrades and the column still held.

Wellington watched the French. Bewilderment and confusion crossed their ranks. Instantly Wellington ordered his own Guards to charge. There was a loud cheer and the British brigade swarmed across the ridge directly at the shattered column. Napoleon's Guardsmen could not believe what they or their comrades were doing. They were throwing down their muskets, loosening their knapsacks in order to hasten their retreat. They were rolling down the hill. Wounded officers, although writhing in pain, tried desperately to stop the rout.

The British continued their charge for some yards. After receiving the fury of French artillery for eight hours, the advance was exhilarating. The men did not want to stop. Their officers could now see a second column of the Imperial Guard. It had paid no attention whatsoever to the destruction of the first column. Their drummers were beating the charge. Ney had disappeared into the smoke at the summit of the British-held ridge. He then had been thrown back like the rest of the Guardsmen. He managed to rally a few soldiers from the first column, and then had taken his place at the head of the second charge.

Wellington's own Guard was now in peril. It could be easily outflanked and destroyed in minutes. There were shouts for it to re-form. Some officer thought that it was under cavalry attack and a loud order of "Form square!" was heard. This was an invitation to disaster. A square could be quickly overcome by advancing infantry. There was a flood of confused orders, and Wellington's Guards stampeded to the rear. But when they reached the summit they obeyed instantly the stout command, "Halt! Front! Form up!"

Wellington noticed the confusion among the survivors of the 30th and 73rd regiments. He ordered Maj. Dawson Kelly, one of his staff, to "see what's wrong there." Kelly rode to find their commander, Halkett. As he was about to speak to the colonel, Kelly saw Halkett fall from a serious wound. A ball had just passed through the colonel's mouth. The commander of the 33rd regiment, Lt. Col. William Keith Elphinstone, ran up. At this moment the two regiments were still in a morass of mangled bodies. Some had panicked and were rushing to the rear. Officers and men who tried to stop them were carried along in the mob, with some of them pressed so compactly in the current of bodies that they were moved for a number of yards without touching the ground. Lieutenant Macready was in the mob. There was nothing he could do to stem the tide. Some seconds before, a close friend who was in agony from a number of wounds had rammed Macready and screamed and screamed, "Is it deep, Mac? Is it deep?" [4]

A sergeant from the 73rd ran up to Kelly saying that the regiment had no commander since all of the officers were dead or wounded. This was Kelly's old regiment and he told the sergeant that he would take command himself. Numerous soldiers from the 73rd heard Kelly's decision and they sent up a tremendous cheer. Lieutenant Macready heard the roar. So did everybody in the 30th regiment. Its effect was spectacular. Everyone instantly stopped and joined the cheers. The crisis for the two regiments was over. Order was quickly restored.

The second column of the Imperial Guard was taking the same punishment that had been suffered by the first. In parade formation, but with skirmishers out, it continued to march through everything that the British could give it. Many survivors of the first column had rallied and were again storming up the hill. The entire battlefield shook, with the Prussians continuing their relentless pressure on the French right and encircling to the French rear. French attacks were still maintained across the face of Wellington's line. The second column of the Guard continued to advance, but "guns fell with ruinous precision upon the dense mass and made them suffer dreadfully: but the men who had often in a doubtful field wrested victory from the . . . foe advanced firmly, their front and flank, as usual, covered by . . . numerous daring skirmishers, the smoke of whose rattling fire concealed at times the advance of the column." [5]

British fire was so severe that French cuirassiers were ordered to charge the guns. They managed to reach a battery and drive back cannoneers who dove into the infantry. A British infantry brigade threatened the attackers and then a squadron of the 23rd British light dragoons was ordered to counter-charge. Their captain had been badly hurt and the command was led by Lt. John Banner, who hit the cuirassiers in the flank and forced them back upon the French infantry. The 23rd was then routed and when the troopers appeared at the British lines they received fire from their own infantry who mistook them for French.

Major General Frederick Adams' brigade, which had been sheltered a little to the rear from the artillery, had been brought directly into the line. The attacking Guards came up in such a way that Adams' brigade, which included Ensign Leeke's regiment, the 52nd, was on the French left. The regiment's commander, Lieutenant Colonel Colborne, watched the charge. He had a plan. It was daring, it could only be executed with great risk not only to his troops but to his whole military career. Fighting in Spain, he had gained a reputation for innovation, but he had done nothing compared to what he planned now. On his left were the British Guard. It appeared that they would take the main attack. If he could wheel his regiment outside the line he would be able to fire directly on the nearest flank of the Old Guard. The destructive fire coming from the British troops directly to the front of the advancing French coupled with the flanking fire from the wheeling 52nd would be sure to destroy the charging enemy. At least that was his hope. First he would wheel the left company of the 52nd to its direct left. It could swing as a gate opens and then stand on the flank of the advancing troops.

The movement had to be fast and precise. Any disorder at all and there could easily be a huge gap opened for the French to plunge through. All they would have to do was just veer a little more to their left.

Colborne explained his orders to his lieutenants. It was about time to act. The Guard was approaching through heavy smoke. Colborne yelled out his command. The left company pivoted with drill field precision. The rest of the regiment began to form up on the front company. Colborne had no orders for this action. It was entirely on his own responsibility. Adams, the brigade commander, rode up quickly and asked what Colborne was doing. Over the roar of musketry Colborne pointed to the French and yelled "To make that column feel our fire." [6] Adams approved of the maneuver so completely that he dashed off to bring up another regiment in support. Through the smoke the vanguard of the advancing French had almost reached the top of the ridge. And then suddenly on their flank they saw the 52nd regiment. The shock of seeing their flank imperiled shook the whole column. For a moment it froze. But seconds later the Imperial Guard recovered. It wheeled some of its troops around and opened a heavy fire against Colborne's regiment. Colborne retaliated with a murderous volley. Other regiments, other units including part of the 95th regiment and the 71st regiment, had been brought up in support. They threw in volley after volley. Colborne's maneuver must be shattering or it would fail. He screamed "Charge, charge!" and the 52nd flew at the Guard with their bayonets.

The Guard quivered. The surprise of seeing troops on its flank, the heavy fire pouring in from the front and the side were too much, and now the British charge. The column began to disintegrate, but slowly, very slowly. To one soldier it seemed that the Guard fell like a giant oak. For a long time it had taken a brutal axing and then it wavered, leaned and plunged. Many officers and men would not retreat. They were rooted in the earth like massive stumps. They died as men die before a firing squad, taking fusillades across their bodies. But most of the column broke in disorder.

"Le Garde recule!" * was a shout of doom. Troops on the right screamed it and pointed in disbelief to the Imperial Guardsmen as they streaked away. French regiments on the left saw them. There was panic. It began with the first shouts and then snowballed into unbelievable proportions. There were still units on the field who had not seen the debacle. But they were like mounds of dry sand in front of a raging torrent. For the moment they kept up the heavy fire against the British. The word triggered a heavy retreat by the French troops engaged with the Prussians who had just joined Wellington's left flank. They flew in disorder. As Napoleon watched from La Haye Sainte he could see his whole empire cascading down the heights, for it was the Guard which held his last measure of power.

It was 8:30 P.M., Sunday, June 18, 1815. Napoleon tried to save his army. He was everywhere, organizing the last reserve of the Imperial Guard, forming it into squares, and trying to use it as a rallying point for his men.

Part of Wellington's troops had continued to pour down the

* The Guard retreats.

hill after the French. The Duke, although realizing French morale was shattering like crystal, felt that the broken regiments might still rally. He hurriedly contacted Vivian and ordered him to charge with his 10th and 18th Hussars. They were to hit in and around La Belle Alliance where Napoleon was now standing with his Imperial Guard. Vivian maneuvered his squadrons through and around British infantry who were still taking heavy fire from the French lines.

Private John Marshall of the 10th heard the bugle sound the advance. He said a short prayer, asking that his life be saved for his wife and children and begging that he would be given strength and courage. Vivian's brigade charged in half-squadrons.

Napoleon knew there was little chance to save his army. He had just received word that Papelotte had fallen, that Plancenoit had been recaptured, and that most of his Young Guard there and the two battalions of the Old Guard were fighting to the end, with the wounded and dying being butchered by Prussian infantry.

There were no plans for retreat. Victory was essential for the Empire. To entertain retreat would have been an open appraisal of disaster. So no plans had been made, and the frantic efforts to manage a retreat at the eleventh hour were failing. Napoleon stood inside a square with his Old Guard as it marched to the rear. Discipline in the French army was dissolving. But it still remained with the last reserve.

Vivian ordered his 10th Hussars in first. Private Marshall rode as fast as his horse would go. He cheered loudly and so did everyone around him. Fleeing infantrymen had no opportunity to protect themselves. Many of them begged to be taken prisoner but the charge was so furious that cavalrymen were seen first cutting one down on the right and then split seconds later, one on the left. The 10th engaged cuirassiers, lancers and some artillerymen in forward gun positions. They found that Napoleon's reserve of squares could not be broken. Vivian, now on his way to charge with the 18th, had almost been killed by a cuirassier, but he watched the Frenchman slip from the saddle. Vivian's orderly who rode with his general had managed to kill the cuirassier with a quick thrust. Units of cuirassiers were rallying. Nearby, cavalry of the King's German Legion was engaged.

Wellington saw the bright flashes of Bülow's guns in the distance. He had a report that the French were deserting some parts of the field. One massive charge might destroy or trap the entire French army. Uxbridge was near the Duke. At that moment the cavalry commander was badly hit. "My God, sir! I have lost my leg!" Uxbridge said. The Duke, without a twinge of emotion, replied, "By God, sir, you have!"

As the 10th continued to slash its way through broken infantry, Vivian was organizing a charge by his 18th. In a loud voice he addressed his cavalrymen who were sparkling with confidence. "Eighteenth, you will follow me," Vivian said.[7] Sergeant Major Jeffs yelled "By Jesus, General, anywhere—to hell—if you will lead us." [8] *

The charge was sounded—an explosion of cheers! The men galloped forward. Just as the attack started a French artillery battery came across their front at a gallop. The artillerymen and the drivers were hopelessly lost, dying on horseback, at the gun and at the limber. In another moment the 18th was among the enemy cavalry, cuirassiers, lancers and then the Imperial Guard. Squares of the Old Guard still stood, but with every disciplined step backward, Imperial Guardsmen staggered from the squares. The reserve was melting away. But Napoleon had rallied many an army on desperate fields.

Sergeant John Taylor had made a cut at the head of a cuirassier. The French horseman, still supremely confident, laughed at Taylor's attempt and swung his sword at the sergeant. This was parried and Taylor thrust again. This time the sergeant's blade was rammed into the mouth of the cuirassier and he rolled from his horse.

Wellington saw the effects of his cavalry charge. Everybody in the line who could, turned to watch him at this instant. He collapsed his telescope, stood in the stirrups and waved his hat in the air to signal a general advance. Cheers rang out around him. They were swept up with volleys of cheers on the right and left. They began to thunder up and down the line like gunfire. Every unit that heard joined in, and in a minute there was a tumult of cheering from the far right which stretched west of Hougou-

* The *Memoirs of the 18th* (*Princess of Wales' Own*) *Hussars* reports that the sergeant said: "By Jagus, General, anywhere—to hell—if you lead us."

mont to the far left which joined the Prussians. Down the ridge streamed all of Wellington's remaining infantry and cavalry that could move.

Grant's cavalry brigade on the right hurried its charge. Lieutenant General Lord Hill, commander of the Second Corps, yelled to the 13th Hussars, "Now 13th, come on!" [9] Lt. William Turner of the 13th had lost his black mare to enemy fire, but now he was on a borrowed mount and he sped forward "over men and horses who lay in heaps . . ." [10] A little east of the Brussels road the Gordon Highlanders charged, their pipes screeching. They tore into a French regiment which stood. They hit it with bayonet, sword, dirk and fist. The enemy crumbled. The 79th Highlanders, the Camerons, had been shot to pieces. Lt. Alexander Cameron was the ranking officer still on his feet. He heard the cheers reverberating and then crashing like a mighty salvo. Waving his sword, he called for the Camerons to attack, "and with loud cheers the debris of the regiment pressed forward." [11] The ranking line officer in the 2nd battalion of the 73rd Highlanders was Lt. Robert Stewart. His colonel and major were wounded. All of the captains had been hit. Three were wounded. Two were dead, John M. Kennedy and Alexander Robertson. Out of the ten lieutenants in the battalion, only three stood. Eight of the ten ensigns were either dead or wounded. Most of the sergeants and corporals were dead or wounded. The rank and file had been badly mauled. Sergeant Morris was still alive to answer the command to charge. The old captain who had shouted over and over, "Tom, Tom, here comes the cavalry!" was dead. He had been saturated with fear, but he had stood to the last. Lieutenant Stewart led his tattered battalion down the hill at a dead run. Maj. Thomas Walker Chambers of the 30th had seen all his superior officers wounded. He had been in charge of the 2nd battalion for some hours now, and when the cheers came he swept his command into the attack.

There had been heavy fire from the French line, even after the Imperial Guard had been repulsed. But now as the men stormed down the hill the fire seemed to stop suddenly and completely.

La Haye Sainte had been abandoned by the French. The area around Hougoumont was being deserted by Napoleon's troops. Legros, the towering French officer who had led one assault after another, his huge body wounded a dozen times, was lying dead in the courtyard with hundreds of his comrades. The whole French army was in flight. British cavalry had reached French artillery through the spray and geysers of a final cannonade. Artillerymen flew from their guns and were sabred, stuck, pierced and slaughtered. The guns were deserted except for the dead. All discipline in the great French army evaporated except in the Imperial Guard. General Pelet with his Chasseurs of the Guard was surrounded by Prussians on the far right of the field. Pelet halted his men on a small knoll. He shouted, *"A moi, chasseurs! Sauvons l'aigle, ou mourons autor d'elle."* [12] (Rally around me, chasseurs! Let us save the eagle or die around it!) The chasseurs rallied. They cut a path through the Prussians to reach what looked like a line of retreat.

The Old Guard Napoleon had organized near La Haye Sainte was being destroyed. But it still held its eagles as it retreated in square. Artillery was brought up at point-blank range to destroy it. Infantry and cavalry tried to storm through the rents, but the Old Guard closed up, finally with so few men left that the squares were abandoned for thin lines of triangles. These units of the Old Guard found themselves at La Belle Alliance. British officers begged the depleted corps to surrender. Hardly a man stood without a wound. Finally it was mangled into almost nothing. Several Guardsmen now stood around their colors, pledging death before the eagles could be swept from them. General Cambronne answered the British with one word: *"Merde!"* The massacre continued. The general was bleeding. He collapsed. A bullet had smashed into his head.

When Napoleon had seen that the Guard he had organized would soon be under furious assault, he, with a few of his aides, had dashed down the road to organize the last of the Imperial Guard. He had just three battalions left. Arriving at the Rossomme farm where he had made his headquarters for a good part of the day, he formed these last battalions. In another desperate flow of orders he tried to stop the rout. At one point he retreated into a square which was coming under fire. He found that he could not form his army here, and again galloped down the road with a thinning suite of aides and attendants.

Before him, behind him, and around him was the broken army.

The cavalry had thrown off its armor. The infantry had thrown away their muskets. The artillery had cut the traces and fled on horseback. Everywhere was a fearful scream of *"Sauve-qui-peut!"* (Every man for himself!) Terror was on every face. Every arm and unit were mixed. The wounded were trampled to death. Brave men, sobbing in defeat, committed suicide. The race was impeded by overturned supply wagons, spilled ammunition carts, collapsing surgeons' tents, and by the horde of civilians who always accompanied the French army—prostitutes, cantinières, burial teams. Officers, their swords broken, blood streaming from their wounds, tried to form small units, but they were knocked to the ground by the torrent. Ney stood with a sword in hand, grabbing soldiers who spun to shake loose. He was caught up in a mass of fugitives. They could no longer hear an officer. They no longer could hear a marshal of France. Blücher urged his men on. He threw in everything he had. Some of his cavalry hit to the rear and caught the refugees head on.

The Highlanders had reached the French guns. With wild cheers and a wilder clamor from their pipes they wheeled the guns around. They touched matches to everything that could be fired—grape, ball, canister, shells, carcass. The hail of iron and incendiaries drenched the swarming masses. The unexpected bombardment killed cuirassiers, hussars, infantry, grenadiers, civilians; blew up wagons, tumbrils, coaches and carts; exploded ammunition dumps.

The last of the Old Guard covered Napoleon's retreat. He headed south along the same way he had come just a few days before. Here and there he stopped to reorganize his army. It hadn't been possible to restore any order. The magic he had was gone. But he would not stop trying. He rode on to organize one last-ditch defense.

Major Chambers was dead. He had led the 30th through the little valley. The French were fleeing and he had stopped to organize his troops. Officers gathered in small groups to share their triumph. Major Chambers was talking about his expected promotion to lieutenant colonel when some desultory firing broke out. A lieutenant in the group volunteered to find out what was happening. After walking a few feet, the junior officer turned around to see the major following him. There was a sharp whistling noise. The major clasped his breast and died. He was one of the last British officers killed in action at Waterloo.

It was dark now. Lieutenant Jackson rode forward with the victorious army. He crossed the spot where "hundreds of French muskets . . . lay in quite regular order as if they had been put down by command." [13] He saw burning farm buildings, the "lurid glare defining the outlines of abandoned guns." [14] He saw a dead Inniskillen [sic] hussar ". . . whose hands were joined and elevated above his breast, as if he had expired in the act of prayer." [15]

It was nearing 9:30 P.M. Wellington had advanced with his men, and had gone as far as the Rossomme farm. Nearby there had been a sharp duel between British and Prussian cavalry—a blunder committed in the last impetuous moments. Men from both sides had died needlessly, believing that they had fought the French. The Duke ordered his units off the road to make way for the Prussian pursuit. His army was too exhausted to do any more.

Near La Belle Alliance he saw the old man riding under a pale moon. Wellington pressed Copenhagen forward to grasp old Blücher's hand. Nearby a Prussian band played "God Save the King."

Blücher had hordes of troops who had reached the field barely 20 minutes before the final convulsion. Wellington told the old man that the British were too exhausted to do any more. They could not move out tonight. "Leave that to me," said the old Prussian. "I will send every man and horse after the enemy."

Chapter Sixteen

On Flanders Fields

THE night was cool. Some said there was a frost, very rare for June. But the coolness could not help the parched throats of wounded and dying. British officers, so many of them wounded, so many utterly exhausted, managed to pick up all the canteens they could carry to ride into Waterloo for water. There was never enough. Often the wells were fouled and it was necessary to ride as far as Braine-l'Alleud for a supply. And when an officer had finally come back and moved from man to man, he would feel that now he could rest. But then there would be a feeble cry for water just a few feet away.

Wellington had ordered ambulances to move the wounded, and in firm tones insisted that the job must continue until all were carried from the field. But it was impossible to reach even a small percentage of the men this night. The field which had seemed so very small during the day took on a different aspect. The darkness seemed to magnify everything. The area was massive, there were too few carts, and the roads were jammed.

Waterloo and all the little villages were littered with wounded who had been brought in earlier in the day. The hospitals were scenes of horror. Exhausted doctors handled one case after another. They spoke softly to their attendants, ordering them to stoke fires under vats of boiling oil and pitch. The wounded soldier had waited so long for attention, and now he dreaded it. Wounds of the hemorrhaging amputees were sealed with an application of the bubbling cautery from the vats. Screams tore at the heart of even the toughest soldier.

In a woman's camp near Waterloo, where the wives and children of British soldiers were sheltered during the battle, five-year-old Elizabeth Gale was cutting up lint for bandages. Her father, Daniel, had been mortally wounded. A four-year-old, Barbara, whose father, a color sergeant in the 3rd battalion, Rifle Brigade, was slowly dying, rode in a wagon over the field that night.

It was nearing 10:00 P.M. when Wellington left Blücher. He started a slow ride back to Waterloo with a few of his aides. They were forced to ride through part of the field because the road was blocked with moving troops and the mess of broken guns and carts. He crossed an area clogged with dead. There were the awful groans of the wounded, compressed under writhing horses and the heavy burden of the dead. Copenhagen made numerous starts as he moved through the area. Wellington did not talk to any of his officers. No one felt like saying a word. The light from the moon touched his face. It seemed that tears were glistening on his cheek.

The thunder had moved south. Some British cavalry had pursued the French for three miles or more, and were returning to Waterloo. Some of the young men were still intoxicated by success and whacked one another on the back like schoolboys returning from a successful cricket game.

The Prussian onslaught was still sweeping through Flanders. Blücher was keeping his word. What was left of Napoleon's army was being mercilessly pursued. Many of the French had made up their minds that to surrender was to die. They had seen Blücher's cavalry cut down their comrades when they attempted to show the white flag. The masses poured down the Charleroi road, the first part of the journey to France. On their heels came the cavalry, lusting in conquest. There was a teasing, diabolical satisfaction which the pursuers experienced in the kill. Frenchmen died under Prussian sabres as flies under swatters.

French cavalrymen took wide detours and had hopes of getting to France. But for infantrymen, the Prussian drums which often meant death were just a few beats away. At Genappe where there had been the sharp cavalry clash just two days before, some officers and a few infantry of the line tried a last defense. They found some cannons which had been following the army during the Emperor's advance. They hurried them into position and barricaded the main street with overturned carts, limbers and wagons. But these were not the same brave men who had fought at Waterloo. Courage had been siphoned away. When the Prussians wheeled up artillery pieces and started a bombardment, the same men who had pledged to make this last desperate stand fled in disorder. This was the last gasp of Napoleon's army in Flanders. The floodgates were opened for the Prussians. The fugitives fled to forests, paths, fields. Some of the wounded crawled into deserted houses, barns and sheds. The Prussians roamed everywhere. They bludgeoned the wounded who lay in bed. They hurled torches into barns and any building where they thought the French had holed up. The streams floated bodies. Many in their rush to escape had been forced off narrow bridges or had plunged into streams and were carried away by the current.

Napoleon found his coach at Genappe, the imperial Berlin with all the trappings of majesty, bejeweled and glittering with gold. But the terrible drums! The Prussian cavalry howled. Napoleon barely had time to jump from his coach and mount a horse before the enemy seized the whole area. There were moments when it seemed that Napoleon would surely be taken. Some of his officers were sorry that he had not died in battle. This was humiliation, this was despair. But if Napoleon was captured to be paraded and finally garroted, the pride of France would shriek forever. The Emperor's officers, plagued by this thought, used their swords to knock a way through the maelstrom.

Blücher arrived in Genappe. A room was found for him in Le Roi d'Espagne. This was the same inn where Wellington had stayed on the night of the 16th, where Jérôme had stayed on the night of the 17th. The old man accorded captured French officers respect, seeing that their wounds were treated and making sure they had food. But these small considerations were lost in the raging brutality that was going on all around him.

The tough old Prussian didn't forget Grouchy. The French marshal had won a minor victory over the Prussians at Wavre, but it came too late, and he had been too far away. Blücher made plans to trap him, sending a corps to march in Grouchy's direction at once.

The Prussian pursuit of Napoleon and his demoralized soldiers continued. Châteaux, mansions, houses, cottages and hovels were sacked of anything the soldiers considered useful. The cognac and wine trains in Napoleon's army were overrun. What the Prussians could not drink they destroyed, and Flanders flowed with wine. Wanton destruction had now become part of their carnival. They smashed windows, demolished statuary and china, ripped furniture, burned books and began throwing both wounded and dead into the wells.

Some of the Emperor's train had lost him. Among them were his secretaries and servants. There were rumors he was dead, rumors he had been captured. Everywhere his aides turned they saw the evidence of a great rout. One of them saw two ambulances which had overturned. Help was secured and the ambulances righted. Most of the wounded inside had smothered. Finally Napoleon arrived at the two-day-old battlefield of Quatre Bras. The stench of the dead was overpowering. Marauding peasants had stripped the corpses of everything.

Napoleon rested for a little at Quatre Bras. He sent a message to Grouchy telling him of the defeat. He dictated other notes for a few intact units which had not been engaged at Waterloo. Then, once again, he continued the long trip back. The French outnumbered their tormentors. If there had not been panic they could have stood. But this was no longer an army. Commands could not be heard. The mob was deaf to everything but the drums.

Private Gaertner had survived. He was exhausted, hungry, in pain from a number of bruises. But he had no serious wounds. He believed now that it was his mother who had saved him. He would not be alive if it had not been for her long vigil and her prayers to Saint Anthony. Old Guardsman Bartholomew Ribault was alive. He had seen his unit almost destroyed, and when it seemed there were not enough men to fight an organized action they worked a way around the fugitives. The Guardsmen still kept their arms and maintained some discipline. The Prussians had learned that death still stood with the Guard. There was less risk following the main stream of fugitives. Colonel Lehmanowsky had been with Ney. The colonel had twenty-three years in the army, but he had never seen a marshal of France in tears. He turned his head. He knew his commander would not want to be seen.

The little boy who had watched the battle from his tree had long since returned home. He had seen the last desperate charges and had finally come down from his perch. He had not been hurt. All around him were men who had died. He would never see anything like this again. He stood the heavy scolding at home without too much complaint. His parents had been out of their minds most of the day.

The woman who cowered so long in the attic of her cottage climbed down. The cow, pigs, chickens, ducks which she had tried so hard to save were all gone. The house was filled with wounded. She should have left with her husband when he begged her to go. But it was up to her to tell him that she had been wrong. It was getting very late and he hadn't returned.

The young girl who had seen the fighting at Hougoumont was exhausted from running across the fields. She had crept into a small forest near the French lines. At dusk she had heard hoofbeats and had seen a man riding slowly on a grey horse as if he were in a trance.*

In Waterloo, Father Bouvrie was doing what he could for the dying. That morning he had canceled both the 7:30 and 10:00 A.M. Masses because his parishioners were all hiding. He must have wondered when was the last time the ancient village had spent Sunday without a Mass.

Wellington went from house to house visiting the wounded and dying. Before the battle, orderlies had chalked billet doors with the names of his officers. Now the billets were morgues and hospitals. Later, Wellington took a lonely meal with just one member of his staff. Captured French generals who had expected to dine with him, according to the custom of war, were coolly rebuffed. The Duke ate in silence, but finally said, "Thank God! I have met him."

There were no more fusillades or cannonades in the little valley south of Mont St. Jean. But occasionally there was a sharp crack of a pistol; a soldier had succeeded in ending his misery, or a looter had killed. These scavengers stalked behind piles of

* Later, friends and relatives told her the man she had seen was Napoleon.

bodies. They preferred to kill silently, and used a sword or knife, but occasionally they were forced during a struggle with one of their wounded victims to fire a pistol. They were soldiers who had temporarily deserted their units. Or they were peasants who could see a rich booty in almost any article that was left on the field. Near what had been the French lines, Lieutenant Colonel Ponsonby was still alive. He had been sabred, pierced with a lance, and had been used as a shield by a young French soldier who had fired over his head. At dusk Prussian cavalry had ridden over him at a full trot, and he was picked up by flying hooves and tumbled over and over again. There had been one act of mercy—a drink of brandy that a French officer had given him hours ago. Ponsonby could not move. Stretched across his legs was a wounded soldier in convulsion, a wound in his side hissing air. Ponsonby couldn't remember how many looting Prussian soldiers had approached him. Several of them stopped to look at him as they passed and one of them went through Ponsonby's pockets although he told him he was a British officer and had already been looted during the battle; earlier a French soldier moving up to the line had robbed him. It was around 11:00 P.M. when Ponsonby saw an English soldier who, he suspected, had been looting, too. Ponsonby shouted for aid. The Britisher pulled off the dying soldier, drew a sword, and prepared to guard the lieutenant colonel for the rest of the night.

On another part of the field, a British officer had regained consciousness but realized that he couldn't see. He rubbed "a mask of congealed blood" from his face.[1] When it was gone he was staring directly into the glassy eyes of a dead officer of the Imperial Guard. Their faces were nearly touching. "A sword-cut had divided the Frenchman's upper lip, and, exposing the teeth, gave to the dead man's countenance a grin so horrible and ghastly . . ." that the officer quickly turned away.[2] He then "made a desperate effort to shake him off . . ."[3] But he found that a horse was stretched across his legs. It was impossible to free himself. He was very cold and thirsty. He tried once more to struggle free, but again it was impossible. He then laid his head upon the ground which was moistened with his own blood and that of the Guardsman. "Just then a voice . . . uttered a feeble supplication for some water."[4] It was a young ensign with a badly injured leg. In another second a man came out of the darkness. He was "dressed in the dark uniform of a Prussian Jäger and armed with a short sword which rifle troops carry..." [5] He approached the ensign, his mind on plunder. There was "the clinking of a purse, and a trinket, a watch or locket glittered in the moonlight..." [6]

The young ensign resisted the looter, but was quickly killed. Then the Prussian moved to examine the dead Guardsman who lay across the body of the wounded British officer. At that moment there was the noise of more plunderers approaching. They were two British infantrymen. The Prussian hid. The British officer asked for the aid of the infantrymen and pointed out the Prussian to them. He was cut down "and ... rolled in the agonies of death beside the unfortunate youth whom but a few minutes before he had so ruthlessly slaughtered." [7] The infantrymen found a musket for the officer, gave him some brandy, and then disappeared.

General Cambronne, who had been left for dead by the retreating Imperial Guard, was still alive. His wound was very serious, probably so serious that the peasants who stripped him of everything believed him dead. Like so many others, he was left naked on the field. The women seemed to be among the worst at scavenging. They moved in small groups and in a few minutes would denude a heap of dead and wounded as if they had plucked a pile of scalded chickens. They did it brutally, tearing clothing from coagulated wounds, and then cackling at the nakedness of the hemorrhaging soldiers. Some of the women carried knives and if a wounded soldier struggled he was killed on the spot.

Lieutenant Jackson found a billet, but when he entered the room he saw a badly wounded French soldier in his bed. After a long search he located other quarters. Anyway, it would have been better if he had gotten drunk instead of trying to sleep. Like so many others that night he went through the whole battle again in a profusion of hideous nightmares. The cavalry would charge and charge and charge. He could never forget the agony of that night.

For so many men the last impressions of the long day were recorded in their minds to be re-played through hours of fitful sleep. They dreamed of priests moving from one dying soldier to another, of anguished women searching the faces of the corpses as they sought their dead husbands. Or could anyone who had seen him ever forget the thirst-crazed Old Guardsman drinking from a basin which had been used to cleanse a wound?

The morning finally came. Wellington had spent half the night writing dispatches and then had ridden into Brussels. Napoleon was nearing France. Blücher was up early to continue the pursuit. Grouchy was becoming more and more anxious about the fate of his Emperor. He had not yet received Napoleon's disastrous report. Sections of Brussels were still confused, with reports mixed on the outcome of the battle. A bright sun magnified every horror on the battlefield while each regiment had officers examining the ground where they had fought so no wounded would be missed. Every effort was made to bring in all the wounded, regardless of nationality, but Wellington's army was forced to take care of its own first, and even now it was impossible to handle all of the British.

Monsieur Hector, the local brewer, had risen very early. He rolled in as many "casks of beer" as his dray could carry and drove to the battlefield.[8] The Scots, many of them severely wounded, nevertheless managed somehow in their agony to drink the whole supply. They never forgot Monsieur Hector. He received grateful letters from them until his death.

The priests were again on the field. The parish priests from Braine-l'Alleud and other nearby villages offered their churches as hospitals. Wellington had asked the townspeople to do all they could for the wounded, and women moved to the field with bandages and water. Acts of kindness and mercy helped erase some soldiers' memories of the brutal peasants. Lieutenant Colonel Ponsonby was found alive, as was General Cambronne. The young officer who had almost been killed by the Prussian was also brought in. Colonel de Lancey lay mortally wounded in a small cottage. Friends were sent to Antwerp to find Mrs. de Lancey who had followed her husband's wishes and left Brussels.

On the western edge of the battlefield toward Braine-l'Alleud, British cavalrymen searching for wounded in a field of rye almost rode over a cat and her six kittens. The cat from Hougoumont sheltered there with her brood, evidently convinced by some instinct that the farm still was no place for her and her kittens. Nor was it. The Hougoumont farm remained one of the most hideous wounds of the battlefield. It was still smoldering with the flesh of soldiers and horses. The cat and her kittens were all safe, but very hungry. The kittens had no problem. The cavalrymen managed to produce some scraps for the mother.

Some time Monday morning the last skeptical Bruxellois was convinced that the allies had indeed won at Waterloo. Waves of panic gradually subsided and when a carload of wounded entered the city there were no longer screams of *"Sauve-qui-peut!"* The city was trying hard to handle the vast number of dying and wounded. The public had been warned by city officials that if the people did not provide what was needed in the way of bedding, mattresses, sheets and linen, these supplies would be confiscated. Finally, a large supply of these materials was piling up at the Hôtel de Ville. All through the city people opened their homes to the soldiers. Some had as many as thirty in their bedrooms, parlors and living rooms. But soldiers could be seen stumbling in the streets from loss of blood. Hundreds of horses had collapsed and were stiffening in death. There was now a fear of pestilence, and British families talked about returning home, but most of them stayed to help. There was much to do. Young ladies long sheltered from any scene of brutality were now moving through areas where the wounded were lying. Servants followed, carrying buckets of drinks which the young ladies ladled out. The Sisters of Mercy were working without let-up. Monsieur Troyans, the lace-maker who enjoyed the heavy patronage of the Britishers during their vacations, closed his plant. He turned his factory into a temporary hospital, and delivered as much linen as he could. His employees were asked to attend the wounded. Although more soldiers from the allied army had been able to make it to Brussels than the French wounded, there was an effort to give the same treatment to all.

The casualties had been high. Wellington's combined losses of killed and wounded were over 15,000 men. The Prussians' total came to over 7,000, and the French had lost at least 25,000 killed and wounded.* This was in addition to the heavy losses at Quatre Bras and Ligny.

Mrs. Deacon found her ensign husband who was recovering from the wound he received at Quatre Bras. Just a little later she gave birth to a girl. She was christened Waterloo Deacon.

* There are no accurate totals of French losses.

By 9:00 A.M., Napoleon had crossed the border. He was now in France and apparently out of danger for at least a few hours. The Emperor was very tired, and it would seem that now he would reconcile himself to the futility of continuing the war. This was not the case. The Emperor moved at once to prepare for another stand against the Prussians and the British. He dictated numerous orders to troops in the back areas. He immediately issued orders to fragments of the army that were swirling along the French border. He dashed off a number of letters. To his brother, Joseph, in Paris, he emphasized that "all is not lost." He talked about rebuilding his forces, including the National Guards, and estimated that he would have thousands ready immediately to bring against the enemy. He spoke of using carriage horses to pull the guns, of a new conscription, of mass levies of troops in the provinces. The Emperor said he had had no word from Grouchy and feared that he had been captured, but that if somehow he had managed to escape, that would give him additional manpower. He wrote with optimism of the armies moving against him, saying that the Prussians "fear the peasantry" and that the Austrians "are slow marchers." But he noted that the "people must help me, not deafen me with advice."

Ahead of Napoleon, in Paris, was waning loyalty. Behind him, his momentous defeat was marked in a thousand different ways. His state papers, torn to pieces by his aides to keep them out of the hands of the Prussians, fluttered over Flanders fields. Much of the Emperor's treasure—priceless diamonds, gold and silver— had been left behind. When the Prussians discovered his train of treasure, word spread to the peasants who fought over leather pouches filled with diamonds and gold and silver coins. Some stole fortunes in minutes. Almost everybody in the struggle got something.

The news of victory had moved to the Belgian coast. On its way it swept into Antwerp at 8:00 A.M., Monday, June 19. Until that moment the city trembled with rumors of a French victory. On Sunday the rain came down in torrents. Shuffling crowds under a canopy of umbrellas waited anxiously for news. Wounded soldiers who had been brought in from Quatre Bras seemed to be everywhere.

Wellington had been beaten, some said. There were the same

cries of horror that had been heard in Brussels. But on Monday morning Miss Charlotte Waldie received unofficial word of the great victory, and so did the waiting throngs. She saw five Highlanders who had been wounded at Quatre Bras. In spite of their bandages ". . . which enveloped their heads, arms, and legs . . ." they were shouting "Victory!" [9] In answer to Miss Waldie's "eager questions," they told her that a courier had just entered the city with word that Wellington "had gained a complete victory . . ." [10] The Scots were now throwing their bonnets into the air and shouting "Boney's beat!" [11] Their tumultuous joy attracted . . . a number of old Flemish women who were extremely curious . . ." [12] One of them grabbed a Highlander and kept insisting that the Scot should in some way communicate with her. But the excited Highlander could not understand Flemish and finally yelled, " 'Hoot, you auld gowk, dinna ye ken that Boney's beat—what, are ye deaf?' " [13]

At Alost, 12 miles nearer the coast than Antwerp, a group was sitting down to dine around noon "at the well-spread Table d'hôte." [14] The news of victory reached the dining room. Down went knives and forks. The plates and dishes were abandoned. "An old fat Belgic gentleman" overturned his soup.[15] Another man "began to caper up and down the room." [16] "A corpulent lady in attempting to articulate . . . was nearly choked . . . with a fishbone; and the demonstrations of joy shown by the rest of the party were not less extravagant." [17]

An agent of the Rothschild banking family had stayed in Brussels. He had gathered the first information available of Wellington's victory and had rushed to the coast. He was far ahead of the official news. In London there had been earlier news of a Wellington defeat, but it hadn't been confirmed. The stock market was nervous. Correct information reaching a speculator could be worth millions. By dawn, June 20, the news reached Nathan Rothschild. "Another man in his position would have sunk his worth into consols.* But this was Nathan Rothschild . . . He did not invest. He sold. He dumped consols. His name was already such that a single substantial move on his part sufficed to bear or bull an issue. Consols fell. Nathan . . . sold and sold. Con-

* Government securities of Great Britain, which were called Consolidated Annuities, or consols.

sols dropped still more. 'Rothschild knows,' the whisper rippled through the 'Change. 'Waterloo is lost.' Nathan kept on selling, his round face motionless and stern, his pudgy fingers depressing the market by tens of thousands of pounds with each sell signal. Consols dived, consols plummeted—until, a split second before it was too late, Nathan suddenly bought a giant parcel for a song. . . ." [18] Consols started to soar.

Major the Hon. Henry Percy, one of the few Wellington aides aside from "Fat" Hill who had not been killed or wounded, carried the official news to London on the night of June 21. With him he took French army flags and two eagles. He also carried a dispatch written by the Duke giving details of the battle. Impatient as anybody would be with such information, he demanded fresh horses and fleet carriages to reach the coast, and then waited anxiously as his ship inched across the Channel. At Dover when he landed again it was fresh horses and fleet coaches and he dashed into London to break the news.

The word of victory flew everywhere. It broke up parties, sent large crowds into the streets singing "God Save the King," and brought out "extras" for one of the few times in the history of the London *Times*. On the front page along with the usual ads the *Times* carried a short story about Wellington's victory which they had gleaned from "a gentleman who left Brussels on Sunday evening . . ." The two inside pages were almost completely devoted to the news of Waterloo and Wellington's dispatch. A partial casualty list of British officers was also included and ran over onto the last page. It is doubtful that the ads in the *Times* had their usual impact.

The victory at Waterloo was the most momentous news in London since Lord Nelson's victory at Trafalgar. The news of Waterloo touched off numerous illuminations, fireworks, bonfires, parades and concerts, as the word spread through England and Scotland on coaches decked with banners and garlands. Trading hours in the stock market saw consols zoom and zoom. The consols Mr. Rothschild had purchased at the depressed market he himself had created went sky high. News of the Waterloo victory had made them soar, and now they were going up, up, up.

Paris knew only of the French victory at Ligny when Napoleon returned to the city on June 21, but the avalanche of disastrous news was right behind him. Parisians had their first hints of defeat when they saw dejected soldiers stumble into the capital. Official Paris knew little more about the rout than the public until the Emperor's ministers, trembling with fear and curiosity, cloistered themselves with him.

The people showed no signs of panic. Although the market fell, it never reached the lows it had made earlier in the year. When Napoleon spoke of yet another last-ditch stand, and the need for more men, more supplies, and more war, official Paris, Ministers, the Chamber of Peers and the Chamber of Deputies were outraged. Some whispered abdication. Some screamed it. Paris and France no longer belonged to the Emperor.

His remaining power was quicksilver slipping from his hands. He still had the broken army, he still had many of the people behind him, but to move ruthlessly against the political juggernaut which was forming against him would mean civil war. It was to the past that the Emperor fled for his final retreat. While men cursed him and Paris wondered what he would finally do, he visited Malmaison. It was Josephine's home where wonderful memories lingered. The past must have greeted him warmly. The pageant of triumphant yesterdays that could parade through his mind was resplendent, perhaps like an endless parade of cheering Old Guardsmen unstained by wounds or defeat.

After shattering emotional scenes and final secret acknowledgment to himself that his authority had perished at Waterloo, he abdicated in favor of his son. This was on June 23rd. The provisional government in Paris which filled the gap from the time of the abdication to the return of King Louis XVIII to the throne decided to capitulate to the allies. The advancing Prussian and British armies encountered some resistance, but by July 6 the French army had retired under government orders and Paris was open to the allies, who triumphantly entered the city on July 7. By July 15 Napoleon, who had hoped to sail to America, found his ports blocked by the British fleet, and surrendered himself to the English. He was now on the *Bellerophon,* and soon would be on his way to St. Helena and final exile.

On that same day, July 15, nearly a month after the battle, visitors to Waterloo were still stunned by what they saw. The aftermath of Napoleon's last battle sickened them. In shallow

graves hundreds of crows and ravens were picking at carrion. De-
composed bodies were everywhere. Thousands of diaries, letters
and book pages fluttered before the wind across the little valley.
Breastplates, muskets, swords, medals were hawked by peasants.
In some corners of the field poppies had started to grow.

Chapter Seventeen

The Years After

Introduction

S O often the story of Waterloo ends with the last shot or in the triumphant procession of the allies through Paris.

All that went on in Paris after Napoleon's first abdication was repeated after his second and final abdication—magnificent parades, decorous parties, the comings and goings of a dozen heads of state, the restoration of Louis XVIII and the relentless advance of shopkeepers' prices. It was all plainly anticlimactic. History had recorded Napoleon's final convulsion at Waterloo.

Yet, in the years after the battle, the legend of Napoleon and the romance of Waterloo made themselves felt generation after generation. It seems that almost anything related to Napoleon or Waterloo took on a fascinating glow.

In this last chapter I have gone some steps beyond the battlefield, but I feel there is no need to present a recital of the anticlimactic allied occupation. Instead, I am concerned with legend, some of the men, and perhaps even some inconsequential events and trivia. But even the trivia fascinates those of us who are caught up in the lure of Napoleon and Waterloo.

*　　*　　*　　*　　*　　*

The alarm sped through the countryside. Around Waterloo, Mont St. Jean, Ligny and in the other little villages there was the sound of sniping. Two divisions of French cavalry maneuvered between Mont St. Jean and Ligny. In the ranks, every man craved revenge for the bitter defeat. Nearby, squadrons of Uhlans galloped. They behaved with remarkable caution. Whenever the French challenged this elite corps it withdrew to the safety of infantry and artillery. On this hot day the atmosphere was chilled with foreboding for these troops. They did not want to engage the French here. For the French the atmosphere seemed charged with victory. They were enchanted with a feeling of invincibility on this field where legions of cuirassiers and Imperial Guardsmen lay, but the Germans would not fight. It was August 20, 1914.

This was the last time that great bodies of horse cavalry were ever to maneuver here. On this day there appeared the same kind of presentiment that visitors have often felt at Waterloo, especially at night while walking through the area where the French maintained their lines until that final moment when everything was lost. There have been stories of mysterious lights flickering near La Belle Alliance. It was here that some of the final reserves of the Old Guard were ruined. The story goes that a dozen Guardsmen, fearing they would lose the eagles in the last struggle, ran to a well and with their banners plunged in to die. Other Guardsmen, seeing their final desperate acts for the Emperor, followed them. These dead soldiers and their eagles were irretrievable. But their spirits are indomitable; hark the lights! so says the legend.

When a wind comes out of the northwest, it is said that sometimes the clear notes of a trumpet can be heard near Caillou, the Emperor's headquarters on the eve of battle. The farm is beautifully preserved and is maintained as a museum. In 1948, Mr. Theo Fleischman, the Belgian historian, became its owner and had it classified an historical monument by royal decree. The house is crowded with memorabilia of the campaign and is the residence of an hospitable caretaker and his wife. In the garden is what looks like a latticed summerhouse. But inside is a jumble of skulls and bones, the contents of a cistern which overflowed with bodies during those dark days after the battle. A passerby may know the story and will tell it. It is said that during the final hour of action, a young French trumpeter died of his wounds near Caillou. He was buried in Caillou's well, but the sounds of his trumpet can never be stilled. The trumpet will call the charge for the Emperor's old soldiers until Judgment Day.

The story that alarmed superstitious peasants in the area concerns the cross of Hougoumont. The château was a complete ruin after the battle and so was the little chapel where wounded British soldiers waited to die. During the fighting the chapel itself caught fire. The walls were scorched, but the flames would only burn to the foot of the wooden cross. Officers who were there verified this strange occurrence, and after the battle, peasants flocked to Hougoumont and seemed insistent on making it a shrine. With succeeding generations the incident was almost forgotten.

One legend that Scots found hard to disbelieve was told by an old piper in the Gordon Highlanders. The men respected their commander, Col. John Cameron, of Fassiefern, Scotland. He had taken them through many difficult campaigns in Spain. He had died from wounds on the evening after the battle of Quatre Bras. But when the Highlanders charged across the field during a crucial point in the battle at Waterloo, the old piper cried out that he saw "Fassiefern," as he was affectionately called, "waving his bonnet in front as of yore." [1]

Sergeant Cotton of the 7th Hussars, who had charged across the field under Grant's command during the last hour at Waterloo, became so fascinated with the campaign that he moved to Mont St. Jean after his discharge. Then, after spending more than fourteen years "as guide and describer of the battle," and interviewing "Waterloo men of every nation" he wrote about the action in *A Voice from Waterloo*. The sources of his book, soldiers revisiting the battlefield, came directly to his Hôtel du Musée, which he ran at Mont St. Jean, so they could arrange for a tour of the field under his guidance, and inspect his "Waterloo Cabinet." This was his museum and it contained battle relics of every description. He interviewed every one of the soldiers, privates as well as generals, about their impressions of the battle. His book is considered a classic.

The sergeant was largely concerned with clearing up misconceptions about the battle. It is regrettable that he did not catalog some of the weird events old soldiers experienced while wandering around the field. There were tales of French veterans in the twilight of a summer evening seeing a ghostly array of cavalry in the direction of Wavre. At night many veterans of both the French and allied armies thought they heard hoofbeats, clanking sabres and incessant groaning coming through the darkness from the little valley. But the aberrations and ghostly events could have been created or at least magnified by a little too much alcohol. Old soldiers on a summer evening would take chairs with comrades on the veranda of one of the modest hotels to gaze across the valley of Mont St. Jean. They would relive the battle until the late hours over much ale, wine or Scotch whisky.

Numerous tales were also told of ghostly events which occurred in London on the night of the great victory. A young bride whose husband fought at Waterloo was at a party in a smart London town house. The affair was gay and very crowded, with the servants extremely busy. There was a knock at the door and the young woman volunteered to answer it. Before her she saw a hussar in the shadows. It appeared that he had been in a terrible battle. His uniform was tattered and covered with mud. She saw a ghastly wound. She extended her hands to help the hussar and then became convinced that she was looking into the face of her husband. At that instant the figure disappeared, and at that instant, it was later determined, her husband was killed at Waterloo.

Sergeant Cotton wanted to lie on the same field with this dead hussar and all the others who fell at Waterloo. He was buried at Hougoumont and this epitaph was inscribed on his stone: [2]

SERGEANT-MAJOR COTTON

Pause, stranger as you pass this hallowed spot
  Where guardian angels hover round unseen!
Reposing here brave Cotton sleeps, whose lot
  On earth has one of dauntless valour been.

At Hougoumont his bleaching ashes lie,
  And mingle with the dust beneath his grave;
Whilst seraphs waft his loosened soul on high,
  To life eternal which awaits the brave.

Bold, as a soldier, faithful, as a friend,
  To enemies forgiving and humane,
He strove through life his country to defend,
  With character unsullied by a stain.

When War's rude thunders rent the loaded air,
  And clashing arm bespoke the dread dispute,

When Heroes pressed the cannon's front to dare,
Each heart for Glory in the wild pursuit.

Amongst them Cotton fought; and lived to tell
To countless eager ears the mighty fray,
In which his comrades and opponents fell,
When victory to Britons gave the day.

His mortal course he thus pursued by choice,
And thus performed the labour from him due;
Till lo! as recompense, from Heaven a voice
Has called to bliss, the "Voice from Waterloo."

Graves of Waterloo veterans can be found almost everywhere. The French combatants, especially the officers, were considered war criminals by the Royalists. Soldiers fled France, were scattered to the winds. Many of them escaped to the United States. Fact and fiction are inextricably mixed when their stories are told. Consider the legend of Marshal Ney who was ordered shot for treason by the Royalists. In 1913, Andrew Hilliard Atteridge wrote about Ney in his *"The Bravest of the Brave."* The author described the marshal's last moments in the Luxembourg Gardens in Paris before a firing squad. "As Major de St. Bias walked back to his men to give them the order to fire, Ney strode forward four paces towards the levelled muskets, took off his hat, and said in a loud clear voice: 'Frenchmen, I protest against my condemnation. My honor . . .' St. Bias gave the order. 'Feu!' and the volley crashed out before Ney could utter another word. The kneeling priest raised his hand in blessing as the smoke rolled over him. Ney had fallen dead on his face on the muddy ground, his hat rolling away . . . Six bullets had struck him in the chest, three in the head, one had gone through his neck, another broken his right arm. One of the 12 bullets hit the wall high up, bringing down a shower of plaster. There was one of the veterans who had refused to fire upon the 'bravest of the brave.' " [3]

But for years now, and the clamor is still heard periodically, many insist that Ney survived and settled in Third Creek, North Carolina. In the old Presbyterian graveyard there, Marshal Ney is said to be buried. A stone reads: "In memory of Peter Stuart Ney, a native of France and soldier of the French Revolution under Napoleon Bonaparte who departed this life November 15th 1846 aged 77 years."

Although the evidence against Ney's escape is overwhelming, the legend says he cheated the firing squad by feigning death, smashing his chest with a vial of crimson substance while shots roared over his head. A beautiful woman, old veterans on the firing squad, attendants at the government's morgue, and charitable nuns were all said to have been part of the intrigue.

So the legend goes: Ney lived on Babylon Street in Third Creek, North Carolina, taught school, made many close friends, and finally died thirty-one years after the battle. In an article in the *Saturday Evening Post* by Herbert Ravelen Sass, dated November 16, 1946, there was this description of the man who claimed that he was Marshal Ney: "His body was scarred with old wounds, and apparently these corresponded to the wounds which Marshal Ney was known to have had. In every physical feature published descriptions of Marshal Ney described Peter Stuart Ney also. Marshal Ney had been one of the best swordsmen in Europe, and the schoolmaster of Third Creek was an expert fencer. So similar were the handwritings of Marshal Ney and Peter Stuart Ney that every handwriting expert who has examined them, including the celebrated David N. Carvalho, has declared them the work of the same man." [4]

Mr. Sass also reported: "While he lived, the outside world knew nothing of him, but in the red hills of Rowan and its neighboring counties the legend of the mysterious schoolmaster grew as he grew older. Three North Carolinians—J. A. Weston, J. E. Smoot and, most recently, Le Gette Blythe—have gathered in as many books much impressive evidence, only a small part of which can be given here. In Statesville one day John Snyder, born near Prague and formerly a soldier in Napoleon's army, saw Peter Stuart Ney and flung up his hand exclaiming, 'Lordy God, Marshal Ney!' " [5]

There are many Marshal Ney legends. One of them which gained considerable acceptance claims that Marshal Ney and Michael Rudulph, an American, were one and the same person. Born a Marylander, Rudulph swashbuckled his way through the American Revolution as a popular, handsome junior officer, and then settled in Georgia. Later, he was commissioned a major to fight the Indians, and in February of 1793 was appointed Adjutant General and Inspector of the United States Army. Shortly thereafter he disappeared and was never heard from again. But reports persisted that he was alive and had been seen in France. Later, there were rumors that he had joined Napoleon's army and that his ability as a soldier, which he had demonstrated so well in America, was taking him to the top. The legend has it that he changed his name to Ney and finally became a marshal of France. One of the scores of accounts which built the legend was the experience of William H. Crawford, the Georgian who was minister to France. Mr. Crawford was not personally acquainted with Michael Rudulph, but he was aware of the prominent Georgia family. During his tenure in Paris, 1813-1815, the man who called himself Ney visited the ambassador constantly. Crawford was befuddled. He could speak only English, and he felt that the man in front of him knew only French. "Did Ney come to listen to the soft Georgian voice, with the hope of chance news of a deserted family?" [6]

One of Ney's aides, Col. John Jacob Lehmanowsky, who fought with the marshal at Waterloo, claimed that he was in prison with Ney in Paris, but managed to escape shortly before he was to be executed. In any event, he made his way to the United States and finally settled in Knightstown, Indiana. In the story of his life, *Under Two Captains,* which was written in Indiana, he exclaimed, "Man or ghost, as he might be, I knew that the figure before me was none other than Marshal Ney." Lehmanowsky claimed that Ney himself or his spirit had somehow arrived in Knightstown.

The colonel himself was a near legendary figure, but through the years many people who knew him well testified in letters to their Indiana newspapers that he was all that he claimed to be. Judging from numerous letters, all of his credentials were in order. He served with Napoleon from the very beginning, and was with him in Italy, Egypt, Russia, Spain and Belgium.

A Pole, he joined the Emperor because he saw hope in the Napoleonic wars for the liberation of at least part of his native country which in the late 18th century was divided among three of Napoleon's enemies—Russia, Prussia and Austria.

A giant of a man, he carried war wounds all over his body and was marked on his face with a scar from a Russian sabre. He spoke several languages, taught school for a while in Ohio, and finally ended up in the pulpit. He married twice and sired fourteen children. Half of them survived childbirth and as late as 1899, four of them were still alive. In that same year, Martin H. Lehmanowsky, of DePauw, Indiana, furnished a biography of his father to the *Salem Democrat*.

The colonel, born in Warsaw in 1773, was alive during the American Civil War. He mourned a close friend, Peter Glen, who was killed during a foray into Indiana by Morgan's Confederate Raiders.

Besides the mystery of whether the colonel saw Ney or his ghost in Indiana, two other mysteries surround him. Aside from state documents, the first book published in Indiana was a biography of Napoleon. Written anonymously, it appeared in 1818, just two years after Indiana was admitted to the Union. Published by Patrick and Booth, in Salem, Indiana, it was thought to be Lehmanowsky's book. At the turn of the century, when a controversy raged over who wrote it, many elderly friends of Lehmanowsky in Indiana insisted that the colonel was the author. It is written well and deals authoritatively with the Napoleonic period.

The colonel is also said to have given Indianians their nickname, but the mystery still isn't unraveled and probably never will be. The old Waterloo veteran was forever talking about the proud hussars who had fought in Napoleon's army, but his Polish pronunciation of the word came out something like "hoosier." A young Indianian who had listened to Lehmanowsky extol the virtues of the "Hoosiers" proudly declared himself a "Hoosier" after a successful fist fight with an out-of-stater. And that's how it all began, it is said.

What of Marshal Grouchy? Blame for the failure of the Waterloo campaign was heaped upon him. After Napoleon's rout, the marshal was left to get his men back to France the best way he could. Blücher did everything to trap him, but Grouchy fought skillful rearguard actions and managed to extricate his army. Many military historians insist that had Grouchy used his abilities as well in pursuing the Prussian army as he did in escaping, Napoleon would have been successful at Waterloo. Grouchy brought his army back intact just in time for the capitulation. His command was taken from him and he, too, was forced to flee.

Grouchy did not linger long on the Continent, but headed for the new center of Napoleonic intrigue—Philadelphia. Many Americans there were receiving Napoleon's officers with open arms. Although American newspaper editorials from Alexandria, Virginia, to New York were decidedly in favor of Wellington's victory and the banishment of the Emperor, most of society in big eastern seaboard cities was enraptured with the invasion of Napoleon's military nobility. Besides, American society had a regal splendor it hadn't had before. Joseph Bonaparte, former King of Spain and Napoleon's most loyal brother, had established his home in the United States. He slipped away from France on an American brig just weeks after Waterloo with the wealth he had hoarded when the Bonaparte family was riding the crest of power. Purchasing Point Breeze, a rambling estate outside of Bordentown, New Jersey, he turned it into a showplace. It became an attraction for all the glittering personalities, grand marshals, grand dames, and beckoned artists as well as politicians. It also became a center for conspiracies of all kinds; new French colonies, south-of-the-border conquests, and, of course, plots to rescue the Emperor from St. Helena.

Grouchy was one of the first of Napoleon's major officers to visit Joseph Bonaparte. He took up residence in Philadelphia, but was a frequent house guest at nearby Point Breeze. He began writing his own version of the debacle of Waterloo and added his voice to the discussion of where the swarms of French immigrants should settle. Between times, he went hunting in nearby Delaware and spent his evenings reminiscing with fellow officers at the tavern on the green in Dover.

Grouchy's sons had arrived in the United States, too. More and more families of Napoleon's officers and soldiers followed. General de Lefebvre-Desnouettes, who had been wounded at Waterloo as the commander of the cavalry of the Guard, came. So did Napoleon's commander of the Third Corps, Lieutenant General Vandamme. General Lallemand, commander of the chasseurs of the Guard at Waterloo, arrived with all kinds of ideas of what the French should do. There were a number of other old favorites of the Emperor, Major Comnes of the Grenadiers, Captain Roual of the Guard Artillery, and Lieutenant Taillade of the Marines. These three men had been with Napoleon from Elba to Waterloo. What they chiefly had in mind was how to put Napoleon back in power. One of the young lieutenants who called on Joseph at

Point Breeze was Michel Bouvier.* Although Napoleon's old officers and soldiers began to merge into French circles in New Orleans, New York, Baltimore and Mobile, they kept in touch with
Philadelphia and Point Breeze.

Joseph's friends argued that there was a need for some entirely
new French settlements in the country. Many of the soldiers and
politicians fleeing France were penniless, and although Joseph
contributed liberally to French charities, it was impossible for any
one man to support them all. Besides, there was a feeling that
chances to rescue Napoleon would be easier if some independent
French communities were established.

It must have been fascinating to have heard Napoleon's officers
and Old Guardsmen discuss the pros and cons of Mississippi and
Texas as possible havens. This is exactly what they did. First they
organized and called themselves the "Association of French Immigrants for the Cultivation of the Vine and Olive." A former
French colonel by the name of Nicholas Parmentier was named
secretary. With Philadelphia as headquarters and Washington his
target, he began lobbying for land grants. Congress was amenable
and allotted the association four townships in Mississippi territory. The terms were easy. Nearly 400 settlers signed up for the
land which went for $2 an acre. Total fees averaged approximately
$460 per person to be paid to the U. S. Treasury over a 14-year
period. Marshal Grouchy and his two sons all secured land allot-
ments. General de Lefebvre-Desnouettes and Captain Roual were
selected as the leaders of the project.

The Tombigbee Valley in what is now Alabama's Marengo,
Green and Hale Counties was their goal, and French families
sailed first to Mobile on the *Macdonough* in 1817 with swords and
satins, guns and guitars. They were ill-prepared to cope with the
hardy pioneer life they found in the wilderness. Unfortunately,
both of their first two villages, Demopolis (city of the people) and
Aigleville (Eagleville), were built outside their land grant. They
established a third, Arcola, in honor of one of Napoleon's victories.

Rugged American pioneers in the canebrake were agog. The
French tried to bring a part of Paris with them—culture, art and
fashionable dress. But it was a long way from the Louvre to a log
cabin. The officers and their wives had shared the glittering so-

---

* Mrs. John F. Kennedy's great-great-great-grandfather.

ciety of Paris with the battlefield. The old enlisted men and their wives knew nothing but the battlefield. Agriculture was not one of their fortes. Most of the olive trees they imported from Bordeaux did not flourish on this soil, and although the pioneers and Indians tried to teach them less sophisticated farming, most of them lost interest in a few years. Many moved into the cities or found a way back to France when conditions permitted. A few did stick it out, however, and even today French names and French customs are alive in Alabama, as are a few of the olive trees.

A second expedition sailed for Texas just a few days after the first group had left for Mississippi. Congress had not backed this venture. In fact, numerous Congressmen were disturbed and so were President James Monroe and his Secretary of State, John Quincy Adams, when they found out about it. Spain and the United States were in dispute over Texas territory. The place crawled with Mexican revolutionists, adventurers, freebooters, desperados and pirates. Jean Lafitte, the French pirate, had made his headquarters in what is now the modern city of Galveston. He had been pardoned by the United States because he had helped General Andrew Jackson slaughter the British at New Orleans. But now he was preying on Spanish ships which were constantly bringing in men and supplies to subdue Spain's Latin American colonies.

It was no wonder that the colonists under the immediate leadership of General François Rigaud were more concerned with military supplies than agricultural implements. The *Huntress* on which they sailed was burdened with field pieces, muskets, sabres and thousands of pounds of powder. General Lallemand, the president of the company, stayed in Philadelphia and then went to New Orleans where he recruited additional colonists.

Washington became increasingly alarmed because reports reached the White House and the State Department almost daily that the French hoped to crown Joseph King of Mexico. The reports were supported by stories that Joseph had contributed large sums for a military expedition into Mexico.

Lafitte welcomed the colonists in Galveston and did all he could to get them started into the interior. They were determined to settle on Trinity River near what is now Liberty, Texas. It was a rough land of Indians and alligators, rattlesnakes and mosquitoes. The expedition seemed doomed from the start. The French ate poisoned vegetables and were saved by friendly Indians who provided antidotes. They smoked the peacepipe and almost choked. Finally after much effort they assembled presentable log cabins and massive stockades. But the pioneer spirit of carving out a place in the land was lacking. They talked constantly about the old days, dressed their children in Old Guard uniforms, and ran their settlement, which they called "Champ d'Asile" (a place of asylum), like a military station.

On May 11, 1818, General Lallemand issued a declaration that stated it was "the natural rights" of men to make homes in unoccupied lands. The manifesto created a storm in Paris. A fund for the immigrants was solicited. It was deposited in a Parisian bank and began to grow. But when a large Spanish force marched from San Antonio to destroy the little colony, approximately 400 immigrants were forced back to Galveston Island. There they were hit by a tropical hurricane and many were drowned. The remaining colonists made their way back to the cities or joined Lafitte's pirates.

Many Old Guardsmen saw "Champ d'Asile" only as a base for rescuing Napoleon anyway. They didn't let its failure deter their preparations for rescuing the Emperor. But it was a long, costly job.

Rumors of escape attempts constantly troubled the British at St. Helena. When Napoleon was confined to his house for a few days of illness the British would become alarmed. "Was the prisoner in the house at all, or was he sliding down some steep ravine to a submarine boat?" [7] Just how many plots were underway or just how far any of them got are other mysteries which have never been answered. The British did receive a report that a boat was being constructed in Philadelphia for Napoleon's rescue. On at least one occasion a dispatch reached the British commander, Sir Hudson Lowe, from Rio de Janeiro, that an attempt would soon be carried out. Some of the Emperor's old soldiers had fled to South America. They were doing what they knew best, soldiering. Many were fighting for Simon Bolivar who was leading one revolution after another. Some of them may have decided that Brazil, which had been under Portuguese rule, would be a good place to launch the rescue operations. It is conceivable also that Lowe may have received his tip from a former British soldier. After Waterloo some of Wellington's men, mostly Scotch and Irish, had signed up in South America as soldiers of fortune. Later some may have deserted to find a refuge in Rio.

One story holds that on the very eve of his surrender to the British, Napoleon had an opportunity to slip away from France aboard a small craft, which its captain, Vildeau, claimed could make the crossing to America. Napoleon, who was a notoriously bad sailor, declined after inspecting the frail craft. It is said that Vildeau later proved that it could be done by sailing from France with a crew of only three to Halifax, Canada, in just six weeks.

There is evidence that a major plot did exist in New Orleans for Napoleon's escape. The conspirators included some of Napoleon's never-say-die Old Guardsmen, some of Jean Lafitte's cut-throats, and a French-American, Captain J. S. Bossière, who came from Baltimore. The captain had been just about every place else, also. Described as a "... powerfully-built man with jet-black hair, large, dark piercing eyes, swarthy complexion and a strangely fierce and savage expression," he had been at sea most of his life.[8] He had sailed on clipper ships as a boy and fought as a mercenary in South America.

Bossière's job was to supervise the building of a sleek vessel and then captain her on the voyage to St. Helena. It seemed that there was plenty of money to get just the clipper he wanted. She was named the *Seraphine* and drew about 200 tons. Long, low, black and rakish, the craft could outsail almost anything afloat.[9] Her tough crew was expected to handle the British sentries who guarded the Emperor.

A former mayor of New Orleans, Nicholas Girod, was involved in the plot, too. It is said that he had a home built for Napoleon during this period. In the New Orleans *Times-Picayune* of March 25, 1923, Mabel D. Gasquet wrote about this house as follows: "Once safely in America, a home worthy of the great man must be ready. So the house at 514 Chartres street was built, remarkably handsome for those days and furnished with the richest that could be bought." [10]

On September 5, 1821, just days before the *Seraphine* was to sail, there was a notice in the French section of the *Louisiana*

Gazette that the Emperor was dead. The news was months old, arriving in the July 14 copy of the Jamaican *Royal Gazette:* "The brig *Amphritrite,* captain Morgan, was boarded on June 23rd, by Captain Anderson of a vessel of the Winchelsea Company, returning from China, which landed at St. Helena, after forty-six days at sea. The captain announced that Bonaparte had died on the 5th of May from cancer of the chest, and that on the ninth of that month he was interred with great pomp at Longwood. Captain Morgan also announced that because of the death of the ex-Emperor, the port of St. Helena was declared a free port of entry for all American shipping." [11]

This news shattered the dreams of Napoleon's old soldiers. Some of them would never believe it, and until they died they accepted the constant rumors that the Emperor was still alive. Wherever there was a French colony there were special religious ceremonies—in Philadelphia, Baltimore, New York, Mobile. In New Orleans the funeral ceremonies required such elaborate preparations that they were not held until December 29, 1821, almost three months after word of the Emperor's death was received.

The affair was costly and a large fund had to be subscribed. The mourners complained that the preparations were taking too long. But artisans were hired to design a cenotaph and a catafalque, and a special program of music had to be composed. There were long rehearsals for the French company of players who "sang several pieces during the celebration of the High Mass." [12]

A huge crowd participated. Old soldiers, wearing their medals of the Legion of Honor, marched in the funeral procession. The cenotaph was considered a work of art. In bold relief on its base were figures of the arts and religion in tears. There was an allegory representing the muse of history who was ordering "a genius to engrave the immortal deeds of Napoleon . . ." [13]

As the years passed, the French government forgave the old soldiers for serving Napoleon. Some of them returned from America, including Grouchy. So did Joseph Bonaparte. But Grouchy, who died at seventy-one in 1847, was always blamed by most Frenchmen for the failure at Waterloo. King Louis Philippe restored his marshal's rank in 1830, the year Louis Philippe took the throne as an elected monarch, but there were always murmurings in Paris that it was Grouchy who had let the Emperor down when he needed him most.

Louis Philippe became king after Charles the Tenth was forced from power by the 1830 revolution. Six years earlier Charles had taken the throne upon the death of Louis XVIII, the sovereign who savored all those mutton chops.

Louis Philippe, after some years on the throne, found that any popularity he had had at the beginning was fading. To shore up his appeal he reached into the past to polish the Napoleonic legend. Statues of the Emperor were resurrected, Empire battle paintings restored, and old soldiers made more welcome.

The French government even managed to convince the British that the body of Napoleon should be exhumed at St. Helena for burial in Paris. Reinterment was planned for December 15, 1840. Old soldiers from everywhere were invited to attend this last march with *le petit corporal*. They came from the United States, South America and most of the countries in Europe.

Following the huge hearse (over a story high), drawn by sixteen plumed and caparisoned horses, came the Emperor's guard of honor. In the buttonhole of each aged and moth-tattered uniform of these Imperial Guardsmen and proud survivors of the Emperor's regiments was a sprig of laurel from the wreaths on Napoleon's coffin. To the sound of muted drums the old soldiers shuffled under the Arc de Triomphe and along the Champs Élysées to the Hôtel des Invalides. That night a weeping Old Guardsman told of a strange wind he had heard along the route, and could only surmise that it was the tribute of his dead comrades to the great leader. This, and a thousand other stories like it, contributed to the Napoleonic legend. Parisians heard, too, that when Napoleon's body was viewed after being exhumed that his features had not been marred ever so slightly by nineteen years in the grave. Many thought this was a miracle.

The legend which Louis Philippe helped resurrect turned on him. It helped promote the revolution of 1848 which forced him to abdicate. Louis Napoleon Bonaparte, the nephew of the Emperor, used the legend for all it was worth and finally made his successful bid for power.

Although even more of the Emperor's soldiers were now returning to France for their pensions, there were thousands who had found new lives abroad. Many of them stayed in the United States for good. When Union troops moved into Mobile during the Civil War, they were impressed with the professional skill of the officers who had designed the fortifications. Part of them had been laid out by General Pierre Benjamin Buysson of the Confederate Army. An old soldier of Napoleon's, he had received the medal of the Legion of Honor and a battlefield promotion from the Emperor himself. He had arrived in New Orleans on Christmas Eve two years after Waterloo, and when the South went to war, he was commissioned a brigadier at sixty-eight because of his engineering skill. In civilian life he "surveyed and mapped" a good part of New Orleans.[14] One of his jobs was to name the streets. He named a wide avenue "Napoleon" and others after the Emperor's victories, "Milan," "Berlin," "Jena."

Lt. Michel Bouvier stayed in Philadelphia to marry Louise Vernou. She came from a noble family who fled to Philadelphia during the French Revolution. Ignoring the French colonies of "Arcola" and "Champ d'Asile," Bouvier became a manufacturer and importer. The young officer made a fortune in his own right, lived to be 84, and when he died, "Philadelphia named a Bouvier Street in his honor." [15]

Private Gaertner, who decided his mother had saved his life at Waterloo by praying to Saint Anthony, settled in Iowa. He found out that his mother had been a little extravagant in her prayers. She had pledged that if he returned safely she would somehow build a church in honor of Saint Anthony. It seemed impossible to keep the promise. But today, near Festina, Iowa, there is a little church, Saint Anthony of Padua. It has a 40-foot belfry, is 14 feet wide, 20 feet long, with four small pews which seat eight persons. In 1885 Gaertner's children decided they would honor the pledge made by their grandmother and the church was constructed. In recent years it has become a tourist attraction. "In the little church graveyard, midst the . . . pines, are buried Johann Gaertner, his wife and others of the family." [16]

Private Siegrist married Miss Salome Strubler four years after the battle of Waterloo and didn't arrive in the United States until 1833. On his way he stopped in Paris for one last look at his capital. He arrived in New York City, went to Buffalo by canal, and then purchased a team of oxen for the journey to Warren, Pennsylvania, where he settled. His granddaughter, Miss Cloie Weiler, remembered that when Waterloo was mentioned, tears would come to her grandfather's eyes.

Missouri became Private Rebo's home. He married a Kentucky girl and settled in Rawls County.

Missouri, like many other states, became infatuated with the Napoleonic legend and the lore of Waterloo. Veterans from both sides helped keep the memory of the Waterloo period alive with the names they gave towns and villages. Along a five-mile stretch of road in Missouri one can travel today through the towns of Wellington, Waterloo and Napoleon. Also in Missouri, towns were named St. Helena, Longwood, and Elba, and two of Napoleon's great victories were commemorated, Arcola and Lodi.

The map of the United States is dotted with the same place names. "Six other states beside Missouri acquired towns named St. Helena; and there are 7 Napoleons, 10 Longwoods, 12 Elbas, 13 Wellingtons, 15 Lodis, and 24 Waterloos." [17]

There was not the imperative need for immigration by men in the allied army. Unlike the French, they did not have to fear courts martial, firing squads or other reprisals by a hostile government. But many of Blücher's men found their way to the United States in later years. They and their descendants settled in New York, Philadelphia, Baltimore and then Milwaukee. Like Waterloo veterans of other nationalities, they accepted their new country and there are records of Prussian veterans fighting in the Mexican, Indian and Civil Wars. Most of the English, Scottish and Welsh preferred to cling to their soil and the old regiments. Yet some came to America to begin the conquest of the West. Stories of Highlanders, still in faded tartans, battling Indians as wagon trains crept across the prairie, are part of the legend of the West. During the potato famine in the '40's, Irish soldiers who had fought at Waterloo made their way to the United States and Canada in large numbers. When they discovered the towns and villages named in honor of Napoleon and his victories, they tried to even things up by naming new settlements Waterloo or Wellington. After all, the Duke was born an Irishman, too.

There is no doubt that a great number of well-known Americans had ancestors in the battle. There were Lees and Grants, and Johnsons and Kennedys, and many more names famous to Americans. Although President Lyndon B. Johnson's forefathers were already in the United States by 1815, he shared some ancestors with the late Winston Churchill. The former Prime Minister had direct ancestors on the field.

There were many Kennedys in the battle and a number of Fitzgeralds.* *The Waterloo Roll Call,* an authoritative list of Wellington's officers prepared by Charles Dalton at the turn of the century, mentions five Kennedys and four Fitzgeralds. Most of them, however, were from Scotland and England. But there were a great number of Kennedys who were enlisted men. Most of them, too, were Scottish, but some were Irish who had joined Highland regiments which often recruited in Ireland. In the Cameron Highlanders alone there were three John Kennedys.

Three of the Gordon Highlanders who had fought so fiercely at Waterloo lived for years after the battle. John Downie, a native of Glenshee, Perthshire, who had been wounded at least three times, was a pensioner at one shilling, three pence a day. He could not understand how the Germans had managed to beat the French in the Franco-Prussian war. "They can't be the same sort that fought against us..." he said.[18] He was still reading his Gaelic Bible without glasses when he was ninety-three. Peter Stewart, who had fought in nearly a score of major battles, always remembered the proud moment when Queen Victoria gave him a sovereign. Afterwards the Duke of Richmond said, "Well, Peter, I suppose you will put the Queen's sovereign on your watch chain." [19] But Peter replied, "I'll hae a dram to her health oot o't first." [20] Nearly one hundred when he died, Pvt. William MacKenzie remembered his old colonel, "Fassiefern," as a fine soldier, but also recalled that he was very strict on those who had a little too much to drink—just a little hard on those who were "heavy on the dram." [21] He often told young boys and their mothers: "If I was young again it's not sitting by the fire at home I would be, but with the lads with the yellow tartan" (Gillean a' bhreacian bhuidhe).[22]

Captain Hill, the fattest man in the British army, whose friends felt sure would be one of the first to die at Waterloo because he presented such a large target, continued his army career after

* The maiden name of President John F. Kennedy's mother was Fitzgerald.

the battle. He died a lieutenant general forty-five years later. Captain Mercer, whose artillerymen had never left the line during the fighting despite Wellington's orders, advanced to the rank of general and lived to be eighty-five. He died in 1868.

As late as 1886, seventy-one years after the Battle of Waterloo, a score of Wellington's officers were still on the "official list" of the British army. Among them was Lt. A. Gardner of the 27th Regiment, that regiment which had taken such heavy losses at Waterloo. The young drummer boy who had stood with him, Private Haughton, was also alive, and six years later there was a report that he was still enjoying good health. Lt. Basil Jackson, who had watched the Highlanders march out of Brussels and who was all over the field at Waterloo, died in 1889 at ninety-four. According to newspaper reports at the time, three British officers who had served at Waterloo still survived.

In 1895 Madame Givron was still alive. She was the young girl whose curiosity drove her close to Hougoumont that Sunday, eighty years before. In 1903, two of the last eyewitnesses of Waterloo died—Mrs. Barbara Moon, the four-year-old girl who rode over the battlefield the night of June 18, 1815, and Elizabeth Watkins, the little girl who had helped prepare the bandages.

There were reports that a few veterans also lived to see the twentieth century. Lieutenant Markiewicz of Napoleon's Polish Light-Horse "was born in Cracow in 1794, fought in the Russian campaign, was decorated in 1813, charged at Waterloo, and was still living in 1902." [23]

Wellington died at eighty-three in 1852. He received every conceivable award, including the prime ministry. Grants voted to him by Parliament for his military services totaled in the millions of dollars. He was lionized everywhere and even after he relinquished the command of the British army he could veto almost any military idea he didn't like. Society flocked to his table, with ladies and gentlemen reporting every scrap of his conversation as soon as they could get out the door. Some men even tried to imitate him. "For some years there was a living caricature of the Duke: this wretched old creature not only imitated the Duke in wearing a blue paletot and the other garments, hat, etc., but he actually wore a crimson under-waistcoat, so as to imitate the Duke's ribbon of the Golden Fleece: this too in morning dress." [24]

Many of Wellington's soldiers criticized him bitterly for showing little charity to the poor, miserable, armless and legless men who had fought under his command. But old veterans went to his rescue when British mobs threatened him in civilian life.

The Duke was despised by many Englishmen, particularly the lower classes. The reasons were obvious. His reactionary policies seemed extreme even in a reactionary age. He opposed reform at a time in England when the Industrial Revolution was taking its toll in the factories and sweat shops. He showed only contempt for public petition, and warned against the "dangers" of the ballot and universal suffrage. He felt that great landed proprietors should have the controlling influence in Parliament, and fought Parliamentary reform. Indeed, to him even the ancient British legislative system would have been the ruin of the nation if it had not had the terror of the French Revolution as an example to temper it. He found newspapers a blight on the nation and accused them of issuing falsehoods and basing their stories on false reasoning. Nothing, he felt, could be trusted to the people.

Even some of his former officers criticized him for not petitioning the government to help the veterans. Most of them had little more than meager pensions, a little prize money from Waterloo, and the first general campaign medal in British history.

Wellington revisited the battlefield with George IV in 1821. He said he couldn't recognize Waterloo and was particularly incensed by plans to build a huge mound crowned with the figure of a lion. It would be erected after much effort by hundreds of peasants at the order of the Prince of Orange so that his part in the battle could be commemorated. Wellington noticed that some knolls had been leveled and various trees destroyed. "They have ruined my battlefield!" he exclaimed.

But perhaps the Duke was mellowing some in later life. At Waterloo anniversary dinners, he seemed almost convincing when he toasted the artillery and the cavalry. He had never neglected to emphasize his disdain for these arms, always insisting that it was the infantry that won the day, nothing else. His funeral was one of the most magnificent pageants in British history.

Alfred Lord Tennyson's *Ode on the Death of the Duke of Wellington* was nearly as monumental as the Iron Duke's great funeral. Two thousand words long, it glorified Wellington in peace and war. These lines panegyrized him as the "foremost captain of his time":

> O friends our chief state-oracle is mute:
> Mourn for the man of long-enduring blood,
> The statesman-warrior, moderate, resolute,
> Whole in himself a common good.
> Mourn for the man of amplest influence,
> Yet clearest of ambitious crime,
> Our greatest yet with least pretence,
> Great in council and great in war,
> Foremost captain of his time,
> Rich in saving common-sense,
> And, as the greatest only are,
> In his simplicity sublime.
> O good gray head which all men know,
> O voice from which their omens all men drew,
> O iron nerve to true occasion true,
> O fallen at length that tower of strength
> Which stood four-square to all the winds that blew! [25]

In his eulogy, Tennyson was at his best when he described the battle of Waterloo: [26]

> Again their ravening eagle rose
> In anger, whell'd on Europe-shadowing wings,
> And barking for the thrones of kings;
> Till one that sought but Duty's iron crown
> On that loud Sabbath shook the spoiler down;
> A day of onsets of despair!
> Dash'd on every rocky square
> Their surging charges foam'd themselves away;
> Last, the Prussian trumpet blew;
> Thro' the long-tormented air
> Heaven flash'd a sudden jubilant ray,
> And down we swept and charged and overthrew.
> So great a soldier taught us there,
> What long-enduring hearts could do
> In that world earthquake, Waterloo!

The man who made "the Prussian trumpet" matter, Blücher, only lived four years after Waterloo, dying at seventy-seven in 1819. Napoleon barely escaped his clutches, and the old man was forever frustrated. He lingered with the army of occupation in Paris as long as he could. During this time he explored numerous ways to torment the French. He haunted the Louvre, cataloging pictures which he felt belonged in Prussia. He tried to blow up the Bridge of Jena because it was named to commemorate a victory over the Prussians. But the attempt went off badly and all that happened was that some Prussian sappers were hurt. The old man was ready to try again, but was foiled by Wellington. He was much amused when he heard that his troops seemed to be eating and drinking the Parisians into utter destitution. He heartily approved of each Prussian soldier drawing three and four rations a day from the complaining Parisians.

The old man, although in his seventies, cavorted with the same excess and energy which had been his style when he was a young hussar. While showing off before some British women in Paris, he fell from his horse and took a blow on the head. Wellington remembered that this gave him "all sorts of strange fancies." [27] Philip Henry, the fifth Earl of Stanhope, recorded a conversation he had had about Blücher with the Duke. Wellington said: "When I went to take leave of him, he positively told me that he was pregnant! And what do you think he was pregnant of?—An elephant! And who do you think he said had produced it?—A French soldier!" [28] Wellington was asked what he had replied to Old Blücher. He said that he could only say he hoped he would get better soon. But Wellington added that Blücher still had these illusions shortly before his death.

Napoleon created a seemingly eternal legend about himself and his empire during his six years at St. Helena. He lived comfortably, but complained constantly of shabby treatment. He wrote his memoirs. Between periods of dictation he attempted to seduce the wives of his staff. His degree of success here is still another mystery.

Recent reports that Napoleon was murdered by arsenic poisoning are reminders of the thousands who wished him dead—political enemies, patriots from a dozen nations, jealous husbands and even some friends of Marie Louise, his second wife. Her affair with the Austrian officer during Napoleon's temporary exile on Elba finally ran full gamut, two illegitimate children. Her friends, knowing of Napoleon's revengeful ways, may have feared what he could do, even from St. Helena, and hired a clever murderer who had the Emperor's trust. Marie Louise finally married her officer after Napoleon's death.

Count Montholon, the court chamberlain who was with Napoleon at St. Helena, is the strongest suspect in the ancient murder case. A close friend of the Emperor, Count Montholon had an excellent personal motive for murder, since he was mentioned in Napoleon's will to the amount of two million francs. Samples of Napoleon's hair have undergone nuclear reactor tests at Harwell, England. A British scientist has stated that the tests prove that the Emperor died of arsenic poisoning. Death by arsenic poisoning would account for the remarkable preservation of Napoleon's corpse, which unnerved superstitious Frenchmen when it was exhumed nineteen years after his death for the state funeral in Paris.

Arsenic was the ideal agent to use for murder. "Medicinal arsenic taken at the rate of a half to five milligrams daily is an aid to the human body's combustion and anabolism. A course of arsenic extending over several months is an effective treatment for general debility and nervous exhaustion." [29] Accepted as a medicine by the Emperor, it would have been easy for a trusted aide to administer a fatal dose.

There is no denying that Napoleon was vindictive enough to reach out from St. Helena for the life of anyone. It is possible that someone who feared for his own life made the arrangements which stilled the Emperor forever. The story of revenge Napoleon sought from his lonely island has never been revealed. But in his will he made sure there was a legacy for a man who had tried to assassinate Wellington. On hearing of this the Duke said that Napoleon "was no gentleman."

This remark would have rocked the Emperor with laughter, although Napoleon was seldom, if ever, that amused. But how could a conqueror, a man of destiny, a man who had broken kingdoms and molded nations, care whether the world considered such a trifle? In fact, how could a man be thought of as a gentleman at all who had grappled with destiny the way he had? Wellington, his greatest adversary, had missed the whole point.

Napoleon left the world what he wanted to leave it—a legacy of legend. It flourishes today even more than he could have imagined, and Waterloo, his great defeat, is still only reluctantly admitted by the French government. The Emperor, who tried to excuse his mistakes at Waterloo, would have liked that. He also would have approved France's shelving of international proposals to mark the 150th anniversary of the battle.

Appendix

THE ANGLO-ALLIED ARMY

COMMANDER-IN-CHIEF

Field-Marshal the Duke of Wellington

CHIEF OF THE STAFF

Colonel Sir William Howe de Lancey, K.B.

ADJUTANT-GENERAL

Major-General Sir E. Barnes, K.B.

COMMANDING ROYAL ARTILLERY

Colonel Sir G. A. Wood

COMMANDING ENGINEER

Lieut.-Colonel Smyth

PRUSSIAN ATTACHÉ AT BRITISH HEADQUARTERS

Major-General Baron von Müffling

FIRST CORPS

Commander, the Prince of Orange

1st Division, commanded by Major-General Cooke

BRIGADES
Major-General Maitland (B): * *2/1st and 3/1st Guards*
Major-General Sir John Byng (B): *2/2nd and 2/3rd Guards*
ARTILLERY
Lieut.-Colonel Adye
Captain Sandham's Field Brigade, R.A.;
Major Kühlmann's Horse Artillery Troop, K.G.L.
TOTAL: 4,061 men **

* B denotes British; H, Hanoverian; K.G.L., King's German Legion.
** This and the subsequent divisional totals do not include the numbers of men in artillery units. The artillery is treated separately on p. 299.

3rd Division, commanded by Lieut.-General Count Sir Charles Alten

BRIGADES

Major-General Sir Colin Halkett (B): *2/30th, 33rd, 2/69th, 2/73rd*

Colonel Baron von Ompteda (K.G.L.): *1st and 2nd Light Battalions, and 5th and 8th Line Battalions*

Major-General Count Kielmansegge (H); (6 battalions)

ARTILLERY

Lieut.-Colonel Williamson

Major Lloyd's Field Brigade, R.A.;

Captain Cleeves' Field Brigade, K.G.L.

TOTAL: 6,970 men

2nd Dutch-Belgian Division, commanded by Lieut.-General Baron de Perponcher

BRIGADES

Major-General Count de Bylandt: *5 Dutch-Belgian battalions*

Prince Bernard of Saxe-Weimar: *5 Nassau battalions*

ARTILLERY

Major Van Opstal

Bijleveld's Horse-Battery and 1 Field Battery

TOTAL: 7,533 men

3rd Dutch-Belgian Division, commanded by Lieut.-General Baron Chassé

BRIGADES

Major-General Ditmers: *6 Dutch-Belgian battalions*

Major-General d'Aubremé: *6 Dutch-Belgian battalions*

ARTILLERY

Major van der Smissen: *1 Horse and 1 Field Battery*

TOTAL: 6,672 men

Total First Corps: 25,236 men, 56 guns

SECOND CORPS

Commander, Lieut.-General Lord Hill

2nd Division, commanded by Lieut.-General Sir Henry Clinton

BRIGADES

Major-General Adam (B): *1/52nd, 1/71st, 2/95th and 3/95th*

Colonel du Plat (K.G.L.): *1st, 2nd, 3rd, and 4th Line Battalions*

Colonel W. Halkett (H): *4 Landwehr battalions*

ARTILLERY

Lieut.-Colonel Gold

Captain Bolton's Field Brigade, R.A.;

Major Sympher's Horse Artillery Troops, K.G.L.

TOTAL: 6,833 men

4th Division, commanded by Lieut.-General Sir Charles Colville

BRIGADES

Colonel Mitchell (B): *3/14th, 1/23rd and 51st*

Major-General Johnstone (B): *2/35th, 1/54th, 2/59th and 1/91st*

Major-General Sir James Lyon (H): *5 battalions*

ARTILLERY
Lieut.-Colonel Hawker
Major Brome's Field Brigade, R.A.;
Captain von Rettberg's Hanoverian Field Battery
TOTAL: 7,212 men

Corps of Prince Frederick of the Netherlands
1st Dutch-Belgian Division, commanded by Lieut.-General Stedman

BRIGADES
Major-General d'Hauw: *6 battalions*
Major-General d'Eerens: *5 battalions*
TOTAL: 6,389 men
Lieut.-General Anthing's Netherland Indian Brigade: *5 battalions and 1 field battery*
TOTAL: 3,583 men
16 men detached from other regiments.

Total Second Corps: 24,033 men, 40 guns.

RESERVE

Commander, Field-Marshal the Duke of Wellington

5th Division, commanded by Lieut.-General Sir Thomas Picton

BRIGADES
Major-General Sir James Kempt (B): *1/28th, 1/32nd, 1/79th, and 1/95th*
Major-General Sir Denis Pack (B): *3/1st, 1/42nd, 2/44th, and 1/92nd*
Colonel von Wincke (H): *4 Landwehr battalions*
ARTILLERY
Major Heisse:
Major Rogers' Field Brigade, R.A.;
Captain Braun's Hanoverian Field Battery.
TOTAL: 7,158 men

6th Division, commanded by Lieut.-General the Hon. Sir Lowry Cole

BRIGADES
Major-General Sir John Lambert (B): *1/4th, 1/27th, 1/40th and 2/81st*
Colonel Best (H): *4 Landwehr battalions*
ARTILLERY
Lieut.-Colonel Brückmann:
Major Unett's Field Brigade, R.A.;
Captain Sinclair's Field Brigade, R.A.
TOTAL: 5,149 men

British Reserve Artillery, commanded by Major Drummond
Lieut.-Colonel Sir H. Ross's Horse Artillery Troop
Major Bean's Horse Artillery Troop
Major Morrison's Company, R.A.
Captain Hutchesson's Company, R.A.
Captain Ilbert's Company, R.A.

Brunswick Corps, commanded by the Duke of Brunswick
Advanced Guard, 4 companies infantry and 1 cavalry detachment; 2 brigades (each 3 battalions) and 2 batteries
TOTAL: 5,376 men

Nassau Contingent, commanded by General von Kruse
3 battalions
TOTAL: 2,880 men

Total Reserve: 20,563 men, 64 guns

GARRISONS

7th Division

7th British Brigade: *2/25th, 2/37th and 2/78th*
3 British Garrison battalions
TOTAL: 3,233 men
Hanoverian Reserve Corps *12 Landwehr battalions in 4 brigades*
TOTAL: 9,000 men

Total Garrison: 12,233 men

CAVALRY

Commander, Lieut.-General the Earl of Uxbridge

BRIGADES
Major-General Lord Edward Somerset (B): *1st and 2nd Life Guards, Royal Horse Guards Blues, 1st Dragoon Guards*
Major-General Sir William Ponsonby (B): *1st Royal Dragoons, 2nd Dragoons Greys, 6th Inniskilling Dragoons*
Major-General Sir William Dörnberg (B and K.G.L.): *1st and 2nd Light Dragoons, K.G.L., and 23rd Light Dragoons*
Major-General Sir John Vandeleur (B): *11th, 12th, and 16th Light Dragoons*
Major-General Sir Colquhoun Grant (B and K.G.L.); *7th and 15th Hussars, and 2nd Hussars, K.G.L.*
Major-General Sir Hussey Vivian (B and K.G.L.): *10th and 18th Hussars and 1st Hussars, K.G.L.*
Colonel Baron F. von Arentschildt (B and K.G.L.): *13th Light Dragoons, and 3rd Hussars, K.G.L.*
TOTAL: 8,473 men

British Horse Artillery Troops attached to the Cavalry:
Commander, Lieut.-Colonel Sir Augustus Fraser
Major Bull's Troop (howitzers)
Lieut.-Colonel Webber-Smith's Troop
Lieut.-Colonel Sir R. Gardiner's Troop
Major E. C. Whinyates' Troop (with Rockets)
Major Norman Ramsay's Troop
Captain Mercer's Troop

1st Hanoverian Cavalry Brigade: Colonel von Estorff
3 regiments: *Prince Regent's Hussars, Bremen and Verden Hussars, Cumberland Hussars*
TOTAL: 1,682 men

Brunswick Cavalry
1 regiment of Hussars, 1 squadron of Uhlans
TOTAL: 922 men

Dutch-Belgian Cavalry Division: Lieut.-General Baron de Collaert
3 brigades under Major-General Trip; Major-General de Ghigny; Major-
General van Merlen
Artillery: 2 half-horse batteries
TOTAL: 3,405 men

Total Cavalry: 14,482 men, 44 guns

ARTILLERY

BRITISH						Guns	Men
7 Field Batteries of 6 guns each						42	
3 "	"	" 4	"	"	(18 prs.)	12	
8 Horse	"	" 6	"	"		48	5,030
K.G.L.							
1 Field	"	" 6	"	"		6	
2 Horse	"	" 6	"	"		12	526
HANOVERIAN							
2 Field	"	" 6	"	"		12	465
BRUNSWICK							
1 Field	"	" 8	"	"		8	
1 Horse	"	" 8	"	"		8	510
DUTCH-BELGIAN							
4 Field	"	" 8	"	"		32	
3 Horse	"	" 8	"	"		24	1,635
						204	8,166

MISCELLANEOUS

Engineers, Sappers and Miners, Wagon Train and Staff Corps   1,240

TOTAL STRENGTH

Infantry   82,062
Cavalry   14,482
Artillery   8,166
Miscellaneous 1,240
Grand total 105,950 men
204 guns

Adapted from Siborne's tables

PRUSSIAN ARMY

COMMANDER-IN-CHIEF

Field-Marshal Prince Blücher von Wahlstadt

QUARTERMASTER GENERAL AND CHIEF OF THE STAFF

General Count von Gneisenau

CHIEF OF THE GENERAL STAFF

General von Grölmann

FIRST CORPS

Commander, Lieut.-General von Ziethen

BRIGADES *
Major-General von Steinmetz
Major-General von Pirch II
Major-General von Jagow
Major-General Count von Henckel Donnersmarck

Cavalry Corps, commanded by Lieut.-General von Röder
Major-General von Treskow
Lieut.-Colonel von Lützow

Artillery, commanded by Colonel von Lehmann
3 horse artillery, 3 12-pdr. and 5 6-pdr. field batteries, 1 howitzer battery
Total First Corps: 31,129 men, 80 guns

SECOND CORPS

Commanded by Major-General von Pirch I

BRIGADES
Major-General von Tippelskirch
Major-General von Kraft
Major-General von Brause
Major-General von Bose

Cavalry Corps, commanded by Major General von Wahlen-Jurgass
Colonel von Thümen
Colonel Count von Schulenburg
Lieut.-Colonel von Sohr

Artillery, commanded by Colonel von Röhl
3 horse artillery; 2 12-pdr. and 5 6-pdr. field batteries.
Total Second Corps: 31,529 men, 80 guns

THIRD CORPS

Commanded by Lieut.-General von Thielemann

BRIGADES
Major-General von Borcke
Colonel von Kämpfen
Colonel von Luck
Colonel von Stülpnägel

Cavalry Corps, commanded by General von Hobe
Colonel Von der Marwitz
Colonel Count von Lottum

Artillery, commanded by Colonel von Mohnhaupt
3 horse artillery; 1 12-pdr. and 2 6-pdr. field batteries
Total Third Corps: 24,141 men, 48 guns

* There was no divisional organization in the Prussian army of 1815, though the brigades were each about the strength of a French division.

FOURTH CORPS

Commanded by General Count Bülow von Dennewitz

BRIGADES
Lieut.-General von Hacke
General von Ryssel
General von Losthin
Colonel von Hiller

Cavalry Corps, commanded by General Prince William of Prussia

General von Sidow
Colonel Count von Schwerin
Lieut.-Colonel von Watsdorf

Artillery, commanded by Lieut.-Colonel von Bardeleben
3 horse batteries; 3 12-pdr. and 5 6-pdr. field batteries.
Total Fourth Corps: 30,862 men, 88 guns

Total Strength, 117,661 men, 296 guns
Adapted from the tables of De Bas. The figures do not include officers or musicians; with these last added, the grand total, with train, etc., is approximately 124,000

THE FRENCH ARMY

COMMANDER-IN-CHIEF

the Emperor Napoleon

CHIEF OF THE STAFF

Marshal Soult, Duke of Dalmatia

CHIEF COMMANDER OF ARTILLERY

Lieut.-General Ruty

CHIEF COMMANDER OF ENGINEERS

Lieut.-General Baron Rogniat

FIRST CORPS

Commanded by Lieut.-General Count Drouet d'Erlon

1st Division, commanded by Lieut.-General Allix (in Allix's
absence Baron Quiot commanded the division)
BRIGADES: Quiot, Bourgeois

2nd Division, commanded by Lieut.-General Baron Donzelot
BRIGADES: Schmidt, Aulard

3rd Division, commanded by Lieut.-General Baron Marcognet
BRIGADES: Noguez, Grenier

4th Division, commanded by Lieut.-General Count Durutte
BRIGADES: Pégot, Brue

Cavalry Division, commanded by Lieut.-General Baron Jacquinot
BRIGADES: Bruno, Gobrecht

Artillery, commanded by Baron de Salles (6 batteries)
Engineers
5 companies

Total First Corps: 20,731 men, 46 guns

SECOND CORPS

Commanded by Lieut.-General Count Reille

5th Division, commanded by Lieut.-General Baron Bachelu
BRIGADES: Husson, Campy

6th Division, commanded by Lieut.-General Prince Jérôme Bonaparte
BRIGADES: Baudouin, Soye

7th Division, commanded by Lieut.-General Count Girard
BRIGADES: Devilliers, Piat

9th Division, commanded by Lieut.-General Count Foy
BRIGADES: Gauthier, B. Jamin

2nd Cavalry Division, commanded by Lieut-General Baron Piré
BRIGADES: Hubert, Wathiez

Artillery, commanded by Baron Pelletier
6 batteries

Engineers
5 companies

Total Second Corps: 25,179 men, 46 guns

THIRD CORPS

Commanded by Lieut.-General Count Vandamme

8th Division, commanded by Lieut.-General Baron Lefol
BRIGADES: Billard, Corsin

10th Division, commanded by Lieut.-General Baron Habert
BRIGADES: Gengoult, Dupeyroux

11th Division, commanded by Lieut.-General Baron Berthézène
BRIGADES: Dufour, Lagarde

3rd Cavalry Division, commanded by Lieut.-General Baron Domon
BRIGADES: Dommanget, Vinot

Artillery, commanded by General Doguereau
5 batteries

Engineers
3 companies

Total Third Corps: 18,105 men, 38 guns

FOURTH CORPS

Commanded by Lieut.-General Count Gérard

12th Division, commanded by Lieut.-General Baron Pécheux
BRIGADES: Rome, Schoeffer

13th Division, commanded by Lieut.-General Baron Vichery
BRIGADES: Le Capitaine, Desprez

14th Division, commanded by Lieut.-General de Bourmont (afterwards by General Hulot)
BRIGADES: Hulot, Toussaint

7th Cavalry Division, commanded by Lieut.-General Maurin
BRIGADES: Vallin, Berruyer

Artillery, commanded by General Baron Baltus
5 batteries

Engineers
4 companies

Total Fourth Corps: 15,404 men, 38 guns

SIXTH CORPS

Commanded by Lieut.-General Count Lobau

19th Division, commanded by Lieut.-General Baron Simmer
BRIGADES: Bellair, M. Jamin

20th Division, commanded by Lieut.-General Baron Jeannin
BRIGADES: Bony, Tromelin

21st Division, commanded by Lieut.-General Baron Teste
BRIGADES: Laffitte, Penne

Artillery, commanded by Lieut.-General Baron Noury
4 batteries

Engineers
3 companies

Total Sixth Corps: 10,826 men, 38 guns

RESERVE CAVALRY

Commanded by Marshall Count de Grouchy

FIRST CORPS

Commanded by Lieut.-General Count Pajol

4th Division, commanded by Lieut.-General Baron Soult
BRIGADES: St Laurent, Ameil

5th Division, commanded by Lieut.-General Baron Subervie
BRIGADES: A. de Colbert, Merlin

Artillery
2 horse batteries

SECOND CORPS

Commanded by Lieut.-General Count Exelmans

9th Division, commanded by Lieut.-General Baron Strolz
BRIGADES: Barthe, Vincent

10th Division, commanded by Lieut.-General Chastel
BRIGADES: Bonnemains, Berton

Artillery

2 horse batteries

THIRD CORPS

Commanded by Lieut.-General Kellermann, Count Valmy

11th Division, commanded by Lieut.-General Baron Lheritier
BRIGADES: Picquet, Guiton

12th Division, commanded by Lieut.-General Roussel d'Hurbal
BRIGADES: Blancard, Donop

Artillery

2 horse batteries

FOURTH CORPS

Commanded by Lieut.-General Count Milhaud

13th Division, commanded by Lieut.-General Wathier de St Alphonse
BRIGADES: Dubois, Travers

14th Division, commanded by Lieut.-General Baron Delort
BRIGADES: Farine, Vial

Artillery

2 horse batteries

Total Reserve Cavalry: 13,144 men, 48 guns

THE IMPERIAL GUARD

Commanded by Marshal Mortier, Duke of Treviso *
Aide-Major-Général de la Garde, Lieut.-General Count Drouot

Infantry, Lieut.-General Count Friant
General Petit, *1st Grenadiers*
General Christiani, *2nd Grenadiers*
General Poret de Morvan, *3rd Grenadiers*
General Harlet, *4th Grenadiers*

Lieut.-General Count Morand
General Cambronne, *1st Chasseurs*
General Pelet, *2nd Chasseurs*
Colonel Malet, *3rd Chasseurs*
General Henrion, *4th Chasseurs* **

Lieut.-General Count Duhesme
Colonel Secrétan, *1st Voltigeurs*
Colonel Trappier, *1st Tirailleurs*

---

* Mortier did not take part in the campaign, but had to remain behind at Beaumont on account of ill-health.

** The 3rd and 4th Grenadiers and the 3rd and 4th Chasseurs were popularly known as the 'Middle Guard' although officially they formed part of the 'Old Guard.'

Notes

Chapter One

1. Leonard Cooper, *The Age of Wellington,* (New York: Dodd, Mead and Company, 1963).

2, 3. Philip Henry, Fifth Earl of Stanhope, *Notes of Conversations with the Duke of Wellington, 1831-1851,* (London: Printed for Private Circulation, 1888).

4-7. Cooper, *op. cit.*

8, 9. Hamil Grant, *The Soul of Napoleon,* (Philadelphia: George W. Jacobs & Co., 1921).

10-12. Lady Jackson (Catherine Charlotte), *The Court of the Tuileries,* (London: The Grolier Society) Vol. I.

Chapter Two

1. Henry Lachouque, *The Anatomy of Glory,* adapted from the French by Anne S. K. Brown, (Providence, R. I.: Brown University Press, 1962).

2. Antony Brett-James, *The Hundred Days,* (London: Macmillan and Co., Ltd., 1964). (From the Journal of Col. Marie Antoine de Reiset, an officer in the king's bodyguard at the Tuileries Palace.)

3. William H. Crawford, Mr. Crawford's dispatches to Washington when he was American minister in Paris. Letters numbered 38 through 41, National Archives of the United States, Washington, D. C.

4. Harold P. Clunn, *The Face of London,* (London: Spring Books, 1952).

5-8. Crawford, *op. cit.*

Chapter Three

1. *The New York Evening Post,* April-May, 1815.

2, 3. *The Philadelphia Gazette,* April, 1815.

4-6. *The Baltimore Telegraph,* 1815.

7-14. *The Alexandria Gazette,* May, 1815.

15-17. William H. Crawford, Mr. Crawford's dispatches to Washington when he was American minister in Paris. Letters numbered 38 through 41, National Archives of the United States, Washington, D. C.

Chapter Four

1. Joel Tyler Headley, *The Imperial Guard of Napoleon from Marengo to Waterloo,* (New York: C. Scribner, 1851).

2. Lady Jackson (Catherine Charlotte), *The Court of the Tuileries,* (London: The Grolier Society), Vol. I.

Chapter Five

1. Henry Lachouque, *The Anatomy of Glory,* adapted from the French by Anne S. K. Brown, (Providence, R. I.: Brown University Press, 1962).

2. Joel Tyler Headley, *The Imperial Guard of Napoleon from Marengo to Waterloo,* (New York: C. Scribner, 1851).

3, 4. John Malcolm Bulloch, *Gordon Highlanders Muster Roll at the Period of Waterloo.* (1927)

5-7. Lt.-Col. C. H. Massé, M. C., *The Predecessors of the Royal Army Service Corps, 1757-1888,* (Aldershot: Gale and Polden Ltd., Wellington Press, 1948).

8. Culinary Arts Institute, *The French Cookbook,* by staff home economists, Melanie de Proft, Director, (Chicago: Culinary Arts Institute, 1955).

9. Lt.-Col. Basil Jackson, *Notes and Reminiscences of a Staff Officer, chiefly relating to the Waterloo Campaign and to St. Helena Matters during the Captivity of Napoleon,* ed. R. C. Seaton (New York: E. P. Dutton & Co., 1903).

10, 11. Headley, *op. cit.*

12, 13. Edmund Wheatley, *The Wheatley Diary,* edited with an introduction and notes by Christopher Hibbert, (London: Longmans, Green and Co., Ltd., 1964).

14. Cecil Woodham-Smith, *The Reason Why,* (New York: McGraw-Hill Book Co., Inc., 1953).

15. Massé, *op. cit.*

Chapter Six

1. Frederick Mainwaring, "Four Years of a Soldier's Life," *United Service Journal,* (1844), Parts II and III.

2. Capt. William Hay, C. B., *Reminiscences, 1808-1815 under Wellington,* Edited by Mrs. S. C. I. Wood, his daughter, (London: Simpkin, Marshall, Hamilton, Kent & Co., Ltd., 1901).

3. Lt.-Col. Basil Jackson, *Notes and Reminiscences of a Staff Officer, chiefly relating to the Waterloo Campaign and to St. Helena Matters during the Captivity of Napoleon,* ed. R. C. Seaton (New York: E. P. Dutton & Co., 1903).

4. Gen. Cavalié Mercer, *Journal of the Waterloo Campaign Kept throughout the Campaign of 1815,* (Edinburgh and London: W. Blackwood and Sons, 1870).

5. Lady Caroline Capel, *The Capel Letters, Being the Correspondence of Lady Caroline Capel and her Daughters with the Dowager Countess of Uxbridge from Brussels and Switzerland, 1814-1817.* Edited by the Marquess of Anglesey, (London: J. Cape, 1955).

6. Jackson, *op. cit.*

7. Harry Ross-Lewin, *With 'The Thirty-Second' in the Peninsula and Other Campaigns,* edited by John Wardell, M. A., (Dublin: Dublin, Hodges, Figgis & Co., Ltd., 1904).

Chapter Seven

1. Lady Magdalene Hall DeLancey, *A Week at Waterloo in 1815. Lady DeLancey's Narrative. Being an Account of How She Nursed her Husband, Colonel Sir William Howe DeLancey, Quartermaster-General of the Army, Mortally Wounded in the Great Battle,* edited by Maj. B. R. Ward, (London: J. Murray, 1906).

2. Sir William Augustus Fraser, *The Waterloo Ball,* (London: F. Harvey, 1897).

3. Maj. Edward Macready, "On a Part of Captain Siborne's History of the Waterloo Campaign," by an Officer of the 5th British Brigade (Maj. Edward Macready, 30th Foot). Colburn's *United Service Magazine,* (1845), Part I.

4. Thomas Morris, late Sergeant, 73rd Regiment, *Recollections of Military Service, including some details of the Battles of Quatre Bras and Waterloo,* (1847).

5. John Naylor, *Waterloo,* (London: B. T. Batsford, Ltd., 1960).

6. Capt. Archibald Frank Becke, *Napoleon and Waterloo,* Revised Edition, (London: K. Paul, Trench, Trubner & Co., Ltd., 1936).

7. *The English Historical Review,* Vol. I, No. 1, January 1886, (London, New York: Longmans, Green and Co., Ltd.).

8. Antony Brett-James, *The Hundred Days,* (London: Macmillan and Co., Ltd., 1964).

9. *Ibid.,* from the writings of Capt. William Verner, 7th Hussars.

10. *Ibid.,* from the writings of Hippolyte de Mauduit.

Chapter Eight

1, 2. George Jones, Esq., R. A., *The Battle of Waterloo with Those of Ligny and the Quatre Bras,* 11th Edition, (London: L. Booth, 1852).

3. Georgette Heyer, *An Infamous Army,* (New York: E. P. Dutton & Co., Inc., 1965).

4. Capt. John Kincaid, *Adventures in the Rifle Brigade, in the Peninsula, France, and in the Netherlands, from 1809 to 1815,* (London: W. H. White & Co., 1892).

5. Records of Observatoire Royal de Belgique, J. Warzee, Astronomer.

6, 7. Charlotte Anne Eaton (née Waldie), *The Days of Battle, or Quatre Bras and Waterloo,* (London: 1853).

8-12. Capt. William Hay, C. B., *Reminiscences, 1808-1815 under Wellington,* edited by Mrs. S. C. I. Wood, his daughter, (London: Simpkin, Marshall, Hamilton, Kent, & Co., Ltd., 1901).

13-15. Lt.-Col. Basil Jackson, *Notes and Reminiscences of a Staff Officer, chiefly relating to the Waterloo Campaign and to St. Helena Matters during the Captivity of Napoleon,* Edited by R. C. Seaton, (New York: E. P. Dutton & Co., 1903).

16-18. Eaton, *op. cit.*

19-24. Gen. Cavalié Mercer, *Journal of the Waterloo Campaign Kept throughout the Campaign of 1815,* (Edinburgh and London: W. Blackwood and Sons, 1870).

Chapter Nine

1. Maj. Edward Macready, "On a Part of Captain Siborne's History of the Waterloo Campaign," by an Officer of the 5th British Brigade (Maj. Edward Macready, 30th Foot), Colburn's United Service Magazine, Part I (1845).

2. Harry Ross-Lewin, *With 'The Thirty-Second' in the Peninsula and Other Campaigns,* edited by John Wardell, M. A., (Dublin: Dublin, Hodges, Figgis & Co., Ltd., 1904).

3, 4. Lt. Frederick Hope Pattison, *Personal Recollections of the Waterloo Campaign,* Printed for private circulation, (Glasgow: 1870).

5. Capt. William Hay, C. B., *Reminiscences, 1808-1815 under Wellington,* Edited by Mrs. S. C. I. Wood, his daughter, (London: Simpkin, Marshall, Hamilton, Kent & Co., Ltd., 1901).

6, 7. Antony Brett-James, *The Hundred Days,* (London: Macmillan and Co., Ltd., 1964).

Chapter Ten

1, 2. John Naylor, *Waterloo,* (London: B. T. Batsford, Ltd., 1960).

3, 4. Lt.-Col. Basil Jackson, *Notes and Reminiscences of a Staff Officer, chiefly relating to the Waterloo Campaign and to St. Helena Matters during the Captivity of Napoleon,* ed. R. C. Seaton (New York: E. P. Dutton & Co., 1903).

5. Naylor, *op. cit.*

6-8. Captain François, *Journal du Capitaine François (dit le Droma-daire d'Egypte) 1793-1830,* publié d'après le manuscrit original par Charles Grolleau, (Paris; 1903-4) 2 Vols.

9. Naylor, *op. cit.*

10. H. Belloc, *Waterloo,* (London: S. Swift & Co., Ltd., 1912).

11. John Malcolm Bulloch, *Gordon Highlanders Muster Roll at the Period of Waterloo,* (1927).

12. Sgt. James Anton, *Retrospect of a Military Life during the Most Eventful Periods of the Last War,* (Edinburgh: W. H. Lizars, 1841).

13, 14. Capt. William Siborne, *History of the War in France and Belgium in 1815, containing Minute Details of the Battles of Quatre Bras, Ligny, Wavre, and Waterloo,* (London: T. and W. Boone, 1848).

15. Lt. Frederick Hope Pattison, *Personal Recollections of the Waterloo Campaign,* (Glasgow: Printed for Private Circulation, 1870).

16-19. Thomas Morris, late Sergeant, 73rd Regiment, *Recollections of Military Service, including some details of the Battles of Quatre Bras and Waterloo,* (1847).

20-22. Pattison, *op. cit.*

23. Naylor, *op. cit.*

24, 25. *Records Assembled by the Royal Scots at Waterloo,* from correspondence with Col. D. A. D. Eykyn, D. S. O., Regimental Headquarters, The Royal Scots, The Castle, Edinburgh.

26. Siborne, *op. cit.*

27. François Thomas Delbare, *French Account of the Last Campaign of Buonaparte,* Translated by Captain Thornton, 78th Regiment, (London: J. Black, 1816).

28. Capt. Archibald Frank Becke, *Napoleon and Waterloo,* Revised Edition, (London: K. Paul, Trench, Trubner & Co., Ltd., 1936).

29-34. Gen. Cavalié Mercer, *Journal of the Waterloo Campaign Kept Throughout the Campaign of 1815,* (Edinburgh and London: W. Blackwood and Sons, 1870).

35. Bulloch, *op. cit.*

36. Lt.-Col. C. Greenhill Gardyne, *The Life of a Regiment. The History of the Gordon Highlanders,* (London: The Medici Society, Ltd., 1929), Vol. I.

37. Belloc, *op. cit.*

38, 39. Edith Saunders, *The Hundred Days,* (London: Longmans, Green and Co., Ltd., 1964).

40. Antony Brett-James, *The Hundred Days,* (London: Macmillan & Co., Ltd., 1964).

Chapter Eleven

1. Capt. William Hay, C. B., *Reminiscences, 1808-1815 under Wellington,* Edited by Mrs. S. C. I. Wood, his daughter, (London: Simpkin, Marshall, Hamilton, Kent, & Co., Ltd., 1901).

2. Lt.-Col. Basil Jackson, *Notes and Reminiscences of a Staff Officer, chiefly relating to the Waterloo Campaign and to St. Helena Matters during the Captivity of Napoleon,* ed. R. C. Seaton (New York: E. P. Dutton & Co., 1903).

3-6. Antony Brett-James, *The Hundred Days,* (London: Macmillan and Co., Ltd., 1964).

7-10. Philip Henry, Fifth Earl of Stanhope, *Notes of Conversations with the Duke of Wellington, 1831-1851,* (London: Printed for Private Circulation, 1888).

11-13. Lt.-Col. Basil Jackson, *Notes and Reminiscences of a Staff Officer, chiefly relating to the Waterloo Campaign and to St. Helena Matters during the Captivity of Napoleon,* ed. R. C. Seaton (New York: E. P. Dutton & Co., 1903).

14. Charlotte Anne Eaton (née Waldie), *The Days of Battle,* or, *Quatre Bras and Waterloo,* By an Englishwoman resident at Brussels in June, 1815, (1853).

15, 16. Lt. Frederick Hope Pattison, *Personal Recollections of the Waterloo Campaign,* (Glasgow: Printed for Private Circulation, 1870).

17-19. Brett-James, *op. cit.*

20. *The Royal Inniskilling Fusiliers,* Being the History of the Regiment from December 1688 to July 1914. Compiled under the direction of a Regimental Historical Records Committee. (London: Constable & Co., Ltd., 1934).

21. Eaton, *op. cit.*

22, 23. Gen. Cavalié Mercer, *Journal of the Waterloo Campaign Kept throughout the Campaign of 1815,* (Edinburgh and London: W. Blackwood and Sons, 1870).

24, 25. Hay, *op. cit.*

26-36. Mercer, *op. cit.*

37. John Naylor, *Waterloo,* (London: B. T. Batsford, Ltd., 1960).

38. Brett-James, *op. cit.*

39-40. Capt. William Siborne, *History of the War in France and Belgium in 1815, containing Minute Details of the Battles of Quatre Bras, Ligny, Wavre, and Waterloo,* (London: T. and W. Boone, 1848).

Chapter Twelve

1-3. Gen. Cavalié Mercer, *Journal of the Waterloo Campaign Kept throughout the Campaign of 1815,* (Edinburgh and London: W. Blackwood and Sons, 1870).

4. Antony Brett-James, *The Hundred Days,* (London: Macmillan & Co., Ltd., 1964).

5, 6. Edith Saunders, *The Hundred Days,* (London: Longmans, Green and Co., Ltd., 1964).

7-9. Brett-James, *op. cit.*

10, 11. Tupper Carey, "Reminiscences of a Commissariat Officer," *The Cornhill Magazine,* (New Series), Vol. VI.

12-14. Brett-James, *op. cit.*

15, 16. Pvt. Matthew Clay, "Adventures at Hougoumont," *Household Brigade Magazine,* 1958.

17. John Malcolm Bulloch, *Gordon Highlanders Muster Roll at the Period of Waterloo,* (1927).

Chapter Thirteen

1. Edith Saunders, *The Hundred Days,* (London: Longmans, Green and Co., Ltd., 1964).

2. Theo Aronson, *The Golden Bees, The Story of the Bonapartes,* (Greenwich, Conn.: New York Graphic Society, 1964).

3-6. Antony Brett-James, *The Hundred Days,* (London: Macmillan & Co., Ltd., 1964).

7. *Ibid.,* recorded by the relatives of Corp. John Dickson, a member of the Scot Greys.

8-11. Capt. William Hay, C. B., *Reminiscences, 1808-1815 under Wellington,* Edited by Mrs. S. C. I. Wood, his daughter. (London: Simpkin, Marshall, Hamilton, Kent & Co., Ltd., 1901).

12. Pvt. Matthew Clay, "Adventures at Hougoumont," *Household Brigade Magazine,* 1958.

13. Charlotte Anne Eaton (née Waldie), *The Days of Battle, or Quatre Bras and Waterloo,* (London: 1853).

14-20. Brett-James, *op. cit.,* from his translation of the writings of François René de Chateaubriand.

Chapter Fourteen

1-6. William Leeke, *The History of Lord Seaton's Regiment at the Battle of Waterloo,* (London: Hatchards, 1871).

7-16. Gen. Cavalié Mercer, *Journal of the Waterloo Campaign Kept throughout the Campaign of 1815,* (Edinburgh and London: W. Blackwood and Sons, 1870).

17. Capt. Rees Howell Gronow, *Reminiscences of Captain Gronow . . . being anecdotes of the camp, the court, and the clubs, at the close of the last war with France,* (London: Smith, Elder & Co., 1862).

18. Thomas Morris, late Sergeant, 73rd Regiment, *Recollections of Military Service, including some details of the Battles of Quatre Bras and Waterloo,* (1847).

19. Capt. William Siborne, *History of the War in France and Belgium in 1815, containing Minute Details of the Battles of Quatre Bras, Ligny, Wavre, and Waterloo,* (London: T. and W. Boone, 1848).

20-24. Maj. Edward Macready, "On a Part of Captain Siborne's History of the Waterloo Campaign," by an Officer of the 5th British Brigade (Maj. Edward Macready, 30th Foot). Colburn's *United Service Magazine,* 1845. Part I.

25-28. Mercer, *op. cit.*

29. Sgt. William Lawrence, *The Autobiography of Sergeant William Lawrence,* (1856).

30. George Jones, Esq., R. A., *The Battle of Waterloo with Those of Ligny and the Quatre Bras,* 11th Edition, (London: L. Booth, 1852).

31, 32. Gronow, *op. cit.*

33. Morris, *op. cit.*

34-39. Mercer, *op. cit.*

40-48. Morris, *op. cit.*

49-51. Siborne, *op. cit.*

52. Sgt. Duncan Robertson, *The Journal of Sergeant D. Robertson,* Perth: J. Fisher, 1842.

53. John Naylor, *Waterloo,* (London: B. T. Batsford, Ltd., 1960).

54. William Wheeler, *The Letters of Private Wheeler, 1809-1828,* edited and with a foreword by Capt. B. H. Liddell Hart, (Boston: Houghton Mifflin, 1951).

Chapter Fifteen

1. Edith Saunders, *The Hundred Days,* (London: Longmans, Green and Co., Ltd., 1964).

2. Sgt. Maj. Edward Cotton, *A Voice from Waterloo. A History of the Battle fought on the 18th June, 1815,* (Printed for the Proprietor, Mont St. Jean, London: 7th Edition, 1889).

3. William Leeke, *The History of Lord Seaton's Regiment at the Battle of Waterloo,* (London: Hatchards, 1871).

4. Maj. Edward Macready, "On a Part of Captain Siborne's History of the Waterloo Campaign," by an Officer of the 5th British Brigade (Maj. Edward Macready, 30th Foot), Colburn's *United Service Magazine,* Part I (1845).

5. Cotton, *op. cit.*

6. Capt. William Siborne, *History of the War in France and Belgium in 1815, containing Minute Details of the Battles of Quatre Bras, Ligny, Wavre, and Waterloo,* (London: T. and W. Boone, 1848).

7, 8. Col. Harold Malet, collected and arranged by, *The Historical Memoirs of the 18th Hussars (Princess of Wales' Own),* (London: Simpkin & Co., Ltd. Winchester: Warren & Son, 1907).

9, 10. C. R. B. Barrett, *History of the XIII Hussars,* (Vol. I, Edinburgh and London: William Blackwood and Sons, 1911).

11. *Historical Records of the Cameron Highlanders.* Vol. I.

12. Henry Lachouque, *The Anatomy of Glory,* adapted from the French by Anne S. K. Brown, (Providence, R. I.: Brown University Press, 1962).

13-15. Lt.-Col. Basil Jackson, *Notes and Reminiscences of a Staff Officer, chiefly relating to the Waterloo Campaign and to St. Helena Matters during the Captivity of Napoleon,* ed. R. C. Seaton (New York: E. P. Dutton & Co., 1903).

Chapter Sixteen

1-7. Sgt. Maj. Edward Cotton, *A Voice from Waterloo. A History of the Battle fought on the 18th June, 1815,* (Printed for the Proprietor, Mont St. Jean, London: 7th Edition, 1889).

8. John Malcolm Bulloch, *Gordon Highlanders Muster Roll at the Period of Waterloo,* (1927).

9-17. Charlotte Anne Eaton (née Waldie), *The Days of Battle, or Quatre Bras and Waterloo,* (London: 1853).

18. Frederic Morton, *The Rothschilds,* (New York: The Curtis Publishing Co., 1962).

Chapter Seventeen

1. Lt.-Col. C. Greenhill Gardyne, *The Life of a Regiment. The History of the Gordon Highlanders,* (London: The Medici Society Ltd., 1929), Vol. I.

2. Sgt. Maj. Edward Cotton, *A Voice from Waterloo. A History of the Battle fought on the 18th June, 1815,* (Printed for the Proprietor, Mont St. Jean, London: 7th Edition, 1889).

3. Andrew Hilliard Atteridge, *The Bravest of the Brave,* (New York: Brentano's, 1913).

4, 5. Herbert Ravenal Sass, "The Mystery of Peter Ney," *Saturday Evening Post,* (November 16, 1946).

6. Marilou Alston Rudulph, "Michael Rudulph, 'Lion of the Legion' " and "Legend of Michael Rudulph," *Georgia Historical Quarterly,* (September and December, 1961).

7. Archibald Philip Primrose, Fifth Earl of Rosebery, *Napoleon, the Last Phase,* (New York: Harper and Brothers, 1901).

8, 9. "The Successors of Laffite," *Louisiana Historical Quarterly,* Volume 24, (January-October, 1941).

10. *New Orleans Times-Picayune,* March 25, 1923, (New Orleans, La.).

11-13. A. E. Fossier, A. M., M. D., "The Funeral Ceremony of Napoleon in New Orleans, December 19, 1821," a paper read before the Louisiana Society on April 30, 1929.

14. James Beard, "A Soldier of Napoleon," *New Orleans Times-Picayune,* December 24, 1911 (New Orleans, La.).

15. Mary Van Rensselaer Thayer, *Jacqueline Bouvier Kennedy,* (New York: Doubleday & Co., Inc., 1961).

16. *Des Moines Sunday Register,* June 14, 1959 (Des Moines, Iowa).

17. Dr. Robert Ramsay, "Our Storehouse of Missouri Place Names," Missouri Handbook No. 2, *The University of Missouri Bulletin,* Vol. 53, No. 34. (Columbia, Mo.: University of Missouri, November 15, 1952).

18-22. Gardyne, *op. cit.*

23. Henry Lachouque, *The Anatomy of Glory,* Adapted from the French by Anne S. K. Brown (Providence, R. I.: Brown University Press, 1962).

24. Sir William Augustus Fraser, *The Waterloo Ball,* (London: F. Harvey, 1897).

25-26. Alfred Lord Tennyson, "Ode on the Death of the Duke of Wellington."

27-28. Philip Henry, Fifth Earl of Stanhope, *Notes of Conversations with the Duke of Wellington, 1831-1851* (London: Printed for Private Circulation, 1888).

29. Gustav Schenk, *The Book of Poisons,* Translated by Michael Bullock (London: Weidenfeld and Nicolson, 1956).

Bibliography

Books

Académie Royale de Belgique. *Classe des Sciences Memoires,* 2ème Série. Collection #4. Brussels: 1924.

Almeras, Henri d'. *Parisian Life under the Consulate and the Empire.* Paris: A. Michel, 1909.

Anton, Sgt. James. *Retrospect of a Military Life during the Most Eventful Periods of the Last War.* Edinburgh: W. H. Lizars, 1841.

Aronson, Theo. *The Golden Bees, the Story of the Bonapartes.* Greenwich, Conn.: New York Graphic Society, Publishers, Ltd., 1964.

Atteridge, Andrew Hilliard. *The Bravest of the Brave.* New York: Brentano's, 1913.

Barnes, A. S. and Co. *A Brief History of France.* New York and Chicago: A. S. Barnes and Co., 1875.

Barrett, C. R. B. *History of the XIII Hussars. Vol. I.* Edinburgh and London: William Blackwood and Sons, 1911.

Becke, Capt. Archibald Frank. *Napoleon and Waterloo.* Revised Edition. London: K. Paul, Trench, Trubner & Co., Ltd., 1936.

Belloc, H. *Waterloo.* London: S. Swift & Co., Ltd., 1912.

Bertaut, Jules. *Parisian Life under the First Empire.* Paris: 1943.

Booth, John. *Blücher in Briefen aus den Feldzugen, 1813-1815,* Herausgegeben von E. von Colomb, General-Lieutenant. Stuttgart: 1876.

Brett-James, Antony. *The Hundred Days.* London: Macmillan & Co., Ltd., 1964.

Bulloch, John Malcolm. *Gordon Highlanders Muster Roll at the Period of Waterloo.* 1927.

Burney, Fanny (Mrs. Fanny Anne Burney Wood). *The Diary of Fanny Burney.* Edited by Lewis Gibbs. London: Houghton Mifflin Company, 1940.

Capel, Lady Caroline. *The Capel Letters, Being the Correspondence of Lady Caroline Capel and her Daughters with the Dowager Countess of Uxbridge from Brussels and Switzerland, 1814-1817.* Edited by the Marquess of Anglesey. London: J. Cape, 1955.

Chesney, Charles Cornwallis. *Waterloo Lectures: a Study of the Campaign of 1815.* 2nd edition. London: Longmans, Green and Co., 1869.

Clunn, Harold P. *The Face of London.* London: Spring Books, 1952.

Coignet, Jean Roch. *Les Cahiers du Capitaine Coignet (1799-1815).* Publies par Loredan Larchey d'après le manuscrit original. Paris: Loredan Larchey, 1883.

Colin, Jean Lambert Alphonse. *L'Education Militaire de Napoléon.* Paris: R. Chapelot et Cie, 1900.

—— *Les Transformations de la Guerre.* Paris. E. Flammarion, 1911.

Collection de Douze Vues de Waterloo. Bruxelles: Gérard, 1835.

Cooper, Leonard. *The Age of Wellington.* New York: Dodd, Mead and Company, 1963.

Corti, Egon Caesar. *La Maison Rothschild.* Paris: Payot, 1929.

Cotton, Sgt. Maj. Edward. *A Voice from Waterloo. A History of the Battle fought on the 18th June, 1815.* Printed for the Proprietor. Mont St. Jean, London: 1889. 7th Edition.

Crawford, William H. Mr. Crawford's dispatches to Washington when he was American minister in Paris. Letters numbered 38 through 41, National Archives of the United States, Washington, D. C.

Creevey, Thomas. *The Creevey Papers.* Edited by Herbert Maxwell. Vol. I. London: J. Murray, 1903.

Culinary Arts Institute. *The French Cookbook.* By staff home economists, Melanie de Proft, Director. Chicago: Culinary Arts Institute, 1955.

Dalton, Charles. *The Waterloo Roll Call.* 2nd Edition. London: Eyre and Spottiswoode, 1904.

De Bas, Col. F., and Le Comte J. de T'Serclaes de Wommerson. *La Campagne de 1815 aux Pays-Bas d'après les rapports officiels néerlandais.* Brussels. 3 vols. 1908.

De Labouie, Lanzac. *The Life in Paris under Napoleon.* 1850.

DeLancey, Lady Magdalene Hall. *A Week at Waterloo in 1815. Lady DeLancey's Narrative. Being an Account of How She Nursed her Husband, Colonel Sir William Howe DeLancey, Quartermaster-General of the Army, Mortally Wounded in the Great Battle.* Edited by Maj. B. R. Ward. London: J. Murray, 1906.

Delbare, François Thomas. *French Account of the Last Campaign of Buonaparte.* Translated by Captain Thornton, 78th Regiment. London: J. Black, 1816.

Dictionnaire Encyclopédique de Géographie (Belgium) Brussels: 1907.

Duncan, Francis. *History of the Royal Regiment of Artillery,* 2 Vols., 3rd Edition. London: J. Murray, 1879.

Eaton, Charlotte Anne (née Waldie). *The Days of Battle, or Quatre Bras and Waterloo.* London: 1853.

Fargeau, Gerault de Saint. *48 Districts of Paris.* 1908-1910.

Fisher, John. *1815, an End and a Beginning.* New York and Evanston: Harper and Row, 1963.

Fitchett, William Henry. *Wellington's Men: Some Soldier Autobiographies.* London: Smith, Elder & Co., 1900.

Fleischman, Théo. *Le Quartier Général de Wellington à Waterloo.* Charleroi: Impr. de Charleroi, 1956.

———— *Bruxelles pendant la Bataille de Waterloo.* Bruxelles: Brepols, 1958.

Fortescue, the Hon. John William. *A History of the British Army.* Vol. X. London: Macmillan and Co., Ltd. 1920.

François, Captain. *Journal du Capitaine François (dit le Dromadaire d'Egypte) 1793-1830,* publié d'après le manuscrit original par Charles Grolleau. 2 Vols. Paris: 1903-4.

Fraser, Sir William Augustus. *The Waterloo Ball.* London: F. Harvey, 1897.

Fuller, Maj.-Gen. John Frederick Charles. *The Decisive Battles of the Western World.* Vols. II and III. London: Eyre and Spottiswoode, 1956.

Gardyne, Lt.-Col. C. Greenhill. *The Life of a Regiment. The History of the Gordon Highlanders.* Vol. I. London: The Medici Society Ltd., 1929.

Gibney, William. *Eighty Years Ago, or the Recollections of an Old Army Doctor. His Adventures on the Field of Quatre Bras and Waterloo and during the Occupation of Paris in 1815.* Edited by his son, Maj. Robert Warris Gibney. London: Bellairs and Company, 1896.

Gigot. *Nouvelle Description Historique de Belgique.* 1817.

Grant, Hamil. *The Soul of Napoleon.* Philadelphia: George W. Jacobs & Co., 1921.

Griffiths, Arthur George Frederick. *The Wellington Memorial.* London: G. Allen, 1897.

———— *Wellington and Waterloo.* London: Newnes, 1898.

Gronow, Capt. Rees Howell. *Reminiscences of Captain Gronow... being anecdotes of the camp, the court, and the clubs, at the close of the last war with France.* London: Smith, Elder & Co., 1862.

Grouchy, Emmanuel Marquis de. *Memoires du Marechal de Grouchy,* par le Marquis de Grouchy. Paris: E. Dentu, 1874.

Gurwood, John. *Selection from Despatches and General Orders of the Duke of Wellington.* London: John Murray, 1851.

Hay, Capt. William, C. B. *Reminiscences, 1808-1815 under Wellington.* Edited by his daughter, Mrs. S. C. I. Wood. London: Simpkin, Marshall, Hamilton, Kent & Co., Ltd., 1901.

Headley, Joel Tyler. *The Imperial Guard of Napoleon from Marengo to Waterloo.* New York: C. Scribner, 1851.

Heitman, Francis Bernard. *Historical Register and Dictionary of the United States Army from its Organization, September 29, 1789, to*

March 2, 1903. Published under Act of Congress Approved March 2, 1903. Washington: Government Printing Office, 1903.

Henckens, Lt. J. *Mémoires se rappartant à son service militaire au 6ème Régiment de Chasseurs à Cheval français de fevrier 1803 à août 1816.* La Haye: E. F. C. A. Henckens, 1910.

Herold, J. Christopher. *The Age of Napoleon.* New York: American Heritage Publishing Co., Inc., 1963.

Heyer, Georgette. *An Infamous Army.* New York: C. P. Sutton & Co., Inc., 1965.

Historical Records of the Cameron Highlanders. Vol. I.

Historical Records of the 32nd (Cornwall Light Infantry), compiled and edited by Col. G. C. Swiney. 1893.

History of Lewis, Clark, Knox and Scotland Counties, Mo. Chicago: 1887.

Hope, Lt. James. *Letters from Portugal, Spain and France, etc.* Edinburgh: 1819.

Houssaye, Henri. *1815.* 3 Vols. I. *La Première Restauration—Le Retour de l'Isle d'Elbe—Les Cent Jours.* Paris, 1911. 2. *Waterloo.* Paris, 1910. 3. *La Seconde Abdication—La Terreur Blanche.* Paris: Perrin et Cie, 1905.

Jackson, Lady Catherine Charlotte. *The Court of the Tuileries.* London: The Grolier Society. Vol. I.

Jackson, Lt.-Col. Basil. *Notes and Reminiscences of a Staff Officer, chiefly relating to the Waterloo Campaign and to St. Helena Matters during the Captivity of Napoleon.* New York: E. P. Dutton & Co., 1903.

Johnston, George. *History of Cecil County, Maryland.* Elkton, Md.; 1881.

Jones, George, Esq., R. A. *The Battle of Waterloo with Those of Ligny and the Quatre Bras.* 11th Edition. London: L. Booth, 1852.

Kelly, Christopher. *A Full and Circumstantial Account of the Memorable Battle of Waterloo.* London: T. Kelly, 1817.

—— *Memoirs and Wonderful Achievements of Wellington the Great. His Crowning Victory at Waterloo.* 1852.

Kelly, William Hyde. *The Battle of Wavre and Grouchy's Retreat.* London: J. Murray, 1905.

Kennedy, Gen. Sir John Shaw. *Notes on the Battle of Waterloo.* London: J. Murray, 1869.

Kielland, Alexander Lange. *Napoleon's Men and Methods.* Translated by Joseph McCabe, with a preface by Oscar Browning. New York: Brentano's, 1908.

Kincaid, Capt. John. *Adventures in the Rifle Brigade, in the Peninsula, France, and in the Netherlands, from 1809 to 1815.* London: W. H. White & Co., 1892.

Knapton, Ernest John. *Empress Josephine.* Cambridge, Mass.: Harvard University Press, 1963.

Lachouque, Commandant Henry. *Le Secret de Waterloo*. Paris: Amiot-Dumont, 1952.

――― *The Anatomy of Glory*. Adapted from the French by Anne S. K. Brown. Providence, R. I.: Brown University Press, 1962.

Lawrence, Sgt. William. *The Autobiography of Sergeant William Lawrence*. 1856.

Leeke, William. *The History of Lord Seaton's Regiment at the Battle of Waterloo*. London: Hatchards, 1871.

Liddell, Col. R. S., collected and arranged by, *Memoirs of the Tenth Royal Hussars (Prince of Wales' Own). Historical and Social*, 1891.

Lossing, Benson J. *A Centennial Edition of the History of the United States: from the Discovery of America to the End of the First One Hundred Years of American Independence*. Hartford, Conn.: Thomas Belknap, 1876.

Malet, Col. Harold, collected and arranged by. *The Historical Memoirs of the 18th Hussars (Princess of Wales' Own)*. London: Simpkin & Co., Ltd. Winchester: Warren & Son, 1907.

Markham, Felix. *Napoleon*. New York: New American Library, 1963.

Massé, Lt.-Col. C. H., M. C. *The Predecessors of the Royal Army Service Corps, 1757-1888*. Aldershot: Gale and Polden Ltd., Wellington Press, 1948.

Memoire sur la Géographie Physique (Belgium) 3rd Vol. 1826.

Mercer, Gen. Cavalié. *Journal of the Waterloo Campaign Kept Throughout the Campaign of 1815*. Edinburgh and London: W. Blackwood and Sons, 1870.

Meyer, Moriz. *Manuel Historique de la Technologie des Armes à Feu*. Paris: J. Corréard, 1837.

Moore, A. B. *History of Alabama*. 1934.

Morris, Thomas, late Sergeant, 73rd Regiment. *Recollections of Military Service, including some details of the Battles of Quatre Bras and Waterloo*. 1847.

Morton, Frederic. *The Rothschilds*. New York: The Curtis Publishing Co., 1962.

Muffling, General. *A Sketch of the Battle of Waterloo to which Are Added Official Dispatches*. Brussels: E. Gérard, 1883.

Napoleon. *Commentaires de Napoléon Ier*. 1867.

Napoleon. *Correspondance de Napoléon Ier,* publiée par ordre de l'Empereur Napoléon III. Vol. 28. Paris: 1869.

Naylor, John. *Waterloo*. London: B. T. Batsford, Ltd., 1960.

Ney, Michel, duc d'Elchingen. *Documents Inédits sur la Campagne de 1815*. Paris: Anselin, 1840.

Official Manual, Missouri Secretary of State, 1897-1898.

Oman, Carola. *Britain Against Napoleon*. London: Faber and Faber, Ltd., 1942.

Pattison, Lt. Frederick Hope. *Personal Recollections of the Waterloo Campaign*. Glasgow: Printed for Private Circulation, 1870.

Ramsay, Robert L. "Our Storehouse of Missouri Place Names," *The University of Missouri Bulletin,* Missouri Handbook No. Two. Columbia, Mo.: The University of Missouri, 1952.

Randolph, Wilfrid. *The Churches of Belgium.* London: G. Routledge and Sons, Ltd., 1919.

Ratcliffe, Bertram. *Marshal Grouchy and the Guns of Waterloo.* London: F. Muller Ltd., 1942.

Records Assembled by the Royal Scots at Waterloo, From correspondence with Col. D. A. D. Eykeyn, D. S. O., Regimental Headquarters, The Royal Scots, The Castle, Edinburgh 1.

Records of Observatoire Royal de Belgique, J. Warzee, Astronomer.

Reeves, Jesse Sidell. *The Napoleonic Exiles in America, a Study in Diplomatic History, 1815-1819.* Baltimore: The Johns Hopkins Press, 1905.

Richardson, Ethel Mary. *Long Forgotten Days (leading to Waterloo).* London: Heath, Cranton Ltd., 1928.

Robertson, Sgt. Duncan. *The Journal of Sergeant D. Robertson.* Perth: J. Fisher, 1842.

Rosebery, Archibald Philip Primrose, 5th Earl of. *Napoleon, the Last Phase.* New York: Harper and Brothers, 1901.

Rosengarten, J. G. *French Colonists and Exiles in the United States.* Philadelphia and London: J. B. Lippincott Company, 1907.

Ross-Lewin, Harry. *With 'The Thirty-Second' in the Peninsula and Other Campaigns.* Edited by John Wardell, M. A. Dublin: Dublin, Hodges, Figgis & Co., Ltd., 1904.

Royal Inniskilling Fusiliers, The. Being the History of the Regiment from December 1688 to July 1914. Compiled under the direction of a Regimental Historical Records Committee. London: Constable and Co., Ltd., 1934.

Saunders, Edith. *The Hundred Days.* London: Longmans, Green and Co., Ltd., 1964.

Scharf, J. Thomas. History of Delaware. Vol. II. Philadelphia: 1888.

Schenk, Gustav. *The Book of Poisons.* Translated by Michael Bullock. London: Weidenfeld and Nicolson, 1956.

Scott, Sir Walter. *The Complete Poetical Works of Sir Walter Scott.* Edited by Horace Elisha Scudder. Boston and New York: Houghton, Mifflin and Company, 1900.

Siborne, Maj. Gen. H. T., edited by. *Waterloo Letters. A Selection from original and hitherto unpublished Letters bearing on the 16th, 17th, and 18th June, 1815, by Officers who served in the Campaign.* 1891.

Siborne, Capt. William. *History of the War in France and Belgium in 1815, containing Minute Details of the Battles of Quatre Bras, Ligny, Wavre, and Waterloo.* London: T. and W. Boone, 1848.

Stanhope, Philip Henry, Fifth Earl of. *Notes of Conversations with the Duke of Wellington, 1831-1851*. London: Printed for Private Circulation, 1888.

Tennyson, Alfred Lord. "Ode on the Death of the Duke of Wellington"

Thayer, Mary Van Rensselaer. *Jacqueline Bouvier Kennedy*. New York: Doubleday and Company, Inc., 1961.

Tournier, *Histoire des Jouets et des Jeux*.

Waldie (See Eaton, Charlotte A.)

Wellington, Arthur Wellesley, First Duke of. *Maxims and Opinions of Field-Marshal His Grace the Duke of Wellington*. With a biographical memoir by George Henry Francis, Esq. London: Henry Colburn, 1845.

Wellington, Arthur Wellesley, First Duke of. *Supplementary Despatches, Correspondence and Memoranda*. Edited by Arthur Richard Wellesley, Second Duke of Wellington. London: J. Murray, 1858-1865.

Wheatley, Edmund. *The Wheatley Diary*. Edited with an Introduction and notes by Christopher Hibbert. London: Longmans, Green and Co., Ltd., 1964.

Wheeler, William. *The Letters of Private Wheeler, 1809-1828*. Edited and with a Foreword by Capt. B. H. Liddell Hart. Boston: Houghton Mifflin, 1951.

Whitehorne, A. C. *The Welsh Regiment (1719-1914)*. Cardiff: Western Mail and Echo Ltd., 1932.

Woodham-Smith, Cecil. *The Reason Why*. New York: McGraw-Hill Book Company, Inc., 1953.

Young, Julian Charles. *A Memoir of Charles Mayne Young, Tragedian, with Extracts from his Son's Journal*. Second Edition. London and New York: Macmillan and Co., 1871.

Magazines

Carey, Tupper, "Reminiscences of a Commissariat Officer," *The Cornhill Magazine*, new series, Vol. VI. (1899).

Clarke, Lt.-Col. I. B., "Waterloo Letters from the Royal Scots Greys," *The Cavalry Journal* (January, 1926).

Clay, Pvt. Matthew, "Adventures at Hougoumont," *Household Brigade Magazine* (1958).

Copin, Jean, "Waterloo: le Folklore de la Bataille," *Le Folklore Brabançon*, Nos. 143, 146, 148, 151, Brussels (1959-61).

English Historical Review, The, Vol. I, No. 1 (January 1886), London, New York: Longmans, Green and Co., Ltd.

Fossier, A. E., A. M., M. D., "The Funeral Ceremony of Napoleon in New Orleans, December 19, 1821," a paper read before the Louisiana Society on April 30, 1929.

Louisiana Historical Quarterly, "The Successors of Laffite," Volume 24 (January-October 1941).

Ibid. Vols. 8 and 13.

Macready, Maj. Edward, "On a Part of Captain Siborne's History of the Waterloo Campaign," by an Officer of the 5th British Brigade (Maj. Edward Macready, 30th Foot). Colburn's *United Service Magazine,* (1845). Part I.

Mainwaring, Frederick, "Four Years of a Soldier's Life," *United Service Journal,* (1844). Parts II and III.

Niemann, Henri, "The Journal of Henri Niemann of the 6th Prussian Black Hussars," edited by Francis Newton Thorps, *The English Historical Review,* Vol. III (July 1888).

Reuter, "A Prussian Gunner's Adventures in 1815," edited and translated by Capt. E. S. May, *United Service Magazine,* (October 1891).

Rudulph, Marilou Alston, "Michael Rudulph, 'Lion of the Legion' " and "Legend of Michael Rudulph," *Georgia Historical Quarterly,* (September and December 1961).

Sass, Herbert Ravenel, "The Mystery of Peter Ney," *Saturday Evening Post* (November 16, 1946).

Taylor, George V., "Scholarship and Legend, William Henry Hoyt's Research on the Ney Controversy," reprinted from *The South Atlantic Quarterly,* Vol. LIX, No. 3 (Summer issue, 1960).

Newspapers

The Alexandria Gazette (Alexandria, Va.)
The Baltimore Telegraph (Baltimore, Md.)
Des Moines Sunday Register (Des Moines, Iowa), June 14, 1959
Indianapolis Star (Indianapolis, Indiana), Sept. 30, 1936
Le Journal de la Belgique, 14 June 1815
The London Gazette (London)
Le Moniteur Universal (Paris), March-June 1815
The New York Evening Post (New York)
Paris Journal (Paris), March-April 1815
Philadelphia Gazette (Philadelphia)
The Salem Democrat, (Salem, Ind.)
The Times-Picayune (New Orleans), Dec. 24, 1911 and March 25, 1923

Index

ate Due